THE HISTORY OF
ABERYSTWYTH COUNTY SCHOOL
(ARDWYN) 1896 – 1973

THE HISTORY OF ABERYSTWYTH COUNTY SCHOOL (ARDWYN)

1896 - 1973

BY

HUW SPENCER LLOYD

PUBLISHED BY THE ARDWYNIAN ASSOCIATION

© The Ardwynian Association

First published in 1996

Printed by Cambrian Printers Ltd, Aberystwyth

ISBN 0 900439 80 7

All rights reserved. No part of this book may be reproduced or transmitted in any form or by any means, electronic or mechanical, including photo-copying, recording or by any information storage and retrieval system, without permission from the Publishers in writing.

Cover photo by W. R. HALL of The Cambrian News, July 1900.

LIST OF CONTENTS

Page

AUTHOR'S PREFACE 9

FOREWORD by W J Phillips 11

INTRODUCTION — The Dawn of New Era 13

CHAPTER ONE — The David Samuel Years 1896-1921 18

CHAPTER TWO — The Lloyd Morgan Years 1921-1928 106

CHAPTER THREE — The D C Lewis Years 1928-1954 134

CHAPTER FOUR — The A D Lewis Years 1954-1971 206

CHAPTER FIVE — The Charles G Suff Years 1971-1973 288

EPILOGUE 304

APPENDICES 307

    The Operas
    State Scholars
    Service and Leadership Awards
    Samuel Exhibitioners
    Chaired Bards
    National Youth Orchestra of Wales
    Welsh Schools' Internationals
    Head Prefects
    Victores Ludorum
    Stimson Gymnasts
    Chairmen of Governors

LIST OF REFERENCES 333

LIST OF SUBSCRIBERS 336

TO DAVID, SOPHIE, JOSHUA and EMILY

AND ALL ARDWYNIANS THE WORLD OVER

AUTHOR'S PREFACE

This book is an attempt to trace the development and the subsequent history of a secondary school founded in the last years of the last century; in common with other Welsh county schools it was a step into the unknown.

For many years, due to grossly inadequate funding, the Governors and staff struggled to develop a school which would fulfil the requirements of the 1889 Education Act which created it and be a credit to the community it served.

During its seventy-six year life, the School had several name changes. The cumbersome 1896-title of the Aberystwyth County Intermediate School, was later shortened to the Aberystwyth County School. In 1928 the name of Ardwyn County School or Ardwyn School was adopted. Following the dictates of the 1944 Education Act it became Ardwyn Grammar School. To the local populace who, from its early days had held it in high esteem, it was always 'the county school'.

All but two of the secondary schools in the county were non-selective when comprehensive education was introduced in the Seventies and retained their names. However when Ardwyn ceased to exist in 1973 its venerated name and hard-won traditions were lost, which saddened many. Although it could be argued that Ardwyn did not need a monument, the successes of its pupils spoke for themselves, I felt there was a need for a record of its achievements and contribution to the life of Aberystwyth and district. I hope that this book fulfils those objectives.

I was fortunate in being able to call upon the experience and expertise of Dr E L Ellis, a former Ardwynian, who readily devoted considerable time to reading the drafts. I am indebted to him for his sound advice, assistance and encouragement.

My gratitude also to W John Phillips, former director of education for Cardiganshire, who sanctioned access to the School log books and Governors' minute books. I also thank him for writing the foreword.

My task has been eased by the full records kept by successive Headmasters. I found the Jubilee Magazine 1946, edited by T J James, an invaluable resource. Tribute must also be paid to the diligence of the editors of the *Ystwythian* and *Ardwynian*-the School magazines, which provided an almost continuous record of the School's activities; they also had the foresight to deposit the issues in the National Library of Wales. I must commend the staff of the Department of Printed Books at the NLW for their courtesy and ready response to my requests for assistance. The County Record Office, Swyddfa'r Sir, provided access to the county council minutes.

I am aware that this record will be in many ways, incomplete, particularly in respect of those pupils who were Ardwynians in the last decades of the School's existence.

Previously, former pupils had their accomplishments and subsequent careers recorded in the School magazine. After 1973, when the School closed, there was no means of recording the high attainments of its *alumni*. Appeals in the local press for information on former pupils elicited a poor response.

I am appreciative of those former pupils who reponded to my request for written recollections of their Ardwyn days which are an important part of the book. Those contributors are recognised in the list of references.

I also wish to thank the following for their assistance:-
Rhiannon Aaron, Meg Bowen, Stephen Cannon, Ron Cullum, Aubrey C Davies, E Jones Davies, Mary Beynon Davies, Mary Llewelfryn Davies, Margaret Evans MBE, Ieuan Ellis, Anthony and Zena Evans, Bethan Evans, Dic Evans, Jane Lloyd Francis, Michael Freeman-curator of the Ceredigion Museum, Stephen Godden, Anna Hubbard (Pugh), Simon Hughes, Wynn Hughes, Evelyn Lumley Jenkins, D James Jones of Cambrian Printers, John Lewis, W J Lewis, R J Lloyd, Hywel B Mathews, Jim Morgan, Peter Norrington-Davies, Bill Owen, Marjorie Penwill, Morfydd Rhys Clark, Rhona Ryle, Brian Sansbury, Charles G Suff, Nona Taylor, W. J. Taylor, Frank Thomas, Beryl and Robin Varley, John Wall, Ifor (Bush) Williams.

The group photographs which have been included are the work of commercial photographers Knipe, Culliford, Pickford & Son, HH and Evered Davies. Many of the other photographs were taken by J C Goodwin.

The line drawings, the work of William David Lewis, Art Teacher 1919-1943 are reproduced from the Ardwyn Roll of Honour, which he compiled.

The support and encouragement of the Ardwynian Association under its chairman John Ellis Williams, was a powerful incentive to complete the work in time for the centenary of the founding of the School in 1996.

I am also indebted to John Ellis Williams for his invaluable assistance with the proof reading.

Finally my grateful thanks to my wife Enfys for her limitless patience, encouragement and for uncomplainingly allowing our home to be the repository for the mass of Ardwyn records, over a lengthy period.

Penpadarn,
Cefnllan,
Aberystwyth

January 1996

FOREWORD

In the history of Welsh education the grammar schools have an illustrious place. Through them generations of pupils from varied backgrounds found their way into higher education and thereafter to enhanced career opportunities. In Aberystwyth, Ardwyn Grammar School fulfilled such a role and in so doing, developed a deserved reputation for academic excellence and achievement. It is fitting therefore that the accomplishments of its staff and pupils should be recorded and Huw Spencer Lloyd, in particular must be commended, for his initiative and industry in embarking upon this task.

It might seem strange, however, that one of those associated with its closure should be asked to contribute this foreword. In this, I can only plead the excuse of the bureaucrat throughout the ages, that I was merely following the dictates of my political masters. The spirit of egalitarianism emerging in the Sixties regarded with suspicion an educational system which separated children at the ages of eleven and the 11+ examination was viewed with undisguised hostility. The architects of the Education Act 1944, had talked about a 'parity of esteem' between the grammar school and its counterpart the secondary modern. In Aberystwyth, the relationship between Ardwyn and Dinas was a good one, but elsewhere the secondary modern was viewed as inferior. It frequently lacked the facilities of the more prestigious grammar school. The answer lay within a comprehensive system and Circular 10/65 exhorted all authorities to reorganise their schools and to establish non-selective schools. Cardiganshire duly complied for, apart from Ardwyn and Llandysul, the other secondary schools on the county were already non-selective and bilateral. Thus Ardwyn Grammar School ceased to exist in 1973.

The process of reorganisation was a difficult one. With limited resources, it was well nigh impossible to fulfil all the expectations of parents and staff of the new comprehensive schools. In spite of their natural regrets at having to prepare for the demise of their grammar school, the staff of Ardwyn participated fully in the planning for the changes. Under the leadership of the redoubtable A D Lewis they fought for every additional resource and together with their colleagues at Dinas, sought to ensure that if changes were inevitable they should at least result in better facilies for all the pupils in Aberystwyth. Not all their aspirations were realised, but at least the new order which emerged was able to absorb many of the traditions of the old. In the early years these provided a valuable foundation for the new comprehensive schools.

Many of my recollections of Ardwyn centre around the meetings of its rather powerful Governing Body. As a comparatively young Deputy Director having to confront such formidable members as Alderman R J Ellis, Alderman Mrs G C Evans and Mrs I C Jones, Mr Arthur Pinsent, Professor Llewelfryn Davies and others, could on occasions, prove to be a daunting experience. In addition there was the presence of A D Lewis, himself a former Deputy Director. In later years 'A D' became chairman of my own Education Committee in Dyfed and a much valued friend. He was proud of Ardwyn and would have been delighted to see the achievements of the School recorded for posterity. His successor, Charles Suff, also ensured that the transition to a comprehensive system was as smooth as circumstances would permit.

Like many other venerated institutions, Ardwyn had to succumb to the national changes in educational perceptions. At the same time, many greeted such changes with a mixture of sadness and scepticism. Harking back to the past can be an arid experience, but it also serves to remind us of those who dedicated themselves to meeting the needs of generations of young people in Aberystwyth and its environs. In recording past achievements this volume should serve as a reminder of the need to maintain the highest standards in the present schools.

W J Phillips

Chief Executive, Dyfed County Council

INTRODUCTION

THE DAWN OF A NEW ERA

The Education Act of 1870 put primary education on a firm footing; soon afterwards, the university colleges provided wide opportunities for education of an advanced character, thus leaving a gap in the intermediate stage. The Aberdare Committee and the legislation based on its report- the Welsh Intermediate Education Act 1889 heralded the dawn of a new educational era.

> The Act provided that a Joint Education Committee should be appointed in every county in Wales, whose duty it would be to submit to the Charity Commissioners a scheme for the Intermediate and Technical Education of the Welsh people. These County Committees soon realized the necessity of agreeing upon general principles in framing their schemes and from conferences held for this purpose emerged the Central Welsh Board, a unique but thoroughly democratic body whose primary task was advisory but it can claim a large share of the credit for the romantic development of our schools. The CWB has never controlled the finances of the schools but by inspection and examination it has played a prominent part in establishing and maintaining the highest educational standards.[1]

In due course the Cardiganshire Joint Committee produced its Scheme which was finally approved on August 1 1896. This established a County Governing Body of twenty-two Governors (twelve County Councillors, one each from the Council and Senate of the University College of Wales, one each from the five School District Managers and three cooptative members) This body controlled the County Intermediate and Technical Fund which received annually (a) the produce of a half-penny rate (b) an equivalent sum from the Treasury (c) a portion of Local Taxation. The Scheme specified a school of 250 pupils at Aberystwyth, a building grant of £2, 586 subject to a sum of £2,400 and a suitable site being contributed by voluntary effort and an annual payment of 34% from the General Fund on a basis of population. It also constituted a body of twelve School Managers appointed as follows: 6 by the County Council (at least 2 women), 2 by the Aberystwyth Corporation, 3 by the School Board (at least one woman) and 1 by the Senate of the University College of Wales.

Long before the first scheme for Cardiganshire was submitted in 1893 the townspeople were determined that Aberystwyth should have an Intermediate School. To this end a meeting was held at the Town Hall on January 22 1891 when a number of influential people met and a movement was initiated to provide a school for the town. John Evans, a solicitor, and Thomas Owen were appointed secretaries and an appeal for subscriptions was launched. At that first meeting nearly £350 was obtained, with plans made to cover the town for a house to house collection with outlying districts included. The collection books are still extant and show how thoroughly the work was done. By June 1891 subscriptions totalled nearly £2,500 and the work of collecting continued for many years. Amounts given varied from £210 to 5 shillings.

each and every gift being thankfully received; each and every gift representing that spirit characteristically Welsh which demands the best in education for our children.[2]

The first entry in Minute Book (Volume 1) of the School Managers of the Aberystwyth Intermediate School records their first meeting held on Thursday March 22 1894 at the Town Hall when Ald. Peter Jones was elected Chairman and the Rev. Thomas Levi Vice-Chairman, with Robert Ellis appointed representative on the County Governing Body. The meeting resolved to advertise for the post of Clerk at a salary of £25 a year. The Chairman informed the meeting that the Town Council had agreed to guarantee a site for the new school and he hoped to specify the location at the next meeting. It will be of interest to recall the names of the first governing body as entered in the records:-

    Ald. Peter Jones Chairman
    Rev. Thomas Levi
    Dr. H. Lloyd Snape, Professor of Chemistry UCW
    Mr.. J. T. Rees, Mus. Bac. Penygarn
    Mr. Richard Rees B. A. Gwarfelin
    Mr. Robert Ellis Chemist, Terrace Road
    Mr. John Evans Solicitor
    Rev. J. M. Griffiths, Vicar of Aberaeron
    Mr. George Davies, Queen's Road
    Mrs. Vaughan Davies, Tanybwlch
    Miss Mary Fryer, Marine Terrace
    Mrs. Phillips (nee Mary Roberts), South Terrace

These members, together with the working committee who had organised the collection of subscriptions were the real pioneers, could rightly be called the Founders of the School and many were to serve the School diligently for some years.
Samuel Evans of 3 Laura Place was appointed Clerk to the Managers in April 1894 and served until his death in April 1899.

At their third meeting, eighteen months later, the Chairman reported that the only land which the Corporation had to offer was a field in front of Stanley Terrace. He expressed doubt about obtaining the sanction of the Charity Commissioners for this site because of its proximity to the railway station and he had therefore approached the Rev. Llewellyn Edwards, Headmaster of Ardwyn, a well-known private school who was prepared to offer his premises to the Managers for a sum of £3,500. The meeting looked with favour on this offer and the Chairman was asked to bring the matter before the Town Council with a view to inducing them to make a monetary grant in lieu of a site. At their next meeting members were informed that the Aberystwyth Town Council were prepared to give a grant of £800, and it was agreed to accept the offer to purchase Ardwyn-'the school on the hill'. The way was now clear to apply to the County Governing Body for leave to open the boys' department of the School and a sub-committee was formed to report on the premises and the additional buildings required. T E Morgan, a local architect was engaged to prepare the necessary plans and certificates to accompany the application.

In January 1896 the Charity Commissioners approved the Ardwyn site but were unable to allow acquisition of the premises until they were satisified that they were capable of adaptation to the requirements of a County School. Further plans were submitted but amendments were necessary to include provision for laboratories, workshops and laundries. These delays were no doubt frustrating for the Founders but by May the Commissioners finally approved the plans and gave sanction for the purchase of the site with the reminder that they needed assurance from the County Governing Body that the necessary funds, in addition to the building grant of £2586, would be forthcoming to defray the costs of the works.

The purchase of the Ardwyn premises was completed on August 31 and a sub-committee appointed to prepare the school for occupation and to make arrangements for awarding scholarships. The Clerk was instructed to inform the subscribers of the action taken, of the financial position and to invite early payment of subscriptions. At the same time advertisements were placed in the *Manchester Guardian*, *Athenium*, *Academy*, *Birmingham Daily Post*, *South Wales Daily News*, *Cambrian News*, and *Aberystwyth Observer* for the following positions:- Headmaster at a salary of £180 per annum with capitation fees of £1:10s for the first 100 pupils and £1 afterwards; a Second Master at a salary of £160 and an Assistant Master at a salary of £140.

There were sixty-seven applications for the Headmastership and after great deliberation David Samuel whose application was supported by testimonials from W Williams, H. M. Chief Inspector of Schools for Wales, Principal Roberts, of Aberystwyth College, Principal Owen, of Lampeter College and Owen M Edwards, Fellow of Lincoln College, Oxford, was elected. For the other appointments there were over one hundred responses and after it was decided that instead of appointing a Second Master, two Assistant Masters at a salary of £150 per annum be appointed, the successful candidates were Thomas Owen and W J Fuller.

The Headmaster elect, David Samuel, a native of Aberystwyth received his early education at the National School and the Aberystwyth Grammar School. In 1872, he entered the Welsh Collegiate Institution, Llandovery and in January 1873 he obtained a scholarship at UCW Aberystwyth- the second term of the College's existence. During his course, he received prizes for Mathematics and Natural Philosophy and in March 1875 he was elected to a Minor Scholarship at Clare College, Cambridge. In January 1879 he graduated 20th Wrangler, taking up a position in the Aberystwyth Grammar School and later 'coach' at a Military Institution in Blackheath. From 1880 to 1885 he served as Second Master of Appleby Grammar School, Westmorland and in 1886 held a similar appointment in the Queen Elizabeth Grammar School, Ashbourne, Derbyshire. From January 1887 to Midsummer 1886 he was Headmaster of the Old Bank (Private) School, Bridge Street, Aberystwyth.

Walter Pearson Fuller was educated at Kingswsood School, Bath, and came to Aberystwyth College where he obtained a scholarship and graduated BA University of London with Classical Honours and listed sixth in the MA examination. He had teaching experience in schools in Birmingham, Shrewsbury and Beaumaris Intermediate School from where he came to Aberystwyth County School.

Thomas Owen, a native of Aberystwyth received his elementary education at Penparcau School under George Thomas. He became a student at the Normal College Bangor, where after two years he obtained a teaching certificate. Following a period as head teacher of Ponterwyd Board School he entered Aberystwyth College becoming senior scholar and gaining the London Matriculation examination with Honours. From 1878 until midsummer 1896 he was Headmaster of the Commercial and Grammar [Private] School, Aberystwyth. At the inaugural meeting in 1891 to launch the movement to obtain an intermediate school for Aberystwyth, Tom Owen was appointed joint secretary.

The sub-committee entrusted with the awarding of scholarships and for making arrangements for opening the school made the following recommendations:-

> That the school be advertised for one year in the *Cambrian News, Aberystwyth Observer* and *Montgomery Times.*
>
> That in the case of two or more children of the same parents attending the School at the same time, the school fees be £5 for the first child, £4 for the second and £3 for the third.
>
> That each pupil be charged a fee of 2/6 per term for the use of books and 1/- per term for athletics
>
> That a field be rented from Mr David Phillips from this date to the end of the Easter Term at a rent of £7.
>
> That Scholarships to the value of £5, to cover school fees be offered for competition to candidates from the grammar schools and public elementary schools of the school district.
>
> That the Aberystwyth County School be opened on Tuesday October 6 1986.

To this end an advertisement appeared in the local papers on September 17 which gave details of the teaching staff with their academic qualifications and the available scholarships.

> Ten County Scholarships of £5 each will be offered for competition. Five of these will be confined to pupils of not less than three years standing in some public elementary school within the Aberystwyth School District. All the Scholarships will be tenable for one year but may be renewed on the recommendation of the Headmaster. The examination will take place at the School on Thursday October 1 at 10am and 2pm
>
> Forms of application and any further details may be had from Samuel Evans, Clerk to the Local Governing Body 6, Portland Street.

A further announcement in the local papers stated that

> Candidates for County Scholarships will be examined in the following subjects:
> 1. English Grammar 2. English Composition or Translation from Welsh to English
> 3. Arithmetic 4. History (Period 1066-1688) and Geography
> Papers will also be set on the following subjects, of which not more than four may be selected by candidates for examination
> a. Algebra b. Euclid Book i c. Welsh Grammar d. Latin Grammar and Translation
> e. Greek Grammar f. French Grammar and Translation g. Chemistry.

Copies of the examination papers are to be found in the first record book, placed there by David Samuel because 'they will be useful for future reference as well as historically of value as being the first set of papers given at this County School.'

At this time a Prospectus was printed and distributed locally; after enumerating the Masters with their degrees and qualifications, it went on:

> The new County School is established under the Welsh Intermediate Education Act 1889. Under the Cardiganshire Scheme, the School will possess a large endowment for educational purposes.
>
> As will be observed from the list, the members of the School staff are gentlemen of high degrees and academic distinction, who have also had long and ample experience in teaching in both English and Welsh grammar schools.
>
> The Curriculum will include subjects usually taught in high class secondary and grammar schools of the country. In addition to the ordinary school subjects, such Technical Branches of Education as Naval and Mechanical Engineering, Navigation, Shorthand, Book-keeping etc will be taught.
>
> Pupils will be trained for commercial and professional pursuits. Classes will be formed to prepare scholars for the following public examinations:-
>
> South Kensington Science and Art
> Oxford and Cambridge Local Board Certificates and Distinctions
> Matriculation at the London and Welsh Universities.
>
> In the higher classes pupils will be prepared for scholarships at the Welsh University Colleges and the older Universities of Oxford and Cambridge. Every effort will be made to make the School a good Classical, Scientific and Technical Institution. Due attention will be paid to Drill, Field Sports and Athletics.

The Prospectus pointed out that the school buildings were situated in an elevated and healthy position with perfect sanitary arrangements and an abundant supply of the famous Plynlimon water, 'which has been one of the chief factors in enhancing the prosperity of Aberystwyth as a fashionable watering resort'.

On Thursday October 1 1896 at 10 o'clock as many as 53 candidates presented themselves for the Scholarship Examination 'a good omen for the future success of the School'. The Examiner, D Thomas HMIS presented his report to the Governing Body which made the following awards:-

1.	John James	Commercial and Grammar School
2.	Richard David Edwards	The Old Bank School
3	(Goronwy Owen	Ardwyn School
	(John Hugh Phillips	Ardwyn School
5	W H Trenwith Davies	Commercial and Grammar School
6.	Gwesyn T Williams	Talybont Board School
7.	Thomas David Jones	Aberystwyth Board School
8.	David Thomas	Aberystwyth Board School
9	Evan Doughton Evans	Aberystwyth Board School
10	Griffith Shannon	Rhydypennau School
11	David John de Lloyd	Carmarthen Board
12	Griffith Daniel Ellis	Aberystwyth Board

The candidates listed varied in age from 12 years to 17 years and as "Free Scholars" were exempt from the school fees of £5 per annum.

D. Samuel M.A., Headmaster 1896–1921

Chapter One

THE DAVID SAMUEL YEARS

1896-1921

Aberystwyth County School opened on Tuesday, October 6 1896. David Samuel noted in the School record book:

> A day which it is hoped will be ever-memorable in the educational history of North Cardiganshire. For more than two centuries there have been schools of undoubted reputation in Cardiganshire. Cardigan, Ystrad Meurig, Lampeter School, St. David's College, Neuadd Llwyd, Llwyn Rhyd Owen, Llanfihangel Geneu'r Glyn, the Aberystwyth Grammar School, have been institutions which in years past have made our County famous as a portion of the Principality which sets a high price on education. Private schools too there have been, such as Mr John Evans's Commercial and Mathematical School in this town which have done acknowledged work in the instruction of Youth. All these institutions were so to speak disconnected points. The new school on the other hand was to be a member(and an important member) of an organic whole. It is to occupy an Intermediate place between the public elementary schools, on the one hand and the University Colleges on the other. It is to complete the educational edifice from the foundation in the elementary school to the topmost summit in the University.

On the opening day, the 55 boys who entered as pupils were given a short examination by the masters and placed in three classes: Form iii, the highest form had 12 pupils, Form ii had 22 and Form i 21. The staff had drawn a code of rules to be observed by the pupils and these were read out by the Headmaster at the first school assembly

School Rules

1. No boy is allowed in any part of the school premises except the playground. The drive and pathway to the school are not to be used as playgrounds.
2. Throwing stones is strictly forbidden; as is also climbing walls and fences and damaging or disfiguring any part of the school property, inside or out, by writing, cutting or any other means.
3. Orderly behaviour is to be observed at all times within the school house. No running, loud talking, whistling or playing is allowed in the schoolrooms or lobby at any time.
4. The staircase is only to be used going to and from the upper schoolroom at the times appointed for lessons there. No boy is allowed to be on the stairs at any other time. In going to and from lessons in the upper room, boys are to go up and down silently and in single file.

5 Each boy is held responsible for the condition of all books lent to him. Books are to be kept in the lockers provided for the purpose and no boy may use a book belonging to another boy.

6 All boys who are late or absent from school at any time and for any reason must bring a written excuse from parent or guardian

7 It is expected that all boys will maintain the character and reputation of the school by orderly and gentlemanly behaviour in the Town and streets at all times.

8 Smoking is strictly forbidden.

Within a few weeks of the opening of the school, the Headmaster gave his first report to the School Governors at a meeting in the Town Hall on Saturday October 24 1896. He outlined the arrangements made for the conduct of the scholarship examinations and the difficulties encountered in accommodating as many as 53 candidates which meant that some took the examination in other premises in the town. David Samuel was aware of the fears in the minds of the elementary teachers and others that the subjects set down for the examination were ill-adapted for such candidates as were invited to compete. All fair-minded persons and schoolmasters who were competent to give an opinion on the subject would agree that the Examiner and the Headmaster had rightly gauged what could be done by the young scholars. He had sent copies of the examination papers to all the head teachers of the elementary schools in the area for their help and guidance and as a means of keeping in touch with the schools from which they would be drawing their pupils.

Included in his report, which is given in full in volume 1 of the record book, is a copy of the time table, provided 'in the full conviction that the scheme of work in the School's first term of existence will have much interest to the historian of the school in the years to come.'

The Headmaster emphasised that the time-table must be looked upon as 'extremely temporary and ephemeral made on the three-teachers plan.' He thought that increased numbers would soon entitle the school to a fourth master, requiring a new scheme of work to be formulated. Pupils would be prepared for the Welsh Matriculation in June, and the Cambridge Locals in December 1897. In order to prepare pupils for the South Kensington Examinations in Science and Art in May and to qualify for grants for science the Governors were urged to appoint a Science Master. Samuel was aware that there was no provision for teaching Drawing, Shorthand, Music and Drill as yet, possibly Drill could be undertaken by one of the Artillery serjeants and Music could come into the plan of work by extending the afternoon work by 15 minutes twice a week. Many parents were particularly anxious to see steps taken to provide for education of girls in the school and the Headmaster wished to be guided by the Governors in the desirability of opening morning school with a Scripture reading and prayers and trusted that they were keeping in view the question of the football field.

It was thought that the boys would present a better appearance about the town if a uniform cap were adopted, the sub-committee had selected green and white as the school colours and steps would be taken to get samples with a suitable monogram.

The David Samuel Years — 1896-1921

In the full conviction that the scheme of work in the School's first Term of existence will have much interest to the historian of the School in years to come, a copy of the Time Table is subjoined:—

Time-Table: October, 1896.

[Handwritten timetable grid with columns for Monday, Tuesday, Wednesday, Thursday, Friday, Saturday, each subdivided into forms iii, ii, i. Entries include subjects such as Script., Scr., Engl., Lat., Arith., Grk., Wr., Euc., Welsh, Alg., Hist., Geo., Fr., Chem., Mech., Engl. authors, Spelling & Dict., Engl. Comp., with teacher codes Hd (Headmaster), F (Mr Fuller), O (Mr Owens). "Interval" appears mid-morning and "Half Holiday" on Wednesday and Saturday afternoons.]

In the above scheme, Hd stands for Headmaster, F & O stand respectively for Mr Fuller and Mr Owens, assistant masters.

The time table was arranged with a view of preparing pupils for the South Kensington examinations, and also for the Cambridge Locals.

School Timetable, October 1896

Concluding his report, David Samuel was confident

> that everything augurs well for the school. There is a tone about the conduct of the Boys which is satisfactory. The rules which have been posted up have had a salutary effect upon their behaviour generally. They come and go in an orderly manner and their conduct in the town has been highly creditable. They are punctual, and when in classrooms they set themselves to their problems and their work and are a pleasure to behold. It was a matter of great regret that the boys who came by morning train missed the first hour of the school day which had a deteriorating effect upon their work generally.

The Headmaster paid tribute to his colleagues for their honest and conscientious work. They worked in great harmony and shared his desire for the success of the School.

Soon afterwards the School obtained a football field. This was a plot of land above the rock called "Grogythan" situated at the back of the school premises. The boys were 'delighted' and School was called together in assembly to elect officers for the football club. 'With much excitement', John Hugh Phillips was elected captain and John James vice-captain. On Wednesday November 11 the opening match on the new field was played against a scratch team designated 'The Wednesday'-the School won easily as they did a fortnight later beating their great rivals-the Grammar School five goals to one. 'The prowess of the players was such as to expect a very good school team if they applied themselves with some regularity to play together.'

Wasting no time, the Governors quickly acted on the advice of the Headmaster and appointed Dewi Ellis as Science Master at a salary of £100 per annum. He was a native of Aberystwyth having received his education at the Old Bank School under David Samuel, the present Headmaster of the County School. He gained a scholarship to Aberystwyth College and gained his degree just before his appointment to the County School where he took up his duties on December 11. This appointment required a change in the time-table with the number of forms increased to four. By this time the number on the register was 69.

During this first term the Governors continued their diligent work and in turn, as members of the visiting committee, spent time in the School, reporting back to the Board on any matters which they deemed needed attention. The sanitary condition of the School premises was one cause for concern and following a report by the Borough Surveyor, TE Morgan the Architect, was instructed to carry out the necessary remedial work. A room had to be equipped for science teaching, £10 was provided for the necessary apparatus. The work of collecting subscriptions continued with each Governor being allocated to a particular town ward or an outlying area. Mrs Hannah Jones was engaged to clean the school and to light fires at 7/6 per week while fires were required and 5/- at other times.

There was a long discussion on homework, opinion being expressed that too much was required from the pupils. The Headmaster was obviously able to alleviate those fears when he reported back. Dr Snape asked about the practicability of introducing German into the curriculum and the Board turned down the offer of purchasing the Barrack Field jointly with the War Office and UCW because of their precarious financial position. The first term came to an end on December 23 1896 with a school assembly

The David Samuel Years — 1896-1921

The Old Ardwyn pre 1896 with a cricket match in progress and a yet undeveloped Llanbadarn road.

The Staff and Senior Pupils, 1899
(seated) J. H. Howells, Tom Owen, David Samuel, Edith Ewart, S. E. Thomas, W. P. Fuller.

when the work of the term was reviewed and the boys commended for their very satisfactory conduct, with the usual groans when the re-opening date was mentioned. The Headmaster announced that next term he would offer, in order to promote the study of Welsh and English Literature, two prizes to candidates who should gain highest marks in an examination based on two Welsh and two English texts.

The examination duly took place in the first week of the Lent term, John James taking the Welsh prize and John Hugh Phillips the English prize, both were Free Scholars. The number of pupils had grown to 73 of whom two were newly admittted 'Close Scholars'. These new scholarships were part of scheme relating to the sale of the old National School in Northgate Street. The money arising from the sale had been invested in the Great Western Railway 5% Preference Stock and part of the yearly income was to be utilized for

> the advancement of education of children who are *bona fide* residents within the Borough of Aberystwyth, who have, for not less than three years, been scholars in the Aberystwyth National School and who have received from the managers of the school such certificates in writing of their good conduct, regularity in attendance, and proficiency as shall be satisfactory to the Trustees. The Exhibitions shall be tenable in the Aberystwyth County School of Intermediate and Technical Education. The scholarships were awarded for a period of 2 years extendible to 3 years.

The first holders were Edward Jones, Bridge Street and Stanley Bertram Masse

In the first week of February 1897, the residents of the town were to see for the first time, county schoolboys resplendent in their new school caps-green and white with the image of the central tower of Aberystwyth Castle in front, a design which was to stand the test of time. An event which was to become a permanent feature of school life in later years, the School Eisteddfod, was not celebrated, instead the pupils had a full day's holiday on St David's Day.

At this time there were changes in the Governing Body due to County Council elections- newly appointed members were Mrs Jessy Williams and CM Williams. There was a change too in the School Board representation, with the appointment of Mrs Mary Jane James, Dolbont. The term of office of the Chairman, Ald Peter Jones had come to an end and he was succeeded by Dr Lloyd Snape with Richard Richards elected vice-chairman There were also elections in School, when, in preparation for the summer, Ivor Evans was appointed captain and John Hugh Phillips vice-captain of the cricket club although at this stage there was nowhere for them to play. The Governors voted the sum of £12 to establish the club in the hope that the Town football club would allow use of part of the Vicarage field for cricket. In mid-May the Charity Commissioners approved the plans for the additional buildings and authorised the Governors to invite tenders for the execution of the work. After six months delay involving re-tendering, the contract was won by Messrs Belham of London at a price of £3195

A sub-committee of the Governing Body, having met to consider the question of scholarships made the recommendation that fourteen scholarships be awarded for the following year. On the advice of the Headmaster, seven of the original twelve Free Scholars were given a renewal and seven offered for competition amongst the boys of the elementary schools of the district who had been in attendance for not less than three years.

The David Samuel Years — 1896-1921

The School reopened for the Midsummer Term with numbers slightly down on the preceding term though with six new boys. Early in the term, Owen Owen, newly appointed Chief Inspector of Intermediate Schools, paid a visit of inspection. He arrived early and saw the school working from the time of roll call to the end of the afternoon. Several classrooms were visited and boys questioned. The presence of the visitor, 'did not disturb the equilibrium of the boys although he was dressed imposingly in the academic gown and scarlet MA Oxford hood.'

In the evening Mr Owen met the Governors in the dining room of the Schoolhouse to discuss the work contemplated by the Welsh Central Board in the organisation and inspection of the County Schools. After congratulating the Governors on the magnificent situation of the school he gave details of the examinations which would take place in July and made recommendations for apparatus &c adding that he was well pleased with what he had seen.

In the same week that the boys started cricket on the Vicarage field, evening classes for those entering the examinations of the Welsh Matriculation and the Science and Arts (Board of Education) were begun. In May, Serjeant WJ Long of the Barracks, gave the first lesson in Drill; he had been engaged at a salary of £5 per annum. 'The first exercises included, the turns, half turns, three-quarter turns, right about turns and form four's. The Boys were interested in their Drill exercises and took as serious a view of this portion of their tasks as could reasonably be expected.'

The first external examinations started in June with six pupils being examined for the Welsh Matriculation followed by thirty-one candidates for the Science and Arts Examination in Mathematics Stage 1, Mechanics and Chemistry. The latter examination had been postponed from the original date owing to the celebrations connected with the Queen's Diamond Jubilee.

The results of the Welsh Matriculation examination proved to be somewhat disappointing, only two pupils figured in the published list- Senior Scholar John James who passed in all five subjects and John Hugh Phillips, another Scholar who succeeded in four out of five subjects.

> this was probably more than we had a right to expect in our first year but we trust that these are only the first fruits of a long series of successes that we shall be called upon to chronicle in the Records of the School.

The first Central Welsh Board (CWB) examinations took place during the last week of the session to bring the first year of existence of the School to a close, 'our Boys had a particularly hard time, some of the papers were of considerable difficulty but the English Literature papers were singularly well adapted for our best pupils.'

When the school opened for its second year, there was obvious disappointment in the number of pupils admitted, some 19 fewer than at the end of the previous term though this number did increase later. Devil's Bridge Board School produced the first two Scholars in a list of six, a seventh scholarship was withheld. Apart from the decision of the Governing Body to begin construction of the new buildings, the main event of the term was the first Prize Distribution held on December 17 1897. The Governors decided that it should take place in the Headmaster's classroom and not in the Public Rooms

The History of Aberystwyth County School (Ardwyn) 1896-1973

"THE SCHOOL will be re-opened (for boys and girls) on TUESDAY, JANUARY 24th, 1899

ABERYSTWYTH COUNTY SCHOOL.

Headmaster:

Mr. DAVID SAMUEL, M.A. (Cantab),
Late Foundation Scholar, Exhibitioner and Prizeman Clare College, Cambridge; 20th Wrangler, 1879, and formerly Open Scholar, U.C.W.

Senior Mistress:

MISS EDITH M. EWART, M.A. (Vict.),
Honours in History; late Head Mistress of Abertillery County School, and formerly Assistant Mistress at Belford College, Liverpool.

Assistant Masters:

Mr. W. PEARSON FULLER, M.A. (Lond.)
Classical Honours in B.A. Exam.; 6th on List in M.A. Exam.; formerly Open Scholar U.C.W.

Mr. THOMAS OWENS,
Late Headmaster of the Aberystwyth Commercial and Grammar School, and formerly Senior Scholar, U.C.W.

Drawing:

Mr. J. H. APPLETON,
Cert. Art Master; Examiner to Science and Art Department, 1892 and 1893; Associate of the Manchester Academy of Arts, etc.

Drill:

Serjeant=Major W. J. LONG.

TERMS:—£5 PER ANNUM (FOR BOYS AND GIRLS).

County School – Prospectus

ABERYSTWYTH COUNTY SCHOOL.

List of Subscriptions towards the Building Fund.

TO THE 20TH JANUARY, 1902.

	£	s.	d.
The Right Honourable Lord Rendel	300	0	0
Mr W. T. Jones, Melbourne	210	0	0
Mr J. M. Vaughan Davies, M.P., Tanybwlch	100	0	0
Mr William Williams, H.M.I.S., Aberystwyth	50	0	0
Mr David Samuel, Headmaster (£100) paid	50	0	0
Rev. Thomas Levi, St. David's Road, Aberystwyth	50	0	0
Mr David Howell, Great Darkgate Street	50	0	0
Mr J. C. Roberts, South Marine Terrace	45	0	0
Mr John Evans, Laura Place	30	0	0
Mr G. D. White, St. David's Road	30	0	0
Mr Peter Jones, Portland Street	30	0	0
Mrs E. L. Williams, Fishguard	30	0	0
Miss E. Charles Davies, North Parade, Aberystwyth	30	0	0
Mr Evan Evans, Solicitor	30	0	0
Mr John Evans, Solicitor	30	0	0
Mr Evan Edwards, The Laurels	30	0	0
Mr Daniel Thomas, Princess Marine Terrace	30	0	0
Mrs Roberts, Bridge Street	30	0	0
Mr R. Bickerstaff, Great Darkgate Street	30	0	0
Messrs. M. H. Davis & Sons, Ironmongers	30	0	0
National Provincial Bank of England, Ltd.	26	5	0
Vicountess Parker	25	0	0
Mr Rd. Morgan, Great Darkgate Street, Aberystwyth	25	0	0
Mr H. C. Fryer, 52, Marine Terrace	25	0	0
Mr Morris Davies, Ffoselrydegaled	21	0	0
Principal Roberts, University College of Wales	20	0	0
Mr J. R. Rees, N. & S. W. Bank	20	0	0
Mr J. Griffith, Waterloo Hotel	15	0	0
Professor R. W. Genese, U.C.W.	15	0	0
Mr Robert Ellis, Chemist	15	0	0
Mr David Richards, North Parade	15	0	0
Mr C. M. Williams, Pier Street	15	0	0
Mr Robert Doughton, Great Darkgate St.	12	12	0
Mr Howell Evans, Chief Constable	10	10	0
Mr J. P. Thomas, Chemist	10	10	0
Mr W. Powell, Portland Street	10	10	0
Professor D. Jenkins, U.C.W.	10	10	0
Miss Fryer, 52, Marine Terrace	10	0	0
The Ven. Archdeacon Protheroe	10	0	0
Mr J. Powell, Little Darkgate Street	10	0	0
Mr David Price, London	10	0	0
Mr T. Lumley Davies, Liverpool	10	0	0
Capt David James, Llanbadarn road, Aberystwyth	10	0	0
Professor Stuart, U.C.W.	10	0	0
Mr. E. Morris, Architect	10	0	0
Mr Edward Evans, Great Darkgate street	8	15	0
Professor Marshall, U.C.W.	8	0	0
Mr Daniel Thomas, Little Darkgate Street	7	10	0
Mr. E. P. Wynne, Chemist	7	7	0
Rev Trepardy Williams	7	0	0
Professor Herford, U.C.W.	6	16	6
Capt. J. G. Bennett, Pier Street	6	0	0
Mr David Jenkins, Maesteg, Glandovey	6	0	0
Mr G. Wilkinson, North Parade, Aberystwyth	6	0	0
Mr J. J. Jones, South Marine Terrace	5	0	0
Mr C. M. Richards & Co., Meat Street	5	0	0
Mr H. Mallory, Llanbadarn Road	5	0	0
Mr Felix, Bryncaerneld	5	0	0
Professor Ethe, U.C.W.	5	0	0
Professor D. Morgan Lewis, U.C.W.	5	0	0
Mr H. L. Evans, Borough Accountant	5	0	0
Mr James James, Ffynonhowell, Llanhystyd	5	0	0
Rev A. P. Edwards, Queen's Road, Aberystwyth	5	0	0
Mr A. J. W. James, Dolybont, Borth, R.S.O.	5	0	0
Professor Anwyl, U.C.W., Aberystwyth	5	0	0
Mr Rowland Morgan, Marine Terrace	5	0	0
Misses Owen, North Parade	5	0	0
Mr David Evans, Great Darkgate Street	5	0	0
Mr Thomas Owens, Queen Square	5	0	0

	£	s.	d.
Miss Katie Powell, Pier Street, Aberystwyth	5	0	0
Mr J. H. Edwards, North Parade	4	4	0
Rev. T. A. Penry, Bath Street	4	0	0
Mrs D. E. James, Cardiff	3	3	0
Mr Edward Ellis, Little Darkgate Street, Aberystwyth	3	3	0
Mr J. Walter Evans, Great Darkgate Street	3	3	0
Professor J. E. Lloyd, Bangor	3	3	0
Dr Abraham Thomas, Aberystwyth	3	3	0
Miss Jessie Roberts, Marine Terrace, Aberystwyth	3	0	0
Mr Samuel Green, Llanbadarn	3	0	0
Mr David Owen, Great Darkgate Street	3	0	0
Mrs C. Ellis	3	0	0
Mr Edward Edwards	3	0	0
Mr Hugh Hughes, Solicitor	3	0	0
Mr William Jenkins, Great Darkgate Street	3	0	0
Rev. Job Miles, Caradog Road	3	0	0
Mr John Hughes, 17, Portland Street	3	0	0
Mr Thomas Hall, Terrace Road	3	0	0
Mr John Phillips, Trefnes Issa, Llanilar	3	0	0
Mr David Thomas, H.M.I.S., Aberystwyth	3	0	0
Miss Getta Jones, Marine Terrace	2	2	0
Mr Angus per Miss Richards	2	2	0
Mr J. Lewis Evans, Great Darkgate Street, Aberystwyth	2	2	0
Mr T. Cruickshank, Queen's Road	2	2	0
Mr E. H. Short, H.M.I.S.	2	2	0
Mr David Rees, Pantgwyrfol, Llanilar	2	2	0
Mr J. Samuel, Bridge Street, Aberystwyth	2	2	0
Mr David Jones, Rest, Trawscoed	2	2	0
Mrs Humpidge, Laura place, Aberystwyth	2	2	0
Capt Davies, 13, Powell Street	2	2	0
Rev Griffith Parry, Llanbadarn	2	2	0
Mr J. Bradbury, Board School	2	2	0
Mr W. R. Jones, Great Darkgate Street	2	0	6
Mr Thomas, Evans, Terrace Road	1	10	0
Rev. William Jones, North Parade	1	10	0
Mr John Thomas, Bridge Street	1	5	0
Mr M. Price, Brynyamman	1	1	0
Mrs Martha Griffiths, Great Darkgate St., Aberystwyth	1	1	0
Mr David Thomas, North Gate House	1	1	0
Mr K. Saycell, Great Darkgate Street	1	1	0
Mr Hughes, 48, Portland Street	1	1	0
Mrs M. Owen, Caradog Road	1	1	0
Mrs Williams, Brighton House	1	1	0
Mr T. J. Samuel, Solicitor	1	1	0
Mr T. Rees, Broncetro, Penygors	1	1	0
Mr Isaac Griffith, Douglas House, Aberystwyth	1	1	0
Mr David Ellis, Rose villa, Llanfarian	1	1	0
Misses Ward, Great Darkgate Street, Aberystwyth	1	1	0
Mr John Roberts, Terrace road	1	0	0
Mr John James, Twlcelanwyn, Penllwyn	0	10	6
Mr John Morris, Penylan, Penllwyn	0	10	6
Mr H. Meredith, Bridge Street, Aberystwyth	0	10	6
Mr John Jones, Garthawr, Llanilar	0	10	6
Capt Cosens, Brompadarn, Aberystwyth	0	10	6
Mr D. R. Davies, Post School, Chancery	0	10	6
Rev. N. Thomas, Llanbadarfawr	0	10	0
Mr William Rowlands, Brenan	0	10	0
Mr Evan Jones, Tancastell, Aberystwyth	0	10	0
Mr J. M. Williams, Brynhwl, Borth	0	10	0
Mr J. H. Edwards, Capel Seion	0	10	0
Capt Richard Davies, Barry	0	10	0
Miss Jessie Davies, Bridge Street, Aberystwyth	0	10	0
Mr David Williams, Talybont	0	10	0
Mrs Clapperton, Terrace Road, Aberystwyth	0	10	0
Mrs Richards, Jenkins, Marine Street, Aberystwyth	0	10	0
Mrs M. Evans, Ceylon House, Llanon	0	10	0
Mr John Jones, Ffynonwen, Llangwyryfon	0	10	0
Miss M. Jones, 42, Marine Terrace, Aberystwyth	0	5	0
Miss E. F. Jones, 44, Marine Terrace	0	5	0
Mr John Jones, Barry	0	5	0
Mrs Kemil, Victoria Terrace	0	5	0
Subscriptions received per Rev. T. R. Morice, without the names of the Subscribers	9	4	0
	£1970	**15**	**6**

NOTE.—In addition to the above the Aberystwyth Corporation has made a Grant of £500 in lieu of a Site.

List of Subscriptions to the Building Fund

The David Samuel Years — 1896-1921

The entire Aberystwyth County School, July 13th, 1897.
Staff from l to r: W. P. Fuller, David Samuel (Head), T. Owen, D. Ellis.

'as some would have liked'. Chairman of the School Managers, Prof Lloyd Snape presided and the Headmaster, reviewing the first year in the life of the School, had no doubt that 'this would be the first of a long series of prize days held in connection with the School'. Since the opening day 103 pupils had enrolled and even those who spent just one term in the School would have gained much through contact with masters and pupils. David Samuel did not agree with Pope's dictum that a little knowledge was a dangerous thing. He spoke in commendable terms of the work done by his charges, making special mention of John James who had gained the Welsh Matriculation, and had received a prize from O M Edwards for an essay on the history of Wales during the reign of Victoria. It was not given to all pupils to win prizes, but this was not a matter of discouragement, for failures were often more instructive and disciplinary than success. At present they were all engaged in laying down the foundation for the future superstructure and too great things should not be expected from a young institution.

Dr Snape, in presenting the prizes, thought that there was a degree of uncertainty about examinations, where examiners had no knowledge save what was learnt by means of the papers; on the other hand there was a degree of certainty in school prizes made after careful examination by their own teachers who took notice of work during the whole year. Addressing himself to those who had not won prizes, Dr Snape urged them not to be discouraged, many valuable habits were formed during their school career, precision, exactitude, reverence, self-control, and withal to think of oneself no higher than one ought to think. Stein, the Russian statesman had said- 'What is put into the schools of a country comes out in the manhood of a nation'. Whilst England still waited for a scheme of state-aided secondary education, Wales had, thanks to the Intermediate Act, the honour of carrying out the first experiment in bridging the gap between the elementary schools and the colleges. There were many problems in realising what they all wanted to see. The scanty population and small rateable value particularly in Central Wales rendered funds small and made it difficult to establish and maintain schools. Given enthusiasm amongst the people, teachers and scholars, even poverty would prove no insuperable obstacle. The three university colleges in Wales had successfully contended with this lack of means and made progress. Aberystwyth College had out-distanced every other university college save London in the contest for places in the pass and honours lists of the University of London. Aberystwyth had become a renowned educational centre and it would be fitting that the Intermediate School placed in that town should become the premier county school of the Principality.

The Headmaster noted in his record book that the proceedings were marked with much enthusiasm. The prizebooks were very handsomely bound and had the words "Aberystwyth County School" beautifully printed in letters of gold on the outside of the cover.

Pupils returning after the Christmas break, found the architect and clerk of works marking out the foundations of the new building and labourers had begun felling trees to the south of the building and demolishing the wall which ran the length of the old playground. By mid-March 'the work had so far advanced that the walls were considerably above the ground. It need hardly be stated that boys as well as the masters took a lively interest in the construction of the new buildings.' The Governors, conscious of the need to publicise the School in order to attract more pupils, agreed to place advertisements in the UCW Magazine, the local newspapers and the *Montgomery County*

Times. They voted the sum of £16 to modify the Science classroom by erecting a gallery to allow pupils a better view of experiments. The problem of unsuitable train schedules was still a matter of concern and the Governors instructed fires to be lit early for the convenience of those pupils arriving by the 7am train ! It was also agreed that only the Headmaster should inflict corporal punishment.

The Governors were reminded by the County Governing Body that the omission of Vocal Music and Drill or Physical Exercises from the curriculum would, after this warning, entail a reduction in th Treasury grant. The Headmaster was requested to provide Vocal Music forthwith and the Clerk was instructed to reply that this was being done and to point out that the reference to Drill was manifestly unfair as this subject was included in the timetable.

In Football, the School team, a combination of past and present pupils, was very successful in many a contest. A victory over great rivals Towyn County School made up for a defeat the previous season and the teams were entertained to tea by the Headmaster in the Chemical Room. There were other 'trials of strength including a match against a College Second Eleven in which our team showed their prowess.'

By the time the School broke up for the Easter holidays, the walls of the new buildings 'had so proceeded that the memorial slab under the central window of the Assembly Hall facing the lawn was inserted in its place. It bore no motto of any kind:this was yet to come'. The health of the boys 'had been marvellously good throughout, considering there was very great illness throughout the neighbourhood as indeed throughout the whole country-an influenza epidemic raging everywhere.'

The Headmaster was absent for the opening of the Midsummer Term having been given leave of absence for a visit to Rome and some other Italian cities during and after the Easter vacation. However he was present to receive the Chief Inspector on his annual visit in May. By coincidence, Mr Skirrow, the Science and Art (Board of Education) Inspector also arrived- both were 'highly pleased with what they had seen during the day'. On his appointment as CWB examiner, Dr Snape was compelled to resign from the Board of Managers of the School. His place as Chairman was taken by Richard Richards who took the opportunity to address the boys when he chaired the lecture given by the Headmaster on his recent visit to Rome.

For some time the subject of entrance scholarships to the county schools had been under consideration by the County Governing Body. The result of their deliberations was that all county schools in Cardiganshire would have the same scholarship examination and the same examiner viz. Mr Darlington H M I of Schools. Elementary schools were issued with a syllabus of subjects to be examined. All candidates would sit papers in Arithmetic, English Composition or translation from Welsh to English and Dictation. In addition they would have to choose at least two subjects from English Grammar, History, Geography, Welsh, Euclid, Domestic Economy, Algebra, Scripture, Needlework, Science. An age limit of 14 years would be imposed on intending candidates. Early in June 1898 an advertisement appeared in the local papers offering six Scholarships to boys entering in September and five to girls entering in January 1899 or as soon as the new School buildings were completed.

In the external examinations towards the end of term, Goronwy Owen, a Scholar of 1896 passed the Welsh matriculation in all five subjects and David Jenkins gained four subjects. These results were identical to those of the previous year. In the Science and Arts examination all candidates presented passed the examinations in Mathematics, Chemistry, and Mechanics. All pupils in the School were entered for the CWB examinations in July, again there were great successes as the Headmaster reported in the Prize Day later in the year.

On July 1 the main roof beams of the new building were in place and the boys watched with great interest and were no less jubilant than the workmen themselves when a red flag was set up to notify the progress. The Headmaster wrote, 'the pupils watched with great wonderment the craftmanship of the skilled workman working on the slab beneath the great window of the Assembly Hall. The stone carver was a young Welshman from Llanidloes, Evan Rees who had also done admirable skilled work at the College, and who owed his career largely to the kindness and support of Lord Rendel'. His floral carving of the sandstone slab has withstood the ravages of time and it is as impressive today as it was to those young admirers over ninety years ago. The same craftsman sculpted the bosses, the finial atop the Hall and the words 'County School 1898' below.

Fifteen candidates, eight boys and seven girls sat the entrance scholarship on Saturday July 30 in the Headmaster's classroom, with invigilation by some of the Governors. For the first time girls had entered a male domain and of the twelve scholarships subsequently awarded six went to girls, three of whom occupied positions 3, 4 and 5 in the order of merit.

There was again disappointment with the numbers enrolled for the start of the the third year. Although twelve new boys arrived, a large number of pupils had left, 'a loss more observable in the fourth form which was stripped of all its former students except two.' During the summer vacation there had been some internal alterations to the existing classrooms and the Headmaster's residence had been closed off from the rest of the school.

There was great elation when the School received news that two pupils had been awarded two of the three scholarships awarded by the Cardiganshire County Council to pupils from intermediate schools in the County based on the results of the external examinations. The achievements were all the more commendable since this was the first occasion that the School was eligible having been established for just two years. When the marks of the CWB examination, on which the awards were based, were revealed the Headmaster commented, 'to have so far outstripped the third candidate was a great distinction of which we are very proud.' The successful scholars, who took up their scholarships at U C W in October 1898 were John James of Bow Street, a farmer's son and Goronwy Owen of Penllwyn, son of a miner. James who had gained distinctions in all twelve subjects sat in the CWB examination, later entered the ministry but died at the early age of 38 years. Owen who obtained ten distinctions went on to gain a B A and M A at U C W, the first Aberystwyth County School pupil to receive these degrees, was decorated for gallantry in the Great War and achieved eminence in the business and political world.

The Governors received regular reports from the Architect on the building progress, decided to have stoves rather than open fires to heat the classrooms and ordered double and triple desks to be made locally to the Architect's design at 19/-and 27/- respectively.

Finances were obviously in a desperate state. They had to refuse a request for a salary increase from Mr Ellis, found it impossible to give form prizes and to subsidise the football club. In December 1898 they were overdrawn at the bank and collectors were asked to visit their respective districts immediately to collect subscriptions.

The Governors, with the newly appointed member Prof R W Genese representing the Senate of U C W, spent some time discussing the position and status of a Senior Mistress who would have to be appointed, with the admission of girls imminent. After considering proposals from the County Governing Body, the Board declared in favour of a separate Girls' school under a separate Head Mistress receiving a capitation fee in respect of every girl pupil while retaining the power of interchange of men and women teachers and for mixed classes. In the event the advertisement sought a Senior Mistress who would have entire charge of girls' discipline in the girls' department at a salary of £180 pa. It also stated that application had been made to convert the girls' department into a separate school. The post went to Edith E Ewart, headmistress of Abertillery County School, who was the only student of her year in Victoria University, Manchester to gain first class honours.

The first Scholarship for Aberystwyth County School pupils tenable at the U C W was established in 1898 by J D Perrott, County Treasurer of Cardiganshire. The exhibition of £10, was for a woman student who had been a pupil for at least two years at Aberystwyth County School or at Brecon Girls' County School and who, as a result of entrance examinations showed the highest proficiency in French or German or both.

Two years to the day on which he was appointed to the Staff, Dewi Ellis accepted an appointment in Wakefield. At a presentation to mark his departure, the Headmaster expressed great regret on his leaving but pleasure on his securing a more lucrative position. A contributor to the Jubilee Magazine published in 1946 remembers Dewi Ellis as 'a teacher of "stinks" who was a most likeable person but out of his element a little with children and who revealed little of the ability which was later to bring him distinction in academic circles.'[3]

The U C W, the School Board and the School Governors agreed to share the services of an Art teacher, J H Appleton, headmaster of Oldham School of Art was appointed as art master. He was highly spoken of as a painter and designer by the principal of the National Art Training School at South Kensington.

The new buildings were progressing well despite the adverse weather. By November, the front of the central hall had reached as high above the great window as the letters 'County School 1898' and there was universal delight when, in particularly bad weather, the finial was in place. The scaffolding was rapidly removed and early in December 1898 the whole of the Central Hall had been tiled.

Unfortunately Prize Day could not be held in the Central Hall as had been hoped a year previously. Richard Richards, chairman of Governors presiding, congratulated the School on the progress made during the year, adding that no boy or girl could wish for a better secondary education than that given at their school, 'there would always be some people deluded by the idea that something at a distance was better than that near to them.' Addressing himself to the sons of farmers, he advised them to become familiar with chemistry, which showed the nature of the soil and how to make it productive, and botany so they would know of the nutritive value of the different grasses.

In his second annual report, the Headmaster regretted that so many able boys had left, many of them for the Civil Service and the banks. He quoted at length from the reports of the external examiners which were 'very pleasing and creditable.' The progress made by the school in the last year could be measured by comparing the 114 distinctions gained that year with 35 the previous year. With Drawing now on the curriculum, all the requirements of the scheme under which the School was established had been satisfied.

Prizes and certificates were presented by Mrs Jessy Williams, a Governor, the prize books bore the motto of the School *"Nerth Dysg ei Ymdrech"*. (the power of learning is in the effort) This is the first reference to the School motto, the circumstances of its adoption are not recorded.

Owen Owen, Chief Inspector of Schools, revealed that the Central Board would like to have just one annual school examination that would suffice for all purposes.

> There had to be examinations, they had a great deal to do in emphasising proper efforts of teaching. There would be, in future, greater emphasis on practical work particularly in Science. This would diminish the gulf between school life and the ordinary life of the world which was to follow it. Ultimately the success of a school was not to be measured by its examination successes, however good they might be, but by the number of strong men it sent into the world, by the number of leaders in thought and action, who were able to look back on their school days as a time of inspiration and a time that gave them strength.

Mr Owen hoped that with such excellent new buildings they would take new heart, new courage and aim to make their school one of the best in the country. Though the School had been in existence for just two years there was much to be proud of.

Principal T F Roberts of the University College, who also spoke, knew that in the county of Cardigan they had a high educational ideal. They would watch carefully the progress of the School, there were signs that it had a great future. The public had responded generously to the appeal for financial support and the Governors would be encouraged to continue to aim for the highest. He emphasised the need for physical fitness and hoped 'that they, being the flower of the younger generation from whom Wales expected hard and good work in the future, would not only have better trained intellectual powers than those who had gone before but that they would also have strong and buoyant physical natures with which to face the work.'

Delay in completion of the new buildings caused the postponement of the re-opening of the School for the Lent Term 1899 so it was not until January 24 that it started its 'mixed' career. It was reliably reported that many glad eyes were noted on both sides on that memorable day.

The David Samuel Years — 1896-1921

During the vacation, a circular had been widely distributed throughout the school district drawing the attention of parents to the admission of girls and to the great successes already obtained as testified by the Chief Inspector. A new advertisement in the local papers drew attention to the staff and their qualifications. The result was that 41 girls and 55 boys registered on the first day with a further 3 girls and 11 boys bringing the total to 110 by the end of the term.

'Some trifling inconveniences were experienced' with the increased numbers but were soon overcome. Three of the classes were mixed, the exceptions being the third and fifth, the latter being a new class, the result of having five teachers. The large first class of 35 were nearly all girls.

The Governors had been informed that at the annual inspection of the School in February, the Chief Inspector would need to see a copy of the regulations respecting licensed lodgings. A set of rules was quickly drawn up with regard to the sanitation of the houses and supervision of the pupils; accompanying the rules was a form of application for a lodging house licence. A copy of the document is extant and indicates that pupils should not be out of the house after 8. 30 pm in winter months and after 9. 30 pm in summer and that boys and girls, unless brother and sister, were not allowed to reside in the same house.

The Governors voted a sum of £45 for a science laboratory and appointed Maude Hughes an honours graduate in botany of U C W to the temporary post of science teacher. The masters' and mistresses' rooms were furnished albeit sparsely although the mistresses were allocated a couch and a small chandelier! The girls had exclusive use of the St. David's Road entrance with the boys now having to use the pathway from Llanbadarn Road.

Samuel Evans who had acted as Clerk to the Governors died suddenly in March and his brother, John Evans, whose term of office as a Governor had recently expired, succeeded him. At this time, the Governors, with a new chairman, George Davies granted a request from George Rees for an order to insert the School advertisement in the new weekly paper (*The Welsh Gazette*) which he was bringing out.

The Headmaster's report to the Governing Body regarding damage to School property was endorsed, a fine would be imposed on offenders as the Governors saw fit; broken windows and lost or damaged books would have to be paid for.

Following his annual visit, the Chief Examiner pronounced himself well satisfied with the work and discipline.

> He was much struck with the excellence of the new classrooms and thought that the Central Hall was the finest he had hitherto seen in Wales.

The School was delighted to learn that as a result of the C W B examinations of Summer 1898, the School stood third on the list of Welsh County Schools-the result being reckoned by taking the number of distinctions gained and the number of pupils on the roll.

With numbers increasing to 133 at the beginning of the Midsummer Term 1899, E M Spencer was appointed temporarily to teach in the lower forms-the sixth member of staff. Before the end of term the Governors were to make two permanent appointments. John H Howell, succeeded Miss Hughes as science teacher. During his course at Aberystwyth College, he assisted at the Old Bank School under David Samuel and was student assistant to Prof Genese in the U C W mathematical department. Mr Howell had taught for three years at King's College, London and had studied at Strasburg under Prof Kohlrausch, a name famous in physical chemistry. His two degrees were obtained at the University of London and at the time of his appointment he was doing research work at Cambridge.

Sarah Elizabeth Thomas who succeeded Miss Spencer was a native of Aberystwyth and had been a pupil of David Samuel at the Old Bank before entering U C W in 1893 gaining London Matriculation. Affectionately known as 'Lallie' or 'Lalla', she was to spend over thirty years in the service of the school mainly teaching English.

As always, the last weeks of the Summer Term were dominated by the external examinations and three pages of the record book show the list of successes written up meticulously by the Headmaster. Once again the School claimed a County Exhibition based on the results of the C W B Senior Examination, David John de Lloyd who was to have a brilliant academic career, was the recipient, passing in seven subjects with four distinctions, including a remarkable 100% in music awarded by Dr Joseph Parry, the examiner.

David Owen Morris, who entered the School as a Free Scholar in September 1899, one of 37 new pupils, remembered his first day.

> September came and I found myself in Form 11a, in the first room leading out of the Hall-the room where all the boys assembled for registration and where the new boys learnt on the first day to answer 'Adsum' even before they had learnt 'mensa'. The girls had preferential treatment for they always assembled in the wider spaces of the Main Hall. The lowest form in those days was Form I, and they probably had the best room in the School, on the first floor of the bay overlooking the Headmaster's lawn, the Scholars however began their careers in 11a. In those early years there was a Junior Certificate to be taken in Form IV, before proceeding to take the Senior, as the School Certificate was then called, in Form V. Very few indeed continued for a further period of study for the Honours Certificate- the rather grandiose name for the present Higher. Most of the pupils proceeding to the University did so armed only with the Senior. In those early days only a small proportion of the pupils stayed even to take the Senior. It had been the custom, in Wales at least, in the epoch before the opening of the County Schools to send children to one of the local grammar schools for only a year or two, and sometimes for one or two terms only, in order to- such was the optimism of the period!- 'complete their education'. This custom had not died out in the early years of Ardwyn and to such pupils Form III was the terminus of their school career. In fact a few of them began and ended their secondary education in Form III, as they were too old to be placed in a lower form when they entered.[4]

David Morris who had a distinguished school and college career, remembers a particularly successful football team at this time with the talented Peake brothers playing for the School-both Bob and Ernie became English League players after gaining amateur

The David Samuel Years — 1896-1921

The First School Hockey Team 1900-1901.
J. H. Howells, Rachel Thomas, Minnie Jones, Lilian Morgan, Mag Brotherton, Lizzie Jones.
Katie Griffiths, Lizzie Morris, Mela Garland, Edith Thomas, Nesta Morgan, Mabel Pearce, Winifred Owen

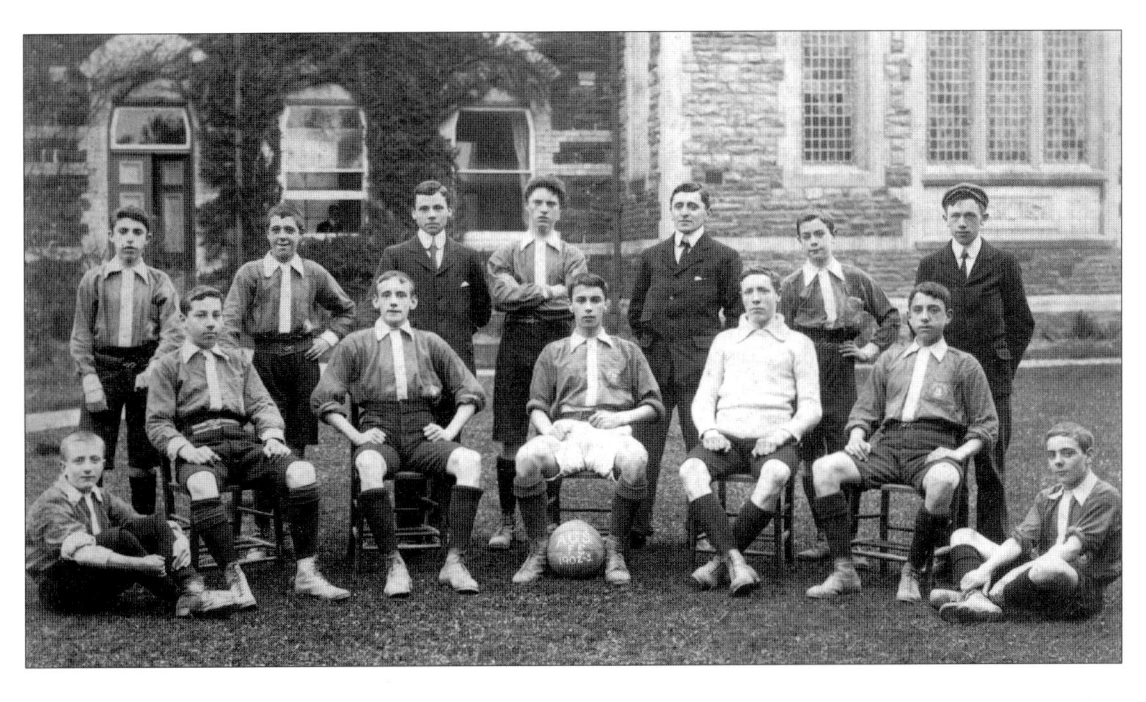

1902-3 Football Team. Staff - T. O. Pearce and N. H. Thomas.

international 'caps' for Wales against England in 1908. Ernie Peake gained eleven senior Welsh 'caps' while a Liverpool player between 1908 and 1914.[5]

Lord Rendel, President of the U C W had generously agreed to open the new buildings on October 26 1899. As Stuart Rendel, Liberal Member of Parliament for Montgomeryshire, he had played a vital part in the passing of the Welsh Intermediate Education Act 1889. *The Cambrian News* reported

> The assembled guests greeted his lordship with cheers and Lord Rendel bowed his acknowledgement. The gathering, which was large and imposing, then proceeded to the main entrance where Mrs Jessy Williams, deputising for Mr. George Davies, chairman of Governors, placed a solid silver key, richly chased, in the hand of Lord Rendel, who inserted it in the lock and amidst great cheering, declared the school formally open. The guests after inspecting the buildings proceeded to the Central Hall where a public meeting was held.

The President, Mrs Jessy Williams, after welcoming Lord Rendel and the other distinguished guests, referred to the adverse balance of £1,300 which remained on the buildings and trusted

> that those friends present would help free them of the debt so as to enable them to carry on the school in such a manner as would be a lasting benefit to the whole county.

Following a report by the Headmaster on the history of the School from its commencement, Lord Rendel started his address by apologising for his ignorance of the financial affairs of the school. 'Let me say at once that if £300 will reduce the deficit to £1000, the deficit is £1000'. (Loud cheers) He told his audience that when he was in Aberystwyth he felt that he was in the cradle of Welsh education.

> Seeing the growth and development of the educational enthusiasms of Wales, those of us who witnessed anything of the origin of the national movement must take pride and pleasure in looking back; it is only just to remember that not so long ago that the distinguishing features of Welsh life were its spiritual neglect, its educational destitution. We have seen something of sectarian jealousies in Wales, yet religion has not suffered;nor has education. Take higher education, of which this is the birthplace. That has never been sectarian, and now take intermediate education of which this fine school is one of the most recent offspring. This is not and can never be sectarian. Without wanting to be controversial, let us see the inconsistency and the unreason for pursuing the sectarian interest in respect of elementary education.

Lord Rendel pointed out that England was learning from Wales; the recent Education Act for England was the result of the great success of Welsh intermediate education. He advised the pupils not to think so much of what they learnt but how they learnt it. A good education meant power to the mind to apply it, to train it in seeing the true relations and proportions of things. He was for simple teaching and was not unfriendly to technical education but was against early specialisation. He did not believe in teaching things technical to those who were not prepared to apply themselves to things purely intellectual. Education should be followed for education's sake. 'We should not take too utilitarian a view of education; it should be put in its proper place. Next to religion, we should remember that education is an essential key to good citizenship.'

Principal Roberts of the U C W, supporting his President, expressed, on behalf of his staff, their deep and lively interest in the prosperity of the School.

> We have anxiously awaited the day on which the Intermediate Schools of Wales should be in actual operation as they are today and we have already felt the influence of the new tide of energy and ability which is making its way into the colleges as a result of the opening years in the working of these schools.

He also represented the County Governing Body, who rejoiced in the opening of the school-the largest school in point of equipment and accommodation for which the scheme provided. 'It is a school which is destined to hold a position higher perhaps than others within the county.'

Ald D C Roberts, the Mayor, expressed pleasure at the excellent way the Managers had expended the contribution of the Corporation. It being a school for the upper part of the county, he feared that the inhabitants of the portion outside Aberystwyth were not taking the interest in it that they ought to take. He recognised that in Borth there was a problem with the railway service but he hoped that surrounding villages would wake up to the fact that the school offered them the best advantages in the way of education.

The Rev T. Levi in moving a vote of thanks to Lord Rendel said that Aberystwyth and Wales generally were indebted to him, the most faithful and generous president of the University College. He was amongst the few who had done an enormous good for education in Wales. 'If Lord Rendel was not a Welshman as he was inclined to think he was, he was good enough to be one.' The Headmaster, chronicling the day's events, wrote

> the proceedings passed with great eclat-the phrases in the 'Song of Praise' in the Book of Ecclesiasticus are peculiarly appropriate to Lord Rendel and others of our benefactors- 'All these were honoured in their generation and were the glory of their times, there be of them, that have left a name behind them that their praises might be reported... their name liveth for evermore.'

The celebrations continued the following day when the Governors entertained the pupils to tea, probably more to their liking than the speeches of the previous day. This was followed by an evening concert in the Central Hall given by the pupils for the Governors, parents and friends. The programme arranged by Miss Ewart and Mr Fuller consisted of song, recitations, choruses conducted by the Headmaster, tableaux and instumental solos on the piano, violin and banjo. S E Thomas recollected

> We had some good soloists among the boys. Willie Hosea's song 'When I was a boy at School' was double encored, and was sung or whistled in the playground for months afterwards[6]

Nesta Morgan and Mollie Owen also took part-they were to become well-known singers in the town and district. This, the first ever School concert, was such a success that another was staged at the end of the Christmas term and became a feature of the School calendar thereafter.

Another 'first' was the establishment of a Literary and Debating Society. The surviving programme lists

    November 3   Debate: The Transvaal War, is it justified?
    November 10   Mock Parliamentary Election
    November 24   Address by the President (Mr D Samuel)
    December 8   Debate: Does education pertain to the happiness of man?

With no reason given, the Governors resolved to terminate the engagement of Serjeant Long and Mrs Hannah Jones and to make enquiries locally for replacements. With the approval of the Headmaster, it was agreed that begining the following session, the whole of Saturday would be a holiday and Wednesday a working day. A further request to the Cambrian Railways to accelerate the morning train from Borth, apparently fell on deaf ears; T. Ivor Rees a pupil from 1903-1907 related how he had to run to catch the 9. 10 am train at Llandre station, arriving too late for the Algebra lesson, hence his lack of progress in that subject.[7] Despite that disadvantage he reached great heights in the Diplomatic Service.

The Governors voted a sum of £5. 18. 0. for the purchase of physical apparatus. 'The first instalment for what must be in the future a fully equipped physics laboratory-a small beginning', so noted the Headmaster.

The Mayor, Ald C M Williams, presided at the 1899 Prize Day held for the first time in the new Central Hall which had been tastefully decorated for the occasion. He congratulated the School on its rapid progress and high status among the county schools of Wales. 'It is only fair that the public should know because there was tendency on the part of some persons not to credit the School with what was really due to it.' (Ald Williams was himself guilty of the same offence in later years)

The Headmaster giving his third annual report, thanked the staff for working 'with the utmost conscientiousness and energy; Mr Appleton the new Art teacher had already seen the fruits of his labour, he had many pupils of great promise.' Commenting on the regulations framed by the Governors for housekeepers with whom pupils lodged, it was important that all pupils should keep good hours and apply their whole energies to the prosecution of their studies which required regularity, application and diligence. The discipline would materially help to form habits of study of the utmost importance in the formation of character and success in life. He was bound to say that the pupils conducted themselves with propriety and their demeanour at all times was not inconsistent with that of well-bred and well-instructed boys and girls. In spite of the upheavals caused by the builders, there was a long list of university, Central Board, and Science and Art examination successes. Prof Genese's prize for geometrical riders was won by William Arthur Lewis 'whose paper was excellent both as regards quality and quantity.' The Head announced that Sir Griffith Evans, of Lovesgrove had offered a scholarship of £10 per annum for two years tenable at the U C W.

The David Samuel Years — 1896-1921

Prof J M Angus who was the guest speaker, urged pupils to pursue a hobby. It seemed to him to be a valuable possession and an important element in a young person's development. In some schools in England with which he was familiar, hobbies formed an important part of the curriculum with an annual exhibition of their leisure interests. He thought much good could be done by encouraging pupils to develop natural bents towards various pursuits, though some guidance might be necessary in case directions were taken which would lead to little advantage.

H C Fryer, Clerk to the County Council, who had been involved in formulating the scheme for intermediate education in the County, stated that in 1881, the total number of boys and girls in public and private schools was nearly 6, 000. In less than two decades later, in 1899 there were 23 County School in Wales with a total of 7,390, besides those in private schools. Aberystwyth was looked upon as a great educational centre for mid-Wales if not for the whole of Wales and when they saw the great strides which the College had made, they hoped that the same progress would be made by the School. He wished to impress upon the pupils the very great importance of establishing a high moral tone in the school. It was a new school, and the pupils had to make its traditions and to form its character. He hoped the character would be a very high one and the tone of the school a lofty one.

The Rev. Prebendary Williams impressed upon the pupils the need to have what the Romans required in their day *mens sana in corpore sano*. He hoped they would pay attention to athletics; education was not merely book learning but the training of themselves for the battle of life.

The new century opened with 116 pupils on the register and a new subject on the timetable. Bertha Jones had been appointed by the County Council to give lessons in Cookery at three of the County Schools viz. Aberystwyth, Tregaron and Aberaeron. Miss Jones held a first-class diploma in cookery and laundry from the South Wales and Monmouthshire College of Cookery and Domestic Arts. A kitchen was set up in the old classics room and on Mondays and Tuesdays, the three lowest classes were instructed in the culinary arts.

St. Davids Day was celebrated on March 2 with an additional half-day holiday on March 1 to celebrate the Relief of Ladysmith in Natal.

The Chief Inspector in his annual visit 'spoke in eulogistic terms' of the progress made in the internal organisation of the school and recommended that a seventh master be appointed to do some high work in the senior form which should be divided into two forms, one of which to be designated form VI.

He told the Governors, that without reflecting on the work done by other schools, the progress made was more marked than at almost any of the schools he had visited.

It was with genuine regret that the School learnt that W P Fuller, who had responsibility for classics, modern language teaching and boys' games, had tendered his resignation on his appointment as Headmaster of Trowbridge High School. In a farewell ceremony in the Central Hall, Mr Fuller was presented with a 14 volume collection of Thackeray's works. On the following day he was given a hearty send-off at the railway station by his former pupils. Fuller was remembered

As being more detached in manner than his colleagues, but a fine teacher with an undoubted knowledge of his classics. He rather fancied himself as a footballer and if energy and dash had been the only criteria he would have been good. One other thing I remember about him is that he jingled his money, wore a very high collar of the choker variety then in vogue, a natty bow tie, and a vast expanse of spotless white shirt. A little aloof, but we liked and trusted him.[8]

Mr Fuller's successor was Nathaniel Henry Thomas a native of Brynaman, Carmarthenshire who had been a pupil of Watcyn Wyn. He was for six years at Llandovery College from where he gained an Open Scholarship to Jesus College, Oxford. He remained at Oxford for four years under Prof Rhys gaining his BA with Honours in Classical Mods in 1899. His appointment was made permanent in July 1900 and he was to have a ten year association with the School.

On the instruction of the Governors, all pupils were to provide themselves with a suitable bag for carrying their school books which were, at that time, the property of the School and lent to the pupils. Miss S E Thomas recalls the reaction of some pupils.

The senior boys, tall hefty lads, were somewhat resentful, they felt that they were passed the age when one carries a school bag. The next morning, each of the fifth-formers brought two books-just enough for the two lessons before the interval. Just after 11 o'clock the town porter arrived, wheeling a huge truck through the girls' playground and deposited in the corridor a heterogeneous collection of bags- carpet bags, portmanteaux, suitcases, cricket bags- bags of all shapes and sizes. Each boy picked up his own bag and took out the books. By this time there was a crowd of pupils and staff and, naturally, there was a great deal of merriment. The next day, however, the boys brought their books in their school bags.[9]

There were two further inspections before the end of term. Hudson Williams of the Bangor College, on behalf of the C W B carried out oral examinations in languages. The Headmaster thought his report was very satisfying particularly his comment that Welsh was taught so successfully 'it is hardly a mere coincidence that in Welsh speaking districts, pupils who have been systematically taught Welsh grammar, have invariably a better grasp of English grammar.' Mr Heller of Birmingham inspecting the practical work in chemistry and physics thought that considering the paucity of accommodation and apparatus, excellent results had been achieved. His recommendations for improvement of the science facilities were immediately adopted by the Governors so that the School could be recognised to teach Natural Science in future.

The C W B examination for the first time included an Honours section, in addition to the Senior and Junior levels. There was again to be great satisfaction with the examination results.

William Tom Williams, one of four boys who sat the Honours examination, spent just one year at the School in 1899-1900.

I soon sensed that here was a School in which the aims were different. Not only different but finer and freer. This was because amongst our teachers there were some who recognised that education was more than book learning and that it was more important to develop and shape our personalities than to cram us for examinations. I remember two in particular. First there was the Headmaster, David Samuel who took us for Mathematics, but could be side-tracked to talk about Welsh literature by the slightest guile on our part. I have since often wondered whether it was because it gave him far greater pleasure to talk about the Mabinogion than to expound geometry that he yielded so readily to our transparent manoeuvres. He was, of course, a brilliant mathematician-so brilliant that he had very little patience with our clod-hopping flounderings. He rarely bothered to draw a diagram on the blackboard; instead he wove a geometrical pattern in the air. 'Now here's the triangle ABC'-and a quick forefinger flashed an insubstantial figure in space. 'If AB is equal to AC, then the angle ABC equals the angle ACB. You can see that, can't you? You can see it, Stephen Owen?' 'No sir,' says Stephen stolidly. 'Oh, Stephen can't see it. Quite simple but Stephen can't see it. ' It was high time for our opening gambit. Was it Arllwyd (who fell in Flanders) or David Jenkins who made the tactical opening? 'Oh Mr Samuel, we went to Llanychaiarn Church last Sunday.' 'Did you now?' And we were off with the complexities of the triangle done with for that lesson.

As a Headmaster, his standard of discipline was different from any I had known. He was no martinet; indeed he wilfully shut his eyes to many of our misdemeanours for he had realised that there was a blessed underlying truth in the saying 'God gave man eyelids as well as eyes.'

Then there was N H Thomas, I was under him for a term only, but I feel that I owe him a great deal. He had a roving mind and was bent on widening our mental horizons. I can't remember that he ever gave us a lesson which proceeded in set fashion from start to finish, his digressions were memorable- stimulating and provocative. We had wandered to some branch of study far removed from our starting-point, when Griff Ellis said, 'But, sir, that's not in our syllabus. ' N H blew up completely and treated us to such a tirade on our cramped and illiberal views on education that I for one, have never forgotten it.[10]

At the start of the fifth session of the School in September 1900 it was announced that David Jenkins, William Arthur Lewis, William Tom Williams and Mathew Henry Evans had gained U C W scholarships; the three County scholarships given by the county council had been claimed by William Tom Williams, David Jenkins and Griffith Daniel Ellis. The latter also gained the Sir Griffith Evans' Scholarship. It had previously been announced that through Lord Rendel's continued munificence scholarships had been established at the U C W for pupils in the counties of Cardigan, Montgomery and Merioneth. His lordship had gifted £250 a year for his life and for five years thereafter. It was another honour for the School when it was announced that the first Lord Rendel Scholar for Cardiganshire was John Arllwyd Jones.

The C W B results at all three levels had 'given immense satisfaction', so much so, that the Governors were moved to record their 'gratification at the splendid successes in the examinations and the scholarships gained.'

The vacant post of School cleaner was filled early in the term when Edward D Jones was appointed as Caretaker and Cleaner at a salary of 18/- a week. He was to be employed for 45 weeks per session and 'would be expected to give his whole time to the work but to be at liberty to find other employment during the summer vacation'. He was to become a great favourite with Staff and pupils. An old sailor who had seen a great deal of the world, the Gyp, as he became to be known, ' had a repertoire of thrilling stories to which the boys listened with rapt attention.'[11]

That year saw the start of a hockey club thanks to the initiative of JH Howell, the Science master. S E Thomas recollected that games were played on a field near the present National Library, the one field had to do duty for both football and hockey. It had one great fault in that it sloped downward on one side.

> The hockey players of today would be surprised to see the 'uniform' of the team that played Tregaron in 1900-long skirts (very useful for stopping the ball), high necked collars, with ties. In spite of this they played well and Katie Griffiths was the best player we ever had. When we played Aberaeron on their ground, it meant for us a three-hour journey in an open horse-drawn charabanc. On one occasion, after making this journey, we had to play between heavy showers and then on the homeward journey we had heavy rain all the way. That rain did not quench our spirits for we all sang lustily, and the girls had a fine repertoire of songs and choruses-the influence of the summer pierrots being evident. Our journey to Towyn was made by train and had none of the adventure of the Aberaeron trip.[12]

Towards the end of term, Revd George Eyre Evans gave a lecture, in the Central Hall, on 'Across America's Prairies'. The proceeds of twelve guineas were devoted to the purchase of about 70 books for the establishment of a pupils' library.

Principal Bebb of Lampeter College was the guest speaker at the prize day in December 1900. As a member of the Central Welsh Board he was particularly interested in intermediate schools and gratified by the great success of the Aberystwyth school. Speaking as a college principal, he thought it was important to get the best possible material from the schools and from what he had heard that afternoon such expectations were more than justified. He was particularly glad that such practical and ordinary things as cooking were taught;he only wished that it was a Monday or a Tuesday so that he might sample the cooking. Education, more than anything, was a matter of cooperation between teachers, pupils and parents. There was a great tendency at the present time of doing too much to make education easy. He hoped that the pupils would always think that the work was hard because as soon as they began to think it easy they began to cease to be educated. Difficulties were a sign of progress-they could not expect to learn cricket by a person bowling them slow balls, and so when they got problems set them in mathematics they improved by tackling them. People were getting alarmed at the present state of trade and the comparison of England with other countries; there was a danger in over-emphasising the importance of technical education and, in their hurry to get results, forgot that without scientific training no great practical results could be achieved. Finally, he trusted that they would be taught to think in order to form the right opinions but they would need to collect material in order so to do-it was no use having the right opinions unless they could express them.

The David Samuel Years — 1896-1921

The Headmaster, in his lengthy report detailing the impressive list of academic successes, regretted that, as elsewhere, large numbers of pupils failed to remain in school sufficiently long enough to reap the full advantages. Arrangements had been made with the College authorities, whereby their students and graduates of the Welsh and other Universities could have practical training in teaching, in order to qualify them for the diploma in secondary teaching. Already a number of graduates had availed themselves of the facilities the County School offered. He was hopeful that discussions then underway between the Board of Education and the Central Welsh Board would remove the need for candidates to continue to have to sit both the examinations of the C W B and the Department of Science and Art. This would simplify the work and make for more efficiency so that energies could be concentrated upon real education. He took heart from the complimentary remarks which had been given, none more so than those of Principal Roberts in his report to the College Council where he had referred specifically to the successes obtained by the School 'as a signal instance of the valuable work being done by the County Schools of Wales'.

In the evening the Central Hall was crowded with an appreciative audience of pupils, parents and friends on the occasion of the annual school concert.

> From beginning to end there was great enthusiasm and all the pieces reflected credit upon those who took part. The tableaux were of exceptional merit, Mr Samuel wielded the baton with his usual precision and confidence-inspiring beat.

The first part of the programme was a cantata entitled "The Hours" (Roeckel), followed by solos, recitations, tableaux, and anticipating future triumphs, scenes from 'Princess Ida', scarf-drill, and a quartet who sang by special request 'The Toy Song' from 'The Geisha. The accompanist was D J de Lloyd a former pupil and County Exhibitioner in the second year of his studies at the U C W.

Finance or the lack of it, continued to concern the Governors and a joint meeting between them and the Guarantors was arranged to discuss the financial position of the School and to produce and circulate a subscription list for the Building Fund. There is no record of the outcome of the meeting but the subscription list is extant and records a total of £1,970.

Thomas Owen, one of the three original members of staff, was taken ill during the Christmas vacation and was unable to resume his duties for the whole of the Lent term. His temporary replacement was W Leonard Darlington. Mr Owen's illness continued into the Midsummer term and two students of the U C W, Ethel Robertson and then Charles Elsden took his place.

The annual inspection brought its customary acclaim for the School. On this occasion the inspection was in the hands of Francis Bond and not Owen Owen as in previous years. He pronounced himself well satisfied with the discipline and conduct of the pupils and the work done by both staff and pupils.

The Revd Thomas Levi succeeded Mrs Jessy Williams as Chairman of the Board of Governors in April 1901. In July the Governors accepted the resignation of J H Howell as science master 'with sincere regret.' He had accepted a post as senior science master at Auckland Grammar School, New Zealand. His colleague S E Thomas remembered that he took a great interest in all the activities of the School.

> As neither Miss Ewart nor I were athletes he kindly undertook to teach the girls to play hockey. He was a very successful teacher for the girls were able to challenge the College 2nd XI and the Tregaron school team. Mr Howell was also greatly interested in the Literary and Debating Society.[13]

A former pupil recorded

> He was the best and most influential teacher of my time. No one ever played the fool with him, not because he was very strict, but because he always seemed to be *en rapport* with every pupil. One thing I remember about him and his charming wife is that they always wore brown clothes from head to foot, a sort of Liberty shade of brown like autumn beech leaves.[14]

As soon as it was known that Mr Howell was leaving, a testimonial fund was set up 'as a mark of the estimation in which he was held by his colleagues and pupils.' At the presentation ceremony, the Headmaster referred to Mr Howells' worth and character and the indebtedness of the school to him in many directions. He expressed his personal regret at his leaving and wished him abundant health and happiness in his new far-off home. A senior pupil D Jonathan Jones said that 'two good institutions, both having noble and glorious aims would be ever gratefully and dearly remembered by Mr Howell-the "College by the sea", where he had been a student and the "School on the hill", where he had been a master. Lizzie Jones, senior girl pupil, 'in a pretty speech', made the presentation of a photographic camera and stand and some excellent photographs of the School, its staff and pupils. Mr Howell suitably replied saying that many of his pupils had brilliant futures and urged them to do work which would reflect credit on their school.

Mr Elsden referred to the work done by Mr Howell in connection with the workmen's club in Progress Hall, 'the interest he had shown and the energy he had thrown into the welfare of that institution.' On leaving Aberystwyth, he was accompanied to the station by a number of pupils and by his colleagues.

Such was the reputation that the School had gained that educationalists from far and wide came to visit. During the previous Easter vacation, several Welsh headteachers were the guests of David Samuel and on the day of the entrance examination, Dr Wendt of Hamburg, who was interested in intermediate education, was greatly impressed with what he had seen and spoke in generous terms of the work done in Wales at this level. In August 1901, the British Chautauquans visited Aberystwyth and spent a morning inspecting the School. One of their party, Dr McClure, Headmaster of Mill Hill School, London, one of the best known educationalists in the country, later wrote to the *Welsh Gazette* to say

> Amidst a host of memories, our visit to the County School stands out very clearly. It is not easy for me to tell you what an impression was made upon me by the School- a

beautiful building with ideal surroundings. My only regret was that I did not meet Mr Samuel, for he has evidently given of his best to the place..... his work is of special interest to me, for I have felt for a long time that the co-education of boys and girls is the best solution. In this country one is but 'a voice crying in the wilderness' and is therefore all the more pleased to find that elsewhere happier conditions prevail. I feel sure that a great work is being done in your midst so quietly and unostentatiously perhaps, that many fail to realise its importance.

The County entrance scholarships attracted 29 candidates, most of whom were from the Aberystwyth Board School. Of the ten scholarships awarded, seven were pupils of that school. Top of the list was Richard Jenkin Ellis, son of a foundryman. R J Ellis was to become a well-known local personality, a long serving town and county councillor and town mayor on two occasions; however he spent less than two years at the School. Ernest Peake who became one of the finest footballers of his generation, was another Scholar in the September 1901 intake.

As a replacement for JH Howells, the Governors appointed Percy George Feek, a science master at Brecon County School. A graduate in physics, mathematics and organic chemistry he had experience in chemical and physical laboratory work having served under Dr Rutherford at Westminster School. He also had knowledge of Sloyd work (Swedish handcraft).

As a result of additional grants for science teaching from the Board of Education it was possible to appoint an additional science teacher. T O Pierce who joined the staff in October 1901, was educated at Friars School, Bangor and University College, Bangor. He remembered the warm welcome he received.

> I was greatly touched by the manner in which all members of staff went out of their way to put me at my ease and I felt that I would get all the help it was possible to give me. The Headmaster gave me a warm welcome and the way in which his mother received me when she found that I came from Llanllechid, which was her home village, was most touching. When I went round the School I was favourably impressed until I came to the Science department.
>
> The conditions were truly appalling; it was not the most ideal condition for a raw student who had never stood in front of a class before to begin a new career, but the general kindness of the pupils, their natural courtesy, their eagerness to help in every way and the sense of loyalty and devotion which they bore towards their School was an encouragement to a teacher which could not be measured. Of course they were not all or always angels..... there were one or two tricks in the old laboratory which seemed to be passed from one generation to an other e. g. to blow suddenly down a gas tube in one room and put out all the burners in the laboratories. The worst occurrence I can remember was when one very innocent investigator joined one end of a piece of rubber tubing to the gas pipe and the other end to the water-tap and then turned both taps on to find which had the greater pressure. He found out, and the gas supply took weeks to recover. It was a relief to leave this part of the building to take a class in mathematics in the new part, in classrooms which were well ventilated and airy. How one envied those teachers who did not have to spend hours in the 'Black Hole.'

> Well do I remember my first Saturday in Aberystwyth, the irrepressible N. H. (N H Thomas,)whose duty it was to supervise the boys' games, persuading me to accompany the football team to Ystradmeurig. It was almost a pilgrimage in those days to a native of North Wales who associated the name with some of the most famous clergy. We started early, the match was duly played and the team dispersed, travelling in some cases many miles to enjoy the hospitality of their opponents. The result was a long delay before we could start on our return journey and a serious effect on a classical temper.[15]

Thomas Owen made a gallant attempt at the commencement of term to grapple with his work at school but broke down at the end of three weeks. One of the U C W students who came to assist in his absence was Charles Valentine who was later to become Professor of Philosophy at Birmingham University

With the increase in numbers there was need to create two sixth forms; the lower sixth being concerned with work for the senior certificate and Welsh matriculation and the upper sixth comprised the honours candidates. With forms I to V there were now seven classes for the first time. The school library was further augmented by the proceeds of a reading of Dickens' 'Christmas Carol' by the Rev George Eyre Evans, in the Central Hall. The mayor, Cllr R J Jones JP, 'complete with chain of office presided.'

The chairman of the Governors presided at the fifth annual speech day and prize distribution in December 1901. The Revd Thomas Levi opening the proceedings, said that there were no prizes given in day schools when he was a boy, neither were there degree masters, he would rather call them degraded. He must have shocked his young audience when he continued- the schoolmaster he had was a drunkard- a failing tradesman- who spent most of his time in the public houses. Often the whole school would set off from the school, like a pack of hounds with the intention of hunting their headmaster from his den in the public house.

The Headmaster reviewed the year which again was one of academic success. David Jonathan Jones had been awarded a county exhibition which meant that in the four years since 1898, the School had secured seven out the twelve scholarships awarded on the results of the C W B examinations despite being the youngest intermediate school in the county. The School had, in this period, supplied 25 students to the U C W. David Samuel regretted the continued absence of his respected colleague Thomas Owen whose long connection with education in the neighbourhood and his energy and enthusiasm in whatever he took up, was well known. 'His unflinching devotion to the County School should on the present occasion be duly acknowledged.' There was also regret that so few of the entrance scholarship candidates came from country districts.

The main speaker, Principal TF Roberts of the UCW said, from the report of the CWB which he had before him, and the reports of the many inspectors who had visited, he could only have a most favourable impression of the School-there was abundant evidence that the work was improving year by year. However he gathered that despite the excellent work carried out by the science teachers, there was insufficient provision in the scientific and technical departments. If the pupils were not provided with the necessary equipment 'it would be a blot and discredit upon the inhabitants of the town and district.' He hoped that everyone present would do all in their power to raise funds so that first class laboratories and equipment could be obtained so that the pupils were not disadvantaged. He then referred to the new Education Bill which Parliament would have before them when it reassembled and hoped that it would practically become a rule that pupils attending secondary school should remain there for a period of four to six years.

Mr Vaughan Davies MP, who had more to say than apparently he ever had in the House of Commons, was concerned that pupils in most schools took up French in preference to other languages. In the mercantile life of the country it would be found that German was almost as important as French. When seeking positions in the mercantile life for Cardiganshire boys, he invariably found the offices crowded with Germans because of the increasing trade with Germany.

The evening concert following the afternoon events was becoming a tradition. Under the baton of the Headmaster, a cantata 'The Enchanted Princess' was performed. A Wynne Davies, U C W who been *locum tenens* at the School during the term, stage-managed the production of 'The Princess' by Tennyson.

In the early part of 1902 there was a movement to form an Old Pupils' Association. Views were widely solicited including those of former members of staff. W P Fuller writing from Trowbridge thought it an excellent idea particularly as the initiative was coming from the former pupils. He didn't think that there was need for too many rules, the main thing was to get them together and keep them interested. Former science master, Dewi Ellis writing from Marburg in Germany enclosed 2/- as a subscription 'I am sending a humble offering, the present state of my financial cupboard does not permit my extracting more from it'. He did not advocate a big programme which was unlikely to be fulfilled. That would bring disappointment and disillusionment. He also warned that 'seeing the School is a mixed one, there is considerable danger attached to such gatherings and opportunities for 'larks' should be removed as far as possible. If an association was formed it must be on a dignified basis otherwise no good would follow - a good tone must be laid at the outset.'

Aberystwyth County School Old Pupils' Association was subsequently formed and the first Reunion took place on Wednesday March 26 1902 in the Central Hall. The invitation to the Headmaster, and the programme, in addition to the letters referred to above, have survived the years. The proceedings lasted from 3pm until 10. 30 pm. The record book contains the signatures of the 97 participants, every name perfectly neat and legible-a tribute to the penmanship taught in the elementary schools of those days. The Headmaster rejoiced in the birth of the Association and was glad that the upper form of the School had been invited since this would impress upon them their sense of responsibility to the School. The President, Goronwy Owen hoped that the reunion would be an annual event and that its success that day would justify its formation. Speeches were interspersed with musical items. D J de Lloyd's piano solo was delivered 'in his usual masterful style.'

E M Ewart, the senior mistress, said she rejoiced, like those who had spoken before her, at the formation of the association, especially as the idea had come from the old pupils themselves and not from the staff. She believed that societies and associations were more durable if they were started by those most concerned in the matter than if they were brought about by outsiders. 'It seems to me that a pupil's duty to his school did not end with his school-days but that he owed a debt of gratitude to his old school and should always be ready to help it on in all that he could'. She suggested that, as new laboratories were needed, the walls of the School could do with a few more pictures and the library might be augmented, old pupils would not forget their duty.

Mr Reggie Evans entertained the audience with *O na byddai'n haf o hyd* and it was evident that 'the words of the music expressed the secret wishes of his heart'. The choir under the conductorship of D J de Lloyd gave a highly appreciated performance of a lullaby composed by the conductor. After the interval, during which all those present signed their names in the record book at the invitation of the Headmaster, a farcical comedy "Disappeared Mysteriously" was staged which was thoroughly enjoyed. The evening ended with dancing and renewal of acquaintances and the new committee charged with organising a second reunion in 1903.

For one pupil the first reunion had other evocations.

> As two schoolboys stood at the open window of the School laboratory to clear their lungs after one of their many unsuccessful efforts to prepare chlorine water, they saw in the School yard a confectioner's handtruck containing several trays filled with fresh choice pastries. It was the Wednesday before Easter 1902, the day on which the first reunion of the Old Pupils' Association was held and those boys were probably the first uninvited guests to partake of refreshments at any School reunion. One of the boys afterwards became president of the Association, and was killed on the Somme in 1916 during his year of office. They had entered the School in September 1900, when Victoria was still Queen; when motor-cars were objects of amazement to human beings, and a source of terror to horses and other animals using the roads. Of greater importance to the average small boy, it was a period when by careful choice and wise investment he could, for one half-penny purchase a pocketful of sweets and ensure for himself a pleasant afternoon provided the teacher failed to see him eating in class.[16]

Proclamation of peace in South Africa on 31 May 1902 earned a half-holiday while the Coronation provided two days extra holiday on the 26 and 27 of June.

> The boys joined in the Grand Procession, marching from the playground to the Smithfield, accompanied by the Headmaster and staff robed in their academicals, a great School banner with the motto enrolled on it, leading on. The smartness of the pupils on the march was universally admired.

As a result of the School entrance examinations, nine scholarships were awarded and for the first time, girls took the larger share. There was a late start to the new session in 1902 because of the extra week's holiday granted to celebrate the Coronation Year of King Edward VII. The School's first girl scholar at the U C W, Rachel Ellen Thomas, a policeman's daughter from Goginan, took with her a county exhibition of £15 and a UCW entrance scholarship worth £20. At the same time, there was joy in Goronwy Owen's achievement in becoming the School's first Bachelor of Arts graduate and the success of former science master, Dewi Ellis in gaining the degree of Ph D from the University of Jura and a post in Dollar, Scotland.

There was great disappointment when Thomas Owen submitted his resignation on health grounds. He was replaced by Charles Eldon who had deputised for Mr Owen during his illness. Tom Owen was remembered as a first-rate teacher of the groundwork of English. 'In appearance he was always faultlessly turned out-everything as he wanted it. I can still see the shine on his shoes and the gold albert across his well curved waistcoat. A dear little man, the very acme of integrity and orthodoxy.[17]

For the first time, on the occasion of the sixth annual prize day, a printed programme appeared, listing the successes of the year 1901-02 with a fine line drawing of the southern aspect of the School by the architect, T E Morgan, on the first page. Annie Griffiths, chairman of the Governors, praised the School on its successes and chided the public who had been slow to acknowledge it. The School, they knew, had been handicapped for want of funds, especially in the science department and although the Governors had frequently made efforts to relieve the pressure, they had not met with the success the School deserved. She appealed to all to support the planned fund-raising events so that the debt could be wiped out and the science department strengthened.

The Headmaster produced statistics on pupil numbers- in the six years of their existence, 294 boys and 180 girls had been admitted. They had stayed for different lengths of time. Of the 132 currently on the register, 72 were boys and 60 girls. There were no pupils under the age of 12; they had 60 between the ages of 12 and 15; 30 between 15 and 16; 25 between 16 and 17 and 17 over 17 years. 'What a crushing reply, observed the Headmaster, 'do these figures give to our ungenerous critics.' He also produced figures on the destination of pupils after leaving school: returned to their homes, 44 boys and 92 girls; taken to trade or business, 71 boys and 10 girls; became clerks &c 36 boys and 12 girls; proceeded to school or college 43 boys and 15 girls; became pupil teachers, 3 boys and 1 girl; unclassed or unknown 23 boys.

The Headmaster paid a tribute of appreciation to Thomas Owen recently resigned. Mr Owen had been involved with education locally for a quarter of a century; his help had been invaluable to them. 'There had been no one on the teaching staff who, for ripened judgement and sound advice, could be equal to him. He had great organising powers and his large acquaintance with the town and neighbourhood served them in good stead.' Samuel recalled the fact that by the resignation of Tom Owen, he was the sole representative of the small teaching staff who began work in the School on its opening in October 1896.

Prof Edward Anwyl of the U C W and vice-chairman of the C W B, was the guest speaker. Addressing himself to the question 'What was education ?', he felt that school played only a comparatively small part in the education of any one of them but the school could play a very important part in cooperation with the parents, who had to be the real educators of the children, to help those children grow up into good men and women, for there could be no higher aim than to make men and women good. He meant good in the active sense; people who strove throughout the whole of their lives to serve the ends of justice and goodness in the community where they may be; people who had high ideals and purposes in life; people whose influence around them was good. One of the problems facing secondary education was how to give those who were not proceeding to higher places of learning, an education which was the very best of its kind and at the same time how also to equip those who were entering higher education.

He hoped that those who were fortunate enough to go on to a higher place of learning, would not look down on those obliged to enter into the work of life. There was nothing more detrimental to true intellectual development than false pride.

It would be a most fortunate thing for their country, if it were possible for those who left school at 15 years or earlier to continue their studies even while engaged at work. There was nothing so depressing as drudgery and there should be something done to relieve the pressure of work on those who had begun work early. He could think of nothing better than the system of continuation classes of other countries which allowed studies to continue while at work. Prof Anwyl thought that pupils were not taught only by teachers; boys and girls learnt a great deal from each other and it was vital that what they learnt was good. There was nothing more important for a school than its tone and atmosphere. When they left school he hoped that they would reflect this tone in their actions and deeds.

The usual concert took place in the evening, the first half devoted to musical items, recitations and fan drill by the girls, followed by an operetta "Cinderella" which was 'much admired by a very crowded house.'

The problem of inadequate provision for science teaching came to a head in January 1903 when the Governors received what amounted to an ultimatum from the Board of Education through the Chief Inspector of the C W B. The Board gave notice that the School would not be recognised as a Secondary School for the current year unless adequate laboratory accommodation was provided within three months. The Governors agreed to proceed immediately with plans for new laboratories and the Clerk was directed to write to the chief examiner pointing out the position and requesting him to induce the Board to reconsider their decision. Conducting the annual inspection on behalf of the C W B, C W Robinson, spoke in the highest terms of the two science masters saying that as far as he knew there were no better Science teachers in any of the Welsh intermediate schools. He advised that, in addition to the present laboratory, the science lecture room be converted to a temporary laboratory with new benches to accommodate 16 pupils. This arrangement would enable continued recognition but only temporarily-the building of the new laboratories 'must proceed with reasonable dispatch'. Robinson also recommended having distinguishing school caps for the boys and hats for the girls.

In May and June 1903, the Governors met on six occasions specifically to investigate a complaint made by a parent regarding the conduct of the Headmaster, Mr Samuel towards her daughter, a pupil at the School.

In the issue of May 29 1903 the *Cambrian News* urged a correspondent not to be in a hurry. 'Wait for the decision of the Managers. We shall see what we shall see'. The editorial notes of the following edition headed 'Reporters asked to leave at A I S Managers meeting' read-' Aberystwyth and district knows more or less inaccurately what the business was and secrecy is out of the question, both in the interests of the School and the public'. In his editorial of the 12 June, John Gibson wrote

> We have never believed and never pretended to believe, in the efficiency of the management. A point has been reached when mere muddle and indecision will not avail. There must be clear and decisive action, the delay is injurious if not fatal, for the pub-

lic are losing confidence not only in the wisdom but in the courage of the Managers to deal with the situation that demands thoroughness and ought not to have been left as this matter has been left from week to week. There is no possibility of evading or shirking the issue which is the future of the School.

In his usual forthright way, he continued the following week-

> Another private meeting of the Managers held on Monday. Four resignations out of twelve in a fortnight. It is said that the matter in hand was finally left undecided and is to remain permanently in that condition.
>
> In our opinion the position of the School has never been satisfactory since it was opened. The Managers have now killed it, but some time may elapse before its death is publicly recognised and officially admitted. The School has lost all when it loses the complete confidence of its own Managers as is indicated by the resignation of one-third of their number.

The minutes of the Managers' meetings gave no detail of their deliberations merely the following statement:

> After lengthy consideration of the evidence and statements made by the accuser and accused and petitions signed by 38 parents of past and present pupils, a resolution was moved and seconded that the Headmaster be dismissed from office. An amendment was moved and seconded that in view of the fact that there was no evidence outside the statements of the accuser and accused, the Managers were inclined to pass it over this time, in the hope that it might prove a warning for better conduct in the future. There were four votes for the amendment and four for the original resolution. At this point, the Chairman, Prof Genese and the vice-chairman J D Perrott intimated their intention to resign and left the meeting.

A subsequent meeting unanimously passed the following resolution:- ' That the Managers are of the opinion that the charges against Mr Samuel have not been clearly proven and therefore they resolve that the matter be dropped. There were two further resignations from the Board.'
The *Cambrian News* editorial of July 10:

> We are not going into details because we are not disposed to deal publicly with a vital matter pertaining to the School which the Managers think ought to be dealt with secretly.
>
> The School has been deprived of public confidence, for when the management is divided it cannot be expected that the public will be united and so the School which should have been the foremost school in Wales practically ceases to exist, for under the present divided counsels, success is utterly impossible quite apart from the matter of vital importance which, to some extent, has dropped into the background, but will certainly and inevitably come to the front again. The hope that the main subject will be lost sight of is ridiculous and their faith that existing mistrust will die down is altogether unfounded.

The same issue carried an account of the Managers meeting of the 7 July chaired by Revd Thomas Levi when the Headmaster presented suggested dates for the next term. The cloud of lingering ill-feeling and simmering animosity was reflected in the discussion.

> JP Thomas: There ought to be more hours of work if the School was to have efficient scholars.
>
> Miss Ewart thought a 14 week term was long enough, everybody was quite exhausted at the end of term.
>
> JP Thomas: You people work about 5 hours a day and talk about hard work. It makes me smile.
>
> R Richards: They do not know what hard work is.
>
> Prof Levi protested about the remarks.
>
> CM Williams: If the Managers wanted the advice of the Headmaster or Miss Ewart they would ask for it. He respectfully asked Miss Ewart not to interfere in a debate unless she was asked. She must pardon him for saying that, but he had occasion to do so before. Surely it was not quite the thing for any member of staff to go there and tell the Managers what they were to do.
>
> Miss Ewart replied that she was simply tendering advice.
>
> CM Williams: The Managers do not want it.
>
> Reference was made to the fund-raising bazaar which in view of the controversy, had been cancelled without the knowledge of the Managers.
>
> Prof Levi was glad the subject had been raised 'now that everything was quietening down nicely after the business that occurred recently'.

However 'the business that occurred recently' was not over.

On the 30 July 1903 at Llanbadarn magistrates court held at the Black Lion Inn, David Samuel, Headmaster of the Aberystwyth County School appeared in answer to a summons charging him with unlawful assault of a 15 years old girl pupil (who was named) on 15 May 1903.

All three local newspapers carried an account of the proceedings, that of the *Cambrian News* completely filling a page. That paper reported that the case had excited great interest in the town and neighbourhood and attracted a large number of people. The pupil was what the newspapers described as, of prepossessing appearance; after starting at the School in 1901 she became a great favourite of the Headmaster and in the presence of others he had put his arms around her.

After hearing from all the witnesses, the magistrates present, JT Morgan chairman, J Hughes Bonsall, Nicholas Parry and Thomas Griffiths took five minutes to dismiss the charge to the cheers of the public.

To add to the air of uncertainty, the School bankers informed the Governors that they had received notices that eleven of the guarantors wished to withdraw. After negotiations with the bank however it was announced that satisfactory arrangements had been made as to the future conduct of the School account.

The second Old Pupils' Reunion came up to the expectations of all and fully maintained the high quality of the first. Despite his illness Thomas Owen had made a great effort to be present to receive a testimonial. John Jones (the School's first Scholar) read

an address, in which was set forth the many valuable services Tom Owen had rendered to the School (a copy of the address was printed in the Jubilee Magazine) The address and a purse of gold was then presented to him on behalf of the old students, staff and present pupils by Miss E A Jones. Mr Owen responded by thanking them all for their kindness. As he had been away from School for two years he had not expected anything, but valued their testimonial all the more because of that. David Samuel hoped that he would be spared for many years to come so that he could enjoy less arduous work and meet his former colleagues and pupils at their annual reunion.
In their business meeting the elected officers vowed to start a School Magazine.
To the regret of all, Thomas Owen died on June 11 1903 at the age of 53 years.

The Headmaster had agreed to a request from the College teacher training department to allow the School to be used for teaching practice-a decision he was to rue later. In July, at the conclusion of their training course, Miss Burritt, Miss Stansfield and Miss Scott were observed 'at the chalk face' by the external examiner Mr Darlington HMIS.

Inspections and examinations took up much of the summer term. The Headmaster recorded that in the C W B examinations alone, 71 different papers were taken. The entrance examination attracted 48 candidates-the highest number to date. In addition to the usual 12 scholarships, Catherine Elizabeth Phillips of Llanbadarn Fawr was awarded the Llanbadarn scholarship of £12; the first time it had been awarded. The endowments, the oldest dating back to 1752, had been applied to education in the National School, but the vicar of Llanbadarn argued that education now came from the rates, so the money was being used to subsidise the rates and not for educational purposes. The School Board were opposed to the vicar but he was supported by the Charity Commissioners and the courts of law.[18]

Former pupils continued to graduate: E Doughton Evans B A Lampeter in Natural Science; David John de Lloyd and William T Williams both with B A Honours in History; Henry Ilar Thomas B A Honours Welsh and Ivor Evans B A Oxon School of Jurisprudence.

In September 1903, the School learnt that Victoria Bonner, Jacob Meurig Jones, and Gwilym Williams had gained U C W entrance scholarships, Victoria Bonner had, in addition, secured the top county exhibition, and Gwilym Williams, a Lord Rendal scholarship.

At the annual Prize Day, the Chairman, referring to the achievement of Victoria Bonner, a miner's daughter from Devil's Bridge, said that pupils of parents of moderate means, if they were diligent and persevering, could in this institution obtain the very best education possible at the present time.

The Headmaster presented figures which indicated the progress of the School. He thought that the total of 56 new pupils was 'quite phenomenal'. For the first time, figures for the number of pupils in lodgings were given;-out of the School population of 124, 16 boys and 24 girls were in approved lodgings. Samuel drew attention to the number of Scholars entering this year who came from country schools. 'Llancynfelin Board School occupied an honourable place as in previous years, and had provided the pupil who had attained the highest place in the whole of the county'. He also gave a summary of the subjects chosen for study in addition to English composition, grammar and literature, history and arithmetic which were compulsory. Mathematics (algebra and euclid) was taken by 109 out of 124 in the school; chemistry and elementary science 121; mechanics 11; geography 66; drawing 74; book-keeping 15; cookery 38; Latin 90 but Greek by very few; French 111 but very little demand for German. Welsh is taken by 66- 'too small a number as I hold.' 'Why is this? There is a growing tendency amongst parents to withdraw their children from Welsh classes on the grounds that it has little commercial or educational value.' The Headmaster refuted this, claiming that a lesson of Welsh grammar or literature could be made as interesting as any lesson in the curriculum.

The address was delivered by Prof D Lloyd Morgan of the UCW physics department and unlike the guest speakers of previous years did not appear to be speaking to the pupils. He outlined the qualities of an educationalist and could not understand why there was a public distrust of educational specialists, perhaps it was thought that they were not men of affairs and were unable to voice opinions on matters other than education. Posing the question 'What is education? A preparation for life?' He thought that it would be dangerous to think that all education for life must be done in school. A lot depended on what was learnt out of school, in the home and among one's fellows in society. This learning was not so deliberate, or intentional and often one was unconscious of it but if ignored it was an important element neglected. The speaker was of the opinion that pupils who had left school early for the world of work should be encouraged to resume their studies when older than perhaps 18 years. He could remember young men who began their education at that age. He hoped that the Welsh educational system would make provision for such cases.

The Rev George Eyre Evans, always a strong supporter of the School, in moving a vote of thanks to the speaker thought that the large and enthusiastic gathering present was sufficient proof of the public confidence in the School and it would take a great deal more than the piping of a voice in the wilderness to tell him that it was not so.

The traditional evening entertainment took the form of a comic opera "King Bulbous" (H Festing Jones) The spacious hall was filled to overflowing and many were unable to gain admittance.

C M Williams took over the post of chairman of the Managers vacated by Prof Genese and was to occupy that position almost continually for the next 12 years. In one of his early meetings it was learnt that the Board of Education were again threatening to reduce the Treasury grant if there was further delay in providing the new buildings. The Clerk was directed to reply expressing the earnest desire of the Managers at all times to comply with the requirements of the Board of Education so far as the funds at their disposal would allow, and their determination to raise the necessary money and proceed with the erection of the new buildings with as little delay as possible. At the same meeting it was resolved that 'a small committee be appointed to inquire into the causes of the present unsatisfactory position of the School and report thereon and upon what steps ought to be taken to place the school in a more satisfactory position and that the Committee shall consist of Prof Macaulay, Prof Levi, Mr Richard Richards and Mrs Annie Griffiths.' At that meeting a request from Mr Feek to be relieved from his duties in order to take up an assistantship in the education office of Derbyshire County Council was granted.

The David Samuel Years — 1896-1921

A move to establish a school magazine to chronicle the activities of present and past pupils was made in February 1904 when a letter signed by N H Thomas, editor and W T Williams sub-Editor was circulated asking for subscriptions and literary contributions. The third annual reunion of old pupils attracted a 'goodly number of old pupils and the proceedings passed off with much eclat.' Mainly as a result of the efforts of the old pupils the first School Magazine was published in December 1904.

For the Headmaster this was a very difficult period and his worst fears must have been realised when the investigating committee reported their findings at the Governors meeting on March 1 1904 (the Headmaster's forty-eighth birthday) The report was read by Prof Macaulay after Prof Levi, Miss Ewart and the Press had left the room.

> The position of the School in the eyes of the public must be regarded as unsatisfactory as evidenced by the recent withdrawal of guarantors, by the recognised difficulty in raising subscriptions for new buildings, and that the school population had never amounted to more than 60% of that for which accommodation was provided, and had been decreasing for the last three years.

The committee, commenting only on poor recruitment and early leaving, were of the opinion that this would not prevail if the public thought that the School was in a thoroughly satisfactory and efficient state. They had applied themselves to such questions as discipline, tone and organisation and to whether, under the management of the present Headmaster, the School could regain the credit it had lost.

Discipline seemed to be fairly good but was dependent on the efforts of individual teachers and liable to break down when classes were taken by inexperienced teachers particularly students of the college training department.

Regarding tone, there was much less of the spirit of strenuous industry and eager competition that might be desirable particularly in the junior forms. The tone was also seriously affected by so many pupils staying for just a year. The fact that more than half of the pupils in the School left during the last session and that no less than 68, out of a total of 116 at present were new to the School this session, was an indication of the problem.

The Headmaster stood accused of being out of touch with the work of the assistant teachers and failing to provide any regular means of consultation with them about the progress of individual pupils or the general welfare of the School. There was a serious deficiency of central supervision and control and sometimes a want of cooperation between the Head and his staff but the committee was unable to say who was most to blame. In the case of important subjects like geometry, the Headmaster seems to have been aware of the considerable weakness but had not seen fit to take remedial action.

The committee was surprised that no internal examinations were organised for forms not presented for the C W B Examinations. Any assessment was left to individual teachers and promotion was determined by the impressions of the Headmaster assisted by teachers' reports. This could only lead to a lack of general keenness and errors in classification. Samuel was further accused of admitting pupils, other than those from local elementary schools, without an entrance examination.

The report was critical of the system whereby a form could have four or even five different teachers each day which meant that no one teacher was responsible for the progress of any particular form or individual pupil. Rather sarcastically they concluded that the Headmaster must be a man of exceptional power if he could supervise everything and be acquainted with the progress of every pupil in the school.

With regard to the C W B examination results of the previous summer, they thought that the results in the higher level were creditable to the School but found it necessary to qualify that faint praise by commenting that there were special circumstances which induced some pupils to stay longer in the School than they would otherwise have done. The results of the lower stage of the examination were unsatisfactory and there seemed little hope that high honours were likely to be achieved in the immediate future.

In conclusion the committee desired to put on record its opinion that the administration of the School required that the Clerk should maintain a neutral and unbiased position and that his work should be of a merely clerical nature.

In his reply to the report, the Headmaster stated that he had welcomed the inquiry when it was instigated but was under the impression that it was to be carried out with his assistance. He doubted whether there had been a 'careful inquiry' and accused the committee of discourtesy in not informing him of their two brief visits to the School. Pointing out that the accommodation provided was more than double what it should be, the attendance (number on roll) was far in excess of the average attendance throughout Wales. The average attendance of pupils in the 95 Welsh intermediate schools was 8, 789 being equal to 4. 36 per 1000 of the population; in the Aberystwyth County School the attendance was 132 being equal to 6. 14 per 1000. Based on the average figures for Wales, the number on roll should be 94 and not 132. In the Headmaster's opinion these statistics totally repudiated the assertion that 'the School had lost the confidence of the public'. Using his undoubted wizardry with figures the Headmaster continued in his Comparative Statement to show that in a two year period the School had obtained five times as many honours certificates as the average for all the schools in Wales. In 1900, 69 County Schools failed to obtain a single honours certificate, the School secured 4; in 1903, 36 schools failed to obtain a single honours certificate, the School secured 6. 'The official facts speak for themselves as to the high position which the School has attained'. Moreover, David Samuel maintained that the majority of parents were not in a position to keep their children in school for long periods and if any improvement was to be effected then the Managers would have to be more liberal in granting bursaries to deserving cases.

The complaint of the short stay of pupils in school was general throughout all the schools of Wales. In Carmarthenshire, even in 1918, only approximately 20% of the 2, 500 pupils leaving elementary schools annually, proceeded to the intermediate schools. Furthermore, the brief stay of many of the pupils in the intermediate schools was evident from the fact that over half of the total number were under 14 years of age. During the school year 1912-13, the average duration of stay in an intermediate school in Wales was 2 years 6 months for boys and 3 years 1 month for girls. Approximately 80% of all pupils left with less than 4 years' schooling. Financial difficulties, as well as the financial attraction of employment and parental doubts about the value of keeping their children in intermediate schools beyond the school leaving age contributed to the situation.[19]

As for discipline, the Headmaster wondered what school would not suffer when classes are taken by strangers or inexperienced teachers. In view of the comments by the committee that the scheme for the training of teachers was detrimental to the School, he had no alternative but to refuse permission to use the School as a practising school for the student teachers. He could now appreciate the arguments of other Headmasters who had warned him against opening the School to the scheme.

On the question of 'not providing regular means of communication', staff meetings did not take place at regular intervals but several evenings at the start and end of term were devoted to discussions on the progress of pupils and the general well being of the School. His lengthy rebuttal comprehensively dealt with all the points put forward and he concluded that the report had totally failed to give a single suggestion for the betterment of the School preferring to give prominence to very trivial matters. It was a matter of great regret that while some local Managers 'threw a veil over the shortcomings of their school', some members of the County School board and their friends considered it their duty to emphasise any small defect, which to some extent, paralysed the work of the Headmaster and staff. 'I have need of the assistance, not the obstruction, of men of academic standing; and while I build up one stone upon another, it is cruel to find a Manager pulling down in another part of the structure'. Mr Samuel contended that the report was biased and that he had absolute proof that the chairman of the committee did not enter into the inquiry with a fair and impartial mind. He hoped that in the future the Managers would sink any differences which may have existed and join hands in working together for the best interests of the School and the rising generation.

At the May 1904 Managers' Meeting when the Headmaster's reply to the investigation was heard, the Board supported the Headmaster's refusal to allow use of the School by the U C W teacher training department. However at the following meeting this resolution was recinded and the Headmaster was directed 'to give permission without delay to the College to use the School for probationary teachers.'

Mr Feek's departure, after two years as science master was marked with the gift of a microscope. Cyril Mortimer Green gave an address and May Thompson the hockey Club captain made the presentation; there was the customary 'send off' at the station. The vacancy was filled by the appointment of Mr Ernest Jones B Sc, MSc, a graduate of Manchester University whose parents hailed from Trawscoed. Aged 23, he was to serve the School for eleven years before leaving to undergo medical training.

Mr Robinson making his annual inspection on behalf of the C W B gave a 'most satisfactory report' to the Governors. They, for the first time, awarded three internal scholarships value £2-10s on the results of an end of session examination and also awarded eight bursaries-the largest number ever given, conditional on the pupil remaining at school for the whole year. These awards were additional to the renewal of scholarships of seven of the previous year's scholars.

There can be no doubt, that as a result of the hostility and calumny shown towards him by his detractors, Mr Samuel felt that he had been stabbed in the back. However there is strong evidence that he was very much loved, admired and respected by his charges and colleagues. T O Pierce, science master 1901-1907 and later headmaster of Pwllheli county school wrote:

Our Headmaster was one of us-a real colleague. Mr Samuel was a remarkable man. He was one of those persons who could have done well at almost any subject, he chose Mathematics in which he gained high honours. It is my opinion that Samuel was primarily a literary man, his love, knowledge and appreciation of good literature, both Welsh and English, was immense. He had a most intimate knowledge of, and admiration for, the Welsh Bible and Prayer Book. When he took the VIth Form in Welsh, in the short time at his disposal, he was able to instil in his pupils a love of the subject which remained with them and which produced in them, a desire to proceed further with its study. Mr Samuel was an excellent musician, in fact *'Dewi o Geredigion'* was a typical Welshman of his time, a man enamoured of his country and its literature, a fine musician and yet able like many another Welshman, to turn his mind and ability to other subjects and stand high among the scholars of the universities of other countries.

As a Headmaster he had many fine qualities. His wide knowledge kept him in touch with the majority of subjects in the School curriculum; he never interfered unnecessarily with the assistant staff in their work, he trusted them and his trust was never betrayed. He was at the same time most approachable, his Staff and pupils, especially the almost monoglot Welsh among them, could depend on him for help at any time. He was their friend. On many a Saturday afternoon I had the pleasure of accompanying him for a long walk in the open country. His knowledge of nature and folk-lore always astonished me and he always deplored the fact that finance kept botany and kindred subjects out of the School timetable. On these occasions he would say 'Pierce, so-and-so lives in that farm, I would like to see his parents. Let's go there' We went and invariably got a great welcome. David Samuel was a lovable man, he was possibly too much influenced by strong-minded outsiders who knew little of the working of a school. I owe him a great debt and can never be thankful enough that my first experience as an assistant master was under a man of this type.

The Governing body of the School was like all governing bodies, they visited the School regularly in turn. Some felt it their business to criticise teachers of years standing. Others would greet you as a friend and ask if they could do anything to help and others would give you the impression that they were duty bound to come round but would like to get away as soon as possible. I feel sure that the outstanding desire in all cases was the success of the School and its pupils.[20]

The Board of Education examinations were confined to Mathematics, Chemistry and Drawing. The results of 1904 are given in detail in the Headmaster's record book. In Mathematics, stage ii, all candidates entered were successful; in stage i out of 18 pupils presented, 16 passed, 8 with distinctions. In Chemistry there were total successes, with 9 out of 15 gaining first class. Obviously the Managers were made aware of these results and the congratulations of the chairman CM Williams, Capt. James and Mrs Griffiths were acknowledged. The C W B results at Honours and Senior level were less impressive with one candidate successful at each level. However Sophie Evans, the Honours candidate took first place in the County Scholarship list and secured an exhibition of £10 at U C W. Mattie Cruickshank, who had left the previous year had been awarded the Perrott Exhibition at U C W value £10.

The David Samuel Years — 1896-1921

Early in October 1904, with 119 on roll, the Governors decided that Mr Elsdon had not fulfilled the conditions of his temporary appointment, and that the School would work with a reduced staff-five assistants and the Headmaster, who would have to devise a new time table to accommodate the change.

Sampling a secondary school time table for the first time was Richard Phillips, a farmer's son. He wrote in the Jubilee Magazine

> Although my body was in school, my mind was away in the cornfields of Llangwyryfon, where I had spent several weeks helping with the harvest. What a wrench it was to find myself in a classroom confined for hours within its walls. It was an even greater change to have a master fresh from College giving his first lesson in science. This new science was very different from my idea of the word, as in the country we had a queer use for it in describing the movement and action of certain individuals- *'Mae e'n gwneud shwd siens wrth weithio.'* Perhaps it was not so very different after all, when the new master in the strange atmosphere of the chemistry classroom with its bottles and chemicals, proceeded to demonstrate how science works. He tried, and no doubt succeeded, to show that polished iron rusts in the presence of air and water. As if we did not know it all the time-the polished breast-plate of the plough rusting overnight in the field, made contact between the new and the old life. I felt that I need have no further fears of this strange world. Another incident that remains is also in some way associated with science with its underlying need for discipline. It happened during tha last period on a Friday afternoon in the Chemistry laboratory, now the Mistresses' room, and T O Pierce was showing what happens when dilute hydrochloric acid has a date with zinc. But there was the opportunity to have a ball game just outside the passage way of the girls' main entrance, and the temptation proved too much for Evan Edwards and myself to resist. Without his usual 'Lo Lo' warning, the Head came rushing out of the Central Hall and slashed at us vigorously with his cane. Naturally we disappeared quickly amongst the crowd of pupils in the lab but the cane pursued us relentlessly. Beakers and test tubes flew in all directions and the hydrochloric acid - zinc reactions came to a sudden end. The subsequent punishment for the sake of discipline was to write the whole of Julius Ceasar by Monday morning! But what could a country lad do when he was going home to the farm that week-end? It was never done. I can also remember the look of surprise on Mr Ashton's face when the usual quiet 'Adsum' became a very loud 'Odyn' at a Monday morning roll-call. I had asked my near neighbour whether we had a soccer match on the following Saturday and somehow his reply was ready when his name was called.[21]

The *Welsh Gazette* reported on December 1 1904 that the eighth Annual Prize Day was one of the most successful gatherings held in connection with the County School. The guest speaker, Sir T Marchant Williams, who had been a fellow student of Mr Samuel at the College 31 years previously, made a virulent attack on the Central Welsh Board generally and criticised the grammar in the annual report compiled by Mr Robinson. Giving a lesson on prepositions taken from their misuse in the report, the speaker felt it was his duty to point out that if the C W B issued reports they should be in a form which did them credit. Sir Marchant, who was Warden of the Guild of Graduates of the University of Wales, censured 'these everlasting inspections and examinations' and thought that pupils were over-examined. (some 25 years earlier Marchant-Williams, then an Inspector of Schools in London, had given evidence to the Aberdare Committee on the position of the Aberystwyth College. Williams a former Aberystwyth student left the College after five months, taking with him an unexplained but exceptionally rancorous hostility towards his *Alma Mater*. Williams who remained excessively opinionated to the end of his life, gave Aberystwyth short shrift.... he would, without further ado transfer the College to Bangor where it would become a much larger college than the one at present at Aberystwyth).[22]

J Austin Jenkins, Registrar of University College, Cardiff was happy to be present because he was a former pupil of the old Ardwyn School pre-1896. He thought that the C W B was an expensive piece of machinery and perhaps was not as efficient as it might be. The previous speaker had mentioned the Welsh National Council, Mr Jenkins thought that it should not contain too many teachers nor too many county councillors; it should represent the academic influences of Wales and also the lay element of academic life but must not be dominated by the industrial South.

C M Williams, chairman of the Board of Governors, presided and in his address referred to plans for additional buildings. To date the premises had cost almost £8,000 with only a small debt of £600 remaining. No undertaking was without its ups and downs; as they knew there had been a little friction (a delightful euphemism !) but that had all been brushed away and the Managers were now working harmoniously together. Using the statistics which the Headmaster had compiled for his defence against the detractors, the Chairman found that the School was second to none and deserved the hearty support of the public.

The prize day programme, in additon to listing the academic successes, reported that eight former pupils had gained B A degrees, two of whom had secured teaching posts in secondary schools and two taken curacies at Barmouth and Aberdare. Other school leavers had joined the Civil Service, the Banks and pupil teacherships in local elementary schols.

Towards the end of term the first issue of the School Magazine, the *Ystwythian* saw the light of day although without any evidence that the Old Pupils, who had promoted the idea, had been actively involved. A contributor to the Jubilee Magazine reveals the background to its birth.

> In 1901 the School library was opened... the books were not such as made a strong appeal to boys, even in those days. For tales of adventure and school yarns the average boy turned to such weekly papers as *The Boys Friend, The Boys' Realm, The Boys' Own Paper* and *Chums* and to the monthly magazine called *The Captain* edited by the great C B Fry. In addition to a long and complete story these papers gave their readers information on all sorts of subjects. One very eager reader of these papers was a boy who came to the School from Jasper House in the town in 1902 or 1903. He was the first to be taught German in the School, and for this reason was promptly called 'The Germ'. Possibly as a result of his intensive reading of school stories he developed a strong desire to start a school magazine and in 1904 he produced the first School magazine, practically all of which he wrote himself. It may be that production has not been continuous since the first number appeared, but in this edition of the School magazine it is right and fitting that the name of Cyril Mortimer Green, the editor and

producer of the first School magazine, who was killed in the First World War should be held in particular remembrance.[23]

It is appropriate to list those involved, all of whom, with the exception of the treasurer, were current pupils.
Joint Editors: Marjorie Markham, Cyril Mortimer Green. Treasurer: Mr Ernest Jones. Secretary: Stanley Edwards.
Committee: Alice Cruickshank, Ella Jones, Katie Phillips, Lizzie Watkins, Blanche Whitby, John Evans, Edward Meredith, Alfred Pickard, Alan Whatham.

The editors wrote-
> We make no apology for its appearance, nor do we seek to justify its publication. To demand a reason for offering a medium for the more extensive circulation of the best thoughts and aspirations of our pupils seem to us superfluous. The expression of one's opinion on paper is so important and so difficult a thing that any opportunity for exercising the same ought to be in itself welcomed. To those of our readers who may be destined to play a prominent part in the municipal or national life of our country - may there not be amongst us a future Prime Minister or a fit helpmeet of a great Proconsul? - we can do no better than invite them to avail themselves freely of this opportunity for thinking correctly and expressing those thoughts clearly, two things without which, as the old Greeks well realised, no one can properly be called educated. The intention is for the Magazine to be issued once each term, one aim being to keep past pupils in touch with their *Alma Mater* 'Let not the breath of your criticism blow too rudely upon it. It is for you to help us to strengthen and improve it with your sympathy'.

The opening article, though unsigned was contributed by N H Thomas, Classics master, was entitled 'School and University Life in Ancient Wales.' The writer proposed, somewhat fancifully that the oldest university was not Oxford or Cambridge but had been situated at Llanilltyd Fawr close to the Glamorgan coast, the first buildings being destroyed by Irish pirates in 446.
Another writer giving advice on what to do on Saturday, commended an old proverb 'Absence from work is no rest, the real rest is change of work.'
The sole contribution from a past pupil was a translation of a Tennyson poem, *Croesi'r Bar* by D Jonathan Jones, a County scholar at U C W, whose contribution to the Jubilee Magazine has already been noted. He was to write again in 1916, as a Royal Navy Chaplain describing the hell in the Dardanelles. Included in 'School Notes' was a report of a presentation of a dinner service to Jones the Caretaker on the occasion of his marriage 'it was an expression of the kindly feeling pupils entertained towards one who described himself as only 'a hewer of wood and a drawer of water' yet by his urbanity, has won our esteem and regard.'
It had been reported that a gentleman had offered to give violin lessons if 20 or more were interested. Lessons would take place from 4.15 to 5.15 pm each day. 'We pity the poor victims of the trigonometry class (David Samuel held extra lessons after school in this subject) but had they been doomed to listen to the discordant tones of 20 violins, life for them would indeed be hardly worth living.'

The History of Aberystwyth County School (Ardwyn) 1896-1973

Mr Samuel's meticulously kept records did not extend to giving great detail of the athletic activities but with the advent of the School Magazine this was remedied and most editions described, often in great detail, the various encounters on the playing fields. In the Autumn of 1904, the school football team under the captaincy of W S Edwards was too strong for Ystrad Meurig 2nd XI winning 7-0, but at home to Aberayron, with Mr Pierce in the forward line they lost 2-5. College Seconds were defeated 2-1 but at Tregaron they went down 2-0. The hockey team, captained by Addie Watkins played just once, against Towyn losing 1-0. After the game ' the players proceeded to School where they partook of a cold luncheon prepared by Miss Ewart assisted by several of her young ladies'. Games players will remember these after-the-match banquets when one had the opportunity to socialise with the opposition as well as satisfying the inner man.

The School magazine sold for 3d, was subsidised by the income from advertisements. It may be of interest to record those businesses which gave their support.
B. Taylor Lloyd 3 Bridge Street- 1/4 plate camera, one guinea, wonderful value for money (the price remained unaltered for many years).
J Hywel Rees Tailor and School Outfitter, City House, (next to Barclays Bank) North Parade.
R Northy Draper and High Class Milliner-Suits 25/-upwards, Tottenham House
Daniel Thomas 22&24 Little Darkgate Street Boys and Youth Clothing
Jack Edwards Stationer 13 Great Darkgate Street
M H Davies 4 Bridge Street, 20 Queen Street(Cabinets and Furniture) 18 Queen Street (Mining Stores and Agricultural Implements) .
Dicks 12 Great Darkgate Street Boots of all kinds.
Thomas and Son Northgate Stores Groceries and Provisions
Hughes & Owen Athletic Outfitters 29 Great Darkgate Street
W R Jones Watchmaker and Jeweller 32 Great Darkgate Street
Oculists Prescriptions made up.

There was great disappointment when, during the last week of term, it was announced that Edith Ewart, had resigned to take up the post of Headmistress of a girls' school in Folkestone. One wonders whether the malevolence of some of the Governors hastened her departure. Miss Ewart was recognised as being a brilliant teacher of history, a good disciplinarian and a splendid Senior Mistress 'whose dignity was sometimes mistaken for austerity.' Her successor, Irene C Dalley was to serve the School diligently for 27 years.

Another change which became a long standing tradition was the staging of the Old Pupils' Reunion on Boxing Day. The 1904 President, D J de Lloyd B A had produced a programme, which as usual showed the great musical and other talents available. The evening concluded with a very humerous comedietta entitled 'Bubbles'.

For the second issue of the *Ystwythian*, one of the editors, Cyril Mortimer Green had left School having moved to Exeter on the death of his father the Rev T Mortimer Green who from 1892 to 1905 held the position of Registrar at U C W.

Cyril's place was taken by David Owen Morris, whose school career had been interrupted for a year as he described in his article, "One of my days at an open-air Sanitorium", in the April 1905 Magazine.

David Owen Morris took the C W B Honours Certificate that year and carried off the premier County Exhibition as well as a U C W Entrance Exhibition. He graduated B A in 1908 and two years later obtained a post as English teacher in the International College, Geneva. In his contribution to the Jubilee Magazine he pays tribute to his teachers... 'many will remember with gratitude N H Thomas a product of Llandovery and Oxford. He was a gentleman of high culture and his teaching, redolent of the best scholarship of an ancient university, I found most inspiring. To study Welsh with the Headmaster and Latin with Mr Thomas for the Honours Certificate in my last year in School, was an unforgettable experience, the more so because I was resuming my studies after being absent through illness for a whole year, most of which I had spent in a sanitorium.[24]

ARDWYN

Gwasgerir plant yr Ysgol Sir
O hyd i'r pedwar ban,
A mwy-fwy'n hanes dynol ryw
Chwareuant ddynol ran.
Enillant glod mewn llawer lle,
Anrhydedd yn eu swydd.
"Nerth dysg ei ymdrech" sicrha
Ym mhobman urdd a llwydd.

Hawddamor Ysgol ar y Bryn,
Boed hir dy ddyddiau di,
Arosed swyn dy enw da
Fel heddyw gyda ni.
Dysg di dy blant o oes i oes
I gyrchu'r uchel nod,
`Er llwydd eu hun, a lles y byd,
A chadw'n wyrdd dy glod.

Tach 29 1905   John James

John James gained first place in the Scholarship Examination in 1896 and is the first name on the Admission Register. As previously mentioned he took the first place in the County Scholarships in 1898. After leaving U C W he trained at Trevecca College, from where he was appointed a minister in New Tredegar and later in Pembroke. He died at the early age of 40 years at Tregaron Sanitorium in September 1919.

Condolences were extended to N H Thomas on the tragic death of his son Henry Morley in a house fire-' his merry face and sweet smile were well known to our pupils'. In Thomas' absence, C W Valentine, U C W who later was to become well-known in the field of psychology came to assist.

The Headmaster recorded that the general health of the staff was not good during the Lent term, the Magazine asked 'Anyone a cure for influenza, which has had such a disastrous effect on the staff? 'One by one they appeared with running eyes, then they did not appear at all.'

The football team continued their season with two matches drawn and two lost. At Aberayron, the School lost 5-1 but complained that the home team played ex-pupils. The hockey team seemed more concerned with the ' eats' supplied. 'On a stormy day, we left for Aberayron at 8. 30, had tea and mince pies on arrival. The Ystwythians had a hard job to keep the opponents out but the home team scored late in the game to win 1-0. We did full justice to a fine tea. We arrived home at 8. 30 pm having rescued three stray fellow pupils at Llanrhystud.' Miss Dalley, who had been a a notable player when at the U C W, played in the forward line for the first time, in the return match with Towyn but failed to prevent the team losing 3-0.

The continued inadequacy of the accommodation for the science department had, once again, resulted in a reduction of the Treasury grant. At the request of the Governors, a meeting was arranged with the C W B Chief Inspector Owen Owen who stressed the need to induce pupils to stay longer at school and suggested lowering the age of entry from 14 years to 13 years; there was need to frame a 4 year curriculum for years 2 to 5 and offer a more advanced and specialised course for form 6. It might then be possible to obtain capitation grants from the County Education Authority under the Education Act 1902 in respect of pupils who had spent the requisite period in the School. At this meeting the Governors considered plans prepared by Mr Morgan the Architect for additional science and technical accommodation and agreed to seek a loan of £1200 from the County Education Authority to finance the project. Ultimately plans were approved and the building contract awarded to Richard Owen whose tender was £865, the lowest received.

In the June 1905 U C W degree list were the names of D J de Lloyd B A who had secured the first ever awarded Mus Bac degree of the Welsh University. On the threshold of an illustrious musical career, de Lloyd, in the College eisteddfod, had led the victorious Male Voice party and his wife to be, Lillian Morgan had won the contralto solo. Rachel Ellen Thomas became the first girl pupil to gain a degree, held the temporary headship of Rhydypennau school joining two former Ystwythians on the staff and later was appointed English mistress at Aberayron County School. Also gaining their B As were Griffith Daniel Ellis and John Arllwyd Jones, both of whom secured posts as grammar school teachers in Truro and Halifax respectively. Twelve years later John Arllwyd was killed in action in Flanders as a Lieutenant in the Welch Regiment.

The guest speaker at the ninth annual prize day was J. Lloyd Morgan M P. After hearing the Headmaster's report he agreed that any school would be proud of such a list of successes. He had just entered Parliament in 1889 when the Intermediate Education Act was introduced in the House. What a tremendous impetus had been given to the cause of education in Wales by its passing. He had read a speech that morning by the Bishop of St. Asaph, in which he had said that there were too many intermediate schools in Wales and they were a danger and a drawback. The speaker could not agree but thought that there was a need to develop technical education to keep up with countries like America and Germany. Neither could he agree with those who advocated boarding school education, he thought that their products were too close to a type. If the intermediate school was good and if the home training was good then this was the best education possible. Some parents sent their children to school to rid themselves of the responsibility. They had an obligation to take an interest in their children's work and to encourage them in their studies. He would say that success in life depended more on the habits which people acquired when at school rather that on which subjects were studied. Industry was indispensable, nobody had a right to expect to succeed in life unless he was prepared to work hard.

Mrs Powell, 'a representative of the noble families of Gogerddan and Nanteos', in presenting the prizes, spoke words of encouragement to those who had not gained prizes. The Founders of the School had put it plainly that the object of work was not to get a prize. Their motto was *'Nerth dysg ei ymdrech'* and not *'Nerth dysg ei gwobr'*

The Headmaster took great pleasure in the publication of the *Ystwythian* offering as it did a medium for past as well as present pupils to be acquainted with the activities and achievements of past and present pupils. He also rejoiced in the loyalty shown by former pupils to their *Alma Mater*, by their gatherings at the annual reunions, as well as in other ways. 'Their devotion to the "school on the hill" shows no abatement as the years roll on'. Six pupils had entered the U C W that term and to date eleven former pupils had taken their B A degree.

The traditional evening entertainment took the form of an operetta "Little Snow-White". The *Welsh Gazette* thought the performance reflected great credit on everyone concerned, with Gwen Williams as Snow-white, the star of the show, and John Richard Jones, a pretty little Prince of Arcadee. Surprise was expressed that no admission charge was made 'so that pupils might enjoy the fruits of their labours.'

The new editors of the School Magazine, Alice Cruickshank and Alan Whatham appealed to old Ystwythians to contribute articles.. The balance sheet for the three issues of the previous year showed that advertising brought in 14/6 and with printing costs £7.17.6d there was a balance of £1.11.3d

To mark the centenary of the Battle of Trafalgar 21 October 1805 an article on the life of Nelson was included. The autumn edition noted that Ebenezer Rhys Thomas had been elected to the presidency of the U C W Literary and Debating Society, the first student to have achieved this honour. The School's first Science teacher Dewi Ellis who recently had gained his D Sc at London and who now held a lectureship (later the Chair) in bacteriology in Glasgow, had given a lecture on microbes at the newly opened Coliseum, Terrace Road, a meeting chaired by David Samuel and organised by the Free Library Committee. The School staff were prominent in many spheres in the town. The Headmaster and N H Thomas were members of the Free Library Committee and had been 'observed in their robes walking from the Hotel Cambria to the site of the new town (Carnegie) library on the occasion of the laying of the foundation stone' (July 1905). The building was opened in April 1906, ' built with the help of a grant of £3, 000 from Mr Carnegie.' Science teachers TO Pierce and Ernest Jones had given a demonstration of Rontgen X-Rays at the Coliseum.

The football team were having a poor season, losing at Machynlleth 5-0 and at Towyn 14-0 'long practice and old age had rendered Towyn perfect' The goal keeper, Dewi Williams had a back-breaking afternoon. The 'footer' team must have also lost to Aberayron if the following contribution is to believed:-

Scene: Charabanc returning from Aberayron.
Voice: We wass go to Aberayron
                   In green shirts with a white line on
                   The game was not a fine one
                   Though the 'scarlets' gave us five one.
                   (sung to 'Did you ever see' ?)

The hockey team fared no better but both teams had their photographs (taken by Mr Pierce) in the Lent 1906 issue.

Also recorded is the result of the Bone-Breakers Hockey XI, all boys except Miss Dalley in goal. They beat a College Second XI 2-0

The Lent issue of the *Ystwythian* was the first one to have the cover adorned with a view of the School reproduced from a fine woodcut by Mr Ernest Jones. This illustration was used continually up to the 1950 issue of the Magazine. Another notable artist, Arthur Doughton Williams, who had gained ten certificates for drawing whilst a pupil- he had made the sketches for plates which were used to illustrate "The History of the Aberystwyth Court Leet" by George Eyre Evans published in 1901, had been appointed draughtsman with Vickers and Maxim, Barrow in Furness.

In the Midsummer issue some light is thrown on the minimal part played by past pupils in the launch of the Magazine. 'The idea had to be abandoned for financial reasons', but the old pupils were delighted that the idea had 'been revived by the more adventurous present pupils. It is not always the last stroke of the axe that splits the wood'. The Old Ystwythians were grateful for space in the Magazine for their Notes and hoped that past pupils would show their love for their *Alma Mater* by supporting the venture with contributions. It was noted, in a recent College concert that the male chorus had sung 'Song of the Siege' under the personal direction of the composer David de Lloyd. With the help of a local appeal, he was able to spend some months in a conservatoire in Leipzig to study composition prior to being appointed lecturer in singing and voice production in the Woolwich Polytechnic. In the Grand National Eisteddfod at Llangollen in 1908, de Lloyd's beautiful part song 'Sleep, sweet baby' was the test piece.

During the Summer Term, there were several extra-mural visits. The senior art class was taken by Mr Appleton and Miss Thomas to the College to study some pictures and other art treasures, permission kindly given by the Principal. The science staff, with a party of senior chemistry pupils, visited the gas works to see the processes employed in the production of coal-gas. A group under the Headmaster visited the Welsh Library to see some early Welsh books and M S S, 'the Welsh Librarian Mr Glyn Davies, rendering valuable services on this occasion.'

There was also time for recreational pursuits which included a cycle run for staff and pupils to Devils Bridge with cricket and tea at The Woodlands, and the traditional trips to Abermad and Llyfnant Valley for a picnic.

The sessional list of U C W Scholars published in June 1906 gave awards to ten former pupils out of the 68 available (16%) There were 21 former pupils at College that term. The degree results included Ebenezer Rhys Thomas B Sc with second class honours in chemistry and Isabella Cruickshank B A. The former had been appointed to Barmouth County School and the latter assistant mistress in a Manchester school.

Professors Levi and Macauly had retired from the Board of Governors and had been replaced by the Rev R J Rees and Prof D Morgan Lewis. The Board had been informed by the County Education Committee that they required all their intermediate schools to be recognised by the Board of Education as centres for the training and instruction of pupil teachers. The July 1906 entrance examination, in addition to the usual elementary school candidates, included 31 pupil teacher candidates of whom 18 were accepted and granted bursaries of between £5 and £1. This innovation helped boost the numbers admitted in the Michaelmas term 1906 to a record 183, an increase of 50 on the the previous session. 'There is no school in Wales where the increase has reached such a high percentage.' As a consequence of this great increase in numbers the Governors acted quickly to appoint John Evans son of the Rev Dr Evans, 'Hawen', and who had recently graduated at Cardiff College. His tenure however was to be a short one.

The 1906 prize day programme records a remarkable family achievement. Four members of the Cruickshank family are named for their various successes. In addition to Isabella previously mentioned, Mattie, later to be appointed to the School staff, and Evan were holding scholarships at the U C W while Alice had gained the C W B Honours certificate in three subjects earning a Perrott Exhibition at the U C W. Youngest of the family Lizzie was to top the entrance scholarship to the School in 1907 but died at the age of 14 years. It was something of a disappointment that the School had failed to attract a County Exhibition for the first time since 1889 though the next year would bring ample compensation.

Ald C M Williams, chairman of the Managers presided and took issue once again with those headmasters of elementary schools in the area who failed to prepare and present their pupils for the entrance examination. Out of 33 schools in the area, only 11 were represented. He commended Llangwyryfon, a small school, which that year, had secured three scholarships. The chairman was pleased that a criticism from the Chief Inspector that the intermediate schools of Wales did not pay sufficient attention to the teaching of Welsh did not apply to the Aberystwyth County School since of the 183 pupils, 160 took Welsh without any compulsion of any kind.

The Headmaster, in presenting his report, said they were gathered at the completion of the first decade of the School's life and history. He believed that there was every reason to be satisfied with their educational results. Visits from the inspectors of the CWB and the Board of Education, some of them unannounced, had produced reports somewhat laconic in their brevity- 'Good work is being done at this school' He was pleased to report that as a result of these visits, the School would be attracting the highest Treasury grants for the 1906-07 school year.

The chief speaker, Principal T F Roberts of the University College said that secondary and primary education now formed one indissoluble whole. Those who were trained in their schools were to live among the people and for the people, and must be trained and educated for that function. Indeed this was the keynote of modern education from the highest grade to the lowest. The emphasis of education must for the future rest upon the needs of the people, and it must derive its inspiration from the life of the people. There was in the labouring community in Wales, a reserve store of ideals and energy, of thrift and simplicity which, if re-echoed in the schools would make them famous as places of education for all classes. The President of the United States, in his manifesto issued a few days earlier, looked forward to great results for the social well-being from education. It was probable, he said, that a thoroughly efficient system of education came next to the influence of patriotism in the bringing about of national success. Principal Roberts would say to the boys and girls, that they now had the conditions for developing the independence, the freedom, and the dignity of their manhood and womanhood which had not been given to any generation of pupils in Wales before. They were not asked to learn in the spirit of the slave, but for the sake of goodness and for the sake of their friends, their parents, fellow citizens and their country. They would then enter upon their work with an enthusiasm and with a joy that would make their studies a pleasure and its own reward.

The traditional evening entertainment in the Central Hall broke all records with the production of the operetta 'Princess Zara' with people queuing for admission long before the start. The *Welsh Gazette* strongly recommended that the largest public rooms in the town should be engaged in future years because a great number failed to gain admission.

The Classical master N H Thomas had secured an award which had enabled him to visit the United States and Canada to study their systems of education. He had been granted three months leave of absence and would be making a full report to the Governors on his return. His replacement was H Madoc Jones B A who 'took delight in rugby, hockey and swimming.'

The Old Pupils Association met as usual on Boxing Day with the President John Hugh Phillips who had been a Scholar and the first soccer captain in 1896. He had left to join a London bank but later changed career direction to become the first Ystwythian to be called to the Bar.

Work on the new laboratories had started in October 1906 and by February progress was such that the whole building was under roof. The builder, Richard Owen had fallen from the scaffolding, but luckily Mr Ernest Jones, from his classroom had witnessed the accident and had rendered first aid. Earlier the Govenors had adopted a suggestion by Prof Morgan Lewis of the U C W physics department, that the room next to the planned workshop be used for advanced work in physics. By October 1907, the new wing, having cost £1, 200 was complete and ready for occupation. Many regretted the reduction of playground space to accommodate the development. One of the science staff however would not be using the new facilities, T O Pierce, who had been horrified at the science provision on his appointment in 1901, had tendered his resignation having been appointed to a post in Llandudno County school. In addition to teaching his subject, Pierce had been coach and umpire to the hockey side as well as reinforcing the football team on occasions. Also leaving, after just one year, was John Evans who was joining Llandeilo County school. His replacement, Mr Joseph Davies BA died before taking up his post. Former pupil and recent UCW graduate, Jacob Meurig Jones filled in temporarily. Pierce's replacement, D P H Ashton was a 21 year-old first class honours physics graduate of Cardiff College who was to give 12 years service to the School.

As a result of the 1907 CWB Honours certificate examinations, of the six County Exhibitions available, the first, third and fourth places went to Alan Watham, Eunice May Davies and Thomas Ivor Rees, respectively. The first named, the son of a Newtonards, Co. Down clergyman also secured a UCW Entrance scholarship and in 1910 obtained a Natural Science scholarship to Clare College, Cambridge. Alice Cruickshank, who had qualified the previous year, claimed a fourth Exhibition for the

School on her entry to the Aberystwyth College that year.

The Midsummer 1907 edition of the *Ystwythian* under the editorship of Eunice Davies and Tom Ivor Rees reported that former pupil Ernest Evans, who, when at U C W had won a Squire Law Scholarship to Trinity College, Cambridge had opened the debate at the Cambridge Union, the subject being 'The House of Lords'. *The Cambridge Review* thought that Mr Evans was excellent and showed great fluency and self-possession. Another, *The Granta* said that Mr Evans 'was the most promising speaker we have listened to this term.' Evans had been elected a member of the Committee of the Union and had gained second class in Part 1 of the Law Tripos. In the following years Ernest was elected to the office of President of the Cambridge Union, gained a law degree, was called to the Bar and in the tradition of many who have occupied the Union Presidency became a Member of Parliament. His older brother Ivor had chosen Oxford for his Law course and obtained his BA in 1903 and MA in 1908. After a short time in London he came home to join his father's law practice. Ivor, Ernest and another brother Evan who died at an early age, had been in the first intake to the School in 1896.

One of Ivor's classmates in those early days was Goronwy Owen, the School's first BA; while teaching in London, he became the School's first M A in 1907, with a thesis on the history of Cardigan castle. The future would see more honours and distinctions coming his way.

At the 1907 prize day, the Headmaster conveyed the opinion of the Chief Inspector who had declared that the new science building was one of the finest, if not the finest in any county school in Wales. He acknowledged the School's indebtedness to the science master Mr Ernest Jones who had devoted an enormous amount of time and energy in the planning and equipping of the laboratories and workshop.

The Address was once again given by Prof Anwyl now chairman of the C W B. He reminded his audience that there could be no true success in a school unless those who governed the school, those who taught in the school and those who learnt in the school, had the same common aim, that aim being the acquisition of knowledge on the one hand and the formation of true character on the other. True education meant the education of the whole man. He came back to a point he had put forward when he had spoken at the 1902 Prize Day saying that children were also taught by each other. He trusted that there was that spirit of fellowship, that *esprit de corps* between the children, which would make them proud of the school to which they belonged. Prof Anwyl was delighted to learn of the Old Pupils Association. A school did not truly succeed if the pupils who left it cooled in the warmth of their affection for the school but a school had been a true success when those who left it continued to feel throughout life, a living and real interest in it.

Sir Edward Pryse, Bart. Gogerddan, replying on behalf of his wife, Lady Pryse who had distributed the prizes, said that this was their first visit to the school. He believed that Cardiganshire took a greater interest in education than any of the Welsh counties and he was gratified to see Welshmen making their mark in different parts of the world.

The vacant post in mathematics was filled by David Brunt, who had recently graduated with first class honours at the UCW. Prof Genese, in his testimonial regarded him as the finest student he had had since leaving Cambridge in 1891. However his stay was a matter of weeks as he was tempted away by a scholarship to Cambridge where he became a Wrangler. In 1935 he obtained a Chair at the University of London and in 1948 was President of the Physics Society and knighted the following year. The vacancy was filled by William Barker BSc a graduate of London University who could teach mathematics, science, drawing and geography. Mattie Cruickshank, a former pupil was appointed initially to a temporary part-time post which later became permanent.

The new facilities for the teaching of science and technical work allowed new developments in the teaching of physics and Sloyd (Swedish handwork). Ernest Jones by visiting Naas in Sweden had obtained qualifications in Sloyd and was paid £10 per annum in addition to £134 for his science teaching.

Many structural changes had been effected, the old laboratories had reverted to classrooms, with the smaller laboratory becoming a splendid mistresses' room and one of the classrooms adjoining the new laboratory had been turned into a demonstration room-the 'Chem Dem' familiar to generations of pupils.

The boys were not having a great deal of success at cricket. In the summer of 1908, the only school played was Towyn. At home, on the Smithfield ground where the surface was somewhat better than at Grogythan and without the slope, the home side lost by a few runs but the return match at Towyn must have been somewhat bizarre if the Magazine report is to believed. 'The pitch was tricky and the home batsmen began to play the ball into rabbit- holes, billiard fashion, of which our fielders knew nothing. Consequently the score increased rapidly by means of the 'lost-ball' method. We were defeated despite Mr Ashton making 30 runs and taking 6 wickets for 19 runs. We enjoyed the tea immensely.'

That same summer John Morris Jones caught his first glimpse of Ardwyn.

> After attending the school at Chancery for so many years it was 'an awe-inspiring sight, a glimpse of the promised land as it were. Along with other hopefuls, I wended my way up Northgate Street and Llanbadarn road to the Central Hall where the annual scholarships were held. On that day I first made the acquaintanceship of Percy George, now on the staff of the University College, and Ifor Morgan of Glanfraed, who lost his life in World War I -friendships destined to be strongly cemented during the succeeding years.
>
> Fortune smiled that day, for the examiners saw fit to include me among the chosen twelve. So when September came I joined scores of others who trudged up the steep lane to the rarefied atmosphere of erudition and learning. Like all other 'freshers', I was ripe prey for the bigger boys who knew the ropes only too well. After being herded into a corner, I was ceremoniously grabbed by the scruff of the neck and hoisted in a most undignified manner by the seat of my pants and duly baptised under the faucet of the north wall, where the high priests were doing a most thorough job of it.
>
> When the roll-call was taken, there was more than one head of damp hair and a glint of amusement in many a teacher's eye, as the new boys timidly mumbled their 'Adsums' when their names were called. Above the entrance hung a motto (I wonder if it is still there) which was duly impressed on the new comers:
>
> > "Dare to be true
> > Nothing can need a lie
> > The lie that needs it most
> > Grows two thereby."

The David Samuel Years — 1896-1921

To us of that generation, Ardwyn was synonymous with one dominant personality, the learned Headmaster, David Samuel, who loved the School with what amounted to a holy ardour. Who will forget ' Sammy ', as he was known to all and sundry? To see him striding through the halls, tall and lean and hungry-looking, with his academic gown flowing behind him and, frequently a yellow cane in his hand, was a picture ever to be remembered. Even the bravest soul would quail at his 'Hello! Hello! Hello! What are you up to now ?

Who will forget his scholarly mien, his vast knowledge and the clever way in which he showed the greenest neophyte how to make the best use of his schooldays. Many of us were privileged to attend his Saturday morning 'Trig' lessons, a labour of love on his part and an outlet for genius pertaining to things mathematical. More than once, staunch Methodist that he was, would he take delight in tripping those of us who were Church of England, whose knowledge of the Common Prayer Book was infinitely inferior to his.

In spite of his strictness, he was a kindly person who burned with a feverish desire to impart knowledge even when doling out punishment. During an art expedition to the Public Library, three of us indulged in some youthful prank that called for punishment and reprimand. The time we spent with him after school for the following fortnight was not spent in useless writing of lines, but rather in wandering through the School from art picture to art picture. He explained what message each picture was intended to convey, who the artist was, and his life experiences. He it was who absorbed the punishment. For us it was pure delight. No one who sat at his feet will ever doubt that his ghost, properly begowned still roams the School and beautiful grounds.

Those of us who had the privilege of roaming through the hallowed halls of Ardwyn may have lost touch with each other, but none of us has forgotten the rich heritage with which the old School endowed us. Long may its traditions endure as an inspiration for those who have the door of opportunity opened for them within its halls, and who go on to wrestle with the everyday problems of our complicated civilisation! Those now at Ardwyn, and legions still to come, will always bear in mind that:

> There's an adventure! It awaits
> Beyond thy wide, mysterious gates.
> Whom shall I meet, where shall I go?
> Beyond the lovely land I know?
> Above the sky, beyond the sea?
> What shall I learn and feel and be?
> Spinx-like, Ardwyn, thou seem'st to say
> Thrills galore wait along the way.[25]

The Headmaster in his report to those assembled for the 1908 prize Day made no apology for 'my intense admiration for scholarship, being an old student of Llandovery and Cambridge, it is perhaps natural that I should think that a school does not perform its proper function if it does not produce scholars. Still I cannot believe that this alone can constitute the be-all and end-all of a school such as ours. Our list shows that we lay great stress on proficiency and success in other walks of life'. The printed list showed that ten former pupils had secured appointments in elementary schools mainly in Wales-many having been trained as pupil teachers in the School, five graduates in secondary schools as well the clergy, banks, Civil Service, ship's purser, hospital dispenser and G W R clerk. Prof Edward Edwards who held the Chair of history at the U C W, and brother of O M Edwards, Chief Inspector, gave the main address. They should be thankful for the work done by the C W B in the administration of education but they should not so fill the time-table that it took away every moment of a child's life leaving no time for leisure reading and appreciation of their culture. Referring to the motto of the School, he thought it happily chosen, and no school had a better one. It meant that the strength or energy of learning was effort. Into the kingdom of learning they could not enter without serious effort. It required effort by the Governors, teachers, parents, some of whom made great sacrifices to educate their children, but most important of all it required an effort on the part of the pupils themselves.

The *Welsh Gazette* reported that the traditional Christmas entertainment by the pupils was worthy of its predecessors with the Central Hall crowded to excess with an appreciative audience. The senior pupils performed the famous trial 'Bardell v. Pickwick' and the juniors, an operetta, 'Rip Van Winkle' with R Maelor Thomas singled out for his performance as Rip. Miss Dalley, Senior Mistress who was responsible for training the pupils in both plays, was congratulated for her devotion. Katie Griffiths, A L C M, one of the pupils, acted as accompanist.

The annual re-union of the Old Pupils' Association continued to be held on Boxing Day. Molly Owen and D O Morris gave a delightful rendering of '*Hywel a Blodwen*' and Evered Davies gave an early indication of his musical talents with an oboe solo. The son of Pier Street photographer H H Davies, he later became well-known as the leader of a very popular local dance band. The second half of the evening was taken up with a farcical comedy where according to the *Cambrian News* report, the acting was not of a high order. In fact the paper was quite scathing in its criticism. 'Mr de Say's acting was marred by his atrocious get-up. One might have thought that a swarm of houseflies has stuck to the grease on his forehead before he came on and he had forgotten to remove them.' David Samuel commented that the report did not give a fair description of the concert, 'it being generally thought that the criticisms were somewhat too severe.'

The funds available for running the School were still inadequate and the Managers had to give careful consideration to every item of proposed expenditure. The Balfour Education Act of 1902 which brought secondary education to England, thirteen years after it had come to Wales, created the Local Education Authority (L E A) which replaced the County Governing Body established in 1896 and provided for grants from the Board of Education. The formation of the Welsh Department of the Board of Education in 1907, with Owen M Edwards its first Chief Inspector, brought increased grants from the Treasury. The School's balance sheet for the session 1907-08 showed the largest surplus, £534, since the foundation of the School and for only the third occasion. This was a turning point financially, each succeeding year produced a credit balance, reaching £2261 in 1912. Grants from the County Governing Body and the Board of Education in 1907-08 were £745 and £373 respectively, with receipts from tuition fees

The David Samuel Years — 1896-1921

£1187. Staff salaries totalled £784 including the Headmaster's remuneration of £269. The chairman of the Governors, Ald C M Williams, speaking at the 1908 Prize Day, thought that the County of Cardigan had never been very generous as far as funding was concerned, giving only the half-penny rate whereas other counties had made substantial grants in addition. He welcomed the increased funding and the remarks of WC Runciman, the Education Minister when he opened new school buildings at Towyn. There he had said that Wales could rely on him to mete out equal treatment to Welsh schools as to English schools. Ald Williams thought that they could face the future with confidence. However the Board of Governors were concerned that many parents were neglectful in the matter of paying tuition fees. Reminder letters from the Clerk threatened that the Headmaster had been instructed to refuse admission if fees were not paid within 14 days of the start of each term. There were obviously cases of genuine hardship despite the increased bursaries, but there is no evidence that the threat of exclusion was ever put into operation, though the problem of early leaving was still prevalent.

The problem of the late arrival of the Borth and Llandre train was obviously insuperable because the Governors, having been petitioned by parents from those areas, circulated all parents for their views regarding a change in the school hours.

    viz.   Morning: 9. 45 am to 1 pm
              Afternoon :   2. 15 pm to 4. 35 pm

The new times were agreed and implemented for a trial period of two terms. No longer would Borth and Llandre pupils miss their early morning Algebra lessons!

Mathew Henry Evans of Goginan was a member of the first intake to the School in 1896 leaving two years later having gained distinctions in the Senior certificate. He obtained a B A in 1904 with Honours in Latin but during his studies for the B D examinations his health broke down and spent a winter in a Bournemouth sanitorium. He recovered sufficiently to complete his course and the 1908 Prize day programme records his success in obtaining his Divinity degree and his appointment as tutor to Wolsey Hall College, Oxford, and assistant to Principal Prys at the Theological College. Despite failing health he embarked on a dissertation for an M A, spending some time at the British Museum. Through the munificence of Mrs Edward Davies of Llandinam, he attended the Leysin Sanitorium in Switzerland but died there on the 7 December 1909, the day the degree of M A was conferred on him in his absence by the University of Wales. He was yet another young victim of tuberculosis, which remained the commonest single cause of death in Wales in the early years of the century, with the people of Cardiganshire particularly vulnerable. Referring to the disease, King Edward VII had asked-'If curable, why not cured?' With notable exceptions, there were no facilities for the comprehensive treatment of the disease in Wales. Following the King's death in 1910, David Davies M P of Llandinam, remembering the numerous memorial clocks and fountains erected after the death of Queen Victoria, conceived the idea of a more objective Welsh memorial to the late King Edward VII. It was agreed that the Memorial should be a national campaign to eradicate tuberculosis. The royal charter granted in May 1910 marked the beginning of the King Edward VII Welsh National Memorial

Association for the prevention, treatment and abolition of tuberculosis. The W. N. M. A. grew to be the fore-most anti-tuberculosis organisation in the British Empire if not the world.[26]

Presenting his thirteenth annual report at the 1909 Prize Day, the Headmaster expressed disappointment with the results of the external examinations-' they were not equal to our merits as they have certainly not been equal to our hopes. It is very trying to a school teacher after putting in his very best into his year's work and expecting great things from hard working and conscientious pupils to find unsatisying results in the examination lists.' Samuel asked for the cooperation of parents and lodging-house keepers in ensuring that pupils observe the school regulations in regard to evening hours and home studies:

> Our town is so peculiarly placed in respect to enticements and temptations to get away from evening work and particularly at certain seasons of the year, that I am anxious to forewarn all whom it may concern that it is my intention to report any delinquency in this matter to the Governors. I speak in this strain not only as a schoolmaster but as a patriot, as one who has the well-being of the country at heart. I fix my eyes not only on the 1910 examination results but on the future of our country in 1920 and 1930 and later, when those who are pupils today under my tuition shall have become grown-up men and women, carrying on the duties of the state in one or other of its departments. The undisciplined slacker of 1910 will have developed into the inveterate loafer of 1920. To prevent this calamity has been and always will be my aim.

Dr Sudborough, professor of chemistry at U C W, in his address would like to insist that every scholar turned out from school, to whatever vocation or calling, should have a knowledge of their own language and a love for the beauties of their own literature. He thought that there was nothing which deserved more thorough attention and organisation in the schools of Wales than the life of the playing fields. As well as bearing on the physical development, the discipline of the playing field was of the greatest importance since it engendered discipline. Another aspect of school-life was that no friendships were so long lasting and true as those formed when one was young at school. What was a school for? The mistake made in most schools was that many members of staff regarded the school as merely the training ground for university. School was preparation for the world at large, to turn out men and women who were fit and capable to take their proper positions in life. Early specialisation in school would not produce pupils of wide outlook.

Following the General Election in January 1910 which allowed Asquith and his government to stay in power, the results of the school election showed the strength of Labour with Mervyn Griffiths polling 44 votes, Herbert Pickard, Conservative- 43, Maurice Hinton Jones, Liberal- 29, and Richard Maelor Thomas, Socialist- 1. *The Ystwythian* reported that 'as usual the Suffragettes were to the fore and displayed a placard with the celebrated legend "Votes for Women" '. So it would seem that the girls did not have a vote, though the Conservative and Labour candidates are reported as being in favour. The same issue of the Magazine carried an article on King Edward Vll, the Peacemaker, following his death on May 6 1910 and an item on Aviation, which the author predicted, had come to stay, aeroplanes in the future would be as common as bicycles.

New School caps appeared early in 1910 'with a beautiful new badge designed by Ernest Jones the chemistry master; the sale of the caps in the School proved a great success and the change in the appearance of the boys was marvellous. We look forward to better effects from the girls.' A brave voice in the School Magazine considered that 'school caps were worn in order to facilitate capture after prohibited hours.' An insight into the girls' dress is given by Dorothy Sulston nee Husslebee in her Jubilee Magazine article.

> It is true that we wore what would now be considered to be fancy dress. Our large black hair-bows tied our long plaits. We were the 'flappers', long skirts and high shirt collars and ties in no way impeded our hockey playing. In our last year we advanced so far as to wear white sweaters; very hot, but, we thought, most impressive, in our team photograph. Trim white boaters were the pride of our lives as well as handy weapons in case of attack-these, of course, fixed with hat-pins. In our most dressed-up moments we tottered along in hobble skirts-known to split at the hem with long strides- and upon our heads we balanced monumental Merry Widow hats which were so large that girls were known to get wedged in doorways and indeed it was always considered advisable to enter sideways like a crab.[27]

The same writer recollected the meetings held to protest when it was learnt that the playing fields at Grogythan, rented from the University, were to be taken to build a mere library. Another remembered-

> A class at drill on the School field, not the present well-kept playing field, nor its immediate predecessor- that sea of mud lying between Plascrug Avenue and the railway, hard by the nurseries. No, this field is an uneven, bumpy stretch lying behind and above the School, to which access is gained by means of a narrow, steep path and a gap in the hedge! A short distance away the first block of the National Library buildings is being erected, and the teacher is finding the activities of the lofty crane an unwelcome distraction. He orders the class to face in the opposite direction, threatening with dire punishment anyone who dares to glance over his shoulder. The little lad obeys with an effort. Little does he dream that the noble building then in course of erection behind him will one day be the source of his daily bread.[28]

Arrangements were made with the Corporation to rent a field on the Flats near Plascrug, which however proved unsuitable for cricket. Summer 1910 saw cricket matches played on the Smithfield or the Vicarage field. The School inflicted defeat on Towyn 57-39 but lost the return match at Towyn where the pitch again proved unreliable. W A Beddoes, who would gain a Rendel Exhibition on the results of his higher certificate examination, topped the bowling and batting averages.

The Governors responded to pupil-pressure for the acquisition of tennis courts, arranging for use of the courts behind the Town Hall, at the same time requesting their architect to draw up plans for tennis courts on the site of the orchard. After much delay the tender of £140 by En Tout Cas was accepted The Headmaster recorded the fruit trees being cut down in 1913 when in full flower prior to the levelling by the contractor. There was great rejoicing at Easter 1915 when the courts were used for the first time. 'All things come to him who will wait' said the *Ystwythian*. Gymnastics were introduced on a more formal basis with the appointment of Miss Olga Haake, a Swedish drill mistress and later, Miss Bronwen Jones, shared with the College, to teach physical exercises to the girls and boys in the Central Hall and later in the College gymnasium.

Miss Dalley's protracted illness in 1910 coincided with a downturn in the fortunes of the hockey team for whom she turned out, but what they lacked in hockey skills they made up for with their repertoire of Pierrot songs- 'Aberayron people thought the motor-coach had brought a concert party.' In the same season the football team conceded fifteen goals in three matches 'but the school custodian deserves mention for his excellent saves.' Worse was to come the following season when in three lost matches, the goal keeper George Humphreys while 'acquitting himself cleverly in goal' was unable to prevent twenty goals. However the introduction in 1913 of School colours and a league system had an immediate effect, with arch-enemies Towyn defeated at football for the first time in ten years. The whole School were awarded a half-holiday!

Swimming entered the curriculum around this time with the Governors funding the evening swimming club on condition the Bath Street Company put their premises in proper order. An attempt to introduce baseball died a natural death with only one game played-between the Knee Crackers and the Bone Crushers.

The first School Sports was staged on 20 June 1912-Emrys Williams remembered it being held ' on that tract of Burma jungle now lying beneath the National Library, with somewhat haphazard handicapping for the mile race ' won by Ernest de Lloyd, who also took the 440 yards in 64 seconds. The Vicarage field was the venue for the Sports the following year where conditions were somewhat more conducive to good athletics. Events included the sack race, egg and spoon, thread the needle, skipping and despatch race (relay?) as well the jumps, sprint and distance races. Llew Bebb won the junior long jump with 11'8 (his son Aled was a fine athlete in the Ardwyn of the 1950s)

The resignation of the classics master N H Thomas in the summer of 1910 after ten years service to the School was regretted by all. He had taken a deep interest in so many phases of School life, the School Magazine owed much to his suggestions. His future career was at the Bar, where 'his wide knowledge of human nature, fine rhetorical powers, ever-ready wit and humour will have ample scope.' His successor F N Pryce was, within six months enticed away to the British Museum to be replaced in quick succession by R A Pritchard and Charles Latham. The latter after a year in the post during which time he gained an Oxford M A, was on honeymoon in the Vosges mountains in August 1914 when war broke out. He was given permission to leave Germany with other British and American nationals and proceeded to Wessel where Mr Latham was detained but his wife allowed to leave. He had written from Frankfurt-on-the -Main in October 25 1914 but was destined to spend the whole of the Great War in a German internment camp.

William Barker who taught mathematics and science also resigned in 1910 and was replaced by a first class honours mathematician Jonathan Jones whose stay again was a short one. Arthur E Williams, another first class mathematician joined the staff and was to remain for four years.

The David Samuel Years — 1896-1921

The first specialist modern language teacher was appointed in 1910. Dr D J Davies a Cardiganshire man, after graduating at U C W, took the degree of Ph D at Marburg, and was a tutor at Skerry's College, Glasgow when appointed. Edwin G Jones a local man was appointed as an additional general subjects teacher though he soon established geography, an increasingly important subject, in the school currriculum. The Governors recorded their thanks to Dr Fleure of the College geography department for his advice particularly in respect of the design of the proposed specialist geography room. Edwin Jones had been a member of the College soccer team and was naturally drafted in to the School XI.

After being appointed art teacher in 1899, J H Appleton retired in 1912. There was no replacement until 1913 when Dan R Jones was appointed from the Art department UCW where he returned in 1919 to become its head. Bertha Jones who had taught cookery on a shared basis with Aberayron and Tregaron since 1900 was highly praised for her work by the Headmaster in his report at the 1911 prize day. Each year, on this occasion, the cookery department staged an exhibition of Christmas cakes where the artistic cookery was much admired. David Samuel's wish to have exclusive use of Miss Jones' talents was granted when, the following year, she was appointed on a three-day week basis. It was not until 1922 that there was the need for her to work full-time. A colleague, T O Pierce considered that the nicest pancakes he had ever tasted were made by her pupils (perhaps that is why he married one of them). Dorothy Sulston was one of many housewives who were grateful to Miss Jones who 'made domesticity into a noble art and taught along with it many valuable truths for the living of life. Ice-cream days in the cookery room were a high spot in life and here I remember the first queues I ever encountered.' Undoubtedly the girls were given a thorough training in the domestic arts under her tuition; one of her pupils, Violet Jones served as domestic science teacher from 1931 until her retirement in 1970 having held the additional post of senior mistress for nine years.

Following a directive from the Director of Education on the curriculum needs of the pupil teacher candidates of which there were 24 in the School, the Headmaster reported that the subjects which were deemed to be necessary for this category of pupil which included needlework, drawing, vocal music, penmanship, did not correspond with the requirements of the Welsh matriculation. If these subjects were included, it would put a severe strain on the teacher candidates particularly since he had found a general deterioration, in recent years, in pupils' writing, spelling, reading and English on their entering the County School.

The triennial inspection in 1910 by the Central Welsh Board, indicated that there had been very great improvements in the School during the previous three years. There was special commendation for the teaching of French, German and history, but too much insistence in English on formal grammar. One inspector, showing remarkable prejudice, thought that chemistry at the Senior stage was not a very satisfactory subject for girls and suggested that cookery should be substituted. It was also pointed out that the teaching staff, with six first class honours graduates, was exceptionally strong, and good work was being done particularly in the higher School.

In 1914, the Inspectors reported the English teaching greatly improved with recommendations made at the previous triennial inspection having been adopted. Finding the children not very articulate, it was recommended that more time be spent on elocution, oral composition, and recitation. Miss Dalley was commended for her exceptional teaching of history. The language course in the School was particularly complete including as it did English, Welsh, Latin, French, German, and to some extent Greek. Welsh, taught as they knew, by a distinguished Welsh scholar (David Samuel) had become a living subject in the School. The School was fortunate in having at the head of the French and German teaching, a man who had lived in those countries. The Inspectors considered that the organisation and discipline was admirable, and that in Ernest Jones, the senior master, the Head had a valuable and efficient colleague.

By 1913 there was again need for additional buildings and a new architect G. Dickens- Lewis, was instructed to draw up plans for a new building on the site of the School garden to include provision for geography, kitchen/laundry, drill and gymnasium room with an art room above. There was to be a terrace for outdoor classes, with cloisters below in the playground. With the estimated expenditure £2800, the Governors applied to the County Council for a loan of £1600 towards the cost and to make such a sum a charge upon the parishes included in the Aberystwyth County School district under the provisions of the Education Act of 1902. With the lowest tender being £3586 the Architect was asked to amend the plans omitting the upper floor. A tender of £2598 secured the contract for a local builder E E Jenkins, the Governors possibly heeding a plea from the North Cardiganshire Trade Union Labour Council to place the contract locally. At the same time, the Governors approved a new hot water heating system throughout the School dispensing with the open fires and gas radiators which were proving inadequate.

The Governors, as well as being concerned with the fabric of the School continued their regular visits of inspection. The chairman, Ald C M Williams, who held that office continuously from 1903 to 1916 reported that in one month he had visited the School every day. He also found time to serve four terms as Mayor of the Borough between 1888 and 1916. In 1913, John Gibson Junior, son of the redoubtable proprietor of the *Cambrian News*, appointed a Governor in 1909, seemed never to have attended a meeting and in 1913 was replaced by Cllr Daniel Thomas, Eastgate, who was to serve diligently for many years. Mrs Powell of Nanteos also joined the Board around this period. On several occasions, the Governors were reminded by the Board of Education that under the 1909 amendments to the Education Act, 20 free places should have been offered and that four additional places should be allocated at once. The Governors appealed on the grounds that the extra free places would cause an undue strain on the finances of the School. The same Act prohibited pupils who had attained the age of 19 years to remain in school.

The School continued to attract eminent men to address those assembled for the annual speech day and prize distribution In 1910 Prof Tyrrel Green of St David's College, Lampeter confined himself to praising the efforts of the intermediate schools of Wales following a recent criticism of them by the Board of Education. The following year, the guest speaker was Sir Edward Anwyl, recently knighted by the newly crowned King George V, and at that time, professor of Welsh at UCW and chairman of the CWB.

The David Samuel Years — 1896-1921

In an outstanding address, he spoke on the diffusion of education, the spreading of it in waves through the whole community, reaching to endless distances both in space and time. Intermediate schools were first thought to be mainly for the training of the exceptionally able children of the community but as experience developed, it was seen that these schools met the needs of a far larger circle of children than those of outstanding ability. It was the duty of schools to see that each child was trained to the highest point of his or her ability. David Samuel in his report to the 1911 speech day audience disclosed that he was completing 25 years' service in the cause of education in his native town. It had given him particular pleasure that, during the year, two honours boards had been set up in the Central Hall.

> If anyone demands proof positive of the excellent work done by the School in the fifteen years of its existence, it stands there as a witness set up on high. It is almost a record among such exhibitions of University successes. I do not say for the quality of its distinctions, though that is marvellous enough, but for the great number of pupils that have graduated within so short a space as a decade and a half. No one has stood before our honours boards with feelings other than those of commendation and wonder. Those names written in gold will always afford me the sincerest satisfaction, for they indicate that during the years that I have served the School, my labour has not been in vain, nor my work unproductive.

One of the names in gold on the honours boards was that of Thomas Ivor Rees, who after graduating with honours in Welsh in 1910, gained a high position in the Civil Service examination and was posted to the British Consulate in Marseilles from where he contributed many articles to the *Ystwythian* under the pen name of *Crwydryn*. Included was a poem in tribute to the Headmaster:

> Deall-agorwr diwyd-yw y dda
> Dafydd doeth drwy i fywyd
> Llawn yw o ddysg hefyd
> Nod i bawb-goleuad byd

By 1914 he was Vice-Consul and was quickly promoted to Secretary of Legation in the Embassy at Caracas, Venezuela where ' his knowledge of Spanish will stand him in good stead'. Later that year he succeeded Mr Harford of Falcondale, Lampeter in charge of the Legation. Subsequently he became *charge d'affairs* in Bilbao, Spain, before taking up the post of consul-general in Mexico City and then *charge d'affairs* in Havana, Cuba. In 1938 he returned to Mexico City as *charge d'affairs*. In 1944, the *Ardwynian* recorded that T Ivor Rees had been appointed British Minister in Bolivia but because of the internal political situation was unable to take up the post immediately. However by 1947 he had become the first British Ambassador to Bolivia serving until his retirement in 1949. T I Rees played a leading part behind the scenes in activities which led to the Battle of the River Plate and the destruction of the German battleship the *Graf Spee*. He was appointed CMG in the 1942 New Year honours lists and the University of Wales conferred the honorary degree of Ll D on him in 1949, the same year as the *Ardwynian* recorded the death of his 92 year old father J T Rees, who had been a member of the first Governing Body of the School.

Elizabeth Jane Lloyd from Llanilar a former classmate of T I Rees was the first woman student to obtain first class honours in Welsh at U C W. She won the Ellis Prize at UCW for the best essay on the Mabinogion and in 1912 won the chief literary prize at the Wrexham National Eisteddfod. The first Master of Science to appear on the Honours Boards was Ebenezer Rhys Thomas, son of Daniel Thomas, Eastgate, who after graduating with honours in chemistry in 1906, spent some years teaching in Barmouth County School before gaining an M Sc at U C W in 1911. This led to a research scholarship in organic chemistry at Emmanuel College, and the Cavendish Laboratory, Cambridge and in 1913, appointment as assistant science master at Rugby School. At the outbreak of war he was commissioned in the Royal Warwickshire Regiment, working on high explosives. Leaving the army with the rank of major he became head of science at Rugby in 1919 before being appointed headmaster of the Royal Grammar School, Newcastle upon Tyne in 1921.

Richard Phillips whose School experiences have already been referred to, was the first recipient of the Loxdale Exhibition open to natives of Llanilar, Rhostie and Llangwyryfon. His entry into U C W in 1910 was a great loss to the football team but earned him a first-class honours degree in chemistry. Later he gained a doctorate and had a long and distinguished career in the department of agriculture U C W specialising in animal nutrition. His great friend and classmate since primary school days in Llangwyryfon, Evan Edwards, graduated at the same time obtaining second class honours in physics and a lectureship in the University of Toronto. The School had benefited from another endowment, the Lewis Thomas Talybont Scholarship, also tenable at UCW, which was awarded for the first time to Gwilym T R Evans. With an honours degree in physics, he was appointed to Aberaman County School and in 1915 contributed a paper to the Cambridge Philosophical Society on the electrical conductivity of solutions. After a short time as lecturer in the physics department at U C W, in 1925 was appointed senior lecturer in Johannesburg University. Cyril Mortimer Green who played a major role in creating the School Magazine in 1904 but who left School early on the death of his father, returned to the town to attend the U C W, gaining a first class Honours in Botany in 1911. He was appointed to the lecturing staff of Kings College, London and later to the National Museum of Wales but like many of his contemporaries fell in the Great War.

The prize day programme of 1912 listed twenty three former pupils attending the UCW with another seven at Oxford and Cambridge of whom five held Exhibitions. The Headmaster proudly recorded that an 'Ardwyn Society' had been formed in Cambridge under the guidance of Mr Austen Keen who had taught in Ardwyn pre-1896 and Mr David Brunt who had taught briefly at the County School in 1908.

Principal Prys of the Theological College who gave the address at the 1912 Prize Day, agreed that talent might win prizes but character alone could win the highest prizes in life. Character was formed by the education they received; education only began in school, it would continue through life. Education was the process by which men and women were made.

Generations of boys will be eternally grateful for the tuition in ballroom dancing given so readily by the girls in those end of term 'hops', Many a school romance originated on the dance floor of the Central Hall, though one was in danger of black looks from the staff and a tap on the shoulder if it was considered that you were monopolising your partner. Dorothy Husslebee at School between 1908 and 1913, described in the Jubilee Magazine how it all began.

> Dancing had been regarded as a most unsuitable occupation for earnest schoolgirls. Was it the Merry Widow hats and their correlation with the Merry Widow waltz? Whatever the inspiration, my generation of girls danced at every possible moment. Daily during interval we careered around the Central Hall, somebody nobly supplying jerky music at the piano. There was, however, one Charles in the lower forms, who certainly played better than the rest of us. This talented boy sat for hours patiently pounding away waltzes, valetas, two-steps, barn dances and lancers, delights which to my horror are now known as 'Old Time Dances'. Thus did Charles Clements start on the road to fame and his good nature and generosity have continued with his playing. There were, it must be admitted, no male partners, we danced with each other. This situation was felt to be so undesirable that we set upon some of the reluctant boys and taught them to dance. Slowly and painfully and with infinite patience, the lessons went on day by day, until at last, we were able to launch our first hop. This was a matter of enlisting the support of our good-natured Head Mr Samuel and Miss Dalley. What a momentous occasion it was; our first little dance with excellent eats provided by the cookery department, all for threepence. Later followed more elaborate dances and thus did the now elegant functions of Ardwyn begin.

The traditional Christmas entertainment which since 1900 had always included an operetta, continued through to 1914 when the War interrupted the production. Dorothy Husslebee again-

> Our concerts were very simple affairs, held in the Central Hall until it became too small for the numbers of people who came to support our efforts. One breathtaking year (1911) we engaged the Coliseum and there I remember, I gave my one and only public performance, singing 'The Quaker Girl' to Charles Clements' accompaniment'.[29]

However Dorothy was being modest, she played a leading part in four of those concerts, as a singer, actress and dancer. She was obviously multi-talented. after leaving school to become a pupil-teacher at Penparke, she won the first prize in design at the Aberystwyth National Eisteddfod in 1916, just one of many successes by the pupils of art teacher, Dan Jones at that Eisteddfod.

A thirteen year old Charles Clements first showed his musical talents in the School concerts singing duets with Edith Richardson (Later Mrs H F Stimson) and taking the lead in the operetta 'The Knave of Hearts' in 1912. It was not until Mabel Parry, and Katie Griffiths, both holding the qualification A L C M, had left School that he came into his own as a pianist. In December 1914, in the last concert for many years, the Headmaster produced the Donizetti opera 'The Daughter of the Regiment' with Edith Richardson in the leading role receiving acclamation for her singing and acting. Her sister Fanny also gave a fine performance as her maid. Charles Clements was the accompanist throughout, aided by R E (Ted) Jones on the drums. 'The concert ended with the National Anthems of the Allies beautifully rendered by the School choir.'

Members of staff continued to contribute articles to the *Ystwythian*. In the term he came to the School, Dr D J Davies recollecting a 'Pleasant Holiday at Besancon', advocated that all modern language teachers should visit countries whose language they teach. He added that he had a high opinion of the German people who were 'kind, generous well-educated, intelligent and quite anxious for peace as we are'. His articles continued in the magazines of 1912-13, after a summer spent revisiting Marburg where he had studied for his PhD. He reaffirmed the great kindness of the German people and how he had learnt to respect and admire them.

The Headmaster anonymously wrote a lengthy essay on *Esprit de Corps*, asserting that no one who had entered heart and soul into school life could contemplate leaving without feeling the deepest sorrow and regret. He explained to those who had not yet learnt to '*parlez vous*' that *esprit de corps* was merely another way of expressing what in school boy language was called 'playing the game'-not just on the sports field, but everywhere endeavouring to promote the welfare of the School and putting a high value on its honour. Before a team can be successful, there must be perfect unity between the players and all must play for the honour of the School and not for exaltation of self. Samuel thought that the games player had excellent opportunities for exercising self-control 'if you are on the losing side, keep your temper; if you are on the winning side show consideration for the feelings of others by not 'crowing'. A sport never 'crows'. He considered that a pupil should guard the reputation of the School as jealously as he does his own and asked them to remember Shakespeare's saying that 'the purest treasure mortal times afford is spotless reputation.'

The Headmaster was probably responsible for a later article on Patriotism where he pinpointed the causes hindering national well-being as being contempt for work, knowledge, and persevering application, and relaxation of parental control and religious authority.

At the start of the 1909-10 session, for the first time there were more girls than boys registered and this remained the case, with two exceptions, for the next ten years. In January 1911, An Shuen Kung, from Shanghai joined the School as a pupil. His grandfather was at one time Chinese Ambassador to the Court of St. James and his father held the post of Secretary to the Chinese Emperor. Kung had been taught English by a Miss Richards, daughter of Dr Timothy Richards, a Cardiganshire man and one of the best known missionaries in China. An Shuen is included in an extant photograph taken at the annual picnic at Llyfnant Valley in May 1911. The party of about fifty had travelled by charabanc ' though some had come on bicycles; we had torrential rain until five o'clock when we had tea at Mrs Waller's hospitable home, having lunched from hampers provided by the girls'. Most of the girls are shown wearing the large hats described previously. When the young Chinaman left for Christ's College, Cambridge, after three years in the School, the Headmaster congratulated him on his excellent conduct and also thanked the pupils for the kind and gentlemanly way they had uniformly treated An Shuen during his stay. He was remembered by his fellows as

> smiling, tolerant and cooperative, he joined joyfully in all activities. An afternoon of tumbles into molehills and softer mounds which pimpled the schoolfield put him off

soccer. A hectic ten minutes in the swimming bath during which he pulled half a dozen of us under water with him, ended his only swimming attempt, but he continued to kick shins as effectively as anyone else in the perilous melees against the walls of the playground.[30]

An Shuen returned to the town during the long vacations to study for the Natural Science Tripos. Recording his degree success of 1916, David Samuel was prompted to say that he was ' as fine a lad as ever entered these portals.' The July 1933 edition of the *Ardwynian* reported that he was the finance minister in the Chinese government.

The year 1914 was to be a memorable one in so many respects. The establishment of a House system was the great novelty of the Lent Term. The basic principle was self-government-the government of the School by the pupils themselves, 'which should add to the efficiency of the School, to its discipline and give to the pupils a sense of corporate life and emulation.' It was also hoped to create a deeper sense of honesty, conscientiousness and honour among the pupils, the development and improvement of School games, and creation of healthy rivalry between the six Houses.

Each House would contain thirty pupils; the boys' Houses were Ceredigion, Dyfed and Powys and those of the girls were Gwynedd, Gwent and Arfon. Each House would have two staff members who would have responsibility for the welfare of their charges including conduct and punctuality and would also recommend courses of study and holiday work. They would act in *loco parentis* in a more special and real sense. This development might surprise those who thought that pastoral work was the creation of the comprehensive school system ! Another innovation was the appointment of prefects to assist the House staff. These were elected by the pupils who were at risk of being disenfranchised for breaches of discipline or slackness in work-'that great evil of the present day'. In a Magazine article, the Headmaster considered that the House system would teach all to take pride in their House and their School. It would train for that larger and fuller sense of community life and solidarity which they ought to have when they leave School or college and find themselves in a village community, city, Principality or an Empire. 'He that is faithful in little will be faithful in much'. 'Loyalty to one's House will develop into loyalty to one's country which is patriotism. '

For the first time, St David's Day 1914, was celebrated with an Eisteddfod rather than the usual Soiree. With the 1916 National Eisteddfod due to be held in the town, at the formal opening of the *Gorsedd* on the Castle grounds on Proclamation Day June 17 1914, the blast of the *Corn Gwlad* from the *Maen Llog* was given on the trumpet by a fifth former David Joseph.

Work on the New Block began in April 1914; by June the foundations were in place after an enormous amount of excavation. The building which was not under roof until near Christmas, was to include a school kitchen and laundry, an art room and a geography room, 'the latter was to be quite a pioneer in its own department as far as Wales was concerned.'

> September 1914. The School is in a ferment of excitement. The Latin master was married during the summer vacation and went to Germany for his honeymoon; war has broken out and he has been interned. The event sets everyone talking, although the

full significance of what is occurring on the Continent is not yet realised. This is the first of a series of pictures darkened by the war clouds of World War 1. In another I see seven strange faces among the pupils, these are Belgian boys and girls-refugees who, driven from their homes, have found shelter in our town and companionship in our School in these dark days.[31]

The number on roll reached the record level of 194 which did not include the seven Belgian children who were given free places by special resolution of the Governors. The Headmaster and staff agreed to place three pence in the pound of their salary towards the Belgian refugee fund for the duration of the war. Soon after their arrival in October 1914, the children and their parents were entertained to tea in the Central Hall where 'the pupils gave songs and two of the Belgian ladies rendered most excellent French melodies. The Belgians were as pleased to see us as we were to have them amongst us.' The group included an eminent violinist M. Nicolas Laoureaux who during the two years he was in the town, gave five violin recitals in the School, accompanied on the piano by his daughter and son who was pianist to the Belgian Court. In his final appearance in 1916, before leaving to become conductor of an orchestra in Harrogate, he was presented with a framed address of appreciation, written in French.

> We have admired the brilliancy of your playing and perfect mastery over this wonderful instrument. As an exile from your country, you have carried with you something which no tyrant, no cruel or brutal circumstances, can rob you of the music which is in your soul and which is a possession forever.

The programme included pieces composed by Charles Clements ARCO who was present as accompanist to M Laoureaux.

Another Belgian refugee, M. de Saedeleer, from Tiegham, Flanders held an exhibition of his paintings during February 1916 in Alexandra Hall, where Principal Roberts of the U C W introduced the artist 'as one of the foremost European artists of the present day.' Included in the exhibition were fourteen paintings of Cardiganshire scenery and ten of his homeland. In recognition of the kindness shown to his daughter Anna Louise, M de Saedeleer, presented a painting to the School; described as a triptych, it represented a view of Tanybwlch and the Ystwyth Valley from the neighbourhood of Crugiau, Rhydyfelin where the artist lived. Generations of pupils will remember the painting which hung permanently in the Central Hall from that date. Staffing problems brought about by Mr Latham's internment and the large increase in numbers was aggravated by the decision of the geography master Edwin G Jones to enlist in Kitchener's Army. He left on December 1 1914 to join the London Welsh battalion of the Royal Welch Fusiliers. David Samuel, referring to him at the 1914 Prize Day said 'he was greatly attached to the School but the demands of the present crisis were so persistent, and the voice of duty so clamant, that he was unmoved by any appeals save those of ardent patriotism which summoned him to the Front.'

> I see a cheering crowd of children at the railway station, they are bidding farewell to their geography master, who has decided to enlist in the service of his country. Some eighteen months later, the whole School is shrouded in sorrow, for the news has come through that that same master had made the supreme sacrifice.[32]

The news that Pte Edwin Jones had been the victim of a sniper on May 7 1916 came in a letter from former pupil, Lieut. Ceredig Ellis RWF, who had spoken to him five minutes before he was shot. Lieut. Ellis died of wounds in France ten weeks later.
Throughout the War, S E (Lala) Thomas, assistant mistress compiled a roll of honour in the School Magazine listing all those former pupils who were serving their Country and writing in the 'Khaki Column' of their exploits (censor permitting). 'Herbert Pickard is home (May 1915) recuperating after a strange experience in Ypres' -presumably a victim of the first gas attack perpetrated by the Germans in April around Hill 60. Wet cloths pressed to the nose were no substitute for the gas masks not yet issued.

News had also been received that Captain Hugh Mortimer Green, Welsh Regiment, was missing in Gallipoli. In a letter dated April 28 1916, Chaplin the Rev David Jonathan Jones on board HMS— described his experiences a year previously off Cape Helles, Dardanelles 'I have never seen such bravery and contempt of death as I saw on that day. The incessant rattle of musketry, and the rat-at-at of machine gun fire will live with me for the rest of my life.' The list of those killed in action or who had died of wounds became longer as the War progressed. The first confirmed victim was Sgt David Rees Davies, a noted School and Town footballer and Secretary of the Old Pupils' Association, who was killed by a bomb in the trenches in May 1916, while performing an act of gallantry. The sinking of the *Lusitania* on May 5 1915 resulted in the death of Frederick Roberts Jones who was on his way home to join the Colours having left the town three years previously for Winnepeg where he was employed as an engineer on the Canadian Pacific Railway. In an editorial, the *Cambrian News* thought that a murderer is more of a murderer in the eyes of the law, if he gives notice of his intention to commit murder- reference to the warning issued by the Germans for Americans not to travel on the liner. Fred who had served an apprenticeship in Green's Foundry after leaving School and was employed by the GWR before emigrating, was the son of Ald Peter Jones, who was the first chairman of Cardiganshire County Council in 1896 and first chairman of the School Governors in the same year.

The *Welsh Gazette* in its issue of December 23 1915 reported that 'The top boy at the Aberystwyth County School this year Edward Rhys Harries who won the Honours certificate in the CWB examinations, has joined the colours and is now serving in the Welsh Guards. He was present in khaki at the annual prize distribution and was given an ovation when he received his prizes and certificate'. A former School football captain, and an all-time soccer great, Ned Harries was just twenty years of age, when he was decorated with the Military Cross by the King for 'conspicuous gallantry and devotion to duty when in charge of a digging and wiring party in No Man's Land. His coolness and courage set a fine example to his men'. J R Richards later Bishop of St David's remembered

> that the War came very close to us as one after another of the senior boys passed from School into the Forces and the names of some we had known began to appear in the lists of casualties. One very pleasant memory is of history lessons with Miss Dalley which were often preceded by extracts of letters received from Old Boys in the trenches. I well remember her telling us how Ned Harries had, at the end of a long letter, added a postscript casually mentioning the fact that he had been awarded the M C, and the pride in her eyes as she told us, was good to see. To John Richards, the War

presented a different kind of dilemma. 'The problem which faced me was whether to take French or German. We were all so splendidly patriotic that we would not touch anything German with a barge-pole, and we were all keen to take French. It seemed, however, that some must take German, and I, for reasons I do not now remember, decided in favour of adopting that very unpatriotic course. I appeased my conscience, as did others in the class, by opening each new exercise book with the belligerent rather than pious wish

'Gott strafe Deutchland !'[32]

The Michaelmas 1916 issue of *The Ystwythian* recorded a total of 224 serving in the Colours, representing one-third of the boy pupils registered. Of this number thirty-four held commissions-one of those officers, Capt Goronwy Owen MA, 5th RWF had been made a Companion of the Distinguished Service Order, 'for conspicuous gallantry and determination in organising and leading a successful raid on the enemy trenches. Capt. Owen covered the withdrawal with great skill under heavy fire despite being wounded'. He received his decoration from the hands of the King in May 1916. By this time sixteen former pupils had made the supreme sacrifice, two had drowned on the same merchant ship which had been torpedoed. It must have been a particularly sad moment for S E Thomas when she had to record the death of Harold, one of her four brothers serving in the army. He had enlisted just four months previously. Another of the Mortimer Green family, Cyril, first editor of the Magazine, had been killed in Palestine while commanding his company, and David Owen Jones who had joined up from School, died of wounds in France. John Arllwyd Jones was the first Rendel Scholar in 1900 and before voluntarily enlisting in the Welsh Regiment, had taught for eight years at Wrexham County School. He went through the great Messines offensive unscathed and in letters to friends he described the dreadful conditions but said nothing could dampen the spirit and ardour of the men under him-Welsh colliers who sang native airs and hymns to bear and brave the worst conditions. Lieut. Arllwyd Jones was killed in the October 1917 offensive in Flanders leading his men to capture a German dugout. The Headmaster reported to his audience at the Twenty-First Anniversary Celebrations in October 1917 that 306 had joined up, nearly forty percent of all the boys who had left School, fifty-five held commissions and the total fallen had reached twenty five. There were many reports of deeds of heroism and valour, some rewarded with decorations. Captain Peter Edwards RAMC, who had qualified as a surgeon at Edinburgh University in 1915 was mentioned in the Dispatches of Sir Douglas Haig. Peter had captained the University football team and starred in the 1909 Town team which reached the semi-final of the Welsh Amateur Cup. In its early history the Town team had played on the field at the Laurels, St David's Road, home of the Edwards family.[33]

CSM David John Davies was also mentioned in dispatches and later, when commissioned was awarded the Military Cross. Lieut Fred Radford added a Military Cross, awarded for gallant conduct on the Somme, to a Military Medal he gained while in the ranks. George Henry Davies RWF was killed in action soon after being awarded the Distinguished Conduct Medal and J Edward Burbeck another noted footballer received the same decoration.

While many former boy pupils answered Kitchener's call for half a million more vol-

The David Samuel Years — 1896-1921

Form VI, 1902
Staff l to r: N. H. Thomas, S. E. Thomas, C. Elsden, B. Jones, D. Samuel, E. M. Ewart, F. G. Feek, T. O. Pierce, M. Valentine.

Annual Trip to Llyfnant Valley, May 13th, 1911.
Extreme right front row, Chinese Pupil An Shuen Kung.

unteers and helped swell the British Expeditionary Force, the girls were equally determined to do their bit and a School Wool Fund was inaugurated to provide wool to answer Queen Mary's call for three hundred thousand pairs of socks for the troops. Girls joined the Red Cross hospital at the Old Bank in Bridge Street after receiving training from Miss Bertha Jones in the School kitchen in the evening. During the Christmas 1914 holiday, the School was taken over by soldiers of the Royal Welch Fusiliers for lectures on military tactics. 'School life this year has had the atmosphere of war hanging over it', commented the Magazine editorial. For the male teachers of military age it must have been a heart-searching period, asking themselves whether duty called them to go or stay. Joseph Pease, Minister of Education, wrote to schools in August 1914.

> If the schools could be kept open and effective, we would have done much. To reassure our countrymen serving with the colours we must maintain the balance and confidence of our life at home, by seeing that the children of this country are happy and occupied, living their normal life, well tended and undisturbed. As far as the educational service is concerned, let us who remain in it make this our first duty. The time of trial is also the time of opportunity. Many boys and girls, in the normal working of the industrial system, are lost early to education, but in its temporary dislocation, can be retained. Let us make for them the best educational provision we can. War involves loss of thousands of men, skilful in their trade, by whose labours our prosperity has been created. Let us seize the chance of giving to our children who must soon take their places, a longer education, a fuller training for the work by which the wastage of war may be supplied and the wealth of nations restored.

His successor, Arthur Henderson offered different advice in October 1915.

> "In view of the increasing gravity of the international situation, the balance of duty has now shifted and the claims of military service relative to those of the education service have now been increased. I offer my colleagues my considered opinion that the need now paramount is the need for men of military capacity to augment and maintain the Forces of the Crown. In their nature, education and war are as far apart as the poles. Education builds, and war destroys. But there is a time when the man who is building must leave his work to guard against a calamity which threatens the building itself; when civilisation must curtail its most constructive work to preserve itself from destruction. That time is now come.

Dr D J Davies and A E Williams appeared before the local tribunal for exemption from military service on conscientious ground. Dr Davies' unconditional exemption was to have unpleasant repercussions later, A E Williams soon moved on to a new teaching post. At the request of the Governors, the Headmaster appeared before the tribunal for the total exemption of science teachers D P Ashton and Emrys Jones and was successful. Emrys Jones had taken the place of Ernest Jones, teacher of chemistry for eleven years, who had decided to change profession to that of medicine 'where the rewards were vastly more splendid.' However his entry to medical school was delayed by a commission in the R A M C for the duration of the War where his scientific knowledge was used in developing anti-gas techniques. Latham's replacement, I W Haime remained for five terms and was succeeded by Judith Jacobs. To replace the late Edwin Jones, a College research student W J Pugh was appointed temporarily. He had published a paper in collaboration with Prof O T Jones on the geology of the district around Machynlleth and Llyfnant Valley; later they were largely responsible for unravelling the complicated geology of north Cardiganshire. Pugh eventually became Director of the British Geological Survey and was knighted. Elsie Brooks at the age of 21 years was appointed to the permanent post of teacher of Geography when W J Pugh returned to full time research. She had the pleasure of teaching in one of the very few purpose built geography laboratories, a privilege denied its designer Edwin Jones. In the advertisements for vacant posts at the School during the War period the Governors insisted that male candidates of military age gave reasons why they were not engaged on military service. They also requested staff to visit lodgings more frequently to check that School rules such as the evening curfew, were not being flouted. The School caretaker Edward D Jones revered by staff and pupils alike resigned in November 1915 after fifteen years service. Some years earlier, in front of the whole school Jones had been presented with the King Edward VII Long Service and Good Conduct medal for twenty years meritorious service in the Royal Naval Reserve in Aberystwyth. He was given three ringing cheers and the Headmaster took the opportunity to draw some useful lessons. Edward Jones was moving to Portdinorwic to take up seafaring, his former occupation; a year later he survived a shipwreck off Hartland Point, Devon. William Jones, Cambrian Place was appointed in his place at a salary of £1. 6s per week. The visiting Governors soon reported that they were impressed with the cleanliness of the School building under the new cleaner. Their prediction that he would become 'an exemplary and conscientious servant' was more than borne out in the following years.

During the War years social and extra-mural activities were curtailed. The 1915 Old Pupils' reunion was cancelled, as so many were at the Front including the President, Sgt Edward D Evans who fell victim to enemy machine gun fire in 1916. There was to be no School Eisteddfod until 1917 but there were occasional appeal concerts to raise money for the war effort. The new tennis courts were well used, but the only hockey game reported was against Aberaeron 'we were trembling with fear but Ceri Coel our goalie ensured a clean sheet'. There were still problems with the School pitch but football was played on the Vicarage Field by kind permission of the College; in 1915, there were victories over Aberaeron and the Old Boys but the 7th R W F proved too strong.

The Magazine continued to flourish filled as it was with news from the Front and the long list of former pupils who had enlisted. Ethel Williams was joint editor in 1914 and from her experiences after leaving School, she contributed an article on 'London 1915'. Women were doing men's jobs; disabled and disfigured servicemen were commonplace, while the parks were filled with drilling soldiers. The greatest difference was seen at night time, London having tasted some of the methods of German warfare, the streets were no longer brightly lit and theatres closed early.

As part of their war effort, the pupils had established a War Savings Association after an assembly of the whole School had heard Mr Ashton emphasising the importance of saving particularly in time of war. He was strongly supported by the chairman of Governors, Rev R J Rees, who urged the pupils to take up the good cause and help their country in its hour of need. There was also a noble response to improve food production. Under the direction of Dr Davies, Emrys Jones and D H Ashton, ground around the rising New Block was prepared by the boys and girls for planting potatoes- 'this was a new branch of 'athletics' which will improve muscular power; we have carried out Virgil's saying of 'Let not the soil be idle.'

Despite the emergency, the New Block was completed and officially opened on the 30 October 1915 by the Rt Hon J Herbert Lewis M P, Parliamentary Secretary to the Board of Education. The printed programme for the ceremony included a description of the new building by the architect G Dickens Lewis and a short historical sketch by the Headmaster which showed that since the opening in 1896, 784 boys and 656 girls had enrolled, 1,440 in total. The contract, carried out by a local man E E Jenkins had cost over £3,00, making the total expenditure on the three additions since the School had opened to over £10,000. The New Block has been so constructed that a second storey could be added when finances permitted. This addition was delayed until 1951. Referring to the subjects which would be taught in the new class rooms, Herbert Lewis had been told by O M Edwards, that the children of the district had a soul for art instancing that wonderful Welsh artist from Penegoes, near Machynlleth, Richard Wilson, the father of British landscpe painting. Who in his early days in school would have dreamt of a geography room? The subject, in Wales, had been transformed from being one of the most arid, sterile and uninteresting of studies into a noble science. From being a mere compilation of useless lists-the capes of Scotland, the lakes of Russia etc., it was now a science explaining his surroundings to a child, teaching him to open his eyes and ears, awakening his interest and developing his reason based on geology and leading to the more deeper and more scientific study of human history. That change was due to the University of Wales and particularly to Dr Fleure. With the School having such fine cookery and laundry rooms, those girls who came for just two or three years and would go home, generally to farms, would have a course that would help them develop into thoughtful and able women. Those who stayed for five or more years would learn how cookery could be the basis for science studies. The speaker understood that plans to build a gymnasium had to be delayed because of financial contraints but in his opinion the best gymnasium was the open air-the new terraces would serve the purpose admirably. They looked forward with undiminished confidence to a future when their country would reap the benefits of the ultimate victory of the cause for which their soldiers were giving their lives. The children of today would be largely responsible for ensuring that the victory shall be well and wisely used.

Following the speeches, the company proceeded to the new building, where Dickens Lewis, the architect, having handed him the key, Herbert Lewis performed the opening ceremony and the building was inspected. Despite the restictions of war the guests lunched well on pheasant, chicken, ham and tongue, roast beef, mutton, beef steak and kidney pies followed by apple pie, velvet creams, prune mould and trifle. All this prepared by Bertha Jones, cookery mistress and her pupils 'who were prettily dressed as waitresses.'

Ald C M Williams who had been chairman of the Governors since 1903, vacated that position in 1916. He pointed out that in the past year the New Building had been completed and paid for and another successful chapter in the history of the School had been closed. He had 'strongly desired and striven for this great improvement.' He remained a Governor and was to be the leading figure in a contentious issue the following year. The oldest surviving Governor, the Revd Thomas Levi died in 1916 at the age of 91, 'after a long and useful life.' He had been pastor of Tabernacle Chapel from 1876 until his retirement in 1903. The Headmaster, in recording his passing, commented that for some years past he had taken no active part in the affairs of the School. The records show that he had not attended Governors' meetings since 1908; R J R Loxdale of Castle Hill, Llanilar was elected to take his place. Revd R J Rees who had succeeded Thomas Levi at Tabernacle, followed C M Williams as chairman of Governors. His four children attended the School, the younger, Morgan Goronwy spent just one session, 1921-22, after being placed first on the entrance scholarship list, emulating his older brother Geraint. His family moved to Cardiff where his father took up a post with the Forward Movement. Goronwy Rees, after a distinguished Oxford career, returned to Aberystwyth in 1953 to become Principal of the University College but ended his career under a cloud.

Prize distribution and speech days continued throughout the war period with guest speakers drawn mainly from the University College. In 1913 Professor Jenkyn Jones made three points, school-time was a period of supreme opportunity, a time for effort and concentration and the need to avoid that pernicious disease-slackness, with the remedy being vivid use of the imagination. The Headmaster referred to the large number of teachers being produced by the School explaining that the Education Authority provided a number of pupil teacher candidates who, after a course of four years sometimes extended to the fifth year, went back to their practical work of teaching in the elementary schools. In a large percentage of cases they proceeded to the University and graduated.

The following year Linda Jones gained the Perrott Exhibition for French and was second on the list for a County Scholarship. The relatively few graduates in 1915 was put down to the War and the Headmaster expressed some disappointment with the C W B results. The guest speaker Prof Stanley Roberts warned against rudeness. A great deal of rudeness and lack of manners was due to a mistaken idea of liberty. If they had liberty then they should remember that everybody else had it also. It was a difficult thing when dealing with people to judge where familiarity began and where true liberty ended.

For the first time in the twenty-year history of the School, the Headmaster, due to illness was unable to present his report to those gathered for the 1916 Prize Day. His report was read by D H Ashton. The Governors had previously congratulated the Headmaster on the excellence of the C W B results which for the first time combined the Honours and Higher examinations. The results included four Higher, eighteen Senior and thirty-two Junior certificates. Some of the boy pupils who had reached the age of eighteen years had received deferment from military service until they had sat the CWB examinations. Valmai Burwood Evans was the only County Exhibitioner, she went on to obtain a first class honours in philosophy, an M A at U C W, a Fellowshp at Somerville College, Oxford in 1923, and in 1925 a lectureship in an American university. The Registrar of the University College, J H Davies was the guest speaker and referred to the success of the intermediate school in Wales. When they were first formed it was predicted that one day there would be fourteen thousand pupils in those schools and twenty thousand students in the University Colleges of Wales. The first prediction had been been realised, there were over sixteen thousand pupils in the schools but sadly the number of students in the Colleges had hardly increased in the last twenty years.

J H Davies spoke, like many of his predecessors, on the qualities which went into the formation of character. An English friend of his thought that an essentially Welsh quality was kindness The Welsh word for kindness was *caredigrwydd*, but there was another Welsh word *cymmwynas* and he challenged his audience to find an English equivalent. He thought that the words 'to do a good turn' came near to it. The difficulty of finding one English word may have something to do with the fact that the Welsh knew more about *gwneud cymmwynas* than their friends across the border. *Parod ei gymmwynas* was a good old Welsh expression which accurately expressed a certain kind of man. He asked the pupils present to respect that quality and try to attain it because it would lead to unselfishness and sacrifice.

At the September 1916 Governors' meeting, Ald C M Williams proposed the following resolution 'that the necessary steps be taken to terminate the engagement of D J Davies, PhD as assistant master at the end of the Michaelmas Term 1916'. It was resolved that the names of those voting for and against the motion be recorded. Upon the motion being put to the meeting C M Williams, Daniel Thomas, Mrs James, and Mrs Richardson voted for it and Revd R J Rees (chairman) Mrs Griffiths, Prof Lewis, Richard Richards and T Doughton voted against it. The minutes of the meeting did not record any reason for the resolution which was narrowly defeated.

The Lent Term 1917 opened with a record 222 pupils and the *Welsh Gazette* reported a highly successful St David's Day eisteddfod that term, the first since the inaugural event of 1914. Gwenllian and Hywela Saer, daughters of D J Saer who for thirty three years held the headmastership of Alexandra Road Boys' School, took prizes for essay writing and pencil drawing. Gildas Tibbott gained first prizes for his translation of Ceiriog's '*Gwanwyn*' into English and Wordsworth's 'Cuckoo' into Welsh; his efforts 'won great approbation from the adjudicator for style and diction.'

Former pupils will have fond memories of the eisteddfod choral competitions particularly the preparations, when lessons were abandoned and breaks extended to allow of practice. 1917 saw the first of these when the choirs were limited to twenty-five voices with boys' and girls' Houses combined. The choir composed of Dyfed and Gwent pupils under the baton of Byron Howell was proclaimed the winner, the conductor receiving a silver covered baton.

'Altogether a very notable day was spent, worthy of the traditions of the School, of the spirit of patriotism, and of the memory of our Patron Saint.'

The celebration of the Twenty-First Anniversary of the opening of the Aberystwyth County School on Saturday October 6 1917. previously referred to, was attended by Herbert A L Fisher MP, President of the Board of Education. He first addressed a meeting of the pupils in the art room, urging them to be proud of their School and Country.

In Wales they had a country which had great enthusiasm for education. There was no part of Europe where there was so much real belief in the power of letters, in the power of music, to elevate and refine character. They must be worthy of Wales and the Empire. In the present war, every trained intelligence, every trained character had been of use to the nation.

Mr Fisher then proceeded to the Central Hall which was filled to overflowing with distinguished guests. He expressed his pleasure at being present at the twenty-first anniversary of such a flourishing institution and thought that the task which devolved upon the intermediate or secondary schools was second to none in importance. Everyone in education agreed that the universities were ill-supplied with students in proportion to the population. The brain of the nation was insufficiently nourished and they must see to it that the intake to university was augmented. Mr Fisher went on to speak of the proposals he was making for the improvement of education in his new Education Act to be introduced in the next session of Parliament. The end of the war would not see the end of competition between Germany and Britain; the only way we could equip ourselves to meet that competition was by ensuring that every individual in the country received as much training and education as he could profitably absorb. Outlining his plan for reform, the President dealt first with elementary education where the first priority was to make the teaching profession more attractive. Teaching was as much a national service as that performed by soldiers, sailors and politicians. The State would in future defray sixty percent of the amount local education authorities spent on elementary teachers' salaries, and they would be empowered to provide nursery schools for children between the ages of two and five. The school medical service would be able to supervise the whole physical course of the child from a very early age until it left the continuation schools. By improving education given in the upper levels of the elementary school, and introducing practical instruction, it should be possible to provide a thoroughly good and progressive education to children up to the end of the fourteenth year.

They further proposed to limit employment for profit in the elementary school period. He had heard reports of children working from four o'clock until nine when school began, and consequently falling asleep during the school period. No exemptions from school would be allowed up to fourteen years and 'half-time' would be abolished. This meant that they would be taking children out of the Lancashire cotton mills, who under the present arrangements were working half-time between the ages of twelve and fourteen.

Turning to secondary education, he said that he had obtained half a million pounds from the Chancellor which should go some way to improve the salaries of secondary school teachers. Too many pupils were leaving these schools before the age of sixteen when they could have proceeded to university. He would be providing extra finance to develop advanced courses. He was aware that large numbers of secondary pupils left for remunerative employment, so he proposed developing continuation classes for those who left school at fourteen. Employers would be compelled to allow this group, who had not received secondary education, to attend continuation classes for eight hours a week for forty weeks in the year. They did not propose these changes because they would be popular but because they were necessary; nothing would ever persuade the President that industry had anything to fear from a general raising of educational standards. He would answer his critics, particularly the Lancashire mill owners who were the largest recruiters of juvenile labour, by saying that any ordinary child from any ordinary elementary school might be called upon to die for his country and that being so, was it not the duty of the State to recognise all its childen as children of the State and to provide for them some form of general education, to fortify their character, to develop their minds and to strengthen their bodies. A great many clauses in the Bill were devoted to the purpose of improving the physical education of the country, such as those which empowered local authorities to provide school games, swimming baths, and playing fields etc. He had been advised by the War Office that not only was the physical health of the working classes, as shown in recent years, deplorable but that it would be an essential of any military organisation in future that there should be a national scheme of physical training for young people during their adolescence. They hoped to give to every boy and girl an education specially adapted to the particular part they would be called upon to play in the economy of national life.

Despite the conviviality of the anniversary celebrations, there was a cloud on the horizon. In the September 1917 meeting of the Governors, C M Williams, who had made very few attendances since the rejection of his motion to dismiss Dr D J Davies a year previously, gave notice that he intended to re-introduce the dismissal motion at the next meeting. Ald Williams, who was the town Mayor, had declined an invitation to meet the President of the Board of Education and to deliver an address at the anniversary meeting 'in view of the question in connection with the staff and the circumstances known to my colleagues.' At the same meeting he protested strongly to a letter from the staff of the School requesting that a minimum of three-fifths of the new State grant should be devoted to the purpose of increasing the salaries of the present members of staff. The salary question was to to come to a head later with serious consequences to the welfare of the pupils. The dismissal proposal was deferred until the November meeting of the Governors, the N U T solicitor, representing Dr Davies, was refused admission. The minutes of that meeting records no discussion, just the voting details where C M Williams, Daniel Thomas, Mrs Jane Jones, Mrs Richards and T Doughton were for the proposition and Chairman R J Rees, Prof Morgan Lewis, Capt David James and R. Richards voting against. The proposition was carried and the Clerk was instructed to give the necessary notice to Dr Davies. However the *Cambrian News* of 23 November 1917 gives a fuller account. Referring to the absence from meetings of C M Williams, Prof Lewis pointedly observed that the School had prospered in his absence, and gave the opinion of a large number of pupils who had said though Dr Davies was a conscientious objector, 'he never attempts to instil his views into us and never mentions any of his opinions in any of his classes.' When pressed by the Chairman to give reasons for his proposal, Williams alleged that Dr Davies was 'a demoralising influence'. Richard Richards retorted that he thought the man was one of the most moral men he could think of. If the reason was not inefficiency, what was the reason? The proposer refused to be drawn further. The same edition of the *Cambrian News* contained a letter from the N U T asserting that 'Prussianism is not confined to Prussia' and asking why no definite charges had been brought and why the N U T solicitor had been denied admission. Later correspondence spoke of 'a grievous scandal'; a former Governor condemned the 'unsupported statements of two Governors', a parent complained that there was no machinery to convey their opinions, another spoke of 'strange happenings in democracies.' The Aberystwyth Free Church Council tabled a resolution protesting strongly against the dismissal of Dr Davies 'without proper cause and as unjust treatment of a public servant and a threat to the integrity of public life.'

At their December meeting the Governors listened to dozens of letters from a very wide spectrum of public opinion from all parts of the Principality including church, chapel, elementary and county schools, trade unions, the N U T, the N U R, and *Cymdeithas Gymreig Tref Aberystwyth*. After a long and obviously heated discussion, where C M Williams was referrred to as a 'dictator', Professor Morgan Lewis moved the following resolution, which was seconded by David James, 'That the resolution passed at the November meeting to terminate the engagement of Dr D J Davies be rescinded'. Further consideration was adjourned to the next meeting but to add fuel to the fire Daniel Thomas moved that the Headmaster and senior staff 'be requested to spend four or five days at one of our high class public schools to study School Organisation and Discipline and that third class rail fares and hotel expenses be paid.' C M Williams give notice that he would call attention to the conduct of large numbers of boy pupils of the County School on Wednesday and Thursday the 21 and 22 November, when they absented themselves from School and paraded the town and acted in a manner highly detrimental to the discipline and reputation of the School and will move that the Headmaster be requested to inquire fully into the matter and to report thereon to a Special Meeting of the Governors. Gildas Tibbott in his contribution to the Jubilee Magazine wrote

> Hullo, here is an unusual picture! All the boys of the School are marching in procession through the streets of the town and demonstrating before the house of the Chairman of the School Governors. What is afoot? One of the masters, they say, is being unjustly persecuted because of his convictions, and so, inspired partly by a sense of injustice, partly by the thrill of taking the law into their own hands, and partly by a desire to evade lessons for an afternoon, they have chosen this method of making their protest.

At their first meeting in 1918, the Governors again refused to admit Dr Davies' legal representative and again heard many appeals on behalf of Dr Davies including one from the Secretary, Penparke Library, with a resolution signed by the villagers protesting against the treatment of Dr Davies, and from D J Saer pointing out the loss his daughter would suffer in her studies if a teacher other than Dr Davies supervised her work. When Prof Lewis' proposition 'that the resolution to terminate the engagement of Dr D J Davies be rescinded ' was moved, it was passed, without the voting details being disclosed. Thus ended a particularly unsavoury episode in the life of the School.

At a later meeting Daniel Thomas withdrew his notice of motion requesting the senior staff to study the organisation of high class schools. However C M Williams was not satisfied with the Headmaster's explanation of the 'strike' of pupils. On a happier note, there was great pleasure when the C W B results of 1917 were published. Six pupils had been successful in the Higher Certificate (now combined with the Honours Certificate), three of these had secured first, second and fifth place out of five County scholarships offered. In addition David John Davies and Muriel Rees (daughter of R J

Rees) had been awarded Scholarships at U C W. A record number of twenty-five senior certificates had been awarded. There had also been a record number of 108 new pupils when the 1917-18 school year opened in September 1917, bringing the total on roll to 263 the highest total yet. The Headmaster recorded that it was gratifying to see the School participating in the increase which was general throughout Wales, attributed to the fact that the middle and lower classes had more money circulating and also to the fact that parents were keener to give their children as good an education as possible, to fit them for the duties of life after the war was over. A further increase in number was expected from the decision of the Governors, following a grant increase, to decrease school fees by one pound to £4 7s 6d to include use of books, from Easter 1918. The Treasury grant for the present year, including the 'Fisher grant', was £1, 646, a notable increase for example, on 1904 when it was £188. Great satisfaction was also drawn from the triennial inspection by the C W B in November 1917. Every teacher had impressed the chief examiner as being faithful and capable. He picked out for special mention the teaching of geography in what must be the finest laboratory in the country. Praise too for woodwork and drawing with the girls urged to take woodwork. The work of boys in the kitchen had impressed the inspector who thought that this trend should be developed as the career of a chef was rewarding and there would be many openings in the future. Dr Davies, the modern languages teacher, had developed greatly in the past three years and pupils under him were full of vitality and energy. Dr Davies was a scholar, with a scholar's knowledge of French and German -'a large acquaintance with phonetics which an ordinary teacher would not know.' The tone and discipline of the School was excellent, this caused by the excellence of the staff and a good sixth form who made the House and prefect system work efficiently.

In the later years of the war, the Headmaster would assemble the whole School usually before a half term holiday. At these memorial meetings, as they were called, he would refer to former pupils who had been killed in action, extending the sympathy of the School to the bereaved relatives and expressing the hope for a complete recovery to those who had been wounded. With great pride he would offer congratulations to his former pupils who had received awards for their distinguished conduct in the field. His record book, during the war years, is filled with press cuttings, usually accompanied by photographs of the killed, wounded and decorated who, brief years before walked the corridors of his School. The war was far from being a male only conflict, apart from raising money to buy wool to knit socks for those in the trenches, the girls, in the absence of school games, were making bandages. Others were leaving for distant places; Beryl Morgan was reported to be in Salonika superintending cooking in a Canadian hospital; Sophie Rowlands, North Parade, a noted singer while at school who had continued her studies at the Royal Academy of Music had been on a concert tour of hospitals in Malta. Nesta Morgan had been similarly engaged in France where she had met up with Katie Griffiths who will be remembered as an outstanding hockey player and team captain who was serving with the Q M W A A Corps.

The Khaki column in the *Ystwythian* was getting longer and ran to five pages in the Midsummer 1917 issue. It recorded the experiences of unnamed former pupils, some of whom had been gassed, suffered from trench fever, wounded, shell-shocked and with a general breakdown in health, the result of two years stenuous work culminating in being buried alive for a time at Ypres. There was news of John Arthur Hughes who had been missing for months, he was a prisoner of war in Germany in the same camp as his uncle. In the last year of the War, the magazine reported that Lt Gerallt Griffiths had piloted the aircraft which had flown over the tank in Trafalgar Square, helping to swell London's contribution to the Great War Loan. Jack Whitby who had emigrated to Australia after leaving School had been home in Aberystwyth on leave from his unit, the Australian Light Horse. It was later reported that he had been invalided home to Australia after being severely injured by an exploding oil-tank in Gaza. On his return to Tooyal after three years military service, he was discharged on health grounds and granted 860 acres of land by the Government of New South Wales.

Though the tide was turning in Europe in the summer of 1918, the War was still claiming the lives of Old Ystwythians, Lt Robert Buttery and L/Cpl Fred Parry were the last to be killed in action though Lt Desmond Macartney-Filgate R F C died as the result of a flying accident in Oxford in June. The School War Memorial recorded the names of forty-six former pupils and one master who made the supreme sacrifice.

List of former pupils decorated for gallantry

Distinguished Service Order	Capt. later Major Goronwy Owen
Military Cross	Lt D. Morris Edwards
Military Cross	Capt E (Ned) Rhys Harries
Military Cross	Lt W A Evans
Military Cross	Lt David John Davies prev MID
Military Cross	Lt Frank Kitto
Military Cross	Lt W A Pickard
Military Cross	Lt Fred Radford M M
Military Cross	Lt Griff Daniel Ellis
Mentioned in Despatches	Capt Peter Edwards
Mentioned in Despatches	CSM David John Davies (later Lt)
Belgian Order of the Crown and Belgian Military Cross	Lt Ivor Prys Morris
Distinguished Conduct Medal	George Henry Davies (deceased)
Distinguished Conduct Medal	Sgt J E Burbeck
Military Medal	Fred Radford
Military Medal	Robert Owen Evans
Military Medal	Epworth Davies
Meritorious Service Medal	T J Keane

The 1917-18 football season was reported to be the best on record. There was a 15-0 victory over a weakened team at Aberayron who were later unable to field a team for the return.

The Magazine ran a full account of two matches against rivals Ystrad Meurig. Their opponents fielded a weakened side including, at the last moment, the Vicar of Llanbadarn, in goal. The Revd J R Davies 'covered himself in glory and in mud', despite letting through fourteen goals. The reporter 'had never met a better set of sportsmen'. The 'famous trio' of H Ll Jenkins, Ifor Jones and Tommy Griffiths,' played classic football'. The return match proved to be the best of the season. 'When our players saw the opponents, they looked liked miniature Goliaths and one wondered how their school buildings could accommodate such huge men. Some of them were not Ystradmeurigians but stalwart youths gathered from various parts of Cardiganshire. However superior skill told and we won 9-1. Tea was provided at the 'Mabws Arms'- 'seldom have the players enjoyed a more excellent repast; indeed we were treated to very unusual occurrences, we had lump sugar in our tea and jam on our cake.'

The prospects for the following season, with several veterans having left to swell the ranks of the Town football team, were not as bright. However Aberayron again suffered at their hands 16-1 and of the three games played against the Wounded Soldiers, two were won. In a critical analysis of prominent team members by 'Dajodas', vice-captain Tom A Griffiths, another star- to- be of the Town team, was picked out as the outstanding player, both Llew James and Idwal Lewis played well together, 'though they play about with the ball a little too much at times.' Tom Garner had no strong shot but was steady and cool. J P Jones, the erratic genius of the team, was maimed by one defect, his inability to shoot with the right foot; but Emrys Jones, was above criticism, 'one of the best goal-keepers there was.'

There was still no hockey for the girls because of pitch problems although the Governors had plans for renovation of the playing fields on the Llanbadarn Flats.. Great use was being made of the tennis courts though School athletics had been curtailed for the duration of the War.

Early in 1918, Martha Cruickshank suffered a breakdown in health and was advised by the Governors to take a long rest, during which time she would not be paid. After attempting unsuccessfully, to return in 1920, she died in August 1921 age 36 after serving the School for ten years. Mr Ashton, after being exempted for the greater part of the War, served in the newly formed Royal Air Force for the last six months of the conflict. Soon after his return he took up a post at the College dealing with the training of discharged soldiers. The School, had appointed Charles Mc Lean F R C O of the College as visiting teacher of vocal and theoretical music, following a visit of the C W B advisor. This had relieved the Headmaster of the duties 'which he had willingly discharged in reference to choral singing.' However Mr McLean soon took up a post in the College music department and it fell to William Jones, who had succeeded Mr Ashton as teacher of physics and who 'played the piano and organ with brilliancy' to step in temporarily. The immediate post-war period saw many staff appointments resulting from the huge increase in pupil numbers. Five of these new teachers were to give, collectively, 144 years of service; T D Salmon, mathematics, 25 years; Irene P Davies, Classics, 29 years; William D Lewis, art, 24 years; David H Jenkins, Welsh, 39 years; E E Forster geography, 36 years.

The 1918 School eisteddfod programme, divided into music, recitations, compositions, and art was the most extensive to date, and became the pattern for future festivals. David Idris Jones remembers his involvement.

> At the School eisteddfod, the subject of the three-minute speech was 'Peace'. The adjudicator's verdict came as a great surprise to me and to most of my colleagues at School, for I had beaten Tom MacDonald, who has since become well known as an

author and journalist; even in those days Tom enjoyed fame as the School's poet. Though I still feel that Tom's speech was better than mine, he made the mistake of stressing the horror of war, whereas I dwelt on the beauty of peace.[34]

The prize for an essay on an incident in School life was awarded to Gwenllian Saer who based her composition on a visit to Nanteos where Mrs Powell had shown the party the 'wonderful cup of healing'. David Samuel had spoken of its supposed origin from the wood of the true Cross and given to the Powell family by the monks of Strata Florida Abbey. Gildas Tibbott again took the prizes for Welsh and German translations with the combined Gwynedd-Ceredigion choir adjudged the best of the three. Festivities continued in the evening where the 'Dominoes' led by T H Garner gave a series of performances. Eluned Gwynn Jones recited some verses and later presented the Headmaster with a well-designed address which made reference to the patron saint with whom David Samuel was linked in a complimentary manner. The verses were composed by the reciter's father Prof T Gwynn Jones. The verses as printed in the Lent 1918 Magazine were:

1 Bu gynt yng Nghymru wr o fri
   A'i enw Dewi Sant,
   Pregethai ef i wylltion wyr
   A charai ddysgu'r plant

2 Oi amgylch ef, er bod y nos,
   Ar ros, a bryn, a phant,
   Tangnefedd a goleuni oedd
   Ar diroedd Dewi Sant.

3 Er myned heibio, er pan oedd
   Flynyddoedd lawer cant,
   Goleuo Cymru Fach o hyd
   Mae yspryd Dewi Sant.

4 A heddyw cedwir dydd ei wyl
   Yn anwyl gan y plant
   A llawen fry yn nefoedd Ior
   Yw calon Dewi Sant.

5 Mae eto yng Nghymru wyr o fri
   Yn canlyn Dewi Sant,
   Yn chwalu nos tywyllwch du
   A charu dysgu'r plant.

6 A'r goreu yn eu plith i gyd
   Fe'i dyfed mil o blant,
   Yw'n Hathro ni, a'i enw ar wyl
   Yw gwyl ag enw'r Sant.

The worldwide influenza epidemic, the so-called Spanish 'flu reached Britain in September 1918. On October 28, the Town Council, acting on the advice of the medical officer of health, instructed all schools and colleges within the borough to close, as a preventative measure.

The Mayor had proclaimed November 20 as a general holiday and a civic procession 'of large dimensions' was formed to parade the town in the afternoon, concluding with a thanksgiving service in front of the Town Hall to celebrate the signing of the Armistice which had taken place on Monday November 11. The Great War had claimed over ten million lives, including three-quarters of a million from Britain -'a lost generation'. Although the School was not in session, 'a great muster of pupils and staff joined in the great procession, preceded by the School banner, altogether making a brave show'.

The Governors had decided not to open the School for the rest of the current term because of the influenza epidemic but to resume on December 31 for an early start to the Lent term and to curtail the Easter vacation by a week 'to catch up the work which had been neglected by the closure.' Prize day had to be postponed to March 1919. The programme showed forty former Ystwythians pursuing courses at the College, eleven of them holding scholarships. As a result of the C W B 1918 Higher certificate examinations, once again the School dominated the list of County awards-out of eight available exhibitions, Hywela Saer, Gildas Tibbott, Gwyneth Richards and Elizabeth Owen had claimed four. Hywela Saer topped the list with distinctions in all four subjects. She later gained her B A with Honours in history and French and in 1925 attended the Sorbonne University, Paris. At this prize day it was announced that T D Jenkins, a former pupil of Aberystwyth Council School had invested £200 in War Bonds to establish a Scholarship to commemorate the services of the late James Bradbury, the first headmaster of the council school. The Scholarship which was open to competition to any pupil of Alexander Road School under the age of fourteen years, would pay the School fees for two years, with any balance used to purchase books for the scholar, chosen by the Headmaster. The first Bradbury scholar was Richard Geraint Rees, son of Revd R J Rees and brother of Goronwy Rees, who gained highest marks in the Scholarship examination of 1919.

Revd R J Rees, having served his three years period, was succeeded by Prof. Morgan Lewis as chairman of Governors, in May 1919. Prof Edward Edwards, brother of Sir O M Edwards and Revd Noah Jones, Devils Bridge joined the Governing body at this time. Having been informed by the College that their gymnasium would no longer be available for School use, the Governors considered building their own but ultimately decided to opt for Swedish drill 'which could be conducted in the open air.' The Fisher Education Act, with its emphasis on physical education, motivated the Governors to improve facilities for physical activities and strenuous efforts were made to obtain adequate playing fields. A site at Maesmawr farm near the level crossing was considered but it was unavailable, so a new lease of the present field on the Llanbadarn Flats with an additional forty yards was negotiated with the Town Council at a yearly rent of £18. G T Bassett, Architect was engaged to plan the layout for football and hockey pitches and to arrange for levelling. The scheme was completed with the erection of two Nissen huts for boys and girls dressing rooms. Ald C M Williams had arranged for D Jones, Butcher to pay £7 a year for the grazing of sheep only on the field, and the sale of the standing hay to the Council thereby realising sufficient to pay the annual rent to the Council.

The Headmaster reported to the Governors on the results of his meeting with H F Stimson, the newly appointed physical training organiser for Cardiganshire. The Central Hall was an unsuitable place for gymnastics and in the classes seen, the exercises had been selected from the 1909 syllabus which were right in principle but were done so indifferently and dispiritedly as to be of no corrective or developmental value to the performers. Stimson pointed out that the 1909 syllabus was not intended for secondary school pupils; it had been superseded by a revised syllabus published in 1919 which emphasised the natural play-activity of the child, the cultivation of team spirit and the development of the power of leadership. In neither class was there any evidence of these important aspects of educational gymnastics. As for dress, the advisor thought that the girls were suitably clad and all wore slippers. The boys however, attempted to exercise in ordinary attire and their movements in consequence were clumsy and restricted. Coats and collars should always be removed and slippers substituted for boots. The teachers conducted their classes pleasantly and conscientiously but their knowledge of the subject was not deep enough to make the work physically effective nor wide enough to maintain interest of the pupil. A specialist teacher for both boys and girls was the ideal to be aimed at and steps should be taken to acquire use of the College gymnasium for morning lessons with provision by the County Education Authority of a specialist teacher.

In accordance with the wishes of King George V, November 11 1919 was observed as Armistice Day, with an impressive service held in the Central Hall. The King's wish of 'two minutes silence throughout the Empire' was carried out, as it was for many years 'on the eleventh hour, of the eleventh day, of the eleventh month'. The old Ystwythians Association had already set up a fund to commemorate the Old Boys who had fallen in the War aiming for a total of £300 for either a stained glass window or a mural tablet to be set up in the Central Hall.

After a lapse of one year due to the influenza outbreak, the School eisteddfod was held on March 1 1920, in the absence of the Headmaster due to illness. Competitions were of a high standard notably the poetry and translations 'which would have done credit to writers much above the age of pupils.'

William O Williams carried off five prizes and led the Gwynedd-Dyfed choir to victory. He added a County Exhibition and the Lewis Thomas (Talybont) Scholarship to his credit by the end of the year.

By the date of the annual prize day, again held in March, David Samuel had recovered and reported that the C W B results were very noteworthy, despite losing half of the first term due to the flu epidemic. He laid great store on examinations; those who struggled to prepare for them were better persons than those who shirked the difficulties attending the tests. The power of learning was in the effort to get it, as the School motto put it. The Headmaster thought that the figure of forty six former Ystwythians attending Aberystwyth College was phenomenal and pointed out that the programme showed six former pupils having recently secured university lectureships. 'Thus there flows from the School as from a fountain-head, a continuous stream of scholars who sustain the fair reputation of the School.' Dr Walford Davies was the guest speaker and he gave 'one of his heart to heart talks' on the place of music in education. He thought that prizes put a stop to the progress of some and were a discouragement to others but always felt heart- warmed when he saw the losers applauding the winners. Their School motto was well supplemented by Mr Gladstone's remark that "Effort succeeds better than success"; effort was the keynote not competition. The professor suggested that schools should stage a weekly concert; by doing something together they would feel better for it. Welsh music was rhythmical and rhythm was the life and soul, the pulse and the heart-beat of music. If only everything could be done with cooperation, the same as a good choir singing, the world would be so much the better. For his own part, he would not mind if solo singing ceased for a time so they could sing concerted pieces for it was in that direction that the great value of their music output lay. Greater attention should be paid to class singing and school concerts, they should be as frequent and as cheerful as a school game.

John Richards, a future Bishop of St David's, gained a College scholarship that year, with three others. He wrote:

> My schooldays were over, I was about to enter college. Since the School opened before the College, I went back on the first afternoon of term. In the corridor I met Miss Thomas (dare I say 'Lala'?) and she stopped dead in her tracks and uttered these words: 'What! back again, John Richards ?' I meekly replied: 'No, Miss Thomas, only for the afternoon. 'She drew a deep breath, said, 'Thank God!' and departed with all the dignity of a long-established Ardwyn institution. What I owe to the School is more than I can put into words. Miss Dalley taught me to think, taught me to learn, making me want to learn. Dr Davies taught me how to learn a foreign language and that knowledge proved of great value to me in Persia. By his bearing he also taught me humility, and helped me appreciate the worth of sincerity. 'Sammy' made me proud to be a Welshman, and taught me practically all I know about Welsh. I am debtor too, to those who for five happy years were my fellow-pupils, and whose friendship made those years such happy ones. They taught me how to live in the community, rejoicing in my membership of it, and in my fellowship with others.[35]

Strange as it may seem, on June 28 1919, a meeting was held in the Central Hall to celebrate Serbian Kossova Day. The University College had undertaken to educate a number of Serbians. Of the fourteen who had arrived, four boys under the age of sixteen years had been admitted as non fee paying pupils. Kossova Day, anomalously, celebrated a defeat rather than a victory for Serbia in 1239. There were certainly victories in 1920 for two of the Serbian boys in the County School sports day, resumed after being abandoned during the War years. On the Vicarage Fields kindly lent by the Students' Association, 'competition was as keen as ever with the standard attained very high'. The Headmaster recorded that 'the achievement by Nikola Pavitch was marvellous, he had thrown the cricket ball fifteen yards further than the winner of the corresponding event in this year's College sports.' His countryman, Ziran Jovanovitch, obtained second place in the senior 440 yards event and sack race and won the 220 yards race. For the first time, a silver cup, donated by Mrs Powell, Nanteos, was awarded to the pupil with the highest number of points won for the House. The champion athlete was Reg

The David Samuel Years — 1896-1921

Farrow and champion House was Dyfed. That year, the traditional Whitweek holiday was inaugurated, with curtailment of the Easter vacation, when the weather was uncertain.

In terms of academic distinction there was a notable start to the new decade. The 1920 C W B results showed that of the thirteeen pupils in Cardiganshire who had sat the Higher Certificate examinations, and were thus qualified for the County Exhibitions, six were pupils from the School and four of these had gained the exhibitions. William Owen Williams had been first in the order of merit and Tom Macdonald though missing a County award gained a College Exhibition. A *'Cambrian News'* article in January 1920 entitled, 'The Poet of Bow Street' described Tom as a boy of 'humble circumstances who worshipped at the shrine of ambition'. From an early age at Rhydypennau School he had written poetry, encouraged by Dewi Morgan of Penygarn, a noted authority on lyrics and a National Eisteddfod winner.

Woodward Owen of Bow Street, recognised his talent and paid for two years of his education at the County School, later receiving bursaries from the Governors. To further finance his education, Tom Macdonald had sold copies of a poetry magazine containing some of his compositions, to his friends. Prof Gwynn Jones, commenting on his writing, stated that his work was very promising showing observation and individuality 'he should have a great future in front of him.'

The School obviously acted on the advice of Prof Walford Davies by staging two musical events in the autumn term 1920. William Jones, teacher of physics and music had arranged a School concert followed by the performance of a play 'Bardell v Pickwick' directed by Emrys Jones, chemistry master. This was the first concert for some six years. At the end of the term, instrumentalists from the College music department, as part of their schools' programme, gave an illustrated lecture on chamber music on the themes 'How tunes are made' and 'How to listen.' 'The music was delightful and the pupils were attentive and appreciative' reported the Head.

The School, invited by Mr Cheetham to his cinema, enjoyed a film showing the adventures of Shackleton and his men in the Antarctic. Apart from the beauty of the pictures, 'it presented noble examples of courage, self-denial, dogged perseverance in the face of enormous difficulties.'

After forty-two years in the scholastic profession and twenty-five years as Headmaster of the Aberystwyth County School, David Samuel tendered his resignation to the Governors at their meeting on December 17 1920, to take effect from July 1921. In accepting his resignation, the Governors wished to record their awareness of his untiring devotion to the School. As its first Headmaster, he had conscientiously ever sought to lay down the foundations of a great School, worthy of his native town. The Governors were united in the wish that he would be long spared to continue, in the leisure time worthily gained, those contributions to scholarship and culture, so congenial to his spirit and by which he has so enriched the periodical literature of his day.

Another long and devoted association with the School was cut when the Clerk to the

Governors, John Evans died in January 1921 after being in declining health for some months. He had been in the forefront of the movement initiated in 1891 to secure an intermediate school for the town, and had served for twenty-two years as Clerk. At the time of his death he held the positions of town clerk of Aberystwyth and coroner for North Cardiganshire.

In his valedictory report to the 1921 Prize day audience, the twenty-fourth he had delivered, the Headmaster recalled that he had begun in 1896, with sixty-five pupils. At the start of the current term there were 365 pupils on the roll. He thought that this number was about as high as the present School building could house and it was likely that for the next session new pupils would be limited to about one hundred. David Samuel regretted the demise of the Junior Certificate, it was always an incentive to work, particularly in the summer term 'when the allurements to slackness are so enticing and the tendency to neglect home study so strong.' 'I am looking on a scene which I shall never see again in my capacity as Headmaster. In my long course of years as a schoolmaster, I have made many mistakes, but I trust that I may claim throughout an honest intention, an absence of private ends, a willingness to be corrected, a dread of making mistakes, a desire to serve the community, and some amount of success. I retire from the field to seek leisure which has been won with abundant toil, when, as Pliny says, it will be impossible for people to charge me with laziness. The development and progress of the School will be to me a concern of constant and never-ending interest, and my wish will always be 'May the School on the Hill ever flourish.'

The guest speaker, Prof J H Atkins of the English department U C W, recognised that school life was a period set apart for equipping the pupil for future work and business. But man could not live by bread alone, a man could earn a good living but if he was ignorant of literature or art, if he were blind to the beauty of nature, and if he went through life unmoved by its mysteries, then he had not reached his proper stature. This could be accomplished by a liberal education, something which would provide interest in future years. Wisdom came ultimately from life, but it came all the sooner from a liberal education. Scientific studies had no doubt a great place in the work of schools, but science without conscience was the ruin of the people. Darwin had lived to realise the great gap in his life. He had said that given his life over again, he would make it a rule to read poetry and listen to music at least once a day.

A leader article in the *Welsh Gazette* recognised David Samuel's record as no mean achievement.

> All who know anything of education will acknowledge that Mr Samuel's noblest and most enduring work during that long period is his unrecorded work. The value and extent of this work can never be shown in the results of examinations; it can be found only in the lives of the multitude of boys and girls who have passed through the School without, possibly, gaining any distinction; but each of whom can say 'my mind to me a kingdom is.'

David Samuel died on 26 May 1921 aged 65 years. He remained at his post up to the start of the Whitsun holidays; following a chill, he had taken to his bed, gradually getting worse and died after a fortnight's illness. The news of his death was received with great sadness by the staff and pupils. The School, which had just reassembled after the Whitsun break, met in the Central Hall, where a vote of sympathy was passed with the family and all lessons abandoned for the day. In the town also there was genuine regret at the death of one who was so familiar and respected a figure in the general life of the community.

There were lengthy obituaries in the local papers with tributes paid to his scholarship and enthusiasm for Welsh literature. He was particularly well-versed in the Mabinogion and in Welsh syntax. A writer in the *Manchester Guardian* spoke of his contributions to Welsh magazines, *Cymru* and *Y Geninen*, 'which were marked by a pleasant and cordial feeling for character and by an idiomatic style which was the man himself-unforced, colloquial, yet suggesting the literary dominie.' David Samuel was a keen eisteddfodwr, his bardic title being *Dewi o Geredigion*. He was frequently selected as adjudicator in literary competitions and acted as examiner for the Gorsedd degree of ovate. At the Gorsedd ceremony at the National Eisteddfod in Caernarfon that year tributes were paid to the literary services of *Dewi o Geredigion*, and the great loss sustained to Wales by his death. Outside his school duties, his greatest interest was centred in religious work particularly in the welfare of Salem Church. When he started his private school in Bridge Street, he became a deacon in Siloh, but joined Salem when that church was built; at the time of his death he was the only survivor of the original deaconate.

At the special meeting of the Governors called on 27 May, a vote of condolence to the family of the late Headmaster was moved and unanimously passed. Miss Dalley and Emrys Jones were asked to act as joint Heads in the interregnum and D H Jenkins, assistant master was requested to take over the teaching of Welsh. At the June meeting, the Governors were informed by T J Samuel, of the bequests made to the School by his late brother. David Samuel had left the sum of one hundred pounds for funding a ' Samuel Exhibition' covering a portion of the School fees, attainable by a boy pupil, who should be a native of Aberystwyth. Additionally, Samuel had bequeathed his mathematical and literary books to the School on condition the Governors provided suitable book cases. The Governors gratefully accepted the gifts and were prepared to comply with the conditions.

C. Lloyd Morgan, M.A., Headmaster 1921–1928.

Chapter Two

THE LLOYD MORGAN YEARS

1921-1928

In the weeks preceding the late Headmaster's death, the Governors had received ninety-three applications for the post of Headmaster. The Governors had acceded to a request from the Welsh Legion of Ex-Servicemen that preference would be given to an ex-serviceman provided that qualifications were equal. From a short list of five candidates, Cecil Lloyd Morgan, M A (Oxon) Headmaster of Haverfordwest Grammar School, was appointed, at a salary of £650 per annum with house.

The Headmaster elect had been born in Denbigh, where his father, a native of Silian, Lampeter, was rector. His early education was at Rossall School from where he gained a scholarship to Corpus Christi College, Oxford. Under the tutorage of Sir Owen M Edwards, Lloyd Morgan read history and graduated BA in 1905 and MA in 1908 when he was on the staff of King Edward VII School, Sheffield. A move to Nottingham High School followed where he was chief master in history and active in school games as well as holding a commission in the Officers Training Corps. He served in the Great War as a lieutenant in the 11th Suffolks; he was in France for some of the heavy fighting in 1916; he was wounded in action twice, the second time, so severely that his right leg had to be amputated. Nevertheless his active service continued and he was promoted to major. When released in 1918 he was granted the rank of honorary major. Prior to the Aberystwyth appointment, Major Morgan had been headmaster at Haverfordwest for two years.

The new Head was taking over at a time when the country was still reeling from the effects of the War. Unemployment had reached one million and within a year the nation was to feel the effects of the Geddes Axe with its drastic pruning of government expenditure especially on education. After several years with a credit balance of over £2000, suddenly in April 1921, the School accounts showed only £311 in credit even after the transference of funds from the deposit account. In May, the Governors agreed to increase the School fees to £5 per annum and later decreed that pupils would have to buy their own text books and mathematical instruments. They had also decided that in view of the large number of applications for admission to the School, an entrance examination would be held for the first time, the subjects examined being English and arithmetic. Those who had gained entrance scholarships (Free Places), and those who had attained more than 75 marks in the Scholarship examination would be exempt. Preference would be given to those who undertook to remain at the school until they reached the age of 16 years.

During his first term, on Armistice Day 1921, the Headmaster and staff, with a group of senior pupils joined in a public procession to the Castle, where His Worship the Mayor, Cllr J Barclay Jenkins, after the two minutes silence had been observed, was to cut the first sod for the foundations of the town War Memorial. On December 27 1921, the School War Memorial was unveiled in the Central Hall. The chairman of the War Memorial committee Ivor Evans, who presided, said:

> Today is a solemn, but at the same time, a proud day in the history of our School, for we are assembled to do honour to the memory of forty-six of our schoolfellows who made the supreme sacrifice during the War. As Rupert Brooke said in his poem to the fallen-
>
> > 'They poured out the red sweet wine of youth,
> > And gave up the years to be.'
>
> We miss and mourn today our late Headmaster. Through his death, every old pupil has lost a friend, for Mr Samuel always took a great interest in the welfare of all his pupils. He had been greatly involved in the War Memorial Committee and it was he who had selected the wording and the motto on the tablet. Though he is not with us in the flesh I am confident that his spirit is not far from this Hall this afternoon.
>
> While we mourn the old Head we welcome the new Headmaster. Major Lloyd Morgan did not know those who fell but he was one of their comrades on the battlefield and was himself dangerously wounded. I do not know where the fallen may be commemorated more fittingly than in their own schools. The spirit they displayed was fostered and developed in them at school. Here the seed was sown and it is fitting that the record of the harvest of duty nobly done should abide in its place of sowing. Not only is the School the most fitting place, it is also the place where the inspiration derived from such a record may prove most fruitful and beneficial.

S E Thomas having read out the names of the fallen, the tablet was unveiled by Major Goronwy Owen, D S O. Trumpeter A Burbeck sounded the 'Last Post' and 'Reveille' and the dedicating prayer offered by the Revd R J Rees.

Major Owen, in the course of his address said:

> He was conscious that he was acting as substitute for one who was no longer with them, for one who had endeared himself to many generations of past students of the School. He was also proud to be present because among the names on the tablet were those of old pupils with whom he had fought side by side in the trenches in France. He could imagine that the staff of the School would bring their pupils to the tablet and point out to them those who gave their all for their country. Many hundreds of thousands of Welsh boys barely out of their teens had felt the call of duty and went out and served their country nobly and well. Little did any of them understand that service meant sacrifice but all service did mean sacrifice.

Another distinguished Old Boy, Major E R Thomas, newly appointed to the Headship of the Royal Grammar School, Newcastle upon Tyne, in a short address thought that the day would come when what had been said and done on this day will have been forgotten, which is why they had erected this memorial.

The Lloyd Morgan Years — 1921-1928

The only way in which immortality could be given to their sacrifice was to live for our country as gloriously as they died for it, then those who come after us will recognise the source of our inspiration and there will move down the ages, an inspiration that will never pass away.

The Headmaster, Major Lloyd Morgan thought that he was probably the only one present who did not know any of those Old Boys who were being commemorated that afternoon. His sense of obligation and privilege was none the less real. As the representative of the teachers and pupils in the School and on behalf of generations yet to come he now accepted from the old pupils, with gratitude, pride and humility, their tribute to their fellow-pupils, the undying dead, who gave their lives for the world's freedom and morality. The Memorial would remind them daily of those twin virtues of duty and loyalty, without which no community, whether it was nation or a school, could prosper or even exist.

The memorial tablet which was tastefully designed in bronze had been fixed to the south wall of the Central Hall. It was surmounted with the School coat of arms in enamel, underneath which are the words, 'Er coffadwriath am Cyn-Efrydwyr yr Ysgol a roes eu bywyd yn aberth ar allor gwasanaeth eu gwlad yn y Rhyfel Mawr 1914-1918.' Then follows a list of the names, and at the foot of the tablet are the following lines from 1 Samuel ch 26-vs 15 &16:-

Y gwyr hyn dda iawn wrthym ni,
Mur oeddynt hwy i ni nos a dydd.

(The men were very good to us, they were a wall to us both by night and by day)

Following their initiative in securing the War Memorial, the Old Pupils, at their 1921 Reunion, where there was a record attendance, made a move towards providing a memorial to the late David Samuel. The dancing, whist drive and miscellaneous events must have been appreciated because a week later, a New Year's Eve dance and whist drive was enjoyed in Ward's Cafe. After the restrictions of the War years the Old Ystwythians were possibly eager to re-affirm their loyalty and affection for their *Alma Mater,* and to keep in touch with each other, following the uncertainties of the immediate past.

The end of term Christmas concert was back to its former status, with a School orchestra performing for the first time as well as violin solos by Esme Silver and J D Williams, folk songs and dances. The play in the second half of the concert was "Scrooge and Marley's Ghost", under the stage management of Norman Hanson and notable for the fine acting of Arthen Owen as Scrooge.

The extra-mural activities continued with Dydd Gwyl Dewi celebrated in the now traditional way. The eisteddfod in 1922 was organised for the first time by D H Jenkins, who had taken over responsibility for Welsh teaching, previously carried out by David Samuel. The programme had considerably expanded and 'the standard of competition reflected great credit on the School and its pupils.' For D H Jenkins it was the first of thirty-seven annual eisteddfodau in which he would be involved. It would appear that the choir competition included only the girls' Houses; Gwent, trained and conducted by Nancy Charman, were the narrow winners.

The Headmaster, in his first annual report to the 1922 Prize Day audience, prefaced his remarks with a tribute to the late Headmaster. 'The shadow of Mr Samuel still hung over the School, but though he was gone, his influence, which was his richest bequest, and his most fitting memorial, still lived'. Major Morgan was gratified that once again the School had use of the College gymnasium and the assistance of Miss Davidson, shared with the College, who undertook physical training with the girls and junior boys. In addition Captain Stimson was training the senior boys. The Headmaster looked forward to the time when every boy and girl in Wales received skilled body training every day of the week. In the county of Cardigan, with its black record of tuberculosis, the schools had a clear duty. They could not by themselves prevent or cure diseases, but they could give the children more power of resistance. Unlike the previous Head, Major Morgan welcomed the demise of the C W B Junior certificate examination believing it gave the School a freer hand in self-management and 'removed part of the tyranny of the examination system. Examinations tended to become the end of education, instead of merely a means of testing progress; it was false judgement which estimated the whole worth of a pupil solely by paper results.' Turning to careers, he observed that there were seventy-seven former pupils currently at universities, colleges, and hospitals, including fifty-one at UCW Aberystwyth. He was surprised and disturbed by the preference shown by women for the teaching profession particularly when, at the present time, such careers as journalists, nurses, doctors, dispensers, solicitors, secretaries, and artistic designers, were open to them. The Headmaster referred to the presence among them of a distinguished Old Boy, Capt. Ernest Evans M P, who had been chosen to second the reply to the King's Speech at the recent opening of the Session of Parliament. Ernest Evans, was one of the group of boys who entered the School in the first term in 1896, had been called to the Bar after his distinguished record in Cambridge and had held the position of secretary to Lloyd George in 1918-20 when he was coalition prime minister. In 1921 he had been elected Liberal Member of Parliament for Cardiganshire. He later became a member of the judiciary.

In a reminiscent speech, Archdeacon Williams of Holy Trinity church, said a hundred years ago, professional letter-writers enjoyed a thriving trade because of the illiteracy of the people. Now they had splendid schools and a high standard of education which enabled them to take their place in life. Following the speeches, there was something of an innovation for these occasions; form two choir gave a rendering of Coleridge-Taylor's 'Viking Song', teams of boys and girls gave physical training demonstrations and the sleep-walking scene from 'Macbeth' was most effectively acted with Gwenllian Saer taking the part of Lady Macbeth. For these new developments to take place it had been necessary to stage the prize day, for the first time, in the Parish Hall. Perhaps this was the reason why the exhibition of cakes, needle work, drawing, wood and metal work and book-binding which had been a feature of such occasions since the early days did not take place.

That the new Headmaster put great emphasis on physical activities is shown by the prominence he gave to the sporting achievements of the School in his record book. He reported in his first prize day speech that the football team had a good season winning

The Lloyd Morgan Years — 1921-1928

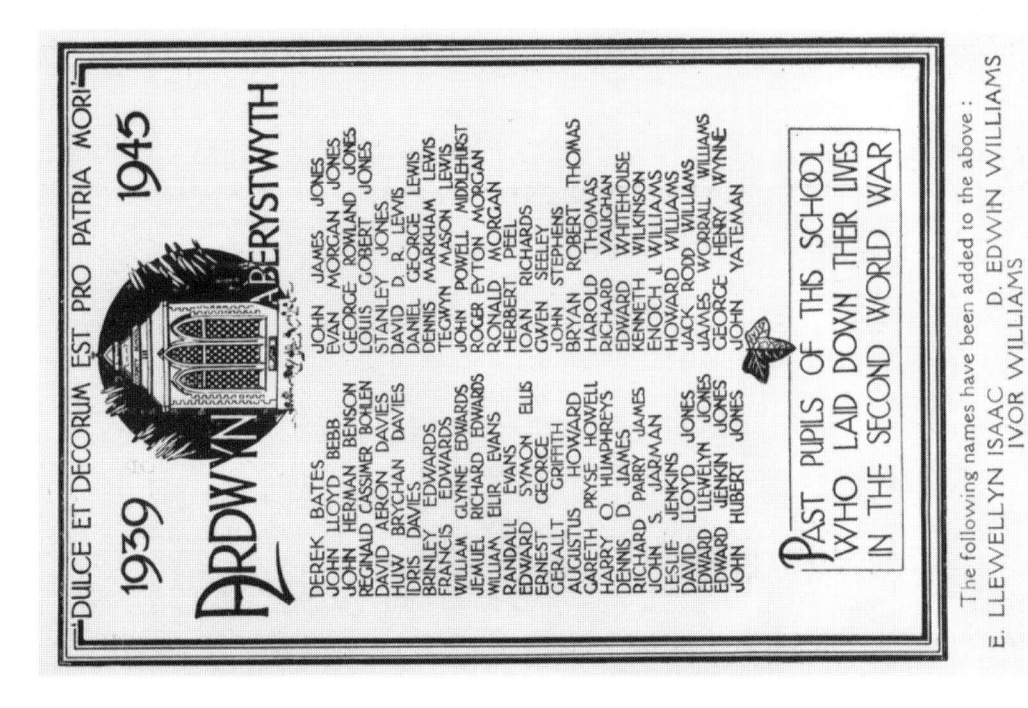

Memorial of World War II, 1939–1945.

Memorial of World War I, 1914–1918.

all matches against school opposition except their old rivals Towyn. The team photograph of the 1921-22 XI shows Reg Farrow as captain. A report of a home game against Towyn, after Percy Evans had put the School two up in the first half, complained 'they fell off lamentably and were only saved from defeat by the brilliant defensive play of Farrow at centre half. It may be fairly said that for the greater part of the second half Farrow played the whole of the Towyn team practically single handed'. The result, a two goal draw was a great disappointment, for there had been great hopes of breaking the Towyn record of sixteen years of supremacy. Reg Farrow must have been a sportsman of some stature since he was boys' athletic champion for three consecutive years. Also in the photograph is Sam Mitchell, football coach and referee, who had been appointed teacher of mathematics and general subjects in 1921; he was to serve the School for thirty seven years. The girls' hockey side had played few matches because of the weather but they had defeated Towyn and Carpenter Hall. Also surviving the years are some snapshots of the 1922 School Sports held at the Vicarage Field, showing the tug-of-war and sack race with some competitors wearing school caps!

No doubt motivated by the General Election of November 1922 which put the Tories in power, the School held a mock-election for the senior pupils. Percy Evans was judged to have made the best electioneering speech and Angharad Hughes dealt with questions most effectively, while Gordon Mathias was an 'attractive Bolshevik.' Against the national trend, Percy Evans (Nat Lib) topped the poll with 40 votes, against Angharad Hughes (Ind Lib) 36 votes, A Burke-Jones (Conservative) 32 and Norman Ellis (Labour) 21 votes. Percy Evans and Angharad Hughes had, earlier in the year, been appointed the first ever School Captains. Reporting to the Governors on possible changes to the curriculum, the Headmaster supported the view of the C W B Inspector that first year pupils were studying too many languages. Major Morgan was of the view that there should be a choice between Latin or German and French or Welsh. Prof Morgan Lewis said the great complaint in the College was the backwardness of Welsh county school pupils in Latin, and that Welsh was being sacrificed for French. At a later meeting Prof Edward Edwards was elected chairman and he welcomed several new Governors including T J Samuel, Town Clerk and brother of the late Headmaster. During his tenure of office, Prof Edwards was to experience what was probably the most difficult period to date in the life of the School. As early as 1918, the teachers' unions had requested the Governors to adopt the national scale of salaries for teachers. The request by the teaching staff for the Governors to take up the Carmarthenshire scales elicited no response, as did a similar move in January 1921 for the newly formed Burnham scales to be a basis for salary negotiations

In January 1922, a salary scale suggested by a joint committee of governors, councillors, and teachers, representing all five County Schools was adopted by the County finance committee and passed by the education committee. This scale was £220, rising to £400 for men graduates and £220, rising to £350 for women graduates-the lowest scale in the kingdom, the maximum for men being £100 below the Burnham award. In March, a new County Council was elected and in April, Ald C M Williams, the long serving Aberystwyth County School Governor, succeeded in having the agreed scale scrapped before it came into operation. In their October meeting, the County education committee agreed on a much inferior scale without any consultation with governors or teachers-the maximum for men on this scale was £150 below the Burnham award.

In common with all the secondary school teachers in the County, the Aberystwyth County School staff rejected the revised October scale and for the first time called for the assistance of their teaching union. To make matters worse the education committee in their January 1923 meeting agreed to place all elementary school teachers on Burnham Scale 1. In that month the School Governors instructed their Clerk to serve notice on each member of staff, discontinuing their services at the end of the current term. At the same meeting, it was resolved to inform the C W B of their action and to advertise for fourteen new teachers. There was no doubt where the sympathy of the chairman lay, Prof Edwards was sure that Cardiganshire would not let its education system run to ruin at the hands of the present administration, and if there was anyone amongst them who tried to secure any temporary popularity by running a false economy stunt, he would live long enough to rue and to repent the part he had played in the matter. C M Williams said that no member had taken such an interest in the school for twenty-five years as he had. He was not against teachers having a fair salary but they should consider the condition of the country at present. There were hundreds of small farmers in debt, wages were down all over the country and they would expect teachers as educated people to try to meet them.. A leader in the *Welsh Gazette* on February 1 put the blame for the crisis on Ald. C M Williams

> He had made a scrap of paper of the scale agreed. The alderman in saying 'that if there was to be a strike then the sooner it came the better', showed a most regrettable attitude. The County Authority was guilty of dishonourable conduct and the responsibility and odium of breaking faith rested entirely upon the Authority and it was grossly unfair to try and saddle the blame for the impending strike upon the teachers.

The dispute was discussed at the Aberystwyth Town Council meeting after Prof Edwards, one of the Council's representatives on the Governing Body of the County School, drew attention to the 'perilous situation which had arisen' and hoped that the intervention of the Council in the dispute would produce an amicable settlement. It was his conviction that the schools would be closed for the summer term with the result that there would be total loss to the county of the whole of the government grant for the year amounting to £8, 500. The damage was even greater when the case of the pupils was considered. Nearly one hundred pupils were entered for the CWB examination in July who would not be allowed to sit if the School were closed. On the other hand if they staffed the School with newcomers they were unlikely to be experienced. Parents had already intimated that if the School were staffed by 'blacklegs' they would not send their children to be taught there. Ald Williams said that they had only heard one side of the case, and the regrettable thing to his mind was that the chairman of the School Governors seemed to be the agitator in this matter and was in a way urging the teachers to strike- 'he was in the pocket of the NUT'. The Council resolved to urge the Education Authority to call another meeting of the parties involved.

Prof Edwards, at the March 1923 meeting of the Governors, reported that there had been 277 responses to the advertisement but 76 had subsequently withdrawn no doubt as a result of the action of the National Union of Teachers in blacklisting the secondary schools of the county. Some of the applicants had no degrees, no teaching experience, were too old and behind some of the applications 'there was grim tragedy.'

For some posts there were no applicants and the Headmaster was most concerned that there was no one with the qualification to take on the exacting and responsible post of senior mistress. Major Morgan quoted from a letter received from one candidate who was withdrawing, 'I must confess that to one who is down and out, I had looked upon a secure post at Aberystwyth as bread upon the waters. I have been unemployed for six months and being a married man I was naturally tempted to consider any present opportunity of repairing my misfortunes but under the circumstances, to sacrifice the chance of obtaining a post seems to me the only course which on principle I could adopt.'

The appointments sub-committee was of the opinion that it would be impossible to staff the School from the applicants. However Ald CM Williams, who had earlier declined membership of the sub-committee insisted that the applicants be reconsidered. It was with his help that a short list of twelve was selected and interviews fixed for late April. By this time the notices served on the present staff had taken effect and the School did not re-open after the Easter vacation. Efforts to staff the School with new teachers continued to be thwarted when it was learnt that seven out of the shortlisted twelve had withdrawn; as a result the Governors agreed to postpone the interviews and made an appeal to the Education Authority and the teachers to come to some agreement. There was a strong objection from C M Williams when he learnt that in the letter of invitation to interview, the Clerk had included a paragraph outlining the dispute between the Authority and the teachers. At the annual meeting of the Governors, when the re-election of Prof Edwards was proposed, Ald Williams thought it would be advantageous to appoint a fresh chairman 'when you have had difficult and unpleasant work to do, I think it is in the best interest to make a change.' However Prof Edwards was re-elected. In a statement the Headmaster made it very clear that he was standing by his staff. He said that the teachers had been called 'grasping' but they had been prepared to accept a scale that was the lowest in the kingdom. They were fighting not for bloated salaries but for the sanctity of bargains and for honest dealing by our public bodies. They had put the issue on a moral plane to which some of their critics seem unable or unwilling to follow and they refused to condone a lie even when the culprit was a county authority. They had taken the only course open to men and women whose privilege it was to teach the young that honesty is among the Christian virtues and they had his entire support. 'Most regretfully I have to inform the Governors that on the day on which it becomes absolutely certain that the old staff will be unable to come back I must hand to the Clerk the notice of my resignation'. Ald Williams, egregious to the last, thought that Major Morgan should have resigned at the same time as the teachers and that in view of the remarks made his position would be intolerable.

With the School having been closed for a week, a number of anxious parents called a meeting of parents of fifth and sixth form pupils in the Town Hall at which a resolution was passed urging the Education Authority to take steps to re-open the School by reinstating the staff under the agreed January scale for twelve months and that in the meantime steps be taken to reach a satisfactory agreement with both parties throughout the County. A telegram was sent to the Minister of Education and copies of the resolution to each member of the education committee.

The *Welsh Gazette* continued its wholehearted support of the teachers in its leader column. The leader in the May 3 issue leader headed 'Bolshevism in Cardiganshire' read:

Bolshevism meant 'the majority' but the ruthless abuse of authority by 'the majority' had given the term a hateful meaning. The Bolsheviks in Russia are using their strength like a merciless giant, destroying the basis of society by repudiating contracts, reducing the country to ruin by exercising their powers in a fashion that is subversive of good government. We are witnessing something the same in Cardiganshire today in the treatment of the secondary schools by the County Education Authority who believe that might is right. What would become of the stability of this country if solemn contracts could be repudiated with every change of government? It is astonishing that the member of the Education Authority who is more responsible than anyone else for the present deplorable state of affairs in the County should have the hardihood to maintain that 'the whole blame is upon the teachers'. If blame must be apportioned, then we are convinced that the bulk of it must be fixed upon Ald C M Williams. It was he, and not the teachers, who took the first active step to break the contact. The teachers are not on strike, they have been locked out because they rightly object to have their salaries reduced below the agreed figure. Every school would be open in Cardiganshire today, and the children would be at their lessons if Mr C M Williams had been content to let well alone.

Llandyssul and Cardigan County Schoola had opened with new staff; in the case of Cardigan, the headmaster and three governors had journeyed secretly to another town and appointed a new staff of seven teachers, while Llandyssul had made the new appointments without the knowledge of the headmaster, who, when the school was re-opened on May 2, had to appeal to the pupils, who supported the old staff, and declined to enter the school. On May 18 all parties involved were summoned to the Board of Education in London and although no statement was issued it was believed that a basis of settlement had been reached. When the full draft of the suggested basis for settlement was revealed, the official language of the document 'was somewhat difficult to understand', the first clause stating that 'that the matter cease to be regarded and treated, as one involving a difference respecting a scale of salaries.' What it amounted to was the acceptance by the teachers of the October 1922 scale for the remainder of the session, with an increase from September 1923 equal to the January 1923 scale, the amount of the increase to be made up by an increase in the school fees to £8 per annum. It was also laid down that the new staffs of Llandyssul and Cardigan schools be dispensed with and all the members of the old staff be reinstated. A mass meeting of the teachers accepted the terms of the settlement 'solely in the educational interests of the children' but expressed regret that the school fees would have to be increased and that they, the teachers, 'would have the stigma cast upon them of being responsible for the raising of the fees.' In a meeting behind closed doors, with the press excluded, the County education committee, decided that they could not accept the basis of settlement and adhered to a previous resolution supporting the governors of Llandyssul and Cardigan schools in appointing new staffs.

Despite this setback, the governors of the three northern schools, whose teachers had resolved to accept re-appointment under the terms of the settlement, re-opened their schools. For Aberystwyth, the ten week closure ended on Friday 29 June 1923 with the CWB examinations due to start on the following Monday-a close run thing. The Headmaster reported that there had been a 75% return of pupils, some had failed to find lodgings, while others had found employment. Only half of those entered for the external examinations had in fact sat papers.

Prior to the closure, the usual spring term events had taken place. For the first time the House gaining the highest points in the eisteddfod received the challenge cup presented by Prof Edwards, the chairman of Governors. The programme listed 37 events, the most extensive to date, including, curiously, a whistling solo for boys and girls won by Percy Evans and Esme Silver who also won the violin solo. 'The enthusiasm of the pupils and the keenness of the competitors reached their climax when, previous to the last item, it became evident that three of the four Houses were equal in points.' The final item was the competition of house choirs, trained and conducted by the pupils themselves. Nancy Charman conducted the winning Ceredigion choir and so the cup was presented to the House captains Patty Gardner and Percy Evans.

The address at the 1923 Prize Day was delivered by the first director of extra-mural studies at the College, The Revd. Herbert Morgan who, like many before him spoke on the importance of character. The pupils should ask themselves how their School had come about. The pioneers were able to do what they did because they lived up to the motto of the school. The school was entrusted to the pupils, they were the real governors and it was for them to hand the school over to those who came after them, unsullied, undiminished in value, and with an enhanced reputation. In his report, the Headmaster spoke on co-education, and wondered how far the advantages of co-education to the girls was secured at the cost of excessive physical and mental strain. No means had yet been devised for over-working boys, that species had subtle forms of protection in the face of danger. Of all the problems confronting parents and teachers today, one of the most urgent was, how far should girls be taught along with boys and how could over-strain in girls be avoided. The era of sexual equality was sixty years away! Major Morgan thought that too much was asked of all pupils in terms of examinations; only those ignorant of the real meaning of education would estimate the whole worth of a pupil or school solely by paper results. For an individual, like a school, was a mass of activities -physical, mental, social, aesthetic, spiritual-that could not be tested by pen and ink or expressed in marks. The Headmaster explained why Aberystwyth County School did not offer advanced courses as did many Welsh secondary schools. By doing so, the School lost a grant of £400 a year but they kept their liberty, did not force their sixth-form pupils to concentrate on three principal subjects but allowed them the opportunity of working in the greatest possible variety of subjects of a really high standard. Sixty two former pupils were at various universities and colleges, including forty-three at Aberystwyth. Twenty-eight had taken degrees in the summer of 1922, including three first class honours science degrees. Percy George, after leaving school in 1912 with a senior certificate, gained a first in economics, went on to Cambridge, and then a lectureship in South Africa before returning to UCW in 1928. B Alfred Edwards, gained another first in mathematics to add to that in applied mathematics earned the previous year. Later with an MSc from Cambridge he continued his studies in the Universities of Zurich and Rome after being awarded a University of Wales Fellowship; a lectureship at King's College, London followed. In 1960, in recognition of his services as Dean of the Faculty of Science at King's College, Alfred Edwards was awarded the

The Lloyd Morgan Years — 1921-1928

CBE. Valmai Burdwood Evans who also had a fellowship was in Rome at the same time. The trio of 'firsts' was completed with Anna Maria Jones becoming the first woman in the University of Wales to gain a first class degree in geography.

Percy Evans, the first pupil to be appointed headboy left in 1923 having been awarded the Headmaster's Prize' for leadership. He started a science course at UCW from where he gained the 'Thomas Jones ' scholarship in surgery to enter Guy's Hospital. After qualifying as a dental surgeon, he spent three years on the staff of Guy's before returning home to take up the post of school dental officer. 'Evans the dentist' as he became known to thousands of Ceredigion schoolchildren served the community for forty-five years retiring in 1976. In 1992, some weeks before he died, age 87 years, he spoke fondly of his days at the County School, remembered Major Morgan, known to all as Hooker, as a disciplinarian 'who wielded the stick to great effect' but was much respected, the 'formidable but kind Miss Dalley', and the fine teaching of William Jones. Percy Evans recognised the sacrifices his parents had made to send him to the County School after he had gained an entrance scholarship from Llanfarian school. His father would milk his cows before setting off for his work in the town. On his return in the evening, the milk would have to be delivered in the village, and the cows milked again. Percy walked to school from Llanfarian, via Penparcau, Penybont Bridge, the Flats, and the cemetery. Lunch would be a cup of tea, bread and butter at the New Quay cafe but after school he had the luxury of a train ride at 5pm, alighting at Llanfarian halt.[36]

With the settlement of the salary dispute, the School quickly resumed its normal life The first tennis tournament in the annals of the School took place in July 1923; the silver cup given anonymously was claimed by Gwynedd who beat Ceredigion in the final. 'The match was remarkable for the brilliant display of tennis by W Gardner'. In the autumn term, the School staged, for the first time, a parents' day, where the public were invited to visit the school on a normal working day, with freedom to inspect all parts of the building and to enter classes unannounced. On display were cakes made by the cookery classes, handwork, demonstrations of physical training both in the School and in the college gymnasium as well as musical items. The experiment was a success, attracting four hundred people; the hope was expressed that it would become an annual event which would bring School and parents into closer touch. A writer in the School magazine now knew what it felt like to reside in the Zoo- 'it was not easy to decide with whom to sympathise most-Mother searching a packed classroom for little Johnny or little Johnny trying to hide behind a blush from the affectionate eye of Mother.' The term also saw the resumption of the traditional Christmas concert when the newly-formed Dramatics Society performed scenes from Dickens' 'Bleak House' and *Yr Hen Crudd*. The School Orchestra under Charles Clements, newly appointed part-time music teacher, played several pieces.

Charles Clements' appointment was due to the resignation of William Jones, who taught physics, mathematics and music with great skill and dedication. Christopher Jones, his replacement in the science department served the School for seventeen years; he quickly formed a Physics Club and his interest in the developing world of wireless spread through the School. Appointed on the same day was Thomas J James. A history tutor at UCW, Tom James had gained college colours in tennis, cricket and soccer; in 1911, his last year as a student at UCW, he was selected to play amateur soccer for

The History of Aberystwyth County School (Ardwyn) 1896-1973

Staff and Sixth Form July 1923.

1920–21 Hockey Team. Captain Irene Ellis.

1921–22 Football Team. Captain Reg Farrow.

The Lloyd Morgan Years — 1921-1928

Gym Display May 27th, 1924 at Vicarage Field, under director of H. F. Stimson.

School orchestra in foreground.

Wales. He resisted the invitation to turn professional for Swansea Town to pursue what was to become a highly successful career as a teacher, interrupted by war service in the Royal Flying Corps. He spent twenty-eight happy years at the School, retiring in 1951 as senior master. Initially he took the place, temporarily, of Miss Dalley on sick leave with an eye problem, but when Miss Muriel Harrris resigned to marry William Jones the former Physics teacher, Tom James was appointed permanently to take her place as history teacher. Another appointment of 1923 was that of Richard D Williams as Clerk to the Governors. The previous Clerk had failed to produce the School accounts in time for their audit and later resigned. R D Williams retained the post until it disappeared when the 1944 Education Act came into operation. His keeping of the accounts for more than twenty years and his knowledge of the Burnham scales 'fully merited the highest praise.'

In 1923, the Old Pupils' Association celebrated their 21st Reunion in what was now the traditional manner- dancing to Evered Davies' band, a whist drive and the performance of a play. They would have rejoiced in the success of distinguished former pupil Major Goronwy Owen in winning the Parliamentary seat of Carnarvon for the Liberals from Labour in the 1923 General Election. After twelve years teaching in London, Goronwy Owen had been called to the Bar and was also a stockbroker.

After an interval of four years, the School magazine was revived. The spring 1923 issue appeared before the salary dispute and included a tribute to the late Headmaster by NH Thomas, Classics master at the school 1900-1910. He recalled that a favourite phrase of David Samuel was 'Let us now praise famous men'. He was certainly not less famous and notable among Welsh headmasters than were Sir Edward Anwyl among Welsh professors, Sir Owen M Edwards among Welsh litterateurs and Llewellyn Williams among Welsh public men. The editorial in the autumn 1923 issue apologised for the loss of the summer edition and commented 'that while not competent to speak of the merits of either side of the case... we should like it to be placed on permanent record that the disorganisation of the school-work had a very deep and far-reaching influence.'

Major Morgan speaking at the 1924 Prize Day paid tribute to those pupils who sat the external examinations in July 1923 who, for two months had been deprived of instruction. Five pupils gained the Higher certificate, two gaining distinctions, that in German, by Brian Ellis, the only one in Wales. In addition, four out of six County Exhibitions came to the School. At School Certificate level (the former Senior) despite the grave difficulties, the percentage of passes exceeded the average for Wales. The Headmaster again referred to the evils of examinations, (as he did in all his reports to the Prize Day audiences)

> The mischief consisted not so much in the amount of knowledge the examiner demanded-though that was often formidable enough- the best pupils could meet his requirements without flinching; but those with moderate abilities have to be hustled through a syllabus which is too long for them, into an examination which is too hard for them. The system bred an inevitable and vicious course of cramming; inevitable because public opinion demanded examination successes; vicious because it involved an unnatural speeding up of a pupil's normal rate of mental development.

Major Morgan thought it should be possible to find something better, 'it would not be easy to find something worse.' A method in vogue in America allowed schools to be 'accredited' to universities for the purpose of passing on their best pupils without any external examinations.

Another innovation announced by the Head was the abolition of orders of merit based on marks. Marks would be given but not communicated to pupils. Pupils would not be graded first, or tenth or twentieth but would be placed in one of four classes- Class I would indicate excellence and Class IV, the reverse, while intermediate shades of good and bad were represented in Classes II and III. He wished to substitute for the competition of one pupil against another, the competition of all pupils against an ideal standard of excellence. While the social and out-of-class activities were increasing-picnics, soirees and a new weekly dancing class, there were now organised games in school hours with good results attained in football, hockey, tennis and swimming. 'The playing fields fostered the civic virtues- avoidance of mean methods, submission to arbitration, cheerfulness in defeat, and moderation in victory'-the old Corinthian spirit *par excellence.*

Hitherto, in this account, there has been little reference to 'Ardwyn' or 'Ardwynians'. The official title was Aberystwyth County Intermediate School, after the Intermediate Education Act which created it. However in the 1924 Prize Day, the Headmaster was prompted to ask

> Why should nearly all the secondary schools in Wales be named alike -county intermediate school - an ugly, official, institutional name ? Uniformity of name tended to produce uniformity of type, of outlook, of prestige. Why should they not adopt officially the name of ARDWYN, which possessed the three-fold merit of brevity, melodiousness, and historical continuity ? Its adoption would help tremendously in that elusive, vital thing called tradition.

It is not clear whether permission for the name change was ever sanctioned by the County Authority since the name was not used in their communications. All internally produced documents such as eisteddfod, concert, and prize day programmes bore the name Ardwyn School or Ardwyn County School. To the townspeople it was still the 'County School' with the local press taking their time in adopting the change. Gildas Tibbott, spent six happy years

> 'at the dear old School on the hill, the Aberystwyth County School as it was then called before the shorter and prettier name, Ardwyn had been revived (and may I add that those responsible for that revival at a later date are to be warmly congratulated.)[37]

The first printed programme bearing the name 'Ardwyn' was that of the educational gymnastics display- 'an innovation as far as Welsh schools were concerned', which took place on the Vicarage field in May 1924. The Governors, with the agreement of the UCW authorities, had secured the part-time services of the College gymnastics tutor Captain H F Stimson and he together with his UCW colleague Miss Davidson, had organised the event. The programme explained that the object of the display was to demonstrate the many and varied activities used in educational gymnastics to stimulate the healthy and proportional development of the growing child. While the team spirit is fostered, specialised athletic activities are not overstressed. Some of the exercises are 'training' exercises where the child works at his own pace. Others are 'control' exercises in which the child moves in unison with the rest of the team. Spectators are asked to view the display as an educative process rather than as an exhibition of athletic prowess.

The programme included massed free gymnastics, folk dancing, vaulting and agility exercises, competitive and demonstration games, apparently involving all the pupils in the School. In the competitive items, points were awarded on a House basis; the winners Gwynedd had a laurel wreath placed on their flag. The photographs taken at the display have survived the years and clearly show the precision with which the programme was conducted by Captain Stimson who is seen standing on a dais under the School flag. Also shown is the School orchestra which played incidental music throughout.

The Summer 1924 edition of the school magazine, carrying the name *Ardwynian* for the first time, reported that the event introduced for the first time, the School flag and the House flags. The display was filmed and shown throughout the following week at the Market Street Cinema.

On the third anniversary of the death of David Samuel a memorial to him was unveiled in the Central Hall by Mrs de Lloyd a former pupil. It comprised a bronze tablet with a simple inscription

ER COF AM
DAVID SAMUEL MA
(Dewi o Geredigion)
PRIF-ATHRO CYNTAF YR YSGOL HON
1896-1921

In addition to the memorial tablet, which remains to this day, a photograph of the late Headmaster and several bookcases were hung in the Hall.

The effects of the teachers' salary dispute were still being felt by the Governors; they were informed by the Board of Education that as a result of the two month closure in the summer of 1923, the Treasury grant would be reduced by an amount of £598. The Governors were also in dispute with the Director of Education who had refused their request to grant more than 25% free places and who had also said that 'in the present financial stringency' the Governors should review the staffing with a view to reducing the number of teachers. The director also wished to know what had happened to the £1,600 which the Governors had on investment. Most of the Governors had little sympathy with the LEA since much of the financial problem was the result of their handling of the dispute. Cardigan and Llandyssul schools were still without Treasury grants because they had been declared inefficient having failed to reinstate the former staff, and were being financed entirely from the rates. The press reports of the Governors' meetings when these matters were discussed are much more informative than the minute book. CM Williams, of course took the side of the County Council (he had been elected their Chairman for the second time much to the disgust of the *Welsh Gazette*) and was his vituperative self in his exchanges with his chairman, Prof Edward Edwards and the Headmaster. On the question of free places, the Governors had awarded thirty-four scholarships to pupils who had attained 144 marks or more in the examination. Aberayron School had chosen the same minimum but in Tregaron free places were awarded to pupils who had scored 134 marks. If Ardwyn was restricted to 25%, then candidates with fewer than 151 marks would be denied a free place. When the Headmaster pointed out that the Board of Education allowed up to 40% which was the basis of their figure of thirty-four places, C M Williams accused him of talking nonsense. The Alderman also supported the move to reduce staff saying that the others schools in the county thought that the Aberystwyth school was over-staffed. When the Chairman pointed out that the Headmaster taught far too much, and had a great deal of administrative work to do, Williams retorted that the former Headmaster had done even more work, to which Prof Edwards replied 'That's why he went to an early grave. The Headmaster produced figures showing that the staff-pupil ratio was 1:24 while that for Wales averaged 1:20. 8 Probably influenced by the publication in the *Welsh Gazette* of a letter with a brilliantly argued case on the free places issue by Major Morgan, the director of education reversed his decision and allowed the extra places.

The provision of school meals to country children had been in the minds of the Governors for some time. Since 1923, hot meals had been provided on two days a week by the cookery classes supervised by Bertha Jones but they would have great difficulty, without extra accommodation and help, in extending the scheme. The Board of Education at this time, enquiried about the availability of mid-day meals, so it was a problem which would have to be faced. Major Morgan thought that the lunch of many pupils-a cup of tea and bun bought in town was very inadequate. A Governor, James Davies, who was headmaster of Rhydypennau school said that they provided hot meals at four pence per meal to between fifty and seventy every day. The cleaner was paid an extra 30/- a week to clean potatoes etc, soup was put on the fire in the morning and allowed to simmer until mid-day. All the vegetables were obtained free from neighbours and the children did the washing up in turns, only one plate having been broken to date- a fine example of rural self-help ! In an attempt to ease matters in the kitchen a refrigerator was obtained and soup served on those days when a cooked meal was not provided.

Betha Jones who had been appointed cookery mistress in 1900 resigned in July 1925 after a year of indifferent health; her successor Jane Williams reorganised the dinner scheme and in her first term, with the aid of Mrs Burns, appointed a kitchen helper at 15/- a week, produced 3,053 dinners for 72 children, five days a week at 6d a meal. The scheme was confined to children in lodgings and those who lived out of town. Given the size of the cookery room it must have been a Herculean task to cater for 72 children in the short lunch break, and one wonders how any cookery teaching could have taken place. At the end of the first term of operation the Headmaster reported a balance of £6-4-9 which was sufficient to pay the wages of the helper. C M Williams who had refused to undertake duties of school visitor -'I shall not be visiting that school until the Headmaster apologises for his conduct when I was up there in June', adding grudgingly that he felt sure that the success of the scheme would be an incentive to Miss Williams to 'put forth an even greater effort, although she had done very well'. Consideration was given to enlarging the cookery room but the estimate of £2000 was thought to be beyond the means of the Governors. It was not until 1928 that a kitchen was built on to the Central Hall; a purpose built kitchen/dining hall did not materialise until 1954.

It was in April 1926 that the Cardiganshire Education Authority had finally to concede defeat on the teachers' salary issue following an ultimatum from the Welsh Department of the Board of Education. Cardiganshire was the only Authority in England and Wales which had still not adopted the Burnham scale for secondary school teachers. As the *Welsh Gazette* pointed out in its editorial entitled 'The End' in the issue of February 4 1926.

> The appeal which was made at the meeting of the Education Commmittee that the members should unanimously agree to grant the teachers the Burnham scale of salaries was excellent in tone, but its belatedness deprived it of all grace.

The Governors discussed the report of the CWB inspection of November 1925 where an additional teacher of English and mathematics had been reccommended. The clamant voice of C M Williams was again to the fore in the debate. With the Burnham decision no doubt ringing in his ears, he thought that the time was not opportune to consider an additional teacher, when the County faced enormous expenditure; what was wanted was reorganisation of the staffing. Prof Edwards, now vice principal of UCW, who had relinquished the chair after completion of the normal three year period again reminded the members that the Headmaster taught for more than half the week and did not have time for the general supervision and organisation on which the success of a county school depended. C M Williams considered that with so many senior, well paid teachers in the School, no supervision was needed. Another member thought that it would be a shame if the Headmaster reduced his time in the classroom, 'his teaching of English was one of the bright spots in the School.' The same speaker agreed that there was a need for reorganisation, on a recent visit he had not been impressed with 'the imperiousness and haughtiness appearing in a teacher.' Not for the first time, the Governors considered the installation of electric lighting when problems with the gas system arose. When the Headmaster said that the light in the School was poor, C M Williams was quick to point out that they had the same light in town and his eyes were not strained in any way. However the change was approved but it was not until 1929 that electricity was installed, allowing its study in the physics curriculum.

When the Governors considered a letter from the University of Wales which lamented the lack of instruction in Greek in the secondary schools of Wales there was some sympathy for the complaint. The late Headmaster had taught the subject to a few pupils. In an earlier meeting when the curriculum was being discussed, some members thought that teaching French, German and Latin to some pupils was a waste of time and money, particularly when 'many children turned out today were unable to write correctly, unable to spell and unable to do anything with figures.' Familiar sentiments which perhaps offer some consolation to those involved in education today, and obviously not a problem confined to the Nineties.

The Lloyd Morgan Years — 1921-1928

*Ardwyn Association F.C. 1st XI, 1927–28. Captain: W. G. Morgan.
This team beat Towyn for the first time in 17 years, 25th February, 1928.*

The First School Rugby XV, 1927–1928. Captain: G. Idris Thomas.

The Board of Education had issued special regulations in regard to medical inspections which stipulated that pupils must be examined medically on entry and once each subsequent year. The Governors welcomed the move; Vice-Principal Edwards drew attention to a pamphlet issued by the Board which revealed 'that there has been a steady and progressive decline in the general physique of country children'. He felt that they were doing great benefit to these childen by providing hot school meals. On the question of medical inspection, doctors had told him that if these had been carried out in secondary school, the very many early deaths could have been avoided. When the inspections were introduced, there were some objections from parents, so it was made a condition of entry that the child must undergo an annual medical examination. There was great satisfaction when Dr Ernest Jones, who for eight years had served as science master at the School before embarking on a medical career, was appointed County Medical Officer of Health in 1926. Countless children will remember his kindliness and good humour during his years in that post.

The effect of the temporary closure of the School in 1923 was to be felt for some years. In 1924, out of 30 who gained the school certificate, 26 were girls and not one boy had sat the higher certificate examination. During the closure many boys had found employment and had not returned to School. The following year, only four pupils in Cardiganshire gained higher certificates, three of them being Ardwyn girls. In 1926, for the first time in the history of the School, there were no higher school certificates awarded. By the following year the balance had been redressed with two boys and two girls gaining the higher certificate and County exhibitions-the Headmaster complained that the value of the latter had dropped significantly. The number of school certificates gained was a record 41 with 13 distinctions. When the Governors reviewed the 1927 CWB examinations results, Ald CM Williams considered them to be be unsatisfactory even when the Headmaster pointed out that there had been a 70% pass rate at the school certificate level. The Alderman had analysed the County results over five years and ' the school does not stand at all well, especially when our school is so large, costs £6000 a year and has a big staff'. Major Morgan challenged Williams to produce the figures, adding that there was no school in Wales which could match their results and suggested, with understandable exasperation, that he should 'cease crabbing.'

Throughout his period as Headmaster, Major Morgan repeatedly condemned the examination system. In his annual report to the 1925 Prize Day audience he pointed out that pupils who required financial assistance to follow a university course were required to sit three examinations; the State scholarships in June, higher certificate in July, and the College scholarships in September. It was little wonder that students entering college were frequently played out before they got there

> Year by year one perceived with increasing anxiety that the examination system of today, intensely specialised and highly mechanised as it was, was the cause of much mental and physical ill-health, especially in girls; it fostered a wrong attitude to learning on the part of the pupil, vicious methods of instruction on the part of the teacher, and in the mind of the public generally, a totally false conception of the meaning and purpose of education. Education should mean 'beauty, wonder, spiritual fineness, and above all creative courage.' I dare to say that in the modern examination system these ideals had their deadliest foe.

The Lloyd Morgan Years — 1921-1928

Major Morgan was pleased to know that the revolt against the examination system was now gathering headway and had even reached the precincts of the Board of Education. More than sixty five years on, he would no doubt have disapproved of the increase in testing demanded by the 1990 Education Act. The Headmaster took great pride in acknowledging the achievements of two former pupils, Goronwy Owen and Ernest Evans. They had been successful Liberal candidates in the 1924 General Election. 'Had any school in Wales, he wondered, ever had two Members of Parliament at the same time?' This distinction was surpassed in 1966, when Elystan Morgan won the Cardiganshire seat for Labour to join John Morris and Jeremy Bray on the Labour benches.

Former pupil Dr David de Lloyd after teaching in London and at the Llanelly Intermediate School returned to Aberystwyth in 1919 to join Prof Walford Davies, in the UCW music department as lecturer. Dr de Lloyd invariably served as an adjudicator at the School eisteddfodau from this date. At the 1926 Prize Day, as well as a physical training demonstration by the senior boys and a sword dance by the girls, there was a performance of a Welsh operetta *'Pwyll a Rhiannon'*, the music of which was composed by Dr de Lloyd and the lyrics by D J Saer, headmaster of Alexandra Road school for 33 years. So successful was the programme that it was repeated a week later, again in the Parish Hall. The press congratulated both the authors and the performers.

> The performers were inspired by the hauntingly beautiful music and the authors grateful that the school possessed singers with voices that could do justice to the beauty of the music and lyrics. We believe that Dr de Lloyd and Mr Saer are as pleased with the performance as the pupils are with themselves and that is saying a great deal.

Later that year Dr de Lloyd succeeded Dr Walford Davies as professor of music, occupying the chair until his death in 1948.

The Parish Hall was again filled for the traditional Christmas concert although on this occasion the play 'Eagerheart' was the only item on the programme. As the Headmaster explained in his introduction, the play was being performed under certain restrictions, the reasons for which were not clear. The names of those participating could not be revealed, nor were they able to perform anything else during the evening. Applause was also prohibited but despite these restrictions, which one press report commended, the play was a courageous and successful attempt to adapt the story of the Nativity to the modern stage. Credit was due to Miss Dalley who had coached the players who were to be complimented 'for presenting the town with something altogether unique.'

Athletic activities continued to thrive; the School sports day now regularly staged on the Vicarage field generated intense competition to secure the Nanteos cup for the House. Dr Abraham Thomas and Col J C Rea had donated silver medals to be awarded to the most successful boy and girl athlete. In 1927 Eira Lloyd, the head girl, had the distinction of winning the victrix ludorum for the fourth successive year. She was also a talented singer who swept the board in the eisteddfod each year.

That year, for the first time, a cross-country event was staged the day before the sports.

Another innovation which stood the test of time was the introduction of life-saving tests during the swimming lessons in the Bath street pool. Major Stimson, recently promoted, and widely recognised as an outstanding teacher of physical education, had successfully coached a large number of boys for the award of the RLSS. In addition, nineteen boys, during the term, had learnt to swim across the baths. For the soccer team, the period 1923 to 1928 proved to be very successful. Some 66 years later, Cadfan Evans remembered with some pride the record of his side in 1925/26, undefeated in 16 games against school teams, losing just one to Lampeter College but much more noteworthy, drawing twice with great rivals Towyn. Cadfan recalled that the captain, Tom Seaton scored 75 out of a record 103 goals scored and that four of the team played for the Town XI.[38] The successes of this period can, to some extent, be attributed to the enthusiasm and coaching skills of young masters -Tom James, Chris Jones and Sam Mitchell. However it was Saturday 25 February 1928 which will go down in the history of Ardwyn soccer -the defeat of Towyn by three goals to one. After seventeen years of failure, at last the impossible had been done and this in an otherwise undistinguished season when as many games had been lost as had been won. 'It was a famous victory' was the title of the account in the *Ardwynian*.

> Three-one, Oh! how we longed for the final whistle. They might do it yet-what agony we endured towards the end of the game. At last it went and it is impossible to describe the ensuing proceedings-all I say is that seventeen years' concentrated emotion was let loose, and eleven boys made history which will always be remembered with the greatest joy by all past, present and future Ardwynians.'

The same account, while giving credit to the forwards, picked out the performance of vice-captain and defender John D Fisher Davies 'who had continually saved the situation.' As well as being a fine athlete-he was the victor ludorum in the 1928 Sports, he gained the Edward Jones scholarship from UCW to the University of Edinburgh Medical School which led to a notable surgical career. The School field at Plascrug, was invariably waterlogged during winter and there were frequent complaints about the quagmire conditions. The hockey fixtures were particularly affected although from time to time the College facilities were available. However, because of pitch difficulties, in 1928, netball replaced hockey as the winter game. Hockey was not resumed until 1935 when new playing fields became available.

The summer games of cricket and tennis flourished in the late Twenties. Cricket was played against Ystrad Meurig, St Mary's College, Towyn School, and St David's College, Lampeter. The Magazine reporting on a game with the latter -'we sent them in first, to face R A Smith who proved to be unplayable. His analysis is worthy of mention- 7 overs, 5 maidens, 1 run, 7 wickets.' This record beat that of G Idris Thomas who in the same match the previous year took 7 wickets for 2 runs. Lampeter were all out for 14 but the School struggled to score 25 to win.

Inter-house mixed tennis matches provided great interest from 1923 when a cup was anonymously donated. The friendly rivalry which had existed with Aberayron from the early days soon resulted in a popular annual tennis fixture with honours being fairly even throughout the Twenties.

In his 1928 annual report, the Head congratulated the soccer XI on its victory against Towyn, which was once thought to be an impossible feat. A rugby football team had been formed that year but were less skilful. He revealed that at one time the possibility of turning over from soccer to rugby had been considered but none of the schools they now played would make the change so the matter was dropped. 'Speaking for myself and from a broadly educational point of view, I should much prefer to see this or any school, playing the rugby code.' The applause which greeted this statement is very surprising in a predominantly soccer area, when one remembers the furore which resulted from the action of a later headmaster in excluding soccer in favour of rugby football. It would seem that a game against Newquay tutorial school was the only rugby fixture played that year-an extant photograph shows the captain to be G Idris Thomas the talented cricketer. There is no further reference to rugby in the records until 1934.

Included in the rugby XV photograph is Dan Evans, who was appointed School cleaner in 1927 following the death of his father-in-law William Jones who had held that post for twelve years.. When the Governors had met to consider his replacement, generous tributes were paid to Jones, as he was known to all. Vice-Principal Edward Edwards considered that they had all lost a good friend. The Headmaster added

> I intensely admired him, I was an old friend of his and he was like a father to me. He never seemed to think of reward in doing his work. He was a remarkably loyal member of the School and it would be difficult to find a man who took greater pride in all its attainments.

In discussing a salary for his replacement, Ald C M Williams was sure there would be plenty of applicants at £2 a week, particularly as it was an indoor job. Prof Edwards thought that he should have a living wage, Jones had been paid £2. 5s. The Clerk knew labourers who were paid more and Major Morgan reminded members that the cleaner worked a 12 hour day. Nevertheless, Williams' niggardly views prevailed and the post was advertised at £2 a week.

The Governors referred to the death of Ald Peter Jones, the first Chairman of both Cardiganshire County Council and the Aberystwyth County School governing body and still a Governor at the time of his death at 80 years. Cllr Daniel Thomas, a former Governor had also recently died.

The director of education had drawn attention to the crowded state of the teaching profession and asked the Governors to consider whether the curriculum needed adapting so that a larger proportion of pupils, particularly the girls, would be better equipped to enter other professions or occupations. The Headmaster pointed out that for several years he had advised pupils to consider careers other than teaching. Major Morgan had always shown a fine grasp of the social and educational needs of his charges; the Governors had asked him to prepare a memorandum in reply to a request from the director to consider reducing the school holidays. The County education committee saw no reason why the holiday periods at secondary schools should differ from those of elementary schools. If the reason was pressure of work then, perhaps the Governors should consider whether that pressure was due, to some extent, to the shortness of the school terms. The Headmaster explained that although fatigue in industry had been well researched, little had been done with respect to fatigue in schoolchildren. He quoted the view of the medical officer to Manchester Grammar School who had said 'the tired boy is necessarily the slow boy and a vicious circle is established. To meet this difficulty, most schools have adequate holidays.' Major Morgan thought that particularly in spring and summer there should be provision for the open-air life and recreation mainly for the demands of growth. He refuted the director's suggestion that the pressure would be less if the terms were longer.

> Pupils instinctively worked and teachers instinctively taught, with a degree of intensity that bore no relation to the ultimate length of the term, except that when saturation point was reached somewhere about the thirteenth week of term, the learning and the teaching began to peter out.

He cited three of the more obvious differences between elementary and secondary school; in the latter, homework was a problem which rarely touched the younger pupil, out-of-school activities were more varied and intense and its pupils were at the most critical and easily disturbed period of their lives, the age of adolescence. It was wrong to consider holidays as periods of idleness, the senior pupils, as examinations approached, were involved in a great deal of private study. However the strain of private work was far less than work done in term time, the pupils could choose their own subject, time and pace. He concluded by strongly recommending that the education committee retain the existing period of holiday and he urged the Board to investigate the problem of fatigue in secondary schools. Major Morgan's report was warmly endorsed by the Governors and submitted to the director.

Major Morgan's period of stewardship of Ardwyn was coming to an end; under his direction the School had made great strides not the least of which was in the field of music. Sir Walford Davies, having discovered three very talented young musicians in his travels around Wales, brought them to Aberystwyth for further training at the College and to Ardwyn to continue their secondary education. The boys, Hubert Pearce (violin and viola), Haydn Lewis (cello), and Idris Thomas (piano) obviously enhanced the already quite strong musical ethos created by Charles Clements. The School orchestra, reinforced by Walford Davies' proteges, won great praise for its performance in the 1927 Christmas concert as did the string quartet of Esme Silver and the three boys. Evelyn Lumley Jones and J Alwyn Jones, in a vocal duet from 'Patience' gave the audience a foretaste of what Ardwyn could do in the operas of Gilbert and Sullivan. The musical talents of these young people were not displayed only in Aberystwyth; they visited many other towns including attending a juvenile music festival at Criccieth, the object of which was to create a taste for native Welsh music among children. The talents of pianist Idris Thomas extended to cricket and rugby as previously noted, and also to poetry-he won the chair in the 1927 and 1928 eisteddfodau.

Criccieth was also the venue for a school trip on the 29 July 1927. The GWR ran a special train which left at 1.25 am to view the solar eclipse in the totality area at Criccieth. In the *Ardwynian* under the heading 'Ardwyn Eclipse Expedition', mathematics teacher Tom Salmon described the day.

> They were a joyous band, full of enthusiasm, devoting their superabundant energy to the study of the mechanical properties of doors and of rapid motion along the corridor, and it is believed that quite new discoveries in the Theory of Relativity were made in this way.
> Darkness gradually gave way to light, when the presence of dark clouds and rain

caused some anxiety, but to the end hopes remained of seeing some of the phenomena accompanying totality. The rain came heavier and heavier as on the bleak uplands we waited and the great darkness for a few seconds blotted out the dripping landscape. There is a silver lining to every cloud. None saw it that day, still there was one-the good humoured and buoyant behaviour of the Ardwyn band under adverse astral influences. The sky was thickly overcast and their clothes were heavy and sodden with rain, but hearts were light and eyes were undimmed, and though quieter coming back they were in no way down cast.

So while we may hope for our descendants of 1999 better attendant circumstances, we cannot wish them anything higher than this: that they may be able to face the greatest of disappointments with that unclouded spirit that characterised this pioneering band of 1927.

The 1928 Prize Day was the second to be held at the College Hall in North Road. This wooden building opened in 1922, could seat 2, 500 people, was built on the initiative of Walford Davies who was able to attract Adrian Boult and the London Symphony Orchestra to perform therein. Unfortunately after just eleven years of use it burned down in 1933 and was never rebuilt. The address at the prize day was given by the Principal of UCW Dr H Stuart Jones. He wanted to impress upon the pupils the advantage they had in living in Aberystwyth 'which in the highest degree, revealed to them the beauties of Welsh scenery, the perpetual hills, and ever-changing sea .' He thought that influences like those had an effect, both physical and moral, on the growing boy and girl. He also wished to impress upon them the importance of the presence in Aberystwyth of two great Welsh institutions: the College, over which he had the pleasure to preside, and the National Library, that treasure house of all that was best in the intellectual world. The principal considered that the justification for the part athletic sport played in their lives was the creation of team spirit. That was necessary in all their life activities because it was the foundation of loyalty-not only should they be loyal to their own group but they should respect the loyalty of others.

In what was to be his last report, The Headmaster was concerned that the County Authority, in an effort to save money, had dispensed with their special scholarships to pupils entering the county schools. Three years previously the School had 22 of these awards, now they none. The School had gained four county exhibitions but their value was just a third of what they had been. Major Morgan considered that the educational ladder was getting narrower and steeper.

In March 1928, Major Lloyd Morgan tendered his resignation to the Governors on his acceptance of the headship of Sir Andrew Judd's School, Tonbridge, which was endowed by the Skinner's Company and aided by Kent County Council. The Governors regretfully accepted his resignation and spoke 'in eulogistic terms ' of his seven years service to the School and congratulated him on his appointment to such an important post. The Governors set in motion the process for appointing Major Morgan's successor and on the proposition of Barclay Jenkins it was agreed that applicants should not be more than 45 years of age and preferably Welsh speaking.

Of the forty applications received, seven were interviewed. In an editorial, the *Welsh Gazette* reminded the selectors that the appointment of teachers was the most important duty of the local authority, particularly now that the influence of the parent was on the wane -familiar sentiments! 'The training of the modern child "in the way he should go" was passing from the home to the school.' The paper was surprised that more 'first class men with outstanding qualifications had not applied for the headship of the Aberystwyth County School.'

However the Governors appointed a 'first class man' in David Charles Lewis, 38 years of age, head of the mathematics department at Swansea Technical College, who had held a similar post at Swansea Grammar School 1911-24. He gained a first class honours degree in pure and applied mathematics at University College, Cardiff in 1910. He had front line war service in the Royal Artillery in France and had reached the rank of major before resuming his career in Swansea. During the hostilities he developed an interest in meteorology and in 1924 gained the M Sc degree for a thesis involving mathematical solutions to atmospheric disturbances. Major Lewis had also lectured in mathematics at University College Swansea.

There was a genuine feeling of regret in the departure of Lloyd Morgan. In addition to his fine administrative qualities he was regarded very highly as a teacher. Rhiannon Aaron neé Morgan wrote:

> We were fortunate in being taught English literature by the headmaster, who had a superlative gift for teaching. His lessons opened windows for us all and in later years in college I never came across any professor or lecturer who could touch him for that power of quickening interest and stimulating imagination. I remember that 'Henry V' was one of the set books that year, and mentally I can still hear the Head storming through the King's speech before Harfleur and his Homeric voice filling III C classroom with the closing shout of 'God for Harry, England and Saint George!' On another occasion when we were doing 'Sorab and Rustum' the Head's reading of the death of Sorab reduced half the feminine members of VA to tears-even the hard-boiled damsels in the back row were quietly weeping before the end. In the Sixth we were privileged to have more of his teaching, especially those of us who did architecture as part of the history course for higher certificate. It was very much enjoyed by those who took it, more particularly since it involved excursions to various parts of the country in search of old castles and buildings. By visiting such places as St David's Cathedral, Shrewsbury, and Stokesay Castle, we all got fired with the Head's own enthusiasm for the subject and as young amateurs we loved talking unintelligibly to our unenlightened acquaintance of Ballflower and Dogtooth, of Perpendicular and Reticulated, of Flying Buttresses and the rest.
>
> In those days the entire Sixth, whether Arts or Science, had to take a certain number of joint classes in English literature, and were made to write essays regularly for the Head. The groans of the physicists and chemists torn from the labs. to read Browning or Swinburn, were vehement and prolonged, but it was extremely good for them and I'm afraid we of the Humanities had little sympathy for their suffering but merely looked down our intellectual noses upon the limitations of science. In summer we often had these large joint English classes under the weeping elm on the lawn-I have very pleasant memories of reading verse in the mingled sunshine and shadow round the big tree on a hot July afternoon.[39]

The Lloyd Morgan Years — 1921-1928

Rhiannon Morgan was the fourth of five daughters of Dr MJ Morgan, North Parade. She recollected, on her first day at School in 1922, the embarrassing comments of some of the mistresses on the behaviour of her sisters in the past and stern warnings not to do as they had done in their day and generation. She had a brilliant school record, consistently winning the eisteddfod essay, short story and drama composition items, not to mention the prize for toffee making. In 1928 she left School as the top exhibitioner in the county to enter UCW. Sixty years later she recollected walking on the promenade in 1931 with fellow Ardwynian Ernest George, both having just learnt that they had secured first class honours degrees, she in English and he in French and remarking 'Hooker would have been pleased'. Rhiannon Morgan was indeed indebted to Lloyd Morgan who took over the English teaching in the sixth form and valued his great dedication which included having his pupils come to his house on Saturday mornings for extra tuition.[40]

At the last Governors' meeeting Major Morgan attended, the chairman, the Revd Noah Jones, said that those who had come in contact with the Headmaster, knew how wholeheartedly he had served the School and it would be a source of great satisfaction to him that his efforts and labours had been abundantly blessed with success. 'We are losing one of the best headmasters in Wales. Major Morgan with his high ideals and sterling character has exercised immense influence on the school and indirectly to the town and district.'

The Headmaster's senior colleague Irene Dalley published her tribute in the *Ardwynian*.

> While he was a gifted teacher of his favourite subject- English, he was far more interested in the people he taught. What would Tommy or Mary be best fitted for? What career should he or she be encouraged to follow? How could it be arranged that the pupil derive the greatest advantage from his Ardwyn years? Realizing that physical fitness was the foundation of mental power and alertness, the dinner scheme came into being and physical training for boys and girls was encouraged in every way.
>
> The credit of the House before that of the individual, the honour of the School as restraint of selfishness and incentive to effort, was the ideal set before the pupils, an ideal which made the St. David's Day eisteddfod, the annual sports, and House and School matches such outstanding events in the School year, such undying memories for individual pupils.

Major Lloyd Morgan, in his contribution to the Jubilee Magazine, described what Ardwyn had meant to him.

> As I look back across the eighteen years since I went away, I have a vivid sense of a vital, dynamic quality in the School as I knew it. Whether it came from the sea and the mountains, or was a natural attribute to the Cardi breed, I do not know. But I do know that it was there, and that it was a quality of such power that a Head was not required to lead; instead, he very gladly followed, and at times was swept along by the torrent. I do not doubt that the same vitality persists in the Ardwyn of today, for it seemed to be inherent and indestructible.

D. C. Lewis, M.Sc., Headmaster, 1928–1954.

Chapter Three

THE D C LEWIS YEARS

1928- 1954

The new Head took over at a time when 'the clouds of post-war depresssion were rolling away and nationally, the future was looking brighter.' D C Lewis was quick to take advantage of the opportunities for expansion. Greater emphasis was being laid on scientific education. As the first (and only) science graduate Head of Ardwyn his priority was to improve the science facilities to meet the ever-increasing demands of the CWB higher certificate and the ever-growing number of pupils. Existing rooms were modified and refurbished to provide new physics and biology laboratories -the masters' staff room was lost to them, to be incorporated into the physics laboratory. At the same time, a new dinner kitchen was added to the Central Hall where the diners were accommodated, 'thus reproducing one of the most valuable benefits of public school and residential college life.' Generations of pupils will remember the routine of rapid erection of the trestle tables immediately after morning school by the boys, while the girls laid the tables. In the early days, tables were allocated on a 'House' system under the supervision of a senior pupil. Then, with lunch over, and afternoon school about to start, tables and benches had to be quickly and tidily stacked under the eagle eye of Dan the cleaner, at the same time avoiding his busy brush.

> I remember Miss Williams, the domestic science mistress, struggling through cookery lessons while at the same time, Mrs Burns trying to be invisible went on with the preparation of School lunches. That came to an end however when the dinner kitchen was built between the two yards and the Central Hall became the dining room. Mrs Burns managed alone, coping gallantly with two enormous gas stoves which seemed to be twice her size and she served out lashings of good appetizing food. The trestle tables were covered with pink oil cloth which had a peculiar smell which, oddly enough, I can remember to this day.[41]

These additional facilities, which were ready for use by November 1929 did little to alleviate the overcrowding-there were now 350 pupils in the school. The Headmaster threatened that unless additional classrooms were provided, he would have to refuse admission to about forty children in September 1930. Neighbouring land was purchased from UCW, but after plans had been prepared, permission was deferred by the County authority in view of the proposed re-organisation of secondary education brought about by the raising of the school leaving age to fifteen in April 1931.

No doubt motivated by a letter in the local press drawing attention to the 'deplorable condition' of the School playing fields, the Governors, with the aid of senior pupils, set about finding suitable sites. The problem was highlighted in humorous fashion by 'Peter' of the *Cambrian News*:

> The frozen bodies of two young lads, it is rumoured have been found on Plynlymon... they were thought to be university students until someone noticed the look of intelligence on their faces. The police were able to identify them as County schoolboys who for some weeks had been searching for a new field. The tragedy does not end there, only a few days ago, after a practice game on the present school field, it was found that five boys were missing. Search was made in the usual hiding places but no discovery was made until a member of the search party accidentally stumbled over a human foot protruding from the mud under which the field lies. Frantic digging revealed the bodies of the unfortunate youths.

Within a few weeks, on the proposal of Col. B Taylor Lloyd, who had been coopted on the playfield committee, the Governors applied to the Town Council for the lease of 'raised land between the gas works and the present playing field of an area approximately 200 by 120 yards for the purpose of a recreation field for the Aberystwyth County School.' This was the site of the former Domen Dre, used as allotments. The allotment holders were requested to relinquish their plots by September 1932, by the following January the area had been cleared, ploughed, harrowed and levelled. The advice of Professor Stapledon of the Plant Breeding Station, on seeding was readily given and acted upon.

> At that time Sam Mitchell took a class of boys for a subject called surveying which had such mysterious words as sine, co-sine, tan, and co-tan. On a fine day, instead of solving surveying problems in the classroom we would walk down to the new playing field where, armed with buckets we would line up and walk the length and breadth of the field picking up stones, broken glass and other small sharp objects. We wondered if at the end of term examinations we would have questions on buckets, stones, and glass![42]

By March 1934 the field, which covered four acres, providing a football pitch at the Llanbadarn end a hockey pitch at the Plascrug end with a perfectly level cricket square in between, was ready for use. The 6th June 1934, the *Ardwynian* reported, 'was a red letter day in the history of Ardwyn for it saw the official opening of our long awaited playing field.' Alderman Morris Davies, chairman of the County Council, which had given splendid financial support, cut the green and white ribbon, and led the procession into the field amid the cheers of the onlookers. Alderman Barclay Jenkins, chairman of the Governors who presided, expressed the hope that in the near future a pavilion would be erected.

The accommodation problem was not eased by a Board of Education memorandum requesting the Governors to regulate the admission of pupils to ensure that classes, as far as practicable, were limited to thirty children and should in no circumstances exceed thirty-five. Despite a visit to the Board in London by the Headmaster and architect to discuss building plans, no progress could be made and by 1937 the situation had become so desperate that plans to erect a sectional hut were being considered. One reason for the delay in the provision of extra accommodation was that the notion of building a separate girls' school, which had been first mentioned in 1898, had arisen again. Following a strongly worded letter from the Board of Education instructing the

Governors to limit new pupils to 90 on grounds of safety, unless other accommodation could be found, the director of education arranged for use of the art room in the public library and for PT lessons to be taken in the Buarth Hall and the Urdd building. Under these arrangements, 120 new pupils were admitted in September 1937 but 14 children had to find places in other secondary schools in the county.

Happily there was more progess in providing a much needed gymnasium; two years after making a request, the Governors accepted a tender of £2700 submitted by E Glyn Davies, Aberarth. As the chairman of the Governors stated at the official opening on 27 January 1939, within nine months, the plans had been formulated, approved and the whole building completed and equipped including a boxing ring. The Head said the day was a great one for Ardwyn; he had voiced the need ten years ago when he had been appointed, now they possessed one of the most modern gymnasia in the country. There had never been a greater need for physical education; some had questioned the need for such a building when the College gymnasium was available, those people did not realise that time was important in a school, half an hour was wasted at each visit to the College gymnasium. In the absence of the secretary of the National Fitness Committee for Wales who had been snow-bound *en route*, the Mayor of Aberystwyth, Ald John John performed the opening ceremony. Under the instruction of Miss Arnold and Major Stimson, the girls and boys gave a fine display of gymnastics.

For some, no doubt, there would be disappointment that journeys to the College gym would be no more. The convent girls were often the cause of a late return to lessons. A Jubilee Magazine article recounted-

> Some of us could hardly wait for the bell if the next lesson was P T. Away we went, ramming on caps, dragging our coats, down the boys' way, along Llanbadarn road, across the College playing fields, and into the gymnasium where Arnold was waiting. With what alacrity we obeyed orders! How we ran, jumped and climbed! All the pent up *joie de vivre* unleashed in one half-hour of bliss. To the devotees of her art, there was no one in the world like Miss Arnold, and we had such confidence in her that had she ordered us to jump over Constitution Hill we should have nothing to fear-provided we remembered to bend our knees on landing.[43]

Six months before the gymnasium had been complete, a pavilion, which had been constructed on the playing fields at a cost of £1000 was officially opened. As well as separate changing accommodation with baths and showers for boys and girls, there was a large recreation room with kitchen which would provide after-the match refreshments.

As in all schools, staff were coming and going, some staying for as little as a year, others devoting the rest of their working lives to the School. In 1925 Bessie Arnold came from Bedales School to start a fourteen year spell as physical training mistress, her services shared by the UCW. At the same time Beatrice M Ogden succeeded Ada Nott who had served as botany mistress for five years. Miss Nott however returned to the town in 1930 to marry J Emrys Jones her former colleague. Dr DJ Davies, at the age of 54, resigned in July 1930 to be replaced by Clara Davies, a first class honours graduate of the UCW where she had been athletics champion for three years and vice captain of hockey. William George Rowlands began his long and illustrious career at Ardwyn at this time, appointed after teaching six years at Alexandra Road Boys' School. While still in his teens he had been badly gassed in the trenches in France. A year, later former pupil Violet Jones was appointed teacher of housecraft a post she held for thirty-eight years

Mathematics teacher IG Richards, after one year, left for Llanelly, his native town; D Aneurin Richards took his place but after two years was enticed to the physics department of the College, however not before establishing the boxing club. He spent the war years as a boffin involved in the bouncing bomb team led by Barnes Wallis. His successor E Cyril Richards spent thirteen years teaching physics at the School. Miss Ogden, after six years service during which time 'her department had become one of the most progressive and successful in the country' left for Cardiff High School. A short time later she donated a silver cup for a House competition in rugby. The Headmaster had convinced the Governors that there was a need for teaching commercial subjects. He pointed out that of the seventy or so pupils who left annually, five went on to university, perhaps six entered teaching and the remainder took up a variety of careers often with a commercial bias. Marjorie Akister, a former sixth form pupil was appointed part-time teacher of shorthand and typing; such was the success of the venture, that within a year, her post was made full-time, with additional duties as the Headmaster's secretary.

At the end of the Christmas term 1932, two long serving and venerated members of staff retired. S E Thomas known to all as Lala, had taught English at the School for thirty-three years, having served under three Headmasters. She had been the leading spirit in innumerable social functions and had a vivid recollection of every pupil who had been in the school. Irene Dalley had been appointed senior mistress in 1905 and during her twenty-seven years service had shown that she possessed exceptional powers of tact, wisdom and leadership. She had taught with great success, while in her early days had played a worthy part in many hockey victories for the School. The Old Pupils' Association organised a function the following June when a tennis match was played between the Old Ardwynians and the staff with afternoon tea provided in the Central Hall. Presentations followed, a grandfather clock to Miss Thomas and a silver tea set to Miss Dalley. During the speeches of tribute, the uniqueness of the event was remarked upon in that for the first time in the history of the School there had been a staff retirement.

Two ladies with distinguished academic records were appointed to the vacant posts; Dr Ethel Jones, who would teach French and act as senior mistress and Dr Nellie Rae, German and classics. A future senior mistress of Ardwyn joined the staff in 1934, Gwyneth Mainwaring, was starting her long association with the English department replacing Clara Davies who followed IG Richards to Llanelly to marry him. Charles Clements had spent thirteen years teaching music at the School, and had been musical director of the first five Gilbert and Sullivan operas performed by the School. When he left in 1935, to take up a full-time lectureship at the UCW, the Headmaster placed on record his deep appreciation of his valuable services to the School and his brilliant interpretation of Gilbert and Sullivan opera. 'His departure has served to underline the importance of music in a secondary school' and expressed the hope that a full time teacher would be appointed. Charles Clements may have left but there would still remain his delightful setting of the Lord's Prayer, which was sung at morning assembly.

The D. C. Lewis Years — 1928-1954

A science graduate William Roberts with a music teaching qualification secured the music post. This appointment marked a new policy by the Governors where short-listed applicants were requested to give a demonstration lesson. From 1925, newly appointed teachers to the School served a period of probation of one year, after which time the appointment would be confirmed if the Headmaster's report was favourable. Roberts quickly proved to be a dedicated and enthusiastic teacher, playing an important part, in his first term, in the ambitious production of 'Merrie England.' His handicraft talents were utilised in the woodwork room, where, the Headmaster later reported, 'the boys were inspired to make useful articles.' He hoped that `the pupils would cultivate such a hobby to prevent the wastage of time in reading ill-chosen books and gossiping on street corners.'

Annie Williams, who had replaced Beatrice Ogden, resigned in 1936 to be replaced as biology teacher by John C Ladd, who had a first class degree in botany, and was an accomplished gymnast, athlete and musician. In his short stay at Ardwyn he used his many talents to the full and there was genuine sadness when he left in 1939 to take up a lecturing post at a Birmingham technical college. That sadness turned to grief four years later, when it was learned that he had died on active service with the R A F in North Africa.

After twenty-two years as chemistry teacher, J Emrys Jones, in 1937, reached the compulsory retiring age of sixty and was succeeded by Laurence E Nelson who, a year later, suffered severe and permanent damage to his eyes in a laboratory explosion which ended his teaching career at 30 years of age.

Within a year of the opening of the new dining facilities, the two lady Governors who had been responsible for the running of the dinner scheme were asked to explain certain items which the auditors had queried. After failing to turn up for two meetings at which the dinner scheme accounts were discussed, the two ladies gave their explanations at a special meeting of the Governors and questioned Mrs Burns the cook, in the presence of the Governors. Following further discussion in their absence, the two ladies were asked to resign their position as Governors of the Aberystwyth County School, but refused to comply. The matter was discussed at County Council level where the board of Governors was criticised for its action against the Council-nominated Governors. The Board of Education which had been consulted, considered it was not their affair; the matter seemed to have been dropped, the two Governors concerned, had by now reached the end of their term in office However it was likely that the Governors considered themselves vindicated when, at the end of the autumn term 1930, the dinner accounts, now being administered by the Head, showed a credit balance of £24. 15. 10 as compared with a loss of 9s 5 p at the same period the previous year. The scheme was now flourishing and within a few months the profits were such that the weekly ticket was reduced by 6d to 2s. The Governors recorded their thanks to DC Lewis and to Mrs Burns the cook.

In 1933 the Education Authority introduced new admission regulations and raised school fees to £6 with reductions for children from the same family. Free Places were replaced by Special Places which were awarded on a basis of 70% of the number of entrants the previous year. However, the award was means tested within a weekly income scale from £2 to £4. 10. 0. In addition it was possible to receive a maintenance allowance. For example a Special Placer from a family with an income of less than £2 would have free tuition and £1 maintenance allowance which would be increased to £3 if there were four dependent children. In the case of a family with an income of £4 a week the full fee would be charged but if there were four dependent children only half the fee would be payable. Free tuition would not be granted to any pupil obtaining less than half marks in the examination; maintenance allowances were granted only to pupils who were remitted the whole fee. Pupils who gained the school certificate qualification and were pursuing an advanced course would be granted a remission of £2 per annum. It must have been a major exercise for RJ Williams the Clerk to the Governors to process all the applications for allowances and obtaining salary details from employers. Although there were provisions in the new regulations for cases of extreme hardship there were many instances of a parent removing a child from the School for reasons of financial stress despite having given an undertaking that the child would remain for four years. Long before it became statutory the Governors provided free dinners for those families in real need. With the gradual development of bus services, fewer country pupils were boarding in town so the Governors gave a travelling allowances even to the extent of giving 6d a week to a pupil from New Cross who had to use his bicycle to travel to the School, there being no bus service.

In 1931 Professor Edward Edwards started his second term as chairman of Governors. He had retired from the chair of history at the UCW in 1930 but retained the Vice-Principalship, a post he held from 1924 to 1932. His old adversary on the Governing board, Ald. C M Williams, had died in 1928 having served as a Governor continuously from 1897, the second year of the School.

One of the first tasks of Vice-Principal Edwards was to offer congratulations on the excellence of the report of the full inspection of 1930 which stated 'the general tone of the School was of a high standard.' H M Inspectors were impressed by the organisation throughout the school and in that respect paid tribute to the Headmaster. The chairman also had to inform the teaching staff that, as a consequence of the national government's financial cuts, a reduction in the Board of Education grant, necessitated a 10% reduction in their salaries. Initially it was for two years but in 1934 it was changed to a 5% cut with full salary restored in 1935.

Having successfully led the campaign for a new playing field Prof Edward Edwards did not live to see its official opening. When he died in September 1933 there was genuine sadness throughout the area. He had given long and dedicated service to the School and many contentious issues had been overcome by his wise counsel and good humour. Now led by Barclay Jenkins, the Governors deliberated at length on the proposed amendments to the Intermediate and Technical Education Fund, last altered in 1912. It was agreed to support the changes proposed by the County Council but a strong protest was made that the Aberystwyth Town Council was denied representation on the Ardwyn Governing Board under the new scheme. The Board of Education duly endorsed the proposals, giving their seal of approval in January 1935, regretting it had been unable to adopt the modifications proposed by the Governors. The Headmaster outlined the effect of the 1935 Scheme:

Throughout the early period, the funds available for running the Schoool were never adequate for the purpose, and every item of expenditure had to be weighed up carefully. As the School increased, it became obvious that a more secure financial background would have to be provided, and a new scheme, sealed in 1935, arranged for the complete maintenance of the School by the County Council. The School Governors became a local governing body appointed by the County Council, and therefore a sub-committee of the County Education Committee, but still possessing the right to appoint its Clerk, the Headmaster and staff. The Governing Body still consisted of twelve members, at least two of whom must be women; eight must be county councillors and four (of whom one is appointed from the staff of the University College of Wales) are not to be members of the County Council.[44]

Some months before the new scheme came into operation, a sub-committee appointed to consider teaching in the School, recommended that a letter be sent to certain members of staff, stating that the Governors were dissatisfied with their teaching. The Governors decided to refer back the proposal which was later rescinded in favour of new recommendations which were agreed upon and circulated to the staff:

1. The retiring age for teachers at the School be 60 years.

2. The Governors being impressed by the growing importance of the scientific studies in a technical and industrial world, would lay stress upon the importance of the efficient and accurate teaching in the various departments of science.

3. In order, on the other hand, that the prevailing scientific bias may not lead to too narrow specialisation, it is desirable on general educational grounds that the Arts subjects should be taught in such way as to secure their cultural effects.

4. That the Governors would urge all teachers to take every available opportunity of attending the refresher or summer courses that are held year by year.

This advice had the hallmark of a science qualified Headmaster anxious that his pupils should be given every chance in the increasingly important and changing world of science. Within a year of the appointment of D C Lewis, the Governors had interviewed a long serving member of the science teaching staff and demanded that his teaching improve.

When the Articles of Government for the revised scheme were issued the Education Authority used the name 'Ardwyn County School' for the first time -so now it was official. Ald Barclay Jenkins continued as chairman of the Governors who included Prof CR Chapple for the first time. Much of their work in the late Thirties was concerned with obtaining extra classroom accommodation for the rapidly increasing numbers. In 1935 the Education Committee cancelled approved expenditure of £10,000 for additional classrooms, in order to build a girls' school at Aberystwyth at a cost of £20,000, a proposal which had not been discussed by the Governors. By 1937 a site had been reserved on Penglais for the new development but with the outbreak of war and changes in the

The Staff, 1946.
L. H. Thomas, B. Morgan, A. K. Vaughan, M. Bowen, I. L. Davies, W. B. Davies, T. Evans,
R. J. Lloyd, A. G. Davies, S. Mitchell, G. Mainwaring, M. T. Chapple, D. G. Price,
H. F. Stimson.
V. Jones, E. E. Forster, I. P. Davies, Dr. E. Jones, D. C. Lewis (Head); T. J. James,
D. H. Jenkins, W. G. Rowlands, E. C. Richards.

educational system in 1945, it was never built; the new classrooms were also delayed until 1951. The Governors were also concerned with such mundane matters as granting £30 for the purchase of the first School wireless, £30 for a greenhouse, and presenting each pupil with a paperknife to mark the Coronation of King George VI. They also allowed the spending of £5 to decorate the outside of the School with bunting and flags because the School could be seen from the National Library where on 16 July 1937 the King and Queen were opening the new central block. They supported the action of the Headmaster in suspending two boys for defacing the School building and resolved that they would not return until the parents paid 10/6, the cost of cleaning. A half day holiday was granted on 4 May 1938 so the pupils could watch Glamorgan County Cricket Club play locally. A complaint by the North Cardiganshire Temperance Association regarding the behaviour of the old pupils at their Boxing Day re-union in the School was not substantiated.

In contrast to his predecessor, D C Lewis considered examinations to be essential, there was no other way to assess the standard of work and attainment. Employers were demanding matriculation, not just a school certificate. In his prize day speeches he always summarised the C W B results and gained great satisfaction in seeing higher and school certificate results gain in quantity and quality year after year. The 1929 school certificate results showed that Marjorie Penwill had gained distinctions in all six subjects sat. During the 1930 inspection the examiners asked to meet her; she recollected serving coffee to them at their morning break. She later studied at the London (Royal Free Hospital) School of Medicine for Women, which had been founded 'with hard

The D. C. Lewis Years — 1928-1954

work and persistence against opposition and prejudice from men, so that women could have a medical education'. Her studies were aided by a Kitchener scholarship because her father had been killed in the Great War. The first in a series of Ardwyn girls who qualified as doctors was Elizabeth Catherine Davies of Llanddewi-brefi who qualified in 1919, her sister Madge was probably Ardwyn's first woman dentist. Angharad Hughes qualified in 1929, followed by Marjorie Penwill 1936, Miriam Davies 1939 and Mary Fleure in 1940.

There was particular pride in the achievement of Miriam Davies who, in 1931, became the first Cardiganshire pupil to gain a State scholarship. This honour was repeated in 1936 by Lillian Williams with a reserve award to Nancy Rees and again in 1939 when a brilliant three distinctions took Gareth Wyn Evans to Cambridge to pursue an illustrious career. In the ten years leading up to the start of the war, Ardwyn pupils gained twenty UCW entrance scholarships, including, on four occasions, the most valuable awards. In his 1930 report, the Headmaster expressed regret that because of overcrowding, of the 130 who had qualified for entry by examination, only 98 pupils could be admitted. With the record number of 367 pupils on the roll, it meant crowding 33 pupils into classrooms which were never designed for that number.

At a time of heavy unemployment, the question of careers for pupils had become especially serious. DC Lewis was instumental in setting up a joint committee with the Aberystwyth Chamber of Trade to provide leavers with suitable opportunities for useful service and to discuss the necessary qualifications for various occupations. He praised the local council for providing career opportunities-pupils had taken up apprenticeships in the health, library and accountancy departments. The Headmaster took great pains to make the public at large aware of the working of his School. He explained that the School was divided into three sections each extending over a period of two years. Every pupil received the same tuition and was introduced to all the subjects in the curriculum during the first two years. At the end of this period, particular aptitudes were beginning to emerge so that choices could be made at the start of the middle stage. Fewer subjects were studied with forms biased towards science, language or English subjects, preserving a fair balance with the school certificate to be taken at the end and possible matriculation which was the first step towards a university degree. The third stage was devoted to preparing for the higher certificate where the pupil specialised in three subjects with a view to university, the Civil Service and some of the professions. The Head was of the view that the higher certificate was too difficult for the average pupil and did not carry sufficient vocational weight in proportion to the work done.

In the first eight years of D C Lewis' stewardship, the school numbers had risen from 320 to 420. To satisfy the regulation of class size, a four-form entry was established in 1937 bringing a record total of 439 pupils. The increase served to highlight the accommodation problem; the School contained over one-third of all the secondary school children in the county. The Head thought that they deserved better treatment in the matter of accommodation and believed that if pupils were accustomed to primitive conditions during the most impressionable period of their training, they could not be expected to maintain the highest standards of civilised life in their adult careers. His report in 1937 gave another glimpse of his educational philosophy when he said that his main task was to train the leaders of the next generation so that they could fulfil their duties efficiently in their chosen vocations, 'their innate abilities must be developed to the utmost so that they can live full cultured lives in the community.' With an eye to the future and the county reorganisation changes, he countered the criticism that their training was too academic for any except those proceeding to university, by listing the subjects taught and pointing out that many were of a practical nature although metalwork and engineering were important omissions. Giving his views on a further raising of the school leaving age,

> The best traditions of secondary education have been built on the principle of voluntary attendance. The unwilling pupil is a serious problem at all stages and a real menace to progress in the higher forms. If compulsory attendance introduces a number of this type of pupil, it will cause serious damage to these traditions.

Welcoming the fall in the average age of admission to twelve years, DC Lewis gave several reasons in favour of early entry. Only the brightest pupils were able to secure a good certificate in four years, a 'year in hand' allowed a pupil to consolidate at the school certificate stage. For entry into the Civil Service it was essential to have attained school certificate standard by the age of sixteen. In the case of the higher certificate, an extra year was even more beneficial. It was at this stage that the best opportunities became available-State scholarships, university scholarships, and the higher branches of the Civil Service. In answer to an educationalist who quoted examples from a local elementary school showing that pupils who had entered at eleven 'had done nothing' while those who had entered at thirteen 'had done well', the Headmaster produced figures from his records which totally contradicted this assertion; he was convinced that entry before the age of twelve years was essential.

In his report to the 1939 Prize Day audience, the Headmaster, for the first time, gave his views on the proposed girls' school. The long awaited Spens report on the future of secondary education had been issued after five years of deliberation. DC Lewis was proud to confirm that most of the recommmendations had been in operation at Ardwyn for many years. However the report had also stated that great importance should be given to the establishment of technical schools, equal in status but quite distinct from the secondary school. In his opinion, Aberystwyth was favourably placed for such a school; the Governors had long realised that the majority of pupils went into business or industry and had adapted the curriculum accordingly. He had no hesitation in saying that a technical school was of prime necessity in the county. With five secondary schools of the so-called academic or grammar type already established, it was proposed to erect another to cater for the girls. With the Spens recommendations, the situation had been altered drastically.

> There are many educationalists who believe sincerely that separate schools are better than co-educational ones;there are many who believe the reverse. My own opinions agree with the latter because co-education provides fuller experiences under more natural conditions and is almost a necessity in this era of small families. Concerning the special conditions of this district, with a natural intake of no more than 90 new pupils annually, I do not believe that any educationalist with experience of secondary schools will claim that two separate-sex schools of about 200 pupils can provide bet-

ter educational facilities than a co-educational one of 400 pupils. In many instances the experience of several similar towns is the opposite. The financial resources of this county are limited and I suggest that the matter of providing a technical school should be given the most thorough consideration before embarking on the present scheme. The one would undoubtedly advance the vocational welfare of the district while the other might easily take away some of the facilties we already possess.

Prize days invariably attracted a member of the clergy or an academic as guest speaker. In 1930, for the first time, an industrialist, D Owen Evans a director of Imperial Chemical Industries took the platform and in his address urged all parents to give their children the best education they could afford, as secondary and higher education were absolute necessities. He could see that they were doing what was right for the Welsh language but urged them 'to receive a taste' of foreign languages which together with a mastery of English was essential for progress in industry and commerce. Having heard the Headmaster in his speech say that a House cup for cricket was needed, Owen Evans responded by promising to remedy the deficiency. The following year the Bishop of St Davids, who, thirty-nine years previously, had been a curate at St Michael's Church, hoped that the the education they were receiving would produce a well trained mind that could think, observe and draw its own conclusions. Dr Prosser was saddened that the curse of gambling had grown in Britain because people did not know what to do with their leisure, much of which had been brought about by world-wide unemployment. He thought there was a need for the pupils to distinguish between leisure and idleness.

Ifan ap Owen Edwards, founder of the Welsh League of Youth- Yr Urdd, a member of the extra-mural staff at the UCW, emphasised the importance of retaining a love of one's country and a knowledge of its language 'which would open the way into wonderful realms of literature which was their heritage.'

Since its formation the School had never failed to attract the principal of the UCW to its prize day platform; in 1934, the year he was appointed, Ifor L Evans gave his address from the stage of the newly opened Municipal Hall later named the King's Hall which was the venue for all subsequent prize days, operas and eisteddfodau. Principal Evans spoke of the importance of the Welsh language and the danger of a generation growing up in Wales 'who would be foreigners in their own land as far as the language question was concerned.' He advised that success at examinations should be thought of as qualifying for something to come afterwards. So many Welsh students were compelled to seek posts in England and it was important that they in Wales kept their product well up to standard.

Principal Thomas Lewis of the Memorial College, Brecon said that for the past forty years the needs of the majority of pupils had been ignored 'we act on the principle that the pupil is made for the curriculum and not the curriculum for the pupil.' He was for free compulsory secondary education for all but not the secondary education provided by the intermediate schools; it was their duty to provide a varied curriculum to meet the diverse requirements. 'In that way pupils would be educated so they might fill a place and play a part in the life of the community, whether it be some humble occupation or some exhalted profession.'

Former pupil Ernest Evans, now MP for the Welsh Universities and a King's Counsel, was the guest speaker in 1939 as he had been ten years earlier. He referred to the Spens report with its emphasis on vocational education and thought that it had particular importance for rural areas like Cardiganshire. There was a great need to draw people to the rural areas and to engage more people in agricultural pursuits. 'We are constantly reminded these days of the perils which war will bring us. One of the greatest dangers would arise from the fact that sufficient use is not made of the land.'

With the stongest encouragement from the Headmaster, sport in Ardwyn flourished during the Thirties, certainly the variety of athletic activities proliferated to a level which few schools could emulate. The standard of soccer in particular, reached an eminence which perhaps few schools in Wales could match. The much celebrated eclipse of the formidable Towyn School soccer team in 1928 was repeated the following season. Reinforced by a very talented footballer from the south Wales valleys, Willie Price, who in the fifteen matches he played that season, scored 46 goals; his most memorable was described in the *Ardwynian*...

> the centre was neatly trapped by Price, who immediately dribbled past two defenders and ultimately placed the ball out of the goalkeeper's reach into the net. It was the best goal scored by the School all season and will be remembered by all who saw it, as the movement which brought our first and well-deserved victory on the Towyn ground.

The writer added 'victories over Towyn in the past two years would surely stop the talk of soccer giving way to rugger at Ardwyn.' After the opening game the following season Price left for Australia with his family who were emigrating, but not before scoring two goals in the vital match with Towyn. Some years later, William Ellis, an Ardwynian seafarer, met him by chance in New South Wales and wrote in the *Ardwynian* that Willie Price had represented N S W and Australia in soccer and toured New Zealand with the Australian XI. He had graduated from the University of Sydney and taught English and history at a high school in N S W.

In the 1930-31 season under the captaincy of John Edwards who was also head boy, Towyn were beaten 7-6 at home. The distinction of completing the 'double' over Towyn fell to the 1933-34 side, playing on the newly completed playing fields for the first time; nine of their twelve matches were won and averaged five goals per match. Perhaps the incentive for this fine effort came from the Head's promise to award 'caps' to regular players. The team photograph of that year shows that promises were kept; 'caps' continued to be awarded until war-time restrictions caused them to be replaced by badges.

There must have been great expectations when the undefeated team of 1935-36 took the field at Llandyssul for their last game of the season; played 11, won 9 drawn 1, was their record which included a 5-0 defeat of their hosts earlier in the season. It was not to be, unaccountably they lost, 'although it must be said that the goalkeeper had been blinded by the sun on one occasion and the home goal appeared to bear a charmed life.' Nevertheless they must have been consoled in the knowledge that the 35-36 season had been the best for Ardwyn to date, despite outstanding players like Bill Bowen, George Garner and Tommy Nepaulin Jones having left School during the season. It was a sad coincidence that three members of that team lost their lives in the war; Dan Lewis,

The D. C. Lewis Years — 1928-1954

James Worrell Williams and Enoch Williams. Playing for his third successive season Enoch Williams captained a largely untried team the following year, which for the first time included a 14 year old star of the future- Eddie Ellis, and Howard Williams the goal keeper, who from 1938 to 1951 did the same job for the Town team. That side lost just one game in fifteen, at home to Llandyssul, who seemed to have taken the place of Towyn as the bogey team. The captain scored twenty-one goals and the side averaged 6. 6 goals per game.

In the five years which Eddie Ellis played for the soccer XI, from 1936 to 1941, the team achieved a greatness which was never equalled. In that period, of sixty-eight matches played only six were lost with 401 goals scored. From 1939, because of the growth of rugby, soccer was confined to one term, with of course, fewer games played. In his last year in School, and in his third season as captain, Ellis' team won the ten games played, scoring 70 goals. In the second game of the season Ellis' seventh goal of seven scored by him, in an 18 -1 drubbing of Aberayron, was his hundredth for Ardwyn. He scored a further 19 goals before a cartilage injury rendered him unfit for the rest of the season. Alwyn 'Chick' Evans was another accomplished player in the team, he went on to play professional soccer for Millwall and Leyton Orient. The captain's report of the 1941 soccer season in the *Ardwynian*, gave a glimpse of the fine literary style which was shown in his acclaimed publications of later years.

> The Ardwyn soccer team has once again proved supreme in Mid-Wales secondary school football. This wonderful record has been due, in no small part to the valuable advice and enthusiasm of Mr EG Davies and in addition, we must pay tribute to the groundsman, Mr Lewis, in keeping the field in wonderful playing condition.
>
> Despite the loss of eight of last year's team, Ardwyn has won every one of the ten matches played. The attack, which this year has been of outstanding merit, has discarded the conventional mode of attack via the wings. Success has been the result of skilful interplay by the forwards and quick bursts through the middle. Allied to this elasticity of attack, School also found a rock-like defence. It must be remembered that the goal-scorer is not all- important, goals are the result of team play.

While the game of soccer prospered in the Thirties, rugby struggled to gain a foothold under what were difficult circumstances. Aberystwyth was traditionally a soccer stronghold and very few schools in the district had adopted the oval ball game at that time. As previously mentioned Lloyd Morgan the former Head was an adherent, but little progress had been made. The advent of a House competition in 1932 for the newly donated Ogden cup prompted a surge of interest, the first holders being Arfon. In the 1934-35 season a team captained by Ifan P Davis seemed to have played just one game- against Dolgelley who had taken up the rugby code three years previously. The *Ardwynian* reported 'the team had given a magnificent exhibition, playing, if not with great skill, with a tenacity of purpose which bodes well for the future of rugby at Ardwyn.' An extract from the *Liverpool Post* was also included 'this was Ardwyn School's first game of rugby and it has the making of a good team. It is hoped that they will devote all their time and energy to one game.' Problems with the offside law, prompted the School Magazine to explain the circumstances when a player was not offside. With staff members, Sam Mitchell and George Rowlands taking an interest, progress was steadily made although few games were won. The biology master John Ladd, a former front row forward in the College pack, being only a few years older than the senior members of the team, was a great asset as an active coach. The correspondent in the Magazine thought that 'rugby was a game of science, which develops the finer points of a boy's character. Even the clumsiest of fellows can do something because the only things needed are what is called grit and fighting spirit.' So much for rugby being a scientific game! There were signs of an improvement in their fortunes when, in January 1937 under Jim Pinsent's captaincy, a win was recorded against a school XV for the first time- despite being two players short due to a misunderstanding, Llandrindod were overcome. The great breakthrough came in the 1938-39 season as Gwilym Williams explained in the *Ardwynian*.

> The division of the football season into a term of soccer followed by a term of rugby, enabled us to gain the support of the soccer players who greatly strengthened the back line. Another feature was the speed and stubbornness of our forwards, who though smaller and lighter than our opponents, always managed to hold their own in the scrums and in the loose play.
> The last, but no means least, reason for our success was the participation of Mr R J Lloyd during the practices and in match play, resulting in our achieving a sense of security and confidence which before was lacking.

Under the captaincy of Peter Joynson, more points were scored and fewer conceded than in previous years but the smallness of the pack was a great handicap particularly against a Town XV which seemed to be the first occasion such a team had taken the field. The captain and vice-captain of the 1940 School XV- Wynne Owen and Ken Allen together with DR Davies, Ivor (Bush) Williams, and Ivor Thomas played a vital part in the formation of the Aberystwyth Rugby Football Club in 1947. In common with the Town soccer club, the rugby club had reason to be grateful for the stream of young well-trained sportsmen joining their ranks from Ardwyn. Following the severe winter of 1940 when most rugby games were called-off, matches were moved to the autumn term, with the soccer team having to put up with the arctic conditions prevalent in the Easter term. The 1940-41 season proved to be the best on record although Wycliffe College, evacuated to the district, proved to be too strong. Cardigan were defeated for the first time, thanks to the educated foot of a player more used to kicking a round ball. In the last minute of the game ' an indisputable dropped goal' by Eddie Ellis won the game for Ardwyn. Later in the term came the double over their great rivals and defeats for Dolgelley and the Old Boys.

In 1929, having replaced hockey as the winter game for the girls, the newly formed netball team was reported to 'have great enthusiasm for the game using every free moment to practice on the courts.'

> In my third year I realised an ambition when I became a member of the hockey team. My excitement however was short lived, for after a rather inglorious season it was decided that perhaps after all netball was more beneficial. And what a fine game it turned out to be; it offered such splendid freedom of movement; the rhythmic catching and throwing was so exhilarating and all those swift little dodges that delivered the ball safely into your shooter's hands. We never regretted the change.[45]

The D. C. Lewis Years — 1928-1954

Soccer XI, 1928-29 - the first to win at Towyn. Captain: George Williams. W. I. Price, seated second on right, later played for Australia.

Soccer XI, 1931–32. Captain: John Lewis.

Soccer XI, 1938–39. Captain: Eddie Ellis.

There seemed to be no disillusionment following a heavy defeat at the hands of Dr Williams' School in the first game played. From the outset there was a shortage of opposition; as many as six matches a season were played against College VIIs providing ideal training against more mature players. Progress was rapid; under the captaincy of Mary de Lloyd, doubles were gained over the College first VII, and Dr Williams' School. A match was won at Llandyssul in such terrible weather conditions that the Llandyssul girls wore caps, macintoshes and wellingtons. Later in the decade the fixture list was expanded to take in the Convent, Barmouth, Cardigan and in 1940, Tregaron were played for the first time, - in the gymnasium because of bad weather. Chatelard, a school evacuated to the area, and the Chelsea PT college were also new opponents. Many former players found places in the College VII so it was some consolation to find, that when beaten by the students, as many as four of their seven players were ex-Ardwynians.

After hockey was resumed in 1935, the young and inexperienced teams won few matches in the early years, but were very appreciative of their own fine playing field particularly when away matches 'were played on quagmires' often soccer pitches. Under the captaincy of Meg Lewis, in the 1938-39 season half the matches were won. By now Machynlleth had become their great rivals; the *Ardwynian* generously reported 'Machynlleth again showed us how to play hockey, although they have no playing field. They did most of the attacking and scored two goals before half time enough to win them the game.'

Playing the Chelsea students on the sands at Borth was a new experience but the 1940-41 XI led by Nest Morgan, with eight of the previous year's team available, were able to defeat all the school teams they met, losing only to the College first eleven and the Old Girls.

A small band of enthusiasts ensured that cricket played an important part in the sporting life of Ardwyn. With the donation of a House cricket cup, interest increased to such an extent that arch rivals Towyn were defeated in 1930. The claim that this was another 'first' was later corrected after *The Ystwythian* for 1909 had been consulted; however this was the first victory on Towyn soil. The pitch problem was apparently solved by a do-it-yourself effort by the captain Herman Benson. 'Due to the untiring efforts of Benson, the School can now boast a respectable pitch on which the home matches may be played.' On the field he had great help from John Edwards and T Henry Edwards, who respectively topped the batting and bowling averages. Herman Benson who was also the School goalkeeper, lost his life in the war. In the first match played on the new School fields in 1934, against Eglwysfach, Gwyn Pryse Howell 'was virtually unplayable' taking six wickets for three runs. The following year, in a side led by Ifan P Davis, Hefin Thomas, in scoring 73 not out broke the existing record. The 1936 season turned out to be a memorable one in that Towyn were beaten twice, a feat never before achieved. A member of that team and an accomplished batsman, Jim Morgan of Talybont, remembered those victories with some pride and also recalled doing the hard work of preparing the cricket square, two years earlier, under the supervision of Sam Mitchell.

Making his debut for the team at fourteen years of age was Jim Pinsent; nurtured by Dewi Ellis who held the captaincy for two years, Pinsent became a a cricketing legend

The D. C. Lewis Years — 1928-1954

in the four years he played. Inspirational leadership from skipper Ken Wilkinson saw the 1938 team undefeated in the fifteen matches played including a double over Towyn. Wilkinson, who lost his life on active service, was top batsman and bowler. The Magazine report paid tribute to Mr Royle, for the dedicated care he took in preparing the wicket in his job as groundsman and to his wife for preparing the cricket teas in the newly opened pavilion. In the same account the captain elect for the 1939 season Bob Williams, aware that only five old caps would be available, appealed for cricketers to start training during the Easter vacation. Another memorable season resulted, losing just one game, to the YMCA. Vice-captain Jim Pinsent, with scores of 76 not out and 89 smashed the previous record score and with Bob Williams established an opening partnership record of 120 against Cardigan, both batsmen having had little sleep the previous night due to the School trip to Dublin! For these achievements Pinsent was presented with a Sutcliffe bat by the *News Chronicle*. By the end of the season, his last for the School before taking up veterinary training, he had recorded his fiftieth 'victim' as wicket-keeper. He had also the pleasure of seeing younger brother Roy establishing himself in the team.

> Cricket showed a steady improvement between 1935 and 1939 and into the new decade. The new field and pavilion made a great difference. Many of the schools we played had rudimentary pitches-some quite lethal. It is interesting to read the scorebooks of the day and realise that a score in the twenties could be a winning one. The Ardwyn wicket however was a fine one producing many high scores. Attitudes to the game also improved with a succession of disciplinarian captains improving standards of dress and cricketing behaviour generally. Even the score books reflect these changes-the earlier ones a garbled mess with sheets erased so that they could be used a second or third time. There were some very fine performances but the team of 1938 led by Ken Wilkinson, an elegant batsman and genuine slow off-spinner, was undefeated. Rhys Jones a slow left arm bowler took nine wickets for six runs in 5. 5 overs against the Theological College on the School field. I wonder if this performance has ever been excelled ?[46]

Tennis also increased in popularity during the Thirties; from the long standing mixed doubles matches played against Aberayron there developed the girls' team with fixtures against Dr Williams' School, Towyn, the Convent and College teams. A boys' team formed later found it difficult to find opposition. The mixed doubles teams appeared to have had the greatest success and in 1937 won all their games, including a first victory over Cardigan. The first string of Meg Lewis and John Middlehurst did not lose a match all season. On one occasion the team was strengthened by the inclusion of the Headmaster and physics master IG Richards but still had to acknowledge defeat at the hands of the College staff.

> Fifty years after leaving Ardwyn, my memories are of a school with high academic ambitions for its pupils. I have happy memories of the athletic side-my father doubled up as science and sports master- and remember modest successes rather than failures. The tennis team, of which I was a proud member, was regarded as wimpish by the cricketers but some of them who were less than enthusiastic could be seen swimming in the Rheidol instead of gracing the cricket field.[47]

In very many ways the School was fortunate to be situated in a town with a university college, with use of its facilities and with many of the members of the College staff well disposed towards the School. In the genial Vice-Principal Edward Edwards they had a great supporter and he, with Dr E A Lewis, long-serving chairman of the college athletic board, were invariably present at the athletic sports held annually on the Vicarage fields from 1920 to 1933 until the new School playing field came into use. The two college professors were later joined as judges by JC Rea, Jack Garner, and B Taylor Lloyd. These three well known local sportsmen, together with Dr Abraham Thomas, and David Evans, the jeweller, provided in turn, the victor and victrix ludorum medals for the top boy and girl athlete.

George Williams, of the boatbuilding family, who captained the soccer team for two years was the premier boy athlete for the same two years in 1929 and 1930; he also was the winner of the cross-country race which, at that time was held a few days before the sports, with points gained contributing to the competition for the Nanteos House athletic cup. Needless to say, with Williams a member of Gwynedd, that House took the cup in 1929 and 1930.

Leslie Thomas, another noted footballer won the cross--country race three years out of four and the victor ludorum twice, sharing it on one occasion with another fine athlete Noel Butler. Butler spent only two years in the School as a pupil but many more as a teacher; he took the victor ludorum twice and his record for the 220 yards and 440 yards events stood for fifteen and seventeen years respectively. When at the UCW, in 1939 he broke the record for the 100 yards which had stood since 1881; he ran it in 10 seconds. At School Noel was never able to beat his great friend and sprint rival David Sansbury in the 100 yards. Sansbury's time of 10. 8 seconds clocked in 1932 stood for ten years. His fine performances on the track were equalled by his accomplishments in the operas where he took a principal role in four productions.

Derek Butler, younger brother of Noel, was another all-rounder; he was victor ludorum in 1934 in the first sports day held on the new field. He also represented the School at soccer, rugby, tennis, was a prominent member of the boxing and swimming clubs, holder of the Stimson gymnastic cup in 1934 and an opera principal. In addition to the sprint race records established during this period, the cricket ball throw was improved by Dewi Wright over a three year period to over 95 yds in 1938, a record which stood until 1950; the mile time of 5 minutes 10 seconds established by Ifan P Davis in 1935 was not bettered until 1960; it was improved again in 1967 when Ifan's son Gary achieved the time of 4 minutes 26 seconds. Ifan was victor ludorum in 1935 as well as being captain of rugby, and cricket and soccer vice-captain. Another capable games player R Killin Roberts was victor ludorum in 1938 and 1939; he was also the recipient of the first of twelve silver medals donated by W Adler a local hairdresser, for the winner of the senior cross-country race. The donor had previously provided the silver cups for House competition in gymnastics and cross-country as a token of his gratitude for the benefits his son Gershon had received at the School.

> I soon found out that I had some talent for cross-country running and some luck too! Luck at finding the railway crossing gates at Llanbadarn were just closing when I passed through, giving me a nice little lead. Now well ahead around the Pendinas

The D. C. Lewis Years — 1928-1954

VIth Gym Class 1933.

monument, across the Rheidol and home ahead of the favourite and last year's winner. The following year my brother and I performed the double, winning the junior and senior races.[48]

The girls too had their outstanding athletes, the victrix ludorum was awarded twice to Gwen Davies and between 1934 and 1938 Vera Jones the netball captain claimed it three times and Pegi Davies twice.

Another activity which flourished in the Thirties was gymnastics. Under the expert instruction of Bessie Arnold and H F Stimson very high standards were achieved individually and in House competitions. The Magazine of July 1938 welcomed a new feature-the boys' gymnastic team competition; the girls' event had been long established. Starting in 1929 and continuing for the remainder of his tenure as physical training instructor Major Stimson selected a boys' gymnastic champion. The first holders of the Stimson cup, were Hywel Ellis and Dick de Lloyd. In the same year de Lloyd equalled his own course record of 67 at the local golf club in winning the Fossett Roberts cup and three years later represented Wales in an amateur golf match at St Andrew's while a dental student. Gym champion in 1930 was John Lewis, who also captained the 1931 soccer XI. After graduating at the UCW, John undertook a course in physical education in Denmark and with fellow Ardwynian Gershon Adler represented Wales at a gymnastic festival in Sweden in July 1939. They, like many other disciples of Arnold and Stimson, joined the teaching profession, teaching their degree subject and physical education and grateful for the opportunities the School had provided.

> Junior boys were taught by Miss Arnold to whom I am personally grateful, for it was due to her enthusisatic teaching that I became interested in practical gymnastics. As one passed into the senior forms, Major Stimson took over and on occasions, lessons in the College gymnasium, would overlap with the training sessions of the college gymnastic club. This allowed us to see and imitate advanced agility exercises so that Ardwyn always had a competent gymnastic team. Periodically, boys were selected to join the College team to give demonstrations in south Wales schools.
>
> The School field was on the site of the present rugby club ground. At that time it was low-lying, badly drained with an uneven surface, becoming a quagmire after a few showers. Form games were not a regular feature of the timetable and it was necessary for the form captain to approach the Headmaster for permission for time off for games. If granted, after the first period in the afternoon, weather permitting, the boys would assemble in the yard to be marched down by Mr Sam Mitchell to the field via the cemetery. The changing room consisted of a Nissen hut which was never cleaned or locked so was it occasionally occupied by gentlemen of the road. As it was never known in advance that there would be a games lesson, country boys would not have their kit but the town boys were able to go home at lunch time and return prepared for the afternoon activity. In the absence of showers, boys returned home covered in evil-smelling mud.
>
> For inter-school matches, classrooms were used for changing, hot water being provided from the domestic science room where the cookery mistress and senior girls were preparing tea for the teams. On reflection one realises the discourtesy we dis-

played in rushing back to School from the muddy field to make sure of getting a bowl of hot water, leaving our visitors to fend for themselves. Matches were refereed by the much loved and respected Sam Mitchell attired in navy blue suit and brown trilby and, if raining, a heavy fawn raincoat.

Cricket, played on the School field, was hazardous, the wicket consisting of a coconut matting laid down on the irregular surface. Scores were low and bowling figures such as eight wicket for ten runs were common place and mainly attributable to the state of the pitch.

In the summer term, swimming lessons took place in the public baths in Bath Street, each pupil paying a few pence entrance fee. Sea water was pumped in and replaced fortnightly; fresh for a few days but decidedly uninviting by the end of the first week.

In the early Thirties, the cross-country race was run from the level crossing in Plascrug following the Lein Fach to Llanbadarn, via Penybont bridge to Penparcau, around the Pen Dinas monument, down through the fields and across the main road to wade through the river Rheidol to the finish at Plascrug. One wondered whether the organiser had walked the course considering the hazards such as the river in flood and crossing a main road.

The organisation of games left much to be desired but one appreciated the efforts of the staff, unqualified in physical education who gave of their best to provide physical activities.[49]

In the 'Ardwynian Association' newsletter of Spring 1991, John Lewis attempted to put the School Yell into words:-

> Arbro, Arbro,
> Countio, countio,
> Arbro, Arbro,
> Countio, countio,
> Vardardee, vardardee,
> Nawr te, Nawr te,
> Hip, hip, hurrah,
> Hip, hip, hurrah,
> HOORAH

He conceded that the spelling was open to correction but hoped that it conveyed the true pronuciation. Ardwynians of the Forties and onwards may be surprised to learn that there was a School Yell or haka. It obviously fell into disuse.

An unhappy consequence of a gymnastic display in 1936 was highlighted by the Headmaster writing in his usual 'Ardwyniana' section of the School magazine

> The Flag has always been the rallying point for all organisations. Countless tales of heroism are related in defence of the flags of regiments, battleships, etc. The loss of our School flag by the gymnastic party at the Royal Welsh Show is therefore unaccountable. After much searching, we have been compelled to acknowledge its loss and to arrange for making a new one. Thanks to the skill and perseverance of Miss Akister,

1939 Cricket Team, Bob Williams, captain.

Rugby XV 1945–46, Wynford Thomas, captain.

Prefects 1939–40.

that loss has been made good and Ardwyn now possesses a flag of which we are really proud. In addition to the School badge, it contains a shield quartered into emblems representing the four Houses. It is unthinkable that our boys will ever desert this flag under any circumstances.

The new flag was carefully preserved, indeed former pupils will probably remember its only use was to decorate the table on the eisteddfod stage. Perhaps that explains its survival to the present day.

Probably unique for a secondary school was the formation in 1938 of a School rowing club. A former pupil Dr Peter Edwards, was chief guest at the second annual dinner of the Old Ardwynians' Association at the Queen's Hotel in 1938. In a provocative address, Dr Edwards, who was superintendent of a sanitorium in Shropshire, spoke of his time at the School thirty one years previously and, following a recent visit, 'was struck by the poverty of the place.' Dr Edwards announced at the dinner that he would give ten guineas annually during his life-time to the School and later agreed with the Headmaster that the donation should be used in the formation and maintenance of a rowing club. Following this initiative, through the generosity of Col JC Rea and Sir George Fossett Roberts, the School acquired the three boats of the defunct Aberystwyth Boating Club which had been formed in 1872 to rival a similar College club. Two of the original boats were given to the School by the two gentlemen who were the only active survivors of the Boating Club. The inaugural launching of the three four-oared boats which bore the names 'Fossett Roberts', 'Jack Rae', and 'Peter Edwards' took place off the slipway at Marine-terrace in June 1938, one boat crewed by 5 boys, one by 5 girls and the third with a mixed crew. The donors were gratified that 'the youth of the town would once again be able to indulge in one of the finest exercises obtainable.' They were thanked, on behalf of the School by Meg Lewis, the head girl. The Headmaster, later urged his pupils to take full advantage of the rowing facilities. 'As one of a team, there is much to learn in balance and rhythm of stroke. May our new-formed club teach us to pull together still more for the benefit of Ardwynians-past, present and future.' During the gales of October 1938, one of the boats was destroyed. The replacement boat, shorter in length and broader in beam was more suitable especially in a choppy sea. It was this boat which gave so much pleasure to so many Ardwynians for almost fifteen years. One recalls the kindly Captain Thomas Lewis of Portland Road who kept a benign eye on the rowing club and on whom one had to call to collect the rowlocks and oars, providing his weather eye considered it safe to launch the *Ardwyn* into the waters of the bay. In 1953 he had to relinquish these duties and with no successor available, the rowing club ceased to exist.

Groups of enthusiasts encouraged by teachers formed the athletics and boxing clubs in the Thirties. Although efforts were made to stage inter-school athletic meetings, the only fixtures were against the College who, understandably, proved too strong. The boxing club came into existence with the appointment, in 1933, of Aneurin Richards. He was 'a noble exponent of the art' and his successor as physics teacher, Cyril Richards, continued his work with the club, using the geography room before the new gymnasium equipped with boxing ring and punch ball became available in 1939. Exhibition bouts were arranged but after- school practices were confined to the Hall the following year due to the lack of blackout in the gymnasium. Following a period of inactivity during the war years, the first House boxing tournament took place in 1947, competing for the Roger Eyton Morgan cup.

The David Samuel bequest seemed to have been held in abeyance until, in 1929, the Headmaster recommended to the Governors that 'Samuel Exhibitions' be granted to two boys who gained the best results in the school certificate examination each year, and in the terms of the bequest, were natives of Aberystwyth. From this date until the closure of the School in 1973 the exhibitions were awarded annually, in some cases more than two awards were made. It is surprising that a similar award for the girls was never founded, though the Martha Roberts essay prize established in 1939, in memory of Mrs M E Roberts, Maesyrhedydd, a former Governor, was restricted to girls.

The second Headmaster C Lloyd Morgan had awarded prizes for service and leadership but in 1929 a gift from an old pupil E R Thomas, headmaster of Newcastle Royal Grammar School, established the Daniel Thomas service and leadership prize for boys. This was in memory of his father Daniel Thomas, a former Governor. The girls had to wait some years for their equivalent award; when IC Dalley retired as senior mistress in 1932, she donated a capital sum to provide an annual prize for the girl who had shown the greatest powers of leadership and had given the best service to the School. In both cases, the prize winners were elected by the pupils from a list selected by the staff.

Although successive Headmasters had frequently referred to the founders of the School, it was not until 6 October 1930, that a Founders' Day assembly was held in the Central Hall. DC Lewis, the Headmaster in his review, thought it was the primary object of a school to look forward but in doing so, there was a grave danger of failing to give credit to those whose voluntary efforts had created the School. 'The path of the pioneer is always more thorny than for those of us who follow on the beaten track.' He was gratified to see persons present who had occupied very honourable positions on the original subscription list which had helped finance the School in the early days. These benefactors had given freely to provide the children of Aberystwyth with educational opportunities equal to those provided in any part of the country. At the 1933 assembly the speakers used, for the first time, the lectern which had been purchased by the Old Pupils' Association with the balance from their war memorial fund. In acknowledging the gift, the Headmaster said 'the lectern in Welsh oak lent grace and dignity to the Hall and paid tribute to the high standard of local craftmanship.' Although the hope was expressed that the Founders' Day assembly would become an annual event, there is no record that it was held after 1935. That year, Lalla Thomas, a former member of staff presented the cricket team with their caps and chairman of the Governors J Barclay Jenkins spoke of the sacrifices in time, thought and money made by the founders and reminded them that the English Bible had been published exactly 400 years previously' 'Whatever your distinctions, I urge you never to forget the Bible and its teachings-the foundation of all developments of the human mind.'

Some six years after the Urdd was founded in 1922, the School branch was formed under the direction of DH Jenkins the Welsh teacher. Members attended the Urdd camp in Llangollen in August 1929, and after their first visit to Caernarfon in 1930, the Urdd

The D. C. Lewis Years — 1928-1954

National Eisteddfod became an annual pilgrimage wherever it was held. Success in the competitions came regularly; in 1933 and 1934 the choir of twelve voices was led to victory by Gwyneth Williams, who as a result of her performances in the School operas, had attracted the attention of D'Oyly Carte. At their first attempt, the football team won the Urdd national competition in 1935 and again in 1936, there was success too for gymnastic and dance teams. Up until 1938 the School magazine regularly reported in Welsh, the activities of *Adran Ardwyn*, and often urged the pupils to speak their native tongue 'so that Ardwyn would became a real Welsh school.' There were no further reported activities until 1956 from which time until the final year of the School in 1973 the Urdd members, trained by Rhiannon Roberts of the Welsh department, distinguished themselves by winning the county eisteddfod cup on many occasions as well claiming several triumphs in the national competitions.

1936 was the year when the School undertook its first educational tour. DC Lewis explained his reasons for the innovative excursion:

> Throughout all ages, travel has been one of the most powerful educative factors. By moving amongst other people and noting their achievements, we are enabled to raise the standard of life in our own sphere and to cement that spirit of sympathy and friendship which is the essence of life and progress. Our earliest forbears were probably in danger whenever they left their caves; even our recent forefathers were able to travel only on foot or horseback and were compelled to view every stranger with suspicion We live in a much more enlightened age and find people everywhere ready and willing to assist us in every way; we merely sit in a coach and are wafted hundreds of miles without any effort on our part. It is our duty to make the most of these advantages and so a School journey was arranged as an experiment. Living as we are in a pleasant spot with green fields, trees and sunny skies over-head, it is esssential that we should gain contact with the great industrial organisations of this land.[50]

Accompanied by the Headmaster and staff, more than 300 pupils set off for Liverpool, a city with a population a hundred times that of Aberystwyth. The planned visit to the Lever Brothers factory had to be cancelled because a railway bridge at Newtown had been washed away. Efficient work by the G W R fixed up an alternative route through Dolgellau, Bala and Corwen. After lunch on the train, the ferry was taken from Birkenhead to Liverpool docks where the party was able to inspect one of the newest liners of the Canadian Pacific fleet-the *Duchess of Richmond*. The Anglican Cathedral-Sir Gilbert Scott's masterpiece, which would be the largest in the country when completed, was worthy of several hours inspection. After shopping opportunities the party journeyed by charabanc through the Mersey Tunnel- 'one of the greatest engineering achievements of the age' to Birkenhead and the train home. Such was the success of the trip that it was resolved to arrange a similar journey the next year.

However it was to be two years before the next excursion- to Birmingham and a tour of the Bourneville estate took place. Impressed by the facilities provided by Messrs. Cadbury for the physical well-being of the workforce, the party was fascinated by the modern production methods, and perhaps surprised that it was an individual production system, where each worker was in charge of one complete operation. The factory even made its own tin and cardboard boxes. After a welcome tea provided by the Cadbury company and a souvenir box of chocolates came the homeward journey and the feeling that they had seen 'an unforgettable example of the efficiency of modern industry.'

Dublin was the venue for the 1939 School excursion which was the last for eleven years. *The Ardwynian* reported

> Over 300 Ardwynians set off by special train for Holyhead on June 8 and apart from raiding every chocolate machine in Merioneth and Caernarvonshire the journey was without incident. Joining the *SS Hibernia* we faced the terrors of the Irish Sea with equanimity, though due to the internal battle of the chocolate and sandwiches, some of the less fortunate were soon showing the School colours on their countenances. After assembling in O'Connell Street the morning was spent sightseeing in small groups, some enjoyed such historic buildings as Trinity College, but the lure of Woolworths proved irresistible to many. After lunch at Clery's restaurant, Phoenix Park was visited, where the gardens and zoo were greatly enjoyed as was high tea in Clery's where although we ate ravenously we couldn't eat sufficient to please the management.

There was great praise for the Headmaster's organisation and for the efficiency and courtesy of the officials of railway, boat and restaurant.

> We went to Bourneville and Liverpool and *en route* I collected my fair share of engine smuts in my eye. A more ambitious trip to Dublin was a great success. I little thought at that time, that within a few years I was to sail the Irish Sea on more urgent business in a naval mine-layer.[51]

On the initiative of the Headmaster, it was decided, in the Christmas term 1929, to depart from the usual School concert and to undertake the production of a Gilbert and Sullivan comic opera, the choice being 'HMS Pinafore' and the venue, the Coliseum. A national newspaper reported on the production as well as printing a photograph of two of the principals:

CHILDREN IN OPERA Creditable Performance at Aberystwyth.

> A significant movement in the training of the young and a happy augury in the future development of operatic and dramatic art in the country was the excellent performance by the scholars of the County School, Aberystwyth of Gilbert and Sullivan's delightful comic opera 'HMS Pinafore'
>
> The singing, acting, dressing and scenic efforts made up a performance that would be a credit to any band of adults.
>
> The principals were all well chosen, and the headmaster and his assistants are to be congratulated on the production, especially the producer Major Stimson. Mr Clements at the pianoforte, with an efficient body of strings, ably supported the company.

Such was the success of the venture that it inaugurated a series of twenty-four annual productions of Gilbert and Sullivan operas. 'Christmastide each year since came to mean for the School, the town and district- Gilbert and Sullivan.' The importance of the operas to the School warrants the separate review to be found elsewhere in this record. Then of course there was the opera soiree for those involved and for the stage-shy pupils who found their way there by dint of being top ticket sellers. The State scholar of 1936 recalled:

> For those who take part, the opera does not end with the actual performances, for there is still the opera soiree to follow-more memories of gay lights, music, dancing and forgive me, a scrumptious repast. One outstanding memory I have of those soirees is that every year, without fail, a certain male member of staff would recite the same poem, which inevitably convulsed his audience. Unfortunately the only line I remember now is: 'and skulking in the gutter was the toad and sewer rat.' I only wish I could reproduce here the accent and intonation of that renowned elocutionist.[52]

While the opera productions had been such a resounding success, apart from the eisteddfod, Welsh language cultural activities, particularly drama had been neglected. The last Welsh drama had been staged in 1928 when *'Y Pwyllgor'* shared the programme with a production of 'Midsummer Night's Dream'. What became a celebrated annual event -the Welsh Night or *Noson Gymraeg* started in 1939 with a concert involving the School orchestra, *canu penillion*, French, Polish and Welsh country dancing followed by the plays *'Y Tebot'* and *'Adar o'r Unlliw'*. The appearance of the orchestra would have pleased the Headmaster since he had voiced his disappointment two years earlier that ten years previously, the School orchestra 'was one of its proudest features and there must be a considerable number of pupils capable of restoring its former glory.' As with most school activities, the enthusiasm and diligence of the staff are indispensable elements and the success of the *Noson Gymraeg* over so many years owed a great deal to the members of the Welsh department and many others. The event was staged annually without interruption for 29 years.

The inaugural *Noson Gymraeg* is remembered by one of the violinists in the orchestra who also acted in the plays.

> The School orchestra conducted by music master William Roberts made its debut. It consisted of twelve violins and a piano. How different from the orchestras and ensembles produced by schools today.
> Producing one of the plays was Mair E Thomas. Her arrival in 1937, to assist in the teaching of Welsh, was like a breath of fresh air. There was little wonder that some of us sixth-formers were in tears when she left in 1940 to get married.[53]

When the second world war began in September 1939, the Headmaster reported that the new session opened with a record 472 pupils which included 45 evacuated from various parts of the country, Aberystwyth having been designated as a reception area under the government scheme. The School was also able to provide laboratory and gymnasium facilities for the students of the Chelsea Physical Training College evacuated to the area; in return the School had use of their film projector 'which enhanced the teaching of many subjects.'

The first of a series of 'Ardwyn and the War' articles in the February 1940 *Ardwynian* noted that in contrast to the outburst of great patriotism and excitement which heralded the war twenty-five years previously:

> This time there were no flags, no bands, no national anthems, no wild enthusiasm, nothing but calm determination to crush Hitlerism and build a new world. Ex-servicemen of the last war are bitterly disappointed at the trend of events but, for the most part, send their sons willingly to serve their King and Country with the sound advice, 'win not the war but also the peace this time.'

The article listed some 150 Ardwynians who had joined one of the three branches of the Services and printed extracts from a letter written by Eddie Lloyd of Borth, a merchant seaman who witnessed the dramatic events of the River Plate and the scuttling of the "Graf Spee".

In the next edition, the Headmaster wrote:

> When fellow Ardwynians are enduring untold hardships and performing countless deeds of valour, we feel somewhat ashamed to state that we have been almost unaffected by the great events which occur around us. If it is good fortune to lead an uneventful life, then Ardwyn has been very fortunate. It is true that we have received and are still receiving pupils from other secondary schools and this has caused greater overcrowding in the lower and middle school than has ever existed previously.

However the School was attempting to make its contribution to the war-effort. The boys presented a petition in favour of forming a Cadet Corps and despite difficulty in obtaining official recognition, progress was made. With the assistance of Sergeant Whyman (Welsh Guards) and WG Rowlands, some seventy cadets were soon 'capable of good foot and rifle drill.'

> We joined the Cadet Corps at School, and after 4 p. m. had our first alarming contacts with the British Army. The School walls reverberated to the agonised cries of a khaki-clad Stentor-Sgt Whyman of the UCW OTC, while we marched and drilled before an infuriating crowd of grinning girls. A more self-conscious body of troops than we, it is difficult to imagine.[54]

At the same time, some of the girls took up Red Cross cadet work while others joined the Girls' Training Corps.

> The G T C held an annual camp in Devil's Bridge, the girls sleeping in army tents. Violet Jones, Meg Bowen and I were the staff in charge with a regular army sergeant instructor. They used live ammunition in their rifles for target practice. The irreplacable Mrs Burns cooked all our meals-she deserved a medal for devotion to duty. Meg took pre-breakfast P T while Violet and I snoozed on. There were talks and walks after which we tended blisters and bites with sympathy. We were visited by our C O the Headmaster, who often brought along V I Ps. Violet and I still chuckle at our introduction to one of them. 'This', said our C O, 'is Miss Violet Jones, one of my mistresses and this is Miss Pegi Davies another of my mistresses.'[55]

The D. C. Lewis Years — 1928-1954

1933–34 2nd Netball Team.

1936 Tennis Team.

1939 1st Hockey Team.

Early in 1941 came the authority for a flight of the Air Training Corps to be formed in the School. ' All boys between 16 and 18 who are physically fit and desire to obtain commissions in the Royal Air Force or Fleet Air Arm should join and take up the work with enthusiasm', so advised the Headmaster. With masters WJ Lewis and Williams Roberts in charge, the cadets soon qualified for uniforms and became 'a smart and efficient unit on parade'. A year later the Army Cadet Force was officially formed with members issued with battle dress, cap badge, shoulder titles, and anklets. It was emphasised that the ACF was not intended to be a rival to the ATC, indeed cadets from both units combined on occasions to act as enemy parachutists for the Home Guard exercises. Ardwyn staff were quickly involved as Local Defence Volunteers which later became the Home Guard. The Headmaster assumed the rank of Lt Colonel when he took command of the North Cardiganshire contingent, with Major George Rowlands in charge of the local volunteers, which included Chris Jones and Hywel Ellis. Sam Mitchell, before joining the army for a second time, was an Inspector in the Special Constabulary assisted by Messrs Tom James, DH Jenkins, and Tom Salmon.

Billy Owen recalled a Home Guard camp on the School field where they were instructed in various ordinances. A flame thrower was being demonstrated when it became uncontrollable and only good fortune prevented a disaster.

George Rowlands also organised the War Comforts Fund which was quickly formed to receive the weekly contributions of almost everyone in the School. Throughout the war, the fund allowed the dispatch of the *Ardwynian* and a postal order to most of the 700 former pupils who served in HM Forces. That the scheme was appreciated was shown by the many letters of thanks which were printed in each wartime issue of the *Ardwynian*. From all over the globe came messages of gratitude for the small gift and also for the recognition that they were not forgotten by the old School. Following an editorial request, many wrote at length, censor permitting, about their experiences; in one of the first 'I was there' articles, Victor Thomas described his involvement in a raid on one of the Lofoten Islands, that successfully achieved its object which was to destroy a cod-oil factory which was supplying oil to the Germans. For good measure the raid captured some Norwegian Quislings and brought back volunteers for the Norwegian forces. Able Seaman Thomas, serving on a landing craft, had an eventful war. He wrote again a year later, of his part in a Commando raid at Boulogne. Howard Williams of Borth, who later lost his life at sea, told of his merchant ship being torpedoed off Dakar.

> From a life- boat, we watched our good ship slide quietly, stern first to her grave. In the meantime, the submarine had surfaced to watch the results of her handiwork. The U-boat commander, speaking in perfect English, asked if we were all right and pointed out two of our crew who were still in the water. She then made off and we were left on our own to make the best of things.

After thirteen days in the open boat they reached Bathhurst on the Gambia river, to receive a great welcome from the Governor, Lord Southorn and his Lady.

For Bill Bowen, *en route* to West Africa, Christmas Day 1940, his first away from home, saw his convoy under attack from German surface raiders and a near miss for his transport ship. 'Thanks to the attention and vigilance of the Royal Navy', he was later able to sit down to a festive dinner of 'hard potatoes, tough beef and gritty cabbage'.

Readers of the *Ardwynian* had already learnt of the end of the *Graf Spee*; another former pupil, Gwilym Willliams, the 1938 leadership prize winner, gave a graphic description of the chase to destroy the *Bismarck* after leaving Malta on May 24 1941 in a cruiser (the censor would not permit it to be named but it was *HMS Sheffield*) in company with the aircraft carrier *Ark Royal*. On that day, the new German battle-ship, with deadly accurate fire power had sunk *HMS Hood*. Aircraft spotted the *Bismarck* in the Bay of Biscay and the *Sheffield*, with superior speed, was despatched to hunt her. The pride of the German fleet was sighted from ten miles away and the dangerous task of shadowing began. Having fixed her position, aircraft from *Ark Royal* took off in a howling gale and overtook the *Sheffield*. The Swordfish planes fired fourteen torpedoes at the *Sheffield* mistaking her, in poor visibility, for the *Bismarck*, they all missed! However a second flight of Swordfish found their correct target damaging the *Bismarck's* steering. That they had scored a hit was apparent to the *Sheffield's* crew as the pilots, passsing over the ship on their return journey to the *Ark Royal* 'had their thumbs up and their faces wreathed in smiles.' Despite being crippled, the long-range guns of the *Bismarck* opened up on the *Sheffield* but all the shells landed in the water around the ship. By now, (after probably the greatest naval chase of the twentieth century), the stricken ship was surrounded by a ring of steel and the might of the Royal Navy, including *HMS King George–V* and *HMS Rodney*, was brought to bear on her. The *Bismarck* was finally despatched by torpedoes from *HMS Devonshire* and sank on 27 May 1941.

> The Hood had been avenged. The jubilant cheers of our men rang throughout the ship, but we all realised that we had witnessed the end of a gallant ship. In the words of our captain 'she went down with her flags flying.' I take my hat off to a gallant ship and a brave ship's company.

Hywel Ellis, who had spent the first year of the war as teacher of art and geography at Ardwyn, joined the Merchant Navy to improve his health. He described arriving in the river Mersey after a stormy voyage, (his brother Dewi was also a crew member,) to be subjected to a March 1943 'blitz' in Liverpool docks.

> It was an awe-inspiring, and in some ways an exhilarating experience. Bombs fell round us in all directions, some between us and the shore, and some between us and a tanker lying close by. Big fires waxed and waned on both sides of the river, and once or twice a great column of ruby flame was seen vomiting richly from some hidden source. High up in the sky the 'ack-ack' twinkled like iron filings on a fire, the whole river festooned with flares and tracer bullets whipped upwards from ships and the shore on every side with a continual rat-tat-tat.

Another member of the Ellis family, William, a Merchant Navy chief officer described how Canada was mass-producing cargo ships similar to the American Liberty shipbuilding programme 'by sheer weight of numbers making the U-boats' task a hopeless one.' He journeyed across Canada to join one of these Fort ships in Vancouver and then after discharging grain and timber in London, it was 'a real wartime cargo' to be delivered to a North African port. However, while at an Italian port, having discharged her supplies for the Eighth Army, Fort A---. was totally destroyed during a bombing raid, with the loss of most of her crew. 'She had done her stuff, contributing to the effort which will bring us final victory.'

Captain Reg Bohlen 'had the privilege' to take part in the Sicilian campaign and described chasing the enemy from the island while the population 'rushed out from their hiding holes to surround us, kiss, pat, shake hands and ply the men with wine.' He expressed gratitude for the 1940 and 1943 copies of the *Ardwynian* which had followed him through Iraq and Persia. He ended his account by saying that he was living in a beautiful Sicilian house with magnificent views and was fit and well. Within a few months Reg Bohlen was missing presumed killed.

Two contrasting reports were sent by G Walford Hughes. The first described his idyllic life in India - 'a country I shall never forget.' He later described his close encounters with the Japanese in Burma where again the 'School mags' got through to the foxholes.

On the same continent, David Elwyn Lloyd Jones was serving with the Assam Regiment on the Burma-Assam border. The idea that they belonged to the 'forgotten army' were dispelled whenever the Magazines and postal orders arrived.

> Half of our men are Christian-many of them coming from the Lushai and Khasi hills who had been converted by our Welsh missionaries. It's odd to hear them in their tents, at night humming Welsh hymn tunes they've learnt in the missions. It is strange and moving, under the stars, to hear the strains of '*Pen-yr-Yrfa*', and '*O Fryniau Caersalem*', come from the natives and to add the Welsh words to the tunes as they float over the air.

Roger Eyton Morgan was an early member of the ATC who secured many proficiency awards before leaving to join the RAF. The ATC notes in the Magazine of February 1944 reported that he had passed out as top cadet of his pilot training school. In the *Ardwynian* of February 1945 he recounted his experiences after leaving England in February 1943 for pilot training in South Africa, flying operations in the Middle East and Europe, before returning to the United Kingdom. Some two months after his article was published, it was reported that he had failed to return from a flying mission over Norway -he was twenty-one years of age.

Ardwynians seemed to have to played a role in many of the naval actions involving the great German battleships. Adding to the experiences of the sinking of the Graf Spee and the *Bismarck*, Gilbert Clark as a Fleet Air Arm officer was present at the attack on another German leviathan, the *Tirpitz*. The largest battleship in the world at the time had taken refuge in a Norwegian fjord and had survived attacks by midget submarines. In July 1944 Gilbert Clarke found himself in the leading Baracuda having to navigate the rest of his flight in a dive-bombing attack on the *Tirpitz* in Kaafjord. More than fifty years later, Gilbert recalled the appalling anti-aircraft fire from the surrounding hills and the presence of a heavy smoke screen which prevented assessment of damage which was thought to be slight. When the *Tirpitz* eventually put to sea in November 1944, RAF Lancaster aircraft with their monster bombs, made no mistake and the pride of the German navy was well and truly sunk.

There were some servicemen who failed to receive the *Ardwynian* because they were prisoners of war. On his release Roy H Fisher related the horror of his experiences in a Japanese P O W camp in the heart of the Thai jungle. His copies of the Ardwynian and postal orders had been kept by his parents awaiting his release.

Lt. Harold Evans R N R spent much of the war in captivity. With the liberating army approaching the camp near Bremen the POWs were made to march for fourteen days, during which time they were fired upon by the RAF. They were eventually released from a camp in Lubeck. In all there were twelve Ardwynians incarcerated, of these, Ivor Williams, and John Yateman died in Japanese camps.

The first year of the war saw several staff changes. The resignation due to increasing ill-health of the much loved physical training teacher Bessie Arnold came as a great shock. During her 14 years years of part time service she had maintained a very high standard and had willingly undertaken additional tasks. The Headmaster in his tribute to her considered that the School owed her a great debt of gratitude for the splendid traditions she had created in dance and games and also for the graceful carriage of the girls.

> We walked the perimeter of the College gymnasium with our text books balanced on our heads, while instructions hurtled through the air like, 'grow tall, chin in, tails and tummy in, feet, feet, feet,' or 'you worm' when a book fell. There was a weekly dancing lesson as well. We danced the folk and country dances of many nations. We were taught basic ballet, free expression, and ballroom dancing including the tango. And the boys, whenever possible were hauled reluctantly in and they too learned ballroom etiquette and dancing. The woman who gave us this vast comprehension, this self-discipline and the social graces, was the incomparable Miss Beatrice Gertrude Arnold. She exhorted us, derided us, extended us and cared for us. No one who knew Arnold will ever forget her. [55A]

Betty Jones newly qualified from the Chelsea college assumed Miss Arnold's duties. The biologist John Ladd left to join the Birmingham Technical College but was to become a victim of the war. Emlyn Glyn Davies took over the biology department but, within two years, was seconded to the War Office for work of national importance. Miss Akister decided on a change of career, she left to marry a future Ardwyn physics teacher Maurice Chapple but later returned to teach commerce and act as School secretary for a period of two years. A distinguished former pupil Hywel N Ellis was appointed as art and geography teacher when W D Lewis relinquished all but his sixth form art teaching. At this time the Governors had decided to discontinue use of the Honours boards which had given David Samuel so much gratification. They were to be replaced by an Honours roll, housed in a casket to be placed in the Hall. W D Lewis produced a beautifully illuminated book, testimony to his artistry and craftsmanship. However the record is incomplete, there being no entries after 1954.

After a year Hywel Ellis resigned to join the Merchant Navy but rejoined the staff in 1943 when fully restored to health. With the departure of Chris Jones to Oundle public school after seventeen years as physics teacher, Sam Mitchell's recall to the army with a commission in the Artillery, and the call-up of RJ Lloyd, many new faces appeared in the science department. Former pupil Pegi Davies became the biology mistress and Doris Mitchell took over some of her husband's teaching for the duration of the war initially, but stayed until retirement in 1960.

> Many of us left Ardwyn in tears, but we left with a sense of self-worth, of loyalty, and responsibility and with a knowledge of friendship and respect. Four years after leaving, I returned to join the staff. It was such a strange feeling as I knocked the door and went into the drab womens' staff room. I felt a kind of reluctance, my rapport was with the young Ardwynians outside. Irene Davies wrapped me in her arms and welcomed me as only she would. Miss Forster was getting her forty winks in her fireside chair. Gwyneth Mainwaring was affirming, listening and knitting. Their welcome made me easy and happy. Later the exuberance of the younger members of staff caused Forster to declare 'there are no ladies appointed to the staff these days.'
>
> To my great and everlasting delight my form was IID (D for Davies). They started at Ardwyn and I started teaching at Ardwyn on the same day. I can remember them all and where they sat in our form room. I'll just mention my first two form captains, Audrey Jones and Geraint Griffith. They were well chosen. I can still see them at twelve years of age. I suppose most people at sometime and maybe some at all times, feel that they are in the right place. I felt just that in Ardwyn. There was contentment and ease and it is a lovely memory I have recalled all my life. Having three sisters, all of whom attended the School, Ardwyn was in our home life too, for nineteen consecutive years. Little wonder that when I left to teach in Bala in 1946, my last walk home was desolate. Only those who loved Ardwyn can miss her.[56]

The chemistry teaching became the responsibility of a retired teacher IT Jones. WJ Lewis was appointed to the staff in 1940 to teach geography and junior school art and with the departure of Dick Lloyd took over the coaching of the first XV having had experience of playing rugby at high level in England. Emlyn Davies was appointed as an additional teacher for general subjects but immediately became head of mathematics. Anna Gwenith Davies joined the English department in 1942 and stayed for five years; her brilliance on the hockey field was utilised to good effect in her work with girls' games. Two masters with nearly fifty years of service between them retired in 1943. Tom Salmon had been mathematics master for twenty-five years and a noted poet and reciter. He had left council school at thirteen to find employment in the tin plate works. He educated himself at evening classes to qualify for entry to university where he gained first class honours in mathematics in 1909. WD Lewis after twenty-four years as art master retired completely but continued to be responsible for the Honours roll for many years. Tom James succeeded Salmon as Senior Master- 'a well-earned tribute to many years of sterling service and loyal devotion to Ardwyn.'

After ten years service, Dr Nellie Rae was informed by the Governors that, as result of the fall in demand for German, her services would probably be dispensed with. She soon accepted a new post in Yorkshire and was not replaced. German had temporarily left the curriculum- was it a case of misplaced patriotism ?

> For German we had Dr Nellie Rae, whose broad Scots accent took some getting used to. She was a first class teacher and we were made to learn by heart not only German

poetry but also passages of German prose, which helped enormously to expand our vocabulary. Although a Scot, Nellie Rae was sensitive to the cold and would sit, on winter days with a hot-water bottle hidden in the folds of her gown (all staff in those days wore academic dress). She drank only water and would wrap her hand in a clean tissue when opening doors.[57]

After a long and successful career at Llandovery College, W Beynon Davies was appointed an additional teacher to teach Welsh and Latin. When WJ Lewis left in 1945, after 4 years of meritorious service, to join the emergency training scheme for teachers in Wrexham, Beynon Davies took over the rugby coaching. W J Lewis later returned to the town to join the staff of the U C W education department and wrote many books of local interest including 'Born on a Perilous Rock' and 'An Illustrated Atlas of Cardiganshire', a copy of which was given to every child of school age in the county, to mark the Investiture of Prince Charles in 1969.

In comparison with many schools, Ardwyn was fortunate in its staffing arrangements during the war, however as the war drew to a close the position worsened. With the protracted illness of physics and mathematics teacher Cyril Richards and the departure of Emlyn Davies, there were periods in the Autumn term 1945 when no teacher qualified in physics and mathematics was available. The teacher appointed for mathematics had been posted to West Africa with the RAF and was not able to assume teaching duties until the following session. The position did ease with the appointment of M T Chapple who was highly qualified in mathematics and physics, and the return of RJ Lloyd from the army. However there was more bad news to come. William Roberts who taught music, woodwork and mathematics announced that he had accepted a post in a London school. The Headmaster in the July 1945 Magazine wrote:

> During nine years of distinguished service at Ardwyn, he set a high standard of effort and leadership and leaves a gap hard to fill. He has been a prime mover in our operas, the ATC, eisteddfod and BBC performances and has given excellent tuition in his teaching subjects. His record of brilliant achievements, together with his energy, ability and driving power will remain as cherished memories in Ardwyn for years to come.

The BBC performance referred to took place in June 1943 when the girls' choir under the direction of William Roberts gave 'memorable renderings of compositions arranged by the music master, ringing the world with sweet melodious song.' D Ronald James RN wrote to say that he had heard the choir on his radio despite being two thousand miles from home and on his way to a dangerous mission. His mind went back to' the old woodwork room where I had tried to sing the same songs'.

> I am grateful to William Roberts for nurturing in me a lifelong interest in music and woodwork. One of my highlights came when he pursuaded David Franklin to give a recital in the School Hall. Franklin, at the time was an army officer, but he had been principal bass in the Glyndebourne opera company. It was truly a memorable experience, one to set against the boredom inflicted by the periodical visits of the Dorian Trio.[58]

The evening before school started in September 1941, I went out for a walk, proudly wearing my brand new school cap. This proved to be a mistake, because I had forgotten the tribalism that existed among and between the juveniles of the town. Up on the Castle grounds I was met and chased by a pebble-and-mud throwing gang, who bellowed out the song that I myself had once been in the habit of singing:

> County School are duffers,
> National School are rats,
> But if you see a Board Schoolite,
> Please take off your hats.

The next morning I awoke with my usual companion-in-trepidation, a churning, aching stomach. Mam came up with my newly pressed clothes; my former Sunday suit, white shirt, School tie, and grey socks. There was no formal uniform then because of clothes rationing.

From beneath the bedclothes I moaned 'I don't want to go'

'George !' shouted Mam to Dad who was breakfasting downstairs. 'He says he doesn't want to go!'

'That's all right, replied Dad calmly. He can go back to Alexandra Road. He won't be able to go to sea, though.'

That stopped me in my tracks. I wanted that more than anything.

'All right,' I scowled, 'but I don't want any breakfast.

On the way up the boys' entrance, we were given some advice by a fourth former. 'Don't struggle', he warned. 'Get it over with and you'll be OK.'

We were met by a frantic mob of wild-eyed third formers who grabbed us, blackened our faces with Cherry Blossom shoe polish and pushed us towards a heaving line making up a gauntlet, through which we were expected to run. As we struggled through, we were pushed, pummelled and beaten, emerging into the big yard, bruised, battered, dirty and dusty.

'You're one of us now,' said a tall gangling youth. 'Join on the end of the line and help bash 'em'.

Our fears forgotten, stomach ache gone, we cheerfully and turn-coatedly did as we were bidden.

We were Ardwynians now![59]

Despite the war-time restrictions on building, a long standing need for new toilet facilities was satisfied in 1942. Soon after, a portable stage was constructed for use in the gymnasium. Financed by opera profits, the new stage allowed the scope of the House drama competitions to be extended. Formerly they had been part of the eisteddfod but the new arrangements required that each House write, produce and act a play of at least fifteen minutes duration to be performed in October of each year.

Dr JSF Philpott had presented a new trophy to be called the Cyril Mortimer Green Dramatic cup, in honour of an old Ardwynian friend killed in the 1914-18 war.

> My first attempt at play writing was a piece called 'Nature Triumphant', in which a scientist came back to life in order to find out what lay on the other side. He was foiled by Nature, in that, although the experiment worked, the scientist was driven insane

The D. C. Lewis Years — 1928-1954

Choir with Music Teacher, William Roberts which broadcast on BBC Radio, June 1943.

Mayor of Aberystwyth Ald. Llewelyn Samuel presenting David H. Trevena with the 'Western Mail' prize for an English essay in the St. David's Day Competition. Also in the picture are the Headmaster D. C. Lewis, G. M. Mainwaring and W. G. Rowlands.

by the knowledge and so could not communicate what he had illicitly discovered. All very serious and clever-clever, but marred by my returning suitably mad, to the stage, being desperately shaken by my wife and the white powder sprinkled off-stage on my hair, rising up in great clouds. I couldn't understand why my solemn efforts were greeted with such mirth. The cup went, quite properly, to Ceredigion for an up-to-the-minute moving little drama written by Nancy Jeremy and called 'From Buchenwald to Brittany'.[60]

A project close to the heart of the Headmaster was a long time becoming a reality. DC Lewis was anxious that the School enhance its technical facilities to fulfil the demands of the 1889 Education Act which was to provide Intermediate and Technical Education for the people of Wales. In his speech to the 1942 Prize Day audience the Headmaster pointed out that the war had already shown that the decisive factors were not numbers or courage. Without suitable equipment the bravest army could be destroyed by a smaller but better equipped one. That year the education committee sanctioned the Governors to proceed with the accommodation for technical instruction in metal work and the internal combustion engine. The plans for a substantial engineering block had to be severly curtailed and by February 1944 a hut had been constructed on land adjacent to the New Block. In order to equip it, a county-wide search was begun to find suitable equipment as the normal channel of supply was unavailable. The County Surveyor provided a portable forge, anvil and vice and a reasonable lathe was found in Llanfarian. Wooden platforms from the Hall were hastily converted into benches and the tools gradually brought into operation under the guidance of WJ Lewis who in addition to his qualification in geography and art held a handicraft teaching certificate. With the departure of WJ Lewis and William Roberts, who between them were responsible for handicraft teaching, the Governors appointed their first specialist in wood and metalwork, Idwal Davies. His ability was quickly recognised and the miniature chair he produced for each School eisteddfod was much prized. At the same time Beryl Morgan took over the music department, to be immediately involved with 'Princess Ida' where 'under her inspiring leadership the party made great strides.' Former pupil Meg Bowen neé Lewis had charge of girls' physical education sharing her duties with the Chelsea college. She quickly 'put new skill into our hockey team and inspired our seniors to start some after-school dancing classes'.

> It was wartime when I first went to Ardwyn-the years of the blackouts, gas masks and rationing. Lessons punctuated by drills in the schoolground trenches;lunches of spam, and a pudding called 'brown' and awful PT classes in the gym given by those students evacuated from Chelsea. Apart from that I cannot really recall that the conflict in Europe and beyond impinged too much on our school life. Yes, we collected for the soldiers and we listened to the horrors of war on the news but daily life meant coping with disciplines and rules within the classroom. Prefects were to be avoided at all costs and the Headmaster was a distant figure. We saw him at morning assembly and important functions but we scattered as soon as we caught sight of him in a corridor.
>
> Teachers make lasting impressions and create permanent effects. Tom Salmon, after a lifetime in the profession, inculcating the intricacies of geometry and algebra; Miss Forster explaining the topography and geography of the Rheidol and Ystwyth vallys

and comparing them with the Rhine and the Rhone; Miss Davies (Davws) seemingly forever reciting the Latin declensions and translating the Iliad; Miss Mainwaring interpreting the great works of Tennyson and Wordsworth; Violet Jones reigning supreme in her spotless kitchen and Mr Chapple hoping for a breakthrough and that I would master the principles of optics and mechanics.

It is only with the benefit of hind sight that one realises how well equipped and how well organised the School was. These were time of enormous social changes and developments in secondary education. The emphasis on good scientific teaching in splendid laboratories could only have been brought about by raising funds within the community.

Herbert Spencer wrote, 'Education has for its object the formation of character', the Ardwyn of my day seemed to embrace that sentiment. What are nowadays termed extra-curricular activities, were given as much emphasis as formal teaching within the classroom, eisteddfodau and Welsh nights; drama and debates and those wonderful Gilbert and Sullivan productions at the Kings Hall. Peter Potts could sing like an angel and Beryl and Beverly Richards were a duo to be reckoned with. To tread the boards as a lowly member of the chorus was a thrill; how I treasure those faded photographs of the 'Gondoliers' and 'Princess Ida'. I'm not sure whether our introduction to classical music had the same effect. Somehow performances by the renowned Dorian Trio failed to capture the imagination and interest but once a term they would give recitals in the Hall-all part of the educative process.[61]

In October 1940, when air-raids were a strong possibility, the Governors discusssed precautions which could be taken. The School-house basement was designated for use as an air-raid shelter although it could accommodate just fifty souls. The authorities of the National Library were requested to inform the School of approaching danger. Following a request from the farmers, permission was given for boys to help with the potato harvest but only on Saturdays! In the March 1943 Magazine the Headmaster observed:

> During October, many neighbouring farmers called for help in harvesting their potatoes. Our boys reponded nobly and on some days we had about fifty at work. It was a noticeable fact-and a regrettable one- that some boys were more ready to pick potatoes on school days than on holidays.

This must have been the first October half-term holiday which became known forever as 'potato week.'

> One morning at the end of assembly the Head asked whether any pupil from the fifth or sixth form would like to help the war effort by potato-picking on a local farm for three days. We would be taken there and back and paid half-a-crown an hour, as well as a meal. We jumped at the chance, gave our names to the duty prefect and turned up the next day, prepared to do our bit and have a holiday as well.
>
> It didn't prove to be the lark we expected. In short in was jolly hard work. The tractor-drawn plough moved up and down the furrows, exposing the potatoes for us to pick. No sooner was one patch cleared than the next was turned over. From our buckets the potatoes were put into sacks and driven away by a Land Army girl in another

tractor. We soon got fed up and tried to enliven the proceedings by pelting each other with small spuds and clods of earth. This brought the wrath of the farmer down on our heads. It was cold, hard work. We looked forward to our dinner, which we ate sitting on sacks, around fires which had been lit to provide warmth. We welcomed the scalding tea which drove the chill from our fingers. The afternoon passed slowly and we were glad when the lorry came finally to collect us and not the sacks of potatoes. The farmer paid us a pound before driving us back to town.[62]

Despite all the distractions caused by the hostilities, the Forties saw an upsurge in examination entries and records were created almost each year. Following the 1940 results, the Headmaster was moved to write:

> The brilliant success of our science fifth at the school certificate proves conclusively that Ardwyn is now able to stand honourably alongside the best science schools in the land. Events of the past year have shown that no nation can live today without a plentiful supply of technicians and scientists, so that this demonstration of our prowess in science is doubly welcome.
>
> The character of any school reflects to a large extent on the character of the headmaster. D C Lewis was a man of firm principles, but appproachable, flexible and innovative in his management of the School. From the beginning of his stewardship he had made great efforts to upgrade the standard of the teaching staff. He was particularly successsful with the science teaching. It was my great good fortune to to be taught physics by E C Richards, chemistry by Nelson so tragically blinded in a laboratory explosion and his successor R J Lloyd. In particular I regard E C Richards as the finest teacher I ever encountered in my school and university career.[63]

The outcome of the 1941 C W B examinations equalled the previous record year of 1939. In reviewing the results at prize day DC Lewis paid tribute to one boy in particular:

> Amongst the eight higher certificates was one of outstanding merit containing distinctions in three subjects. But for a slight age disqualification this performance would have undoubtedly gained a state scholarship for their head boy, Eddie Ellis. Earlier in the year he had won the most valuable scholarship offered by the University College of Wales together with the Machynlleth Eisteddfod Prize and had proved a most inspiring captain and record goal scoring member of the football team. His election to the Daniel Thomas service and leadership prize was a fitting climax to a brilliant career of all-round achievement.

In 1941-42 session, of the twelve scholarships offered by the UCW, five were claimed by Ardwyn boys; so perhaps the record twelve CWB higher certificates which monopolised the county order of merit and earned a special commendation from the LEA, did not come as a surprise. Evan John (Jack) Jones with three distinctions, obtained a state scholarship and entrance to St John's College, Cambridge. A futher two state scholars four years later in Paul Roberts and John Watkin brought the total to six for the previous fifteen years. Both candidates had earlier won the two major UCW awards. There was also pride in the fact that fifteen out of seventeen candidates had gained the higher certificate and as a result qualified for the newly introduced County major award. In his report in 1947, DC Lewis explained the value of the County award whereby possession of a higher certificate guaranteed a substantial grant for a university career.

The Headmaster expressed disappointment with the higher certificate results the following year but was compensated by the achievement of the 1939 state scholar Gareth Wyn Evans in securing the rare distinction of a first class in the Cambridge mathematical tripos. The same honour fell to Paul Roberts in 1950 who after a year at the UCW, had gained an open scholarship to Gonville and Caius College Cambridge in 1947. Other notable achievements recorded in 1947 were first class honours of the University of Wales to Dewi Ellis in French, David Trevena in physics and Eddie Ellis in history. The latter had also gained a Welsh amateur international soccer cap and scored a brilliant goal in the first minute of the game against England.

Records tumbled in 1948 when the sixth form produced no less than twenty-six higher certificates from twenty-nine candidates, including two reserve state scholarships.

The decade ended on a high note in the field of academic achievement. Two of the four open scholarships offered by the UCW came to Ardwyn; in all, the sixth form claimed four of the seventeen awards available. There was even better news to come-a record number of seventy six school certificates and included in the nineteen higher awards was a state scholarship to William G Edwards who chose to study medicine in Lincoln College, Oxford.

During the war, sporting activities continued unabated. The soccer XI after its invincible era, needed two years to regain its supremacy. John Hugh Edwards captained the side for three seasons from 1942, winning all ten matches in the winter of 1944. He also broke the high jump record and was head boy in 1945, the year he left to join the Services. Five of that team later played for the Town XI; John Ellis Williams played over 170 games for the Black and Greens, scoring 99 goals. In the 1948-49 season when Eddie Ellis scored a record 67 goals for the Town club, 'John Ellis Williams, a small but beautiful balanced player, created many of the openings with his intricate dribbling.'[64] Another future Town soccer star, Wynn Hughes led the School side with great success for the next two seasons. He also captained the rugby XV, and represented the School at cricket and tennis. It was not surprising that his chosen career was in the field of physical education. Tom Williams emulated the earlier feat of another versatile sportsman Islwyn Fisher Davies, in captaining the rugby, soccer and cricket sides, but did it for two successive years. Both served as head boy before leaving for national service. Another gifted athlete was Colin Lewis who captained the 1942-43 rugby XV, when he was head boy and had the distinction of running the 100 yards in 10.4 seconds to beat David Sansbury's ten year old record by .4 second; he also gained the victor ludorum. Harry Hallam, another multi-talented sportsman succeeded him the following year as rugby captain, was victor ludorum in two successive years and head boy in his last year.

The standard of rugby had improved sufficiently for coach W Beynon Davies to obtain fixtures with Carmarthen Grammar, a strong rugby school. It fell to Wynford Thomas' side of 1945 to break new ground; though losing both home and away fixtures, the School team were not disgraced. The only other school in the county which played rugby was Cardigan who were always difficult to beat, probably because they played rugby both terms.

In 1948, both Aberaeron and Lampeter turned to the oval ball and within a few years became a force to be reckoned with. They always seemed to be able to field huge forwards which was a great advantage. The period 1947 to 1949, under the captaincy of Tom Williams, was one of the most successful -just three defeats in eighteen matches. This feat was due in part to the development of a junior team providing a nursery for the senior XV. Holyrood preparatory school which had been evacuated to Abermad mansion, provided keen opposition for the juniors but due to the age and small size of their boys, they insisted that the opposition was carefully matched, on size and weight rather than on age. This was something of a novelty for RJ Lloyd who had again taken over responsibility for rugby on his return from the war, but it made good sense in such a vigorous contact sport. Nevertheless a visit to Abermad was always something to look forward to if only for the delicious teas which invariably included a boiled egg fresh from the mansion farm. These were still times of food rationing of course.

The standard of play in hockey and netball in the early Forties probably suffered from the games being played simultaneously. There were complaints of the poaching of players from each code and lack of interest. There was a marked upturn when Meg Bowen was appointed in 1945 to be the physical education specialist and a term was devoted to each game. Marian Hughes captained the hockey team for two years when, of the 24 games played just 4 were lost. Under the captaincy of Beryl Richards, opera star and victrix ludorum, the netball team had some success.

Cricket failed to reach the heights of the late Thirties until well into the decade. It would appear that there was difficulty in finding opposition possibly due to many schools having inadequate facilities for the game. No games were played in 1945 'due to unforeseen circumstances.' Later however there were some good performances; in the first of his two years of captaincy, Tom Williams' side lost just one game-to Towyn. This period coincided with the arrival of RD James to teach geography, a knowledgeable, dedicated cricketer, who despite a physical handicap caused by a war injury, brought great enthusiasm to the game. With an eye to the future, his policy was to introduce juniors into the senior XI to gain experience; 12 year old Keith Garbett, on his debut batted for one and a half hours for 17 runs, just failing to save the game. Under the direction of Roy James, Ardwyn cricket reached great heights in the following years.

In the 1940 Sports, the victrix ludorum was gained, for the first time, by a junior athlete Marjorie Williams, who repeated the feat the following year. Head boy, David Rowland Edwards was victor ludorum, winner of the 100 yard and 440 yard events and runner up in the long and high jumps. Many records created in the previous decade were improved. Mair Evans who had held the junior 100 yard record since 1937 added the senior record in 1941. Both times were not improved for more than ten years. A familiar face for so long at the sports was missing in 1944; Col JC Rea, who had acted as judge for many years, had died to the great regret of all. That year Idris Ivor Jones tied with Harry Hallam for the champion title, with Ellen Watson a clear winner of the victrix ludorum. The long jump record of 17 feet 9 inches held jointly by Idwal Owen and Noel Butler was bettered in three successive years- by David White in 1947, by Trevor Evans, and Meurig Magor who recorded 18 feet 3 3/4 inches. At the same meeting Magor improved Noel Butler's 440 yard time, which had stood for seventeen years, recording 56. 4 seconds.

Earlier in the year, Magor had scored fourteen goals in two matches for the Soccer XI and won the senior cross-country title in a record time of 25 minutes and 45 seconds. In addition to claiming the long jump record, David White, in 1947, broke the 220 yards record held for fifteen years by N Butler and the high jump record made the previous year by John H Lewis. He was a very worthy victor ludorum. Other fine boy athletes of that era were brothers John R and Peter Jones who each won two senior cross-country races between 1943 and 1946. In 1944 John won the mile with Peter third, the following year the positions were exactly reversed. Of the girls, Menna Davies, who had led an unbeaten netball team, was girls' tennis captain, and gained the victrix ludorum in 1942. Towards the end of the decade, Joyce Jones and Beryl Richards both fine games players, were victores ludorum two years in succession. After sharing the Nanteos athletic cup with Ceri in 1944, Arfon were to claim it for the following five years.

With the closure of the Bath street swimming baths in 1936 swimming instruction had disappeared from the curriculum. The Headmaster was pleased to report that almost ten years later, swimming lessons would be resumed; permission had been obtained for the use of the College baths. Senior boys had cut a foot path across the College gardens to link up with the Library path, so that travel time to and from the baths would be minimised. Each pupil would have the opportunity of spending an hour under expert tuition in perfect conditions once a fortnight. The Magazine reported 'that appreciation of the valuable opportunity to learn to swim under a first-rate instructor in Mr Blaze, in a magnificent swimming bath, had been amply demonstrated by the keenness shown in the House swimming galas held on June 22 1945.' Events were hotly contested, however Gwynedd retained the cup they had held during the ten years the competition had lapsed. The awarding of a point to every pupil who completed a length became a feature of the annual gala, in many cases it was the first occasion for them to accomplish this feat. The reporter in the Magazine, while applauding the success of individuals, thought it desirable that the Cup be won by that House which excelled in team events rather than reliance on one or two outstanding swimmers. A vital adjunct of the use of the College baths was in the training for life-saving. The girls initially had led the way in this activity but in 1949, thanks to the diligence of the good natured Mr Blaze and keen interest of the pupils, an impressive list of successes in the awards of the Royal Life-Saving Society was achieved. The award of merit-silver medal was gained by Beryl Richards and Marian Hughes, with bronze awards to twenty others.

The first boxing tournament for the Roger Eyton Morgan trophy in 1947, provided excellent entertainment with the cup going to Powys, who won three out of eight events. Gratitude was expressed to the donors of the cup whose son, a former pupil, had failed to return from a wartime bombing mission. In this and subsequent competitions, what was lacking in skill was more than made up for in courage, though in view of the little training undergone by the combatants, the benefit of the event was perhaps questionable. At this stage in their athletic careers, correct preparation and training should have been emphasised.

The results of the long established House gymnastic competition for the Adler cup were rarely reported upon but following the 1947 competition the Magazine explained that each team of six had to devise and carry out an eight- minute sequence of rhythmic exercises followed by tests of agility on the box, buck, beams and mat. The judges thought that most competitors had been too ambitious and in concentrating on feats of agility there was a danger that the real purpose of physical training would be lost. The Headmaster was even more forthright when he presented the cup to Wynn Hughes the Ceredigion captain. He commented on 'the tendency in recent years towards very small teams competing in highly specialised exercises; this did not help promote keenness throughout the school and in future he wished to see larger teams in which every fit pupil would take part.'

When the 1944-45 session opened it was confidently expected that the war in Europe would soon be over. However May 8 1945 was a long time coming. The Headmaster wrote in the July 1945 *Ardwynian*:

> At a time when one has to keep a ear open to each news broadcast for fear of missing the announcement of another thrilling victory, it has not been easy to concentrate upon the peaceful events of Ardwyn. This period of tension reached its climax as VE-day approached and a very excited School assembled on its eve in order to decide upon a suitable means of celebration. We guessed-and fortunately guessed rightly- that VE-day would be declared that evening and would be a day of national thanksgiving. Our prefects felt that the second day called for celebration and decided to organise a fancy-dress carnival through the town. Many pupils responded to their appeal in gallant style and provided Aberystwyth with a feast of costume and colour which thrilled the spectators into contributing £25 to the Welcome Home Fund. An excellent piece of organisation on the part of our pupils which deserves the highest praise.

In the same issue of the *Ardwynian* it was deemed to be appropriate, with the overthrow of Germany and the imminent defeat of Japan, to summarise the contribution made since September 1939. Exhaustive enquiries had revealed that 711 old pupils had answered the call, including 69 to the women's Services and 3 Bevin Boys. Fifty-seven had made the supreme sacrifice, including three who had died during the blitz in London and Coventry. Many had survived serious wounds, in one case necessitating amputation of both legs following injury at sea.

There was great rejoicing when POWs Harold Evans, Arvian Jones, Vivian Lewis, David JP Edwards, Idwal Pugh, Monty Thomas, Ernest Northwood, Bert Harget, Richard Mills were repatriated followed by Roy Fisher and Evan William Owen after the Japanese surrender. Ivor Williams and John Yateman had died while in Japanese hands.

While all who served had given meritorious service, there were those who had their bravery or devotion to duty recognised by the award of decorations. Those honoured were:-

Distinguished Service Cross-	D Idris Jones
Military Cross-	Richard M Caul, Huw Morus Jones
	Peter Yateman, D Elwyn Lloyd Jones

The D. C. Lewis Years — 1928-1954

Military Medal-	Gomer Francis, Geoffrey Thomas.
Distinguished Flying Cross-	George A Isbell
Distinguished Flying Medal-	Evan Owen.
Order of the British Empire-	Leslie Davies
Member of the British Empire-	J I Jones, J Albert Jones.
Mentioned in Dispatches-	Trevor Bennett, Edgar Brown, Ieuan Davies, John Edwards, Arvian Jones, Ceredig Jones John Mason, John P Middlehurst Edwina Mills, Alec Vaughan.

Less spectacular were the efforts of the Ardwyn staff and pupils, in the work of the three cadet units formed, the collection of over £10,000 during the special weeks devoted to War Weapons, Warships, Wings for Victory, and Salute the Soldier. In addition there were the subscriptions to the Comfort Fund which financed despatch of the *Ardwynian* with postal order, to all corners of the globe. Involvement also in the Home Guard, Special Police, Fire-guards, Civil Defence, not forgetting the salvage collecting, potato harvesting and the gathering of hips and plants for medicinal purposes.
The vital role of a former Ardwynian girl in the war effort did not come to light for another forty five years.

> Having won a state scholarship on the higher certificate results in 1936, I went to University College, London, full of gratitude for the sound grammatical grounding I had received at Ardwyn. I took my degree in French and German in 1939 just before war broke out and not wanting to teach I took a brief and hurried secretarial course. Within a year I found myself at Bletchley Park where I remained until the war was over.
>
> Until comparatively recently none of us who worked at Bletchley would have dared mention the name, such was the secrecy surrounding it. But publications in recent years have made known that Bletchley was a highly important code-breaking centre where, at the height of the war thousands of German messages were intercepted and deciphered daily. We had there some of the best mathematical and linguistic brains in Britain, but there were thousands of us lesser mortals doing shiftwork all round the clock in huts in the grounds of this large country mansion. We were a mixture of Forces and civilians, the majority of us civilians billeted with families in the surrounding villages. Army transport was provided and security was tight.
>
> The work was highly secret and we only knew our own little bit of it. My work in hut 3 involved a knowledge of German, for it was here that the coded messages were handled and sorted. The pressure was great and the long hours exhausting, but like everyone else in wartime we kept going. It is acknowledged that had it not been for the Bletchley achievement, the war would have gone on much longer.[65]

There was great pleasure taken in the honour conferred on the Headmaster Lt Col DC Lewis by his appointment as Deputy Lieutenant of the County in recognition of his work in the military defences services during the war.

Major HF Stimson who had acted as Deputy Controller of the Civil Defence service during the hostilities, had also been honoured with the award of the M B E.

The Ardwyn Old Pupils' Association held their Victory Welcome Home Dinner and Dance in June 1946, when nearly 200 guests, for the most part, men and women who had been demobilized from the services, attended. Old friends met exchanging their experiences of the war years as well as of their schooldays. The Hall had been tastefully decorated and after an excellent dinner prepared by the newly appointed cook George Edwards, speeches of welcome were made by the Headmaster and other members of staff. Old pupils representing all branches of the services responded and Hywel N Ellis, the Association president, thanked all who had helped make the evening a success. For the second part of the festivities, guests were conveyed to the King's Hall to dance to the music of Evered Davies and his band, with the M C, Major Stimson, ensuring that it all went with a swing.

The ending of the war coincided with a period of great educational change with the implementation of the ambitious 1944 Education Act. Probably the greatest and most beneficial aspect was that secondary education would be free. From April 1 1945, no pupil would pay fees and text-books would be provided free of charge. 'Not before time' would be the reaction of those who had experienced the all too common occurrence previously of seeing a child who had gained a school place on merit, only to find, despite possible remission of fees, the place would have to be refused because of financial hardship. In the days when six or more children in a family was not uncommon, and with one wage earner, it would be impossible for each to receive secondary education. The pages of the minute book of the Governors' meetings are filled with applications for exemption of fees from parents who had to declare their weekly wage -roadman £2, farm labourer 18/- with board, painter £2, widow with pension 15/-. The same book records requests from parents to withdraw their children to become wage earners to help support the family.

Under the new Act, every child between the ages of 11 and 15 years would have to receive secondary education. DC Lewis in considering the future status of Ardwyn, expressed the view that it would be unthinkable that the wheels of progress should be reversed, that the trend towards the practical which had characterised the School during the later years should be retarded, so that the School would become a purely academic institution. Schools would have to be designated as grammar, technical or modern and a decision regarding the status of Ardwyn would have to be made by the local authority. The Headmaster was confident that another requirement of the Act, religious instruction, could be provided without the appointment of a specialist teacher. In addition to the morning service, the staff had agreed that form teachers would teach the subject for a twenty minute period three times a week. It was not until 1948 that the School officially became Ardwyn Grammar School, and as the Headmaster had predicted, it was not seriously affected by the working of the Act. By this time, the annual intake was around 120, a figure which represented fifty per cent of the age group. When one considers that in larger towns the percentage entering grammar schools was as low as ten per cent, perhaps it is not surprising that many found the strongly academic course too difficult, with just fifty per cent of the intake gaining a school certificate. Forty years on there was a public outcry that children were leaving the comprehensive schools without any examination qualifications!

As a result of the operation of the new Education Act, the post of Clerk to the Governors would be assumed by the Director of Education. After the Clerk, RD Williams, had read the minutes for the last time at the Governors' meeting of 23 July 1945, the chairman paid tribute to his faithful and efficient work over a period of twenty two years. Both DC Lewis and his deputy TJ James, writing in the Jubilee magazine, acknowledged his valuable contribution to the School.

> When I was growing up I did not think it at all unusual that my father should sit at a big desk most evenings and tap away at an old Oliver typewriter from time to time. I also took it for granted the fact that he should give advice to people who called at our house clutching official forms of some kind or other. It was later, much later, that I realised what a remarkable man he was, and how fortunate I was to have been born in No 18 Glanyrafon Terrace, in Trefechan.
>
> In this tiny council house, my father Richard David Williams and my mother brought up six children, of whom I was the youngest. Four of them went to university, my sister Lilian having the rare distinction of winning a State scholarship. The house was full of books-books which did not merely 'furnish a room' but were read. 'If you don't know a word, look it up in the dictionary' Dad would say, advice I follow to this day. I did not particularly appreciate it at the time because I took everything for granted.
>
> Dad- 'RD' to all who knew him-sat at that desk because he was Clerk to the Governors at Ardwyn County School. This spare-time job brought him a certain amount of extra income and a great deal of satisfaction. To some extent it met his inner need for the kind of fulfilment he did not obtain from his workaday life: by trade he was a painter and decorator, having his own small business in Aberystwyth between the wars. He had the intellectual capacity to have gone to university, and the spiritual capacity to have become a man of the cloth, but the openings which would have been his right a generation or two later were denied him. He was born in 1887, the son of a local fisherman, and to the distress of his elementary school master, was prevented from going to Ardwyn after performing well in the 'scholarship' because the family needed him at work bringing home some money.
>
> What my father enjoyed about being Clerk to the Governors, I think, was not just the chance to display his grasp of figures-he had studied accountancy at night-school-and to write carefully-drafted minutes in that neat sloping hand of his, but the sense of being part of an academic world, if only in a minor way. He could not have taken part in the Governors' discussions but would have followed them intently. Then there were the papers and documents from the Government, the County Council, the University and other public and private bodies. All these would have broadened personal horizons which otherwise would have been intolerably limited.
>
> My mother was totally supportive, and not simply because the extra cash must have spelt the difference, in the bad times, between just managing and not managing at all. She knew he was capable of much better in life, and that being Clerk to the Governors of Ardwyn, although a long way short of his potential, was important to him.[66]

> In my first year, the 1944 Education Act had not come into force. My earliest picture, even before I entered the portals of Ardwyn, is of going with my parents to Galloway's to buy text books. Another picture is of a long queue of pupils forming each term after the end of the school day to pay our £2 fee to the Clerk to the Governors.
>
> The most vivid picture from that first year was of events surrounding the end of the war. We knew that peace would soon come when IT Jones, the white haired chemistry teacher standing in for RJ Lloyd while he was on active service, told the girls sitting nearest the windows, to peel off the shatter resistant material which had adorned the windows for the previous six years.
>
> In my second year the physics lab was our form room. As we had most of our lessons there I sometimes wonder how much physics was taught in the School at that time. However the back of the room was ideal for Welsh and English class dramatics. One picture that has stuck firmly in my mind is that of our portrayal of the assassination scene from Julius Caesar. We the conspirators, had poked Caesar firmly with our swords, alias rulers, and he had fallen dramatically on the floor. When we got to the line 'Stoop, Romans, stoop, and let us bathe our hands in Caesar's blood', an evil thought entered our minds individually and without premeditation. The result was that the 'dead' Caesar began to wriggle and laugh uncontrollably as we tickled him with as little mercy as that shown by the original conspirators. On glancing apprehensively over our shoulders we were relieved to see that the teacher, Gwenith Davies, was enjoying the joke immensely. That Caesar is now a respected member of the judiciary.
>
> Another picture from that time is our introduction to one of the wonders of modern technology. One day a member of the class produced a new-fangled writing instrument, which did not have a nib but rather a minute ball as the point of contact with the paper. To our great surprise the ink dried instantaneously. The boy came from a well-to-do family so his father was able to afford such an expensive instrument for him.[67]

After twenty years as School cook, Mrs Burns intimated in 1943 that she wished to retire. The Governors recognised her efficient and dedicated service and applied for permission to raise her salary for the remaining period of her service. However, following negotiations, the Headmaster reported that she would take on the role of supervisor/cook with an assistant appointed. With more than 250 pupils taking dinners, plans were prepared for an extension to the dining kitchen which had been built in 1929 when seventy pupils took meals. Before the extended kitchen came into operation in 1947, Mrs Burns had finally retired being succeeded by George Edwards. The Headmaster was confident that the new facilities would be capable of providing meals for the whole School when the proposed scheme for providing free meals for all pupils came into operation. Sadly that advancement never came to fruition although free milk became available during the mid-morning break.

> It is not unusual for a son to go to the same school as his father, but when father follows son, as happened in my case, then it is.
>
> I left Ardwyn in April 1946 to join the Merchant Navy as a cadet. My father, George Edwards, started work as cook supervisor at the start of the summer term that year. He became totally and deeply attached to Ardwyn staff and pupils. I used to marvel

The D. C. Lewis Years — 1928-1954

at the hours he would put in. Most days he would leave the house at seven a. m. and return well after six in the evening. He spent Saturday mornings with the wholesalers placing his orders and the afternoons completing his accounts, menus and paperwork. On Sundays and even in the holidays he would walk up to the School to check on the kitchen. I well remember that on Shrove Tuesday he left even earlier in order to make sufficient pancakes for everyone.[68]

Some of the guest speakers at the wartime prize days were staff of the University of London evacuated to the town. In such times, it was natural that many took democracy and freedom as their main theme. Professor Sissons reasoned that the power of thought was not a birthright-it had to be won. 'The very essence of a democracy was that they had no dictator intellects to work for them, we think for ourselves.' Professor Chapple appealed to pupils to cultivate a civic courage which would be needed to replace, in due course, the martial courage which was currently being displayed. 'If you are too lazy to acquire the habit of thinking straight, and too cowardly to act straight then your place is under a dictatorship.'

Dr Philpott of London University, who later presented a new House cup, spoke on freedom- freedom of working or slacking, freedom of the open mind, freedom to see, freedom to hear, freedom to sum them up and freedom to decide.

Principal G A Edwards of the Theological College reminded his audience that so many great men had begun with limited opportunities but, with great courage and determination had triumphed.

The newly appointed Director of Education for Cardiganshire Dr J Henry Jones, in 1946, emphasised the importance of religion in education, saying that ideas could not be put into practice without the driving force of Christianity.

Dr Mountford, Vice-Chancellor of the University of Liverpool, whose two daughters had attended the School stressed the need for natural ability to be accompanied by hard work. There was place in a school for the ordinary person as well as the exceptional one. School was a place for training for the obligations and responsibilities to come.

The Chief Inspector of Schools for Wales, Dr William Thomas whose team of inspectors was about to descend on the School spoke of how science had revolutionised the world and how atomic energy could be of the greatest benefit to mankind. It seems inconceivable that the problems of half a century later, the disposal of atomic waste and nuclear fallout resulting from nuclear accidents on the scale of Chernobyl, were not foreseen to temper the euphoria.

In preparation for the fiftieth anniversary in 1946, of the founding of the School, the Governors and the Old Pupils Association formed a joint committee to organise the celebratory events. Arrangements were made for a week of festivities with all meetings in the School. In addition, it was decided to produce a special Jubilee issue of the School magazine under the editorship of the senior master T J James. Former pupils were invited to send their reminiscences of their schooldays; an attempt was made to cover the whole period of the School's existence. The week of celebrations started with a service of commemoration on Sunday October 6; on the following day, instead of lessons the pupils were treated to enthralling tales of the old Ardwyn from distinguished old pupils, including Sir Goronwy Owen former MP for Caernarvonshire who was number four on the School register in 1896.

Governors of the School, 1946.

The celebrations continued with a display of gymnastics by the senior boys led by Major Stimson and the girls under the guidance of Meg Bowen, skilfully performed a variety of dances. Visitors also enjoyed the numerous displays put on in the science laboratories and in the wood and metal working rooms.

The School's most distinguished musicians-Professor David de Lloyd and Charles Clements arranged the first of two musical evenings. Dr de Lloyd conducted the College string orchestra while Charles Clements gave solo performances on the piano.

Katie Wilkes sang two solos written by the organisers to further delight the audience.

Great interest was shown in the re-enactment of the House dramatic competition when four one-act plays written, produced and acted by the pupils were presented. Powys were awarded the trophy by former member of staff T O Pierce.

Evelyn Lumley Jenkins succeeded in getting past and present pupils to take part in a miscellaneous musical evening which also included a small choir of girls under the leadership of music teacher Beryl Morgan.

> All roads led to the School field on the last day, for old and young were engaged in deadly combat in soccer and hockey. The middle-aged gentlemen, despite shortage of breath, slowness of manoeuvre and splendid corporations, managed to draw the game, four goals all, thanks to the tactfulness of the referee T J James. Meanwhile the youngsters were being rather merciless on the hockey field and the not-so-young had to admit defeat by eight goals to nil in a game refereed by Meg Bowen.
>
> After the matches came the grand finale, for all the present pupils and staff were entertained to tea in the Central Hall by the old pupils. Full justice was done to the good fare provided and a memorable week had come to an end.
>
> Fifty years ! it is a long time and Ardwyn has travelled a long way. Great changes are foreshadowed in the world of education and the role of the School may change

but, whatever the future may hold, it is the duty and privilege of its sons and daughters to consolidate the splendid work already accomplished.[69]

In contrast to the early years of the School when school inspectors seem to have been frequent and regular visitors, there had not been a full inspection of Ardwyn since 1938. DC Lewis described the upheaval the 1948 visit caused:

> Last March, seventeen inspectors came at various times, each devoting at least two days to his specialist subject. These visits were spread over a month and caused considerable disorganisation of our end-of-term arrangements. Most of our visitors were able to make suggestions which should help to improve the work in classroom whilst all were agreed that the School was seriously overcrowded. As a result of their pressing representations, the County Authority has prepared plans for Ministry approval which will go far to remove our present handicaps and provide buildings worthy of the School.

Immediately following the inspection, HMIs met with the Governors to present a preliminary verbal report. The main points recorded were:

1. The chief difficulties of the School arose from over-crowding and the large percentage of children who were not of grammar school standard. It was recommended that admission in future be confined to at most a three form entry of about ninety.
2. Premises were deficient, there was an urgent need for more girls' offices, larger cloakrooms, and a new kitchen-dining room. Additional classrooms and a library were also required.
3. Attention was called for a linguistic policy more in keeping with the character of the area and for the use of Welsh as a medium of instruction in other subjects such as religious instruction.
4. The curriculum was varied and good work was being done under difficult circumstances
5. Science teaching was suffering for lack of practical facilities; the large science sixth form should be split for practical work.
6. There was no equipment for religious instruction, a special initial grant should be made for this subject to purchase Bibles and atlases. Classes should be split into sets according to the pupils' home language. A specialist teacher was a further desirability.
7. Physical training was excellent and should be maintained at its present standard after the departure of the Chelsea college.

When the confidential written HMI report was considered by the Governors, it was variously described as 'discouraging to teachers', and 'possibly querulous in tone'. One Governor declared that the inspectors had not fulfilled their roles as friends, guides and counsellors and that certain passages in their report should be challenged. During the discussion it was stated that 26 out of 29 pupils had gained the higher certificate that year, though there was little to suggest in the report that the School would have achieved such a record success.

The 1939-45 War Memorial was the work of the former art teacher, WD Lewis. The names of fifty seven old pupils who fell are inscribed on parchment at the head of which is a simple but tasteful design and the words *'Dulce et Decorum est pro patria mori.'* The work of framing the parchment was undertaken by Edward T Lewis, who had lost two sons, both Ardwynians, in the war. The service of dedication took place on 6 October 1947, in the Central Hall, where relatives and friends, together with senior pupils of the school, joined in paying tribute to those who had made the supreme sacrifice. The chairman of the Governors, Ald D Rees Morgan performed the unveiling and in dedicating the memorial, the Rev Richard Davies recalled his own days at Ardwyn and his personal knowledge of some of those who had fallen.

In 1992, the two war memorials were removed from the old School building and with the kind permission of Ceredigion District Council, the Ardwynian Association arranged for them to be placed in the foyer of the town hall. On the 11 November 1992, an appropriate date, the memorials were rededicated by G Walford Hughes, an old Ardwynian who had served in Burma during the second world war.

By 1947 the deprivations of war time were behind and the years which followed were ones of great change and improvement.

There were changes in the internal organisation of the School, and in the external examination system. Compulsory religious instruction for all forms was met by changing the School day into eight periods, four each in the morning and afternoon sessions. This arrangement also allowed each form to have a double period of games weekly instead of once a fortnight.

In 1949, the Central Welsh Board (CWB), which had been established in 1896, (after the passing of the Welsh Intermediate Education Act of 1889 which created the intermediate schools) became merged into the Welsh Joint Education Committee (WJEC), which would meet all the educational needs of Wales except those provided by the University. DC Lewis was honoured by membership of the Committee, a tribute to his high standing in Welsh education. In 1951 there followed the replacement of school and higher certificate by a General Certificate of Education (GCE) to be taken in three grades- ordinary, advanced and scholarship with new matriculation requirements for university entrance. The ordinary level examination could not be taken before the age of sixteen years; to accommodate the five year O-level course, first year pupils would enter Form 1 from session 1949-50 session and not Form 2 as previously. A decision between arts or science courses in the third year, prompted criticism of too early specialisation. The Headmaster advised pupils to concentrate on pursuing an advanced course to qualify for the scholarships and grants which were forthcoming. 'Our advanced courses will be given the highest priority and we hope to run first and second year sixth courses separately in the more popular subjects.'

> Sooner or later we had to face the ordeal of our first major examination, the CWB school certificate. I can still feel the fear and foreboding of those sessions. My picture is of long rows of individual folding desks in the gym and Hall, with gowned figures proceeding in a dignified manner between the rows, glancing from left to right to ensure that we were not cribbing. During the morning sessions in the Hall, Dan the caretaker would come around to mark the position of each leg of every desk with a chalk mark on the floor. In this way the desks could be replaced in their exact positions after they had been removed to make way for the serving of dinner.[70]

It had long been a concern of the Governors that country pupils often had to wait in town until 5pm before being able catch buses for home. From 1948, pupils living

beyond the three mile limit were conveyed on special buses provided by the local authority. The advantages of the new system were obvious but it deprived some pupils of participation in after-school activities. In an effort to alleviate this, the staff encouraged the formation of lunch time clubs. Activities burgeoned and the Magazine regularly reported on the progress of the dancing, record, badminton, table tennis, dramatics and debating clubs. The latter was the brain child of John Morris with David Jenkin the first president. The opening debate 'That spuds should not be peeled' was overwhelmingly lost. A more serious election week generated great interest, high emotions, innumerable addresses, posters and, it was reported, fights. The election lasted for two days and 'JM' recalled that the terrible noise made many of the Conservative and Communist candidates' valuable remarks inaudible. The result was a tie between John Morris (Liberal) and Sian Davies (Welsh Nationalist) each with 58 votes followed by Labour 36, Conservative 18 and Communist 2. The trial of B Sykes for murder, with Mr Justice Beynon Davies presiding, in the Geographic Hall, presaged the future careers at the Bar, of Mr John Morris for the defence, and Mr Elystan Morgan for the prosecution. Going from strength to strength the Club staged a further mock election in December 1948 when John Morris (Liberal) had a landslide victory with Francis Edwards (Conservative) just beating Elystan Morgan (Welsh Nat) for second place. With the departure of many stalwarts including John Morris 'gone the merry Morris din', there was some concern about the future of the debating club. Sensibly, rather than being 'run by the genius of one boy', a committee with joint presidents James Jenkin and Elystan Morgan organised a full programme. Included were a junior debate on the merit of sport, an all female debate on the eccentricities of male clothing, mock police courts, an Ardwyn model parliament, and most notable, a Soccer v Rugger debate.
'During January 1950', wrote 'EM':

> the School echoed in miniature the national political turmoil. Each day witnessed a new strife among the youthful demagogues. Blood and thunder was mixed with Gladstonian oratory. Noble sentiments were mixed with enthusiastic fervour as the candidates exploited the spoken word in an attempt to win over the electorate. Heckling was developed into a fine art and unwanted elements were ejected by the stalwarts of the rugby team.

This was the third election campaign for Elystan Morgan; he was to fight many more in the real world. For Elystan it was a handsome victory at last, the Welsh Nationalists polled 99 votes, with James Jenkin(Liberal) 67, Cecil Jones (Labour) 66 and Dorothy Edwards (Conservative) 57.

> The invitation to project one's thoughts back to schooldays at Ardwyn (in my case 1944-50) is both an alluring and chastening prospect. The allurement lies in re-living experiences which in so many cases had an uplifting and inspiring effect upon one's life. The sobering reality, however, is that so many decades have flitted by since those days so that one better understands the thoughts of the author of the 90th Psalm 'we have spent our years like a tale that is told.'
> But enough of morbidity; the years at Ardwyn-for my generation at any rate-constituted a period of bountiful hope and aspirations. The world was then emerging

from the greatest conflict experienced by humankind; the late 1940s gave signs of that 'revolution of rising expectations', which in succeeding decades was to effect people in every continent. Such developments inevitably dominated the atmosphere of our school days and brought to our lives a sense of buoyancy perhaps not enjoyed by either preceding or succeeding generations.

However much one seeks to concentrate one's mind upon those days which stood in the shadow of cataclysmic events, it is often not the significant skyline of the period that first appears, but a cascade of scenes of such vivid reality and recall as if they had occurred but last week.

I can hear the shuffling, chatter and petty mischief at the beginning of morning assembly giving way to the full-throated gusto with which 'Hills of the North rejoice', 'Rank by rank again we stand' and *'O llefara addfwyn Iesu'* and other splendidly powerful hymns were sung; the thunder of a battalion of boots along the corridor; the clang of laden school bags falling on the hot-water pipes in the lobby; the gentle voice of Dr Ethel Jones that was never raised beyond a whisper and the stentorian rebuke of Roy James to me when playing an agricultural stroke at the wicket - 'Go back to the bush, boy'. I can still smell the stench of the gas works waste on the playing field and the vile odours of rotten eggs coming from the chem. lab. I can see the names on the memorial plaque of those who fell in the war followed by the quotation from 1 Samuel *Y gwyr hyn fu dda wrthym ni... mur oeddynt i ni ddydd a nos.* For some inexplicable reason I can recall every line and detail of the coloured drawing of the Roman siege Gallistra on the wall of the room of 'Miss Davies Latin.'

With such general and public recollections came some of the more personal and intimate nature. High in that category are memories of rather numerous occasions I was summarily sent to the Headmaster's study for a caning. The same scenario was repeated several times:-

'Yes, boy, what do you want?'

'I've been sent for punishment Colonel.'

'What have you done boy?'

'I was misbehaving in class Sir.'

'Why were you doing that lad ?'

'I was showing off Sir.'

'Sit down Dafydd (for some reason he always called me by my first name) I want to talk earnestly to you.'

From that moment the numbness of anticipatory dread in the region of my posterior disappeared. DC Lewis, some years later, showed the same sympathetic humanity when six of us took the School boat to Clarach in stormy weather, and were lucky enough to be carried back by the turn of the tide.[71]

In 1948 the Chelsea physical education college had moved from Borth to new premises in Eastbourne which left a gap in the School's visual aid resources, since the School had made good use of their film projector. A modern film projector costing £238, fund-ed by opera profits, was quickly acquired and led to the formation of a film club. It soon enlisted more than half the School as members, providing mid-day entertainment in the gymnasium twice a week.

The rowing club which seemed to have had a period of inactivity, was revived in the summer of 1947 after the boat, which had been in need of repair, was worked on by the woodwork department supervised by the master Idwal Davies who was always ready to give of his time. A number of captains were appointed and the rule was made that the boat could be launched only if a captain was available to cox and take complete charge of the boat whilst out at sea. Another rule was that the boat could not be taken out of sight of Hywel Ellis' house 'The Chateau' near Castell Brychan. Previously, perhaps, conduct on the high seas had left much to be desired.

> Though not a sportsman, I did take part in one open air activity, the rowing club. I remember on one occasion when we rowed under the pier along its length, one member of the crew stood up and grabbed one of the cross-pieces of the pier's structure. Of course the boat did not stop and he was left hanging above the water while we rowed a leisurely and wide circle back to pick him up. When we reached him he was being accused by somebody up above of trespassing! Being a prospective lawyer he proceeded to argue that he could not be so accused unless a warning notice had been provided to that effect, and that he was prepared to fight his case in a court of law.[72]

In response to the HMI's report, the local authority quickly prepared plans for additional buildings costing £50,000. It was thought unlikely that there would be approval for the full outlay immediately. Surprisingly the plans included provision for boarding accommodation for boys and girls outside the School. Work started early in 1950 with the building of a new house for the Headmaster so that he could vacate the existing accommodation in the main School which would be converted into staff rooms, girls'-cloakrooms and a library. Additionally the roof of the New Block would be removed, the walls built up and the roof replaced to provide four new classrooms above the existing rooms. Thus the full plans for the New Block came to fruition some thirty seven years after they had been made. By October 1952 the Headmaster was able to report that the alterations were almost complete. During the construction work there had been the greatest pressure on accommodation with the loss for a year of the four rooms in the New Block. The metal work room became two classrooms in the interim and all sorts of expedients were adopted.

The provision of a hut by the Air Ministry as headquarters for the Ardwyn ATC squadron was gladly accepted and quickly equipped as two classrooms.

> My father remembered the building and opening of the New Block. I remember its closure for a year so that an additional storey might be built on top of it. The sixth form with the smallest numbers were obliged to find room wherever possible, such as the senior mistress's room and the woodwork room. The prep. class sometimes had to meet in the staff dressing room of the gym and I remember one class being taken half way up the stairs to the laboratories. Looking back on it, the work had been very well done. The School had retained its character and was vastly different from the brick, concrete and glass factories which one saw so often elsewhere.[73]

1952 saw the formation of the Aberystwyth College of Further Education which was linked to the School with the Headmaster as its principal. A purpose built building was soon erected in the School grounds to provide a science laboratory and drawing office. The aim of the college was to provide vocational and technical education for pupils over the age of 15 years. Day-release classes for craft apprentices in the building, engineering, gas and electrical trades and for scientific assistants were established and enthusiastically attended. A branch of the college in the town provided a full-time commercial course. At Ardwyn, facilities were shared, the additional science laboratory being a valuable asset.

The School opera productions continued to be the highlight of the local musical calendar. The three performances and matinee were sell-outs, with queues for booking seats forming at 3 a. m. before sense prevailed and a system for drawing tickets from a drum was introduced. Although each performance brought forth general acclaim, there were dissenting voices. Following the 1947 production of `The Rebel Maid', a correspondent in the *Welsh Gazette* expressed his views:

> For many years now we have had to expect light operas of this sort from Ardwyn, and on each occasion I have experienced this keen disappointment. My 'Cardi' soul revolts at the waste involved-the waste of talent, the waste of money, and the waste of time.
>
> It is obvious that there is always considerable talent at Ardwyn. The principals in the cast of 'The Rebel Maid' were delightful-in spite of the fact that one of them was badly mis-cast. There is no doubt about the talent, but for how much longer are we to see so much promise being put to such footling ends. Is a production of this kind worth the considerable labour, time and money lavished upon on it ? I am given to understand that the bill for costumes alone ran to several hundred pounds. Such an annual production should have educative value in itself, not only for the cast but for the audience as well. The school effort should not be dissipated on trifling nonsense of this sort.[74]

The criticism did not go unanswered:

> Mr Edwards seems to have misunderstood completely the value of the Ardwyn light operas, and to have displayed in passing, his rather limited view of the meaning of education.
>
> Ardwyn has created a very high reputation for itself as a school providing not only education of a strictly academic sort, but also extra-curricular activities of many kinds, all affording opportunities for the pupils to develop a social and cooperative sense. Amongst these activities I would rank the operas as being the most important. As an old pupil I remember with pride the corporate effort voluntarily made by so many staff and pupils, irrespective of whether their place on the final night was on the stage or not, and the enjoyment we all got out of making some little contribution to the joint effort. Would it shock Mr Edwards' obviously materialistic attitude if I suggest that the enjoyment of the pupils derives mainly from the pleasure that they give to others ?
>
> Mr Edwards objects to the type of production being chosen as being 'footling'. The virtue of the Gilbert and Sullivan operas and of others of that kind, is that they are within the scope of school children. Anything more ambitious would impose an

undue strain on voice and physique, and the joy would go out of the whole thing. I would assure Mr Edwards that the educative value of the productions is by no means negligible from the formative point of view, though perhaps not measurable by the restricted and functional interpretation of education upon which he appears to base his criticism.[75]

There always seemed to be an abundance of talent available to fill the principal roles in the operas. However in some cases there were reluctant participants.

It was a great disappointment to me as a tone-deaf child that the school drama was effectively the annual G & S opera, which dominated the autumn term, culminating in a series of performances in the King's Hall. After I had read the lesson in assembly for the first time as a prefect, I was stopped in the corridor by the Head, and complimented on my reading. 'Very good, Edmunds. We need a King Hildebrand in "Princess Ida". You'd better do it.
'But sir, I'm a droner.'
'You read the lesson very well. You can play Hildebrand.'
'But sir I can't sing'
'You read the lesson very well.' And so it went on. There was no-one else, so I had to do it. Poor Miss Beryl Morgan-on whom I had quite a crush-had her burden as music director heavily increased, and I went through hell. Oh, it was fine in the speaking bits, in my blue velvet robe and gold crown, but as soon as I had to open my mouth and try to sing, my voice became a feeble, embarrassed mutter. Never again.[76]

John Edmunds, at Ardwyn 1940-1947, entered the UCW with a scholarship and left with a first class honours degree in French. He became a familiar face on the television screen in the late Sixties and early Seventies hosting 'Top of the Form' and BBCtv newsreading. He also found time to research a Ph D and in 1973 returned to Aberystwyth to found and direct the UCW drama department. After twelve years came early retirement and university teaching in Mexico. In the early Nineties it was back to the London stage, directing and acting and translating French and Spanish drama. Ardwyn left an indelible impression on him:

I am always amazed at how some people have forgotten their schooldays; who taught them what, even. To me it was so exciting. Subsequently I taught in two London grammar schools and a public school. They weren't a patch on Ardwyn in the quality of staff, the imaginativeness of the educational experience offered, or in the friendly family atmosphere.
 I was always fascinated-as a theatre buff from an early age-with the ritualistic aspects of school (the fact that teachers wore gowns I thought amazingly exotic) I loved the way the Head swept into the Hall to take assembly wearing his mortarboard, only to remove it immediately for prayers, and put it on again simply to turn round and walk out.
 One might think that, with so much energy expended on the opera and the eisteddfod-as well as the usual sporting activities- academic work would suffer. Not much chance of that; DC Lewis had the nerve to require every member of staff to keep a log of what they had done with every class throughout the week and every piece of

homework set. These were written up, usually at the extended form-teacher period on Friday afternoon, handed in, inspected over the week-end and returned on Monday. Then there were the examinations in the penultimate week of every term, the whole School being reorganised to fit a special exam time-table. Some how, the papers were marked, gone over in class and the results handed in to the office by the end of term, and those pupils who had achieved a first-class average were mentioned in final assembly. So we worked and played hard all the time, and were stretched in all directions. An Ardwyn pupil was challenged with the highest expectations and given the most positive encouragement in an atmosphere that was ordered and caring.

During the five post-war years there were twenty-five staff appointments made, of which five stayed until retirement. Many left after just a year, the scarcity of housing being a contributary factor to the high turnover so there were calls for the council to make special arrangements for the housing of teachers. Pegi Davies, who had been biology mistresss throughout the war years and who had been prominent in so many School activities left to take up a post in Bala. Her successor AK Vaughan stayed for one year before being spirited off to join the teachers' emergency training scheme. A similar fate befell E Cyril Richards, for thirteen years physics and mathematics master, a post which he had held with distinction. One of many of his pupils who achieved prominence in his subjects was Dr Gareth Wyn Evans, a state scholar of 1939 and long serving member of the mathematics department of University College Swansea. When Cyril Richards died in 1993 age eighty six, Dr Evans in a tribute wrote:

> In applied mathematics in the sixth form, we worked out problems in dynamics and statics; some of these were monstrously difficult and neither I nor occasionally he, could solve them. There was never any false pride, the blockbusters were taken to the Headmaster DC Lewis, who I never knew to fail. Richard's attitude to physics was different. For him it was not just a technical matter but rather a search for an understanding of the natural world and the limitations of that understanding. It was an attitude bordering on metaphysics which was common enough in those days but which was destroyed utterly a few years later by the coming of the atom bomb. I would meet him occasionally when he visited his family in Swansea. He had integrity and a direct honesty; I always felt more relaxed and complete after meeting him. Ardwyn, clearly meant much to him. I was there as a pupil expecting to learn, he as a teacher who learned much.

Having reached the retiring age of sixty years, Irene Davies the Latin teacher, had her application for extension of service denied by the Governors and Haydn James was appointed in her place. She was however, asked to teach religious instruction for the 1947-48 session but eventually resigned at Christmas that year to take up a post in Romford, obviously disenchanted after twenty-nine years service to the School.

> 'Dafws Latin' she was called, just as 'Mrs Jones the Fish' designated the wife of the fishmonger. When we first moved to Wales as 'private evacuees', I thought it was because she had eyes like a cod, but no such wit. The Latin-monger Irene Davies, was not actually schizoid, but she certainly had a double personality; a timid, nervously smiling, ingratiating soul outside the classroom, she became a fiery fiend within it.

> Find the verb! How many times do I have to tell you? The harsh, weary voice would hammer away until the Livy, or Cicero, or Virgil turned itself into acceptable English. Never any discussion or explication of the content; philosophy, history or literature was exploited for its syntax and vocabulary. The medium was all, no wonder most of us detested Latin.
>
> Yet I chose the subject in the sixth form, weakly won over by an unexpected appeal in the corridor. Hopping bird-like from one foot to the other, a strangely vulnerable Dafws Latin wondered whether I had thought of continuing with her subject, so useful for French which I intended to pursue at the university. I hadn't, but looking down (for she was tiny) at the round olive face topped by jet-black hair parted and plaited into what we called ear-phones, I suppose I was touched. Well, yes, I must have been, for I had not mastered Latin, didn't enjoy it, and indeed never learned to read it with ease.[77]

When Hywel Ellis suffered a further breakdown in health and had to resign, the Headmaster recognised the value of his teaching of art, geography and German and the contribution he had made to the rowing club, gymnastic teams, drama production and army cadets. His able presidency of the Old Ardwynian Association during the period of the Victory dinner and Jubilee celebrations had assured the success of those events. The art teaching was continued by Leslie Thomas for two years and FS Baldwin for four years.

David G Sansbury returned to his *Alma mater* to teach biology for the rest of his career. After four years of 'energetic, capable and enthusiastic service' Meg Bowen and Beryl Roberts neé Morgan, left to undertake home duties. In particular their work for the operas had been brilliantly successful.

In 1949 W Leslie Davies took over the teaching of Classics and remained at his post until his untimely death in 1973. That same year Gwyneth Winkler a former pupil, who had been living in east Germany when it was over-run by the Russian army, was permanently appointed to teach Latin initially but later re-introduced German, a subject which had regained its popularity. Mansel Jones whose talents had been recognised during a period of training at the school, was snapped up as a teacher of general subjects with a view, no doubt, to succeeding to head of history.

The start of the new decade saw the retirements of two long serving members of staff. Dr Ethel Jones had served as senior mistress and French teacher for seventeen years.

> Dr Jones has earned a high place in the affections and regard of staff and pupils. Keen and efficient as a teacher, she was also a guide, philosopher and friend and the best tribute we can pay to her is to recall the warm regard of hundreds of old pupils and the kindly wise beneficent influence she had on them. She was fond of a comment made by a small boy sitting the entrance examination supervised by Dr Jones. 'I don't think she was a teacher: she looked more like a mother.'[78]

HF Stimson was retiring after twenty-eight years service, shared between the School and the College. He was recognised as one of the outstanding gymnastic teachers of his day.

His colleagues at Ardwyn will remember Major Stimson as an outstanding example of a superb craftsman, whose genius as a teacher could transform routine method into something which inspired even the least able to do their best-and then a little more. Innumerable Ardwynians over the past twenty-one years will recall with the greatest delight his productions of the annual opera in which every rehearsal-so much more important to the pupil than the actual performance-was a lesson in singing, speech training and deportment.[79]

Looking back at those happy days at Ardwyn, I begin to wonder where the time has gone. It seems that it was only yesterday when 'Stimmie' would get in touch during school holidays to get the gymnastic team together because there was a garden fete or some such event. The lads would rally around, keeping their PT kit at the ready and off we would trundle to perform. They were great days. Looking back, it was quite remarkable that 'Stimmie' could inspire such a group response. His favourite saying as he walked into the gym was, 'No wonder the Germans laugh'. This didn't do much for our egos. He did make one promise to my year which we decided to take him up on. He promised tea and cakes for the whole class if he could walk in one day to find every boy doing a handstand. One magical day it happened. He was as good as his word. A few weeks later he took us all to tea at W Wynne Owen.[80]

The replacement staff were Gwendolyn Herbert from Halifax, who became senior mistress, with Denise Taylor, a French national, in charge of French teaching. Gerwyn Williams the reigning Welsh Rugby Union full back, direct from Loughborough college, became the first full-time physical education master to be appointed. In line with the increased importance of the subject, physical training had by now become physical education. It would be appropriate to pay tribute to those non-PE trained teachers who, usually without any financial incentive, assisted with games coaching, in addition to teaching their subject specialism, and usually spent every Saturday morning refereeing or supervising matches. Many had gained such enjoyment from active involvement in their sport that this was a means of repaying their debt. The girls also had a newly qualified PE teacher in Zoe Latus who succeeded Jean Elliott who had left after just one year to join her husband. Ronald Everson an Aber graduate and a College gymnastic champion started a twenty-three year dedicated stint as senior mathematics master.

Another long connection with the School was severed at the end of the 1950-51 session. After twenty-eight years of devoted service, the last eight as senior master, T J James had reached retirement age. Sam Mitchell who succeeded him as senior master, wrote in the October 1951 magazine:

> In a distinguished academic career at the College, Tom James had an equally successful sporting career gaining colours in soccer, cricket and tennis, culminating in a Welsh amateur soccer cap in 1911. He kept wicket for the College side for three years, a rare pointer to his character. The scoring batsman or the devastating bowler earns the plaudits of the crowd whilst the wicket-keeper 'has to be on his toes'-mentally and physically throughout the match and shares none of the limelight.
> Although his playing days were over when he entered Ardwyn, he took a keen

interest in every branch of School sport; his refereeing of a soccer match was a model which many referees in local football could copy to their advantage

Every past and present pupil knows how much they are indebted to Mr James not only for the teaching received but also for that extra 'something' which transcends actual teaching. It is certain that he will be remembered with gratitude and affection by all who came in contact with him.

In his tribute, the Headmaster spoke of Tom James' loyalty and devotion to the School and how his teaching had inspired so many of his pupils to gain high distinction in his subject. As senior master he had zealously carried out his duties with the highest standards of tact and efficiency.

In acknowledging his retirement gift Tom James said that it was his intention to purchase a wireless set with the money and with the surplus he would provide himself with a comfortable chair in which he could muse upon that which had been and soften his regrets at what had to be. He rejoiced that he had had the privilege and pleasure of helping pupils prepare for the time when they had to face life on their own. He rejoiced too in their successes, which brought credit to themselves and reflected glory and credit to their teachers and the School.

Tom James the history master, was a fine teacher, a quiet disciplinarian and a gentleman. In my final year, the history lesson, on a Wednesday afternoon was held in the biology room, which overlooked the college playing field. On occasions, Mr James would request us to 'study privately' so that he could view the progress of a soccer match through the window.[81]

Tom James was a very fine teacher who made the past come to life; imparting information was the least of his concerns, his main purpose was to prompt thought, even speculation. I remember him with admiration and gratitude; to this day the structure of some of his lessons remains with me.[82]

The choice of the 1949 opera, the twenty-first of the series, was 'The Pirates of Penzance' - the third time for it to be performed by the School. The newly appointed music teacher Gerwyn Thomas was unable to start until the Easter term which of course had serious implications for the opera production. For the first time, a pupil figured prominently in the task of musical direction along with Arthur Hughes, the temporary music teacher. Gareth Davies, a sixth form music student, in the Headmaster's words 'proved a tower of strength in rehearsing for our opera production and in directing the work at the performance'. In many respects he mirrored the earlier Charles Clements in that he was invariably to be found playing the piano in the Hall or music room surrounded by a bewitched audience. In his last year he virtually won the eisteddfod for Powys, winning four events and leading the House choir to victory. Gareth went on to the UCW on a music scholarship and gained his ARCO at the age of nineteen. After graduation came national service spent playing in the orchestra of the Irish Guards. He was drawn then to the stage where he was musical director of many West End musical 'hits' such as the 'The Music Man', 'Cabaret' and the much acclaimed 'Fiddler on the

Roof' with Topol. In addition to his theatre work, he enjoyed a busy career in radio, television and recording studio. Gareth was commissioned by the B B C to write a work for voices and orchestra which was broadcast live on March 1 1969, entitled *'Cotiau Coch Gogerddan'*. The musical world was robbed of his talents when he died at the early age of forty.

> On the Saturday before the week of the opera, pupils would queue outside the King's Hall to book seats for those to whom they had sold tickets, the keen ones arriving as early as 6 am to make sure of the best seats for their customers. The performances were always a sellout.
>
> Then came the big week. Everyone had to be at the King's Hall by 10 am on the Monday for costume fitting. The dress rehearsal would start at 2 pm and continue until 9 or 10 pm. Those pupils living in the country would stay with friends in town for the week.
>
> During the tea break, the whole cast would be assembled on stage for a photograph, the big magnesium flash, a real crash, bang, wallop affair, would scare the daylight out of many.
>
> On Tuesday afternoon, the principals would parade up Eastgate Street to Evered Davies' studio in Pier Street to have their photographs taken. When the 'Pirates of Penzance' was performed in 1949, the policemen marched smartly in pairs, with truncheons at the ready headed by 'Sergeant' Brian Martin, much to the surprise and amusement of onlookers.[83]

During the three years she taught English, Mary Jones had endeared herself to her pupils and there was a genuine sadness when she left in 1950 following her marriage to W Beynon Davies. Her successor Heulwen Edwards (Beech) gave six years devoted service to the School.

After three years, the last, as head of history, Mansel James moved to Trinity College Carmarthen, as history lecturer, later becoming principal of that teacher training college. As well as being an inspiring teacher, he was responsible for the resuscitation of the Air Training Corps which, five years after the departure of its commander William Roberts in 1945, seemed to have been moribund. The provision of their own headquarters -the ATC hut at the School- encouraged a muster of over thirty cadets who enjoyed flights from their camps at RAF stations as well as studying for proficiency examinations. By the time David Sansbury took over as commanding officer, the squadron had been firmly re-established and went from strength to strength providing the cadets with exciting and challenging experiences. The award of a flying scholarship in 1953 allowed Roger Griffiths to be the first Ardwyn cadet to qualify for a pilot's licence.

> The Air Training Corps or Mansel's Air Force as we called it. I was a founder member in 1950 and recall the mad scramble for pieces of uniform when the crates arrived-the jubilation when I managed to acquire a complete set of trousers, jacket, topcoat and beret. Drill in the School yard and flying for the first time in an Avro Anson from St Athan during the first camp. Ten hour flights in Sunderlands from Pembroke Dock with gunnery and depth charge practice. Finally learning to fly in a de Havilland Tiger Moth in Manchester as I left Ardwyn in 1953, when DG Sansbury was the CO (His son is now my GP at Swansea).

> We were well served by our science teachers at Ardwyn. RJ Lloyd was a successful and popular teacher of chemistry, responsible for a stream of eventual graduates and a number of PhDs in my year alone. I also owe a great debt to Maurice Chapple. The 'dreaded physics' that I had been warned about by my seniors turned out to be a never ending source of interest to me. MT Chapple instilled in me a love of physical science as I discovered how things like the electric bell, the car jack and the telescope worked. It was he who launched me into a career as an aeronautical engineer and I shall be for ever grateful to him. I often wonder whether our teachers fully appreciate the good they do and the far reaching effects their influence has on their pupils.[84]

It was no surprise when Gerwyn Williams left to join a London school, after two years. Former pupil Noel Butler, one of the finest athletes produced by the School, joined the staff to teach history and physical education as well as assisting with the ATC.

Roy James, appointed in 1948 to lead the geography teaching had made an immediate impact in the classroom and on the games field. However in order to receive hospital treatment for a serious hip injury sustained on war service, he was away for most of the 1952-53 session. Much to his joy he was able to return in time to resume coaching of his beloved game -cricket.

A movement to increase the partnership between teachers and parents gained momentum nationally after the war. Inspired by keen and interested parents, the first meeting of the Ardwyn Parents'-Teachers Association took place in January 1950, with nearly two hundred parents and staff present. Professor Richard Aaron was elected chairman of the Association and a draft constitution was discussed. The early meetings produced strongly worded resolutions to the Governors on the deplorable state of the buildings and furniture, some of which had been in the School since its formation, and the need for a new kitchen -dining room. Dr Ernest Jones, the county medical officer of health, reported that the dining conditions were unsatisfactory from the point of view of health. Roderic Bowen MP had been notified by the Minister of Education that the erection of a kitchen-dining room was prevented by existing legislation. However the Headmaster was authorised to purchase lockers and new furniture. Another matter discussed was the inadequte provision made by the LEA, compared with other counties, in the matter of grants and awards for university education and other categories of student.

It had long been a declared ambition of DC Lewis to have an electronic organ installed in the Hall. As far back as 1938 an organ fund was started from opera profits. However the intervention of the war and the diversion of funds for the purchase of Red Cross equipment and the distribution of School magazines and gifts for the serving troops delayed matters. In the 1952 prize day, the Headmaster announced that the organ fund had been re-established. He believed that an organ could be a most valuable asset to religious services and to the music teaching in the School. Since 1939 there had been a three-fold increase in the cost but he was confident that with the promise of £500 from the P.T.A; together with a School target of the same amount, the money would be found. The withdrawal of the promised £500 from the LEA, due to government cuts, was a set-back particularly as the Head naturally wished to have the organ in place before his retirement. With a concentrated effort during the 1952-53 session-'a session that would go down in the history of Ardwyn as organ year', the fund quickly grew. Weekly contributions by staff and pupils, profits from concerts, plays and Welsh Night raised over £300. The PTA reached its target with a whist drive, jumble sale and a Spring fair, which together with generous donations from the public, allowed the purchase at £1,685, of the best electronic organ available. The Headmaster was due to retire in August 1954 so it was with a great deal of pride that he was able to announce in his last prize day that the Compton organ had been installed and 'had made a tremendous difference to morning assembly and is already helping several pupils to become organists.' At the service of dedication in September 1953, Charles Clements had given a masterly recital which showed the value of the acquisition.

As part of the School's effort to generate funds for the organ, the senior pupils staged 'The Chiltern Hundreds' at the Little Theatre. This was entirely the effort of the pupils with no adult assistance-the Headmaster knew little about it until he saw the production on the stage. The success of the production prompted a lengthy leading article in the *Welsh Gazette* of the 5 March 1953.

> As a result of the Education Act of 1944, an education is so much easier today than it was ten or twelve years ago and many have come to believe that advantages without any great effort or sacrifice on the part of the pupils tend to kill initiative and make them take things for granted.
>
> The pupils of Ardwyn have shown that this fear is without foundation. Without any aid from their teachers the pupils presented in about six weeks, a play in the local theatre. They made all the arrangements, such as booking the theatre, selling the tickets and ushering the members of the audience to their seats. The two performances they gave were, for young people of their age, of an exceptionally high standard that compared favourably with the productions of professional repertory.
>
> Activities of this kind, which are outside the formal school curriculum are important in the education of young people. They teach them how to shoulder responsibility and how to act on their own initiative. It is to be hoped that children everywhere can show the same independence of mind and initiative that is characteristic of the present generation of higher form pupils at Ardwyn. They have created a new tradition which can be enriched and developed by succeeding generations of pupils. This is leadership at its best.

The production of 'The Gondoliers' in December 1951 was to be the last in the series of twenty-three operas. In an effort to reduce costs, Violet Jones had designed and largely made the costumes of the girls' chorus. Due to a huge increase in the cost of production and with receipts diminished, the Headmaster announced that he was compelled to close the series but would seek some alternative which would avoid the very heavy costs of scenery, costumes, orchestra and production. The choice was a Christmas concert held in the King's Hall and included a boys' gymnastic display, a girls' dancing display, performance of a one-act play and a nativity play. The wide array of costumes used were again designed and made in the School, many by the pupils themselves. The profit of £100 boosted the organ fund, and the Headmaster admitted that the concert gave a better picture of the School's activity.

The D. C. Lewis Years — 1928-1954

In one final effort to reach the target figure for the new organ it was decided to produce just one more opera. In Coronation year, 'Merrie England' was a fitting choice;. Major Stimson, now retired, once again agreed to produce it. This final production maintained the high reputation built up since the first opera in 1929, with the £200 profit finally clearing the outstanding deficit on the organ. When Major Stimson, who had produced all the School operas, was requested to give his usual rendering of 'Sergeant Major' at the opera soiree, it was to be his last appearance at the School, for he died in June 1954.

With the impending retirement of TJ James, who had served as Magazine editor for at least seventeen years, it was decided, by the new staff editors Gwyneth Mainwaring and AR Pugh, to produce one magazine recording events of one School year. The first edition covering session 1950-51 was produced in October 1951 and certainly looked different. Larger in size and greater in content than the previous editions, it sported a new cover designed by the art master FS Baldwin, with a stylised School crest showing six towers of a castle instead of the traditional keep of Aberystwyth castle. In the second issue the Headmaster warmly complimented the editors on the success of the first. 'The production of a true and faithful record of session 1950-51 in such an attractive form, is a most praiseworthy effort and has undoubtedly enhanced the prestige of the School.'

Within the covers, every aspect of School life was recorded including the trip to Cork- the first School excursion since the Dublin visit of 1939. With rationing still in force in the United Kingdom, the food and confectionery shops were a revelation. One remembers the visit to Blarney castle and the acrobatics of those intent on kissing the Blarney Stone, including the future MP, Elystan Morgan whose powers of oratory were already extraordinarily developed. On the return journey, kindly customs men turned a 'blind eye' to the bulging bags filled with sugar, tinned fruit and of course nylon stockings. In the years which followed regular annual excursions were made to London in 'Festival of Britain year', Edinburgh, Bristol and Oxford.

WG Rowlands contributed an article 'An hour with a world celebrity', which described a visit made to the London home of the Rt Hon Winston Churchill, by members of the Corporation of Aberystwyth. Soon after the war that body had agreed to confer the freedom of the borough on the wartime premier in recognition of his leadership and inspiration during the conflict. A silver casket containing the freedom scroll had been prepared but five years had passed and the great man had not been able to travel to the town to receive the honour.

> Mahomet could not come to the mountain so the mountain went to Mahomet, a deputation of six was selected to make the journey to London. 'What has this to do with Ardwyn you may ask?' The answer is a good deal as five of the party had connections with the School. Cllr RJ Ellis, the Mayor, Cllr J A Hughes, ex-Mayor, Cllr EO Savage, cameraman and HDP Bott, Town Clerk are all old Ardwynians, while the writer, as you know has been a member of staff for over twenty years. Ald David Thomas, Mayor elect, cannot claim the same distinction, although his wife and daughter are old pupils. The ceremony itself was short and dignified and took place in the garden. We all felt we had been greatly privileged to have spent an hour with a truly great man, one chosen by destiny to lead his country 'in its finest hour.'

By the end of the Forties, sporting horizons were being extended with the formation of county teams, national trial matches and championships. In the early Fifties, the netball team reached heights not previously attained. Under the coaching of Zoe Nicholls neé Latus, only two games were lost in four seasons. Hilary Evans and Mary Owen captained undefeated sides while Sheila Meigh and Janet Ward were only slightly less successful leaders, losing to the experienced UCW VII and St Padarn's Convent, the latter defeated in the return match. However in trial matches for the national team the players realised that they had some way to go to match the standards of the south Wales girls. However during their college years, Janet Ward and Audrie Evans had the distinction of playing for their country.

During the same period the hockey players had undistinguished years apart from the 1950 team led by Jane Mason which suffered just one defeat at the hands of Newtown.

In athletics there were changes in track and field events in line with the requirements of the county and national programme. Age categories became junior, middle and senior with the tug-of-war, egg and spoon race, three-legged race replaced by the more serious shot, weight, javelin, discus, triple jump and walking events. Specialist coaching and rigorous training produced high standards; the 1952 sports meeting produced twenty-six new records, many of course in recently introduced events. Dafydd Rhys Thomas was an outstanding athlete of this era gaining the victor ludorum on two occasions and creating a new long jump record of 19ft 4ins. Hefin Elias who created a record in winning the senior cross-country race three years in succession, was equally talented on track and field, being twice victor ludorum. He improved the 880 yards time, threw the shot over 33 feet but was incorrectly reported to have broken the mile record with a time of 5 min 25 sec; Ifan Davis' mile, run in 1935 was 15 seconds faster. The mile record was again reported to have been improved by M Pusey in 1954 but the time of 5 min 16. 4 sec reported in the *Cambrian News* did not better the 1935 record. The victorious netball captain Mary Owen earned the victrix ludorum in 1951 and 1952, the result of winning the sprint events.

In the county athletic championships, the School regularly gained section cups and many Ardwynians won their way into the Cardiganshire team competing in the national championships but at this time made little impression on the athletes of the larger counties.

Hefin Elias captained an unbeaten soccer team in 1952 in which the brilliant goalkeeping of Ronald Thomas played a large part. After leaving School, Thomas gained a Welsh youth 'cap' against England. Two years later, in what was the last season for soccer in the School for sixteen years, the untried team led by Iwan Jones lost just one game. Carrying on the family tradition, Dyfed Elias showed a talent which attracted the attention of English League football scouts.

During the two years when Gerwyn Williams was in charge of boys' games, the rugby results were unspectacular. But perhaps his influence was felt the season after his departure when an experienced first XV led by Brian Martin had its most successful season for many years, being unbeaten. Highlights were a well-earned draw against Pembroke Dock played for the first time and defeat of Cardigan for the first time in six years. R J Lloyd, helped by Roy James was once again involved in the rugby training.

The D. C. Lewis Years — 1928-1954

Prefects 1949–50.

Hockey Team 1950–51. Captain: Jane Mason

Netball Team 1950–51. Captain: Hilary Evans

For the boys, it was always a proud Friday when they were first chosen for the School rugby or soccer team. It meant going to the men's staff room to collect the green and white team shirt and walking around with it in full view to show that you had made it to the School team. No doubt the girls felt the same pride when they made their sports teams.[85]

For ten years, starting in 1951 readers of the *Ardwynian* were treated to reviews of the cricket season by Roy James who coached the team for sixteen years. The reports revealed the depth of his knowledge and intense love for the game. Full of constructive criticism, expert advice and anecdotes drawing on his long association with the game, these chronicles were also literary gems, eagerly awaited each year by cricketers and others alike. Under his coaching, he dedicated many after- school hours to it, great strides were made by individuals and the team became increasingly successful over the years in their matches against school and adult sides. The secret of the consistent success probably lay in the selection policy of introducing a few younger players each year to rub shoulders with the experienced. Keenly contested House matches also revealed a wealth of talent to be utilised in the future. 1952 was reported as being a triumphant season for the cricket XI - not one game lost in fourteen matches played, though there were anxious moments in a drawn game with the powerful College staff side. The closing matches were played under increasing strain but Newtown were defeated on their own ground. The real crisis came with the visit to the bogey ground at Machynlleth. The School were dismissed for 32 by lunch. 'It looked all over but hostile bowling supported by aggressive close-in fielding put the home side out for only 12.' One boy who had played for three seasons was picked out for special praise. 'No side could be a poor one, with an opening bowler of the calibre, speed and experience of Alan Jones, whose final record of 195 wickets during his school career is not likely to be beaten for a long time.' In his last year Alan's success earned him a place in a south Wales touring XI to the south of England.

In this period, the success of Ardwyn cricket produced an improvement in local cricket generally. Many adult teams were boosted by the inclusion of former Ardwynians, so the sides previously beaten with ease were proving more difficult. The reviewer thought that there was no game other than cricket in which keen skilled youngsters could take on average adult players, and more than hold their own. In describing the School ground as one of the loveliest in West Wales he acknowledged the fine work of groundsman John Lewis in preparing the wicket 'without which good batting would not have been possible. If only the School XI could always play on its own lovely ground and not, as they did so often, have to perform in semi-cut grass in rural hay fields'. Roy James was also generous in his praise of the senior girls who gave up their leisure time on Saturday afternoons to prepare the teas. To him there was no summer activity other than cricket. His singlemindedness is expressed in one of his reports.

> The occurrence of school and county athletic sports during May and the encouragement of mixed tennis affected regular attendance at net practices. Ardwyn cricket should not be allowed to decline from being the most consistently successful school game- boys and girls- for several years.

Academic distinctions continued to flow into the School. Between 1950 and 1953 seven State scholarships were gained in addition to seventeen university entrance awards. In 1951 the School gained the only three State scholarships which came to Cardiganshire, and five university entrance awards including three open scholarships. Not all sixth formers proceeded to university. The 1950 head boy Norman Nichols was probably the first Ardwynian, certainly in peace time, to enter the Royal Military College at Sandhurst. One of his contemporaries, John A C Morgan from Talybont, joined the Fleet Air Arm and became the first Ardwynian helicopter pilot. As a naval lieutenant operating from *HMS Theseus*, he was awarded the M B E for his rescue work during the Suez crisis in late 1956. Sadly he was killed in an air accident while on active service in Borneo in 1965.

In his penultimate annual report in 1953, D C Lewis regretted the action of capable girls leaving at the age of fifteen to take up posts which he thought were unworthy of their capabilities and could not provide them with adequate opportunities to use their talents. He believed they should have proceeded to the sixth form. He again emphasised that no pupil should enter Ardwyn with the intention of leaving before reaching the age of sixteen. If they felt strained or discouraged at their lack of progress after two years or if they desired to leave at fifteen then they should apply for transfer to the secondary modern school. Maintaining academic standards was a prime concern, particularly with indications that it was becoming more difficult to gain a pass in the new external examination system.

The guest speaker at the last speech day attended by D C Lewis as Headmaster of Ardwyn in March 1954 was Morgan Goronwy Rees who was in his first session as Principal of the U C W. The Headmaster in his introduction said-

> I must state how proud we are to have such a distinguished Ardwynian on this platform today. Former pupils have gained very high distinctions in many vocations but only one has become a principal of a university college. Goronwy Rees was a pupil at this school for just one session owing to the removal of his home to Cardiff but we have watched his career with great pride and pleasure. A School magazine contained this brief statement-'Hearty congratulations to Goronwy Rees of Cardiff High School on his history scholarship to New College, Oxford; he is well remembered as an exceedingly live wire in IIA in 1921-22.' The following year the Magazine reported that he had won a State scholarship and had proceeded to Oxford where he gained many distinctions including a fellowship of All Souls. We feel sure that under his able guidance as principal, the University College of Wales will rise to great eminence and wish him every success in his responsible task.

Principal Rees, in his address said-

> Unless one is a genius who manages to preserve throughout life the fresh eye and fresh mind of children it is almost impossible to enter their minds or even to re-enter one's own mind as a child. This is one of the fundamental difficulties of education.

Wishing success and happiness to those leaving Ardwyn, he hoped that some of them would enter the U C W where they would be assured of a cordial welcome.

> The relations between the town of Aberystwyth and the College are matters which are very close to my heart as the only principal of the college who was born in the town. I cannot think of any better means of strengthening those relations than a close, continuous and ever-increasing connection between Ardwyn School and the College, both of which have their homes in Aberystwyth.

The Principal's stay in the town was short. In 1957 he was forced to resign following the publication of a series of articles in a Sunday newspaper on Guy Burgess, the spy who defected to Moscow in 1951. A national newspaper had revealed that the source of the information from which the articles were written was Principal Goronwy Rees of Aberystwyth.[86]

In his last report, the Headmaster glanced backwards over a quarter of a century. In 1927, when he was appointed the School had 310 pupils, that had increased to the current total of 535 and over that period he had been responsible for the education of 3,300 Ardwynians. The new block had greatly improved accommodation but conditions had become cramped again following the admission of 135 new pupils in 1953. He appreciated that the local authority had a difficult task in setting a satisfactory line between grammar and modern pupils but he was convinced that no grammar school could take 60% of the pupils in its district up to general certificate of education standards.

He paid tribute to the Governors who had served with him, in particular Ald D Rees Morgan who had been in office when he was appointed and who had served as chairman of Governors for fifteen years.

After reviewing the considerable building developments which had taken place during his time, he hoped that the new dinner unit would not be too long in coming now that the site in the adjacent college garden had been secured.

> When I arrived at Ardwyn during the autumn of 1948, I felt as though I had landed on another planet. Previously I had attended a boys' boarding school where attitudes between staff and pupils were confrontational and there was considerable violence in class and in the playground. Fights between pupils would often take place in the fives courts. Moving to Ardwyn from such an environment made one feel at first that the place was unreal; staff were friendly, relaxed and encouraging. I did see two members of staff hit pupils, but this was the exception and not the rule. I did not witness one fight between pupils.
>
> For me, DC Lewis was a great Headmaster; he always kept sufficiently distant to be held in awe, but in personal relationships he was always interested in pupils, kind and encouraging. I recollect his coming in his car to our home in Gogerddan to fetch my brother Dyfed and sister Dilys to an exam for which they had failed to turn up. Assemblies with DC Lewis were always dignified occasions.
>
> There never seemed to be a dull moment at Ardwyn as I look back from this distance. There was always preparation for some activity or other, debates, opera, eisteddfod, School and House sporting events as well as some academic work to be enjoyed.[86A]

The D. C. Lewis Years — 1928-1954

The School said farewell to its Headmaster in the final assembly of the 1953-54 session. Sam Mitchell the senior master was to first to pay tribute to D C Lewis who, having completed twenty-six years, was the longest serving Ardwyn headmaster. Mr Mitchell, after relating the state of the facilities before the time of D C Lewis, enumerated the developments which had resulted from his vision, and dogged persistence- new science laboratories, a new school field with pavilion, the gymnasium, engineering workshops developing into the further education college. *Y Noson Gymraeg*, the operas and his ultimate effort the acquisition of the organ, were all his initiatives. Sam Mitchell concluded by saying that the Head's finest virtue was that he trusted his staff and never interfered with their teaching or their departmental duties. This made for a happy school.

The senior mistress Gwendoline Herbert added her tribute by saying that the Head 'expected the best from the staff and then left us to do it in our own way but at the same time was at least one jump ahead.'

Former senior master T J James referred to the period of steady expansion -new buildings, new outlooks, new activities, new records- academic, sporting cultural and social.

> 'You were out to get the best for the School and you had the faith, courage and persistence to get it. You spared no efforts in the interest of the School and your efforts were crowned with success.'

In expressing his thanks for the generous gifts, D C Lewis spoke of the privilege that had been his as Headmaster. He acknowledged the support given to him by the staff saying that he had never had to deal harshly with any of his colleagues during the twenty-six year period. His wife too had given him the strongest support and had always shown interest in his work.

The retirement gift was too large for the Central Hall so the presentation was made on the School lawn where the rowing dinghy with outboard motor was presented by the head boy David Morgan. Head girl Janet Ward formally named the new boat 'Ardwyn'. D C Lewis would make good use of the craft since his new retirement home was situated close to a north Pembrokeshire beach.

A. D. Lewis, M.A., Headmaster, 1954–71.

Chapter Four

THE A D LEWIS YEARS

1954 - 1971

The successor to D C Lewis was no stranger to the School. Alban Dewi Lewis at the time of his appointment was Deputy Director of Education for Cardiganshire. In addition to his official duties he had visited the School on many occasions to act as judge at the annual House boxing competition.

A D Lewis was a native of Cardigan who had received all his formal education in the county. He graduated from the U C W in 1935, with first class honours in English and obtained a teaching diploma the following year. In the athletic side of College life he had been equally successful, obtaining colours in rugby, rowing and boxing, becoming the middle-weight champion of the University of Wales and a U A U finalist in 1936. He later played first-class rugby for Birkenhead Park and Bath.
In his last year as deputy director, the University of Wales had conferred on him the degree of M A for research in English literature.

The new Headmaster declared his philosophy and aims at the first P T A meeting he attended. He paid tribute to the work of the Association and stressed the essential contribution which parents could make to the development of the School, for the attitude of children to their teachers generally reflected the ideas which they acquired at home. He was anxious to develop a personal acquaintance with all the pupils, for each one of them was a personality in his own right, with his or her peculiar problems and interests. Referring to Welsh-speaking children, he said that he always expected them to address him in their native tongue; 'no child could be encouraged to acquire self-confidence and the gifts of natural expression except through the medium of his first language.'

The Headmaster emphasised the importance of keeping a constant watch on the academic development of the child; the choice of a career at an early stage in his school life was admittedly difficult, but there was a danger from indecision and drift. Nothing was more frustrating and disappointing to the school leaver than to find himself without a subject required for the vocation of his choice.

Later in the year at prize day, many of his remarks were given in the Welsh language-the first time for an Ardwyn Head to do so. He declared himself to have great faith in the grammar school though far too many of them had paid but scant attention to the Welsh background of their pupils. He wanted his pupils to use the Welsh language as naturally in Ardwyn as they did at home. A D Lewis also thought that the grammar school had done little to train those destined to earn their living in the countryside-in agriculture and related occupations. It might be said that this would be vocational training, the very negation of grammar school education. However he asserted that the grammar school since its earliest days had provided a vocational training for rulers, administrators and professional people.

He went on:-

> I am glad to say that Ardwyn has seen in recent years, a considerable increase in the number of its budding scientists and technologists. But in developing scientific training we have a great responsibility. It is essential that young scientists have a broad background of human sympathy and understanding and a sense of moral responsibility. It just will not do for scientists to claim that they are only concerned with an abstract search for truth, that their function is to discover, with no responsibility for the use made of their discoveries.
>
> We are concerned at School with something much more difficult than acquiring and imparting knowledge, important though that is. We are concerned with the development of character and personality. Our efforts to impart knowledge, however successful they may be, will avail us little unless we can promote a healthy growth mentally and spiritually.
>
> Honesty, kindness good behaviour, good manners-these are the things which I consider important. To be able to run a home well and be useful in society-two simple aims applicable to everyone.

Controversy came early in his stewardship. News of the decision that association football was being dropped in favour of two terms of rugby football came as a bombshell to a town steeped in soccer tradition. The story seemed to have emerged in January 1954, at the start of the customary soccer term. In the 7 January edition of the *Cambrian News*, the main headline on the sports page was 'Exclusion of Soccer at Ardwyn- A Hasty Decision, say former pupils.' John Ellis Williams, Alun Jones and Eddie Ellis, former pupils and well-known amateur soccer players, one a Welsh international, said that at Ardwyn they had played and enjoyed both codes, thereby increasing their range of interest and participation in organised sport.

> The decision is a poor reward to all past pupils who, though primarily interested in soccer, entered with enthusiasm into the new game because they were assured that the introduction of rugby would in no way prejudice the future of soccer at the School. The School records show that the Ardwyn rugby team began to enjoy a modest success when soccer players were persuaded to play rugby. Ardwyn with a very fine soccer tradition, was among the best soccer schools in Wales. In rugby, fine game though it is, she can claim no more than mediocrity. Must the fine soccer tradition be destroyed in order to strengthen rugby.
>
> There is everything to be said for the playing of both games, virtually nothing for an attempt to force rugby exclusively in an area which is primarily soccer in tradition with not much more than a mild interest in rugby.

The *Welsh Gazette* of 3 February 1954 reported the plight of Bow Street FC in possibly having to withdraw from the Welsh youth cup competion. With four Ardwynians in their team and the School prohibiting pupils from playing soccer for local sides if matches clashed with School rugby matches there was great concern that a team could not be fielded. There was talk of holding a public meeting to protest at the decision.

Comment was not confined to the local press. In his weekly article in a national newspaper, a much respected Welsh professional footballer, Ivor Allchurch talked of 'petty dictatorship which deprived schoolboys of an elementary freedom to play the game they loved ', and 'the alarming spread of the exclusion of soccer in secondary schools.'

The move to drop soccer seems to have been a unilateral decision by the Headmaster. There is no record of the matter being discussed by the Governors. Wynn Hughes a former School rugby and soccer captain had been appointed in 1954 to teach physical education. He recalled that there was no consultation, he was simply told of the decision in January 1954 at the beginnning of what should have been the 'soccer term'. His protests were ignored and he was informed that the boys would do as they were told. Howard C Jones recalled that some boys, to feed their love of soccer, formed their own team, the Park Avenue Rangers which later supplied players like Geraint Jenkins to the town team.

> My brothers Hefin and Dyfed had contributed a great deal to sport in the School. By the time I arrived in the School the Headmaster had decreed that there would be no soccer played. It still irks me, though only a little by now, some forty years later. My brother Dyfed had the good sense to drop the rugby ball each time it was thrown to him. Perhaps partly as a consequence, he became a Welsh youth soccer international playing against England, Scotland and Ireland. I was 'daft enough' to catch the ball and run with it. When I made a request to the Headmaster to be left out of the School XV one Saturday morning because I had a Welsh youth trial match in the afternoon, he refused permission. I decided then that I would never play rugby after leaving School. For many years I happily played soccer for Guy's Hospital attracting zero spectators while on an adjacent pitch my colleagues were regularly playing rugby against first class opposition.[87]

Despite his alienation and disillusionment, Elwyn Elias progressed further than most in the Welsh secondary schoolboys' rugby trials and was an out-standing rugby full back, cricketer and runner. One wonders what rugby honours would have come his way were it not for the uncompromising attitude which prevailed at the time. He was head boy in 1961 and elected to the Daniel Thomas leadership award before entering Guy's Hospital to start his medical studies. Great honours have come to Elwyn in his professional life. After clinical research in several of the London hospitals and in the universities of Chicago and Yale he gained his MD degree. Since 1979 he has headed the liver transplant unit at the Queen Elizabeth Hospital, Birmingham, which has become the busiest such unit in the UK.

It was one of the great regrets of D C Lewis that the School was unable to produce an orchestra during his time. He took the first steps in 1953 when the services of a brilliant instrumentalist and conductor, Ralph Davies, an old Ardwynian, were secured.

Betty Jones Davies, head of music 1952-73 recalled the birth and growth of the orchestra:

In 1953, a small group of pupils met regularly on Friday afternoons. It was a mixed group of players, some in the earliest stages of instrumental tuition -violins, two 'cellos and a clarinet. This was the beginning of the School orchestra which was to grow and flourish in the succeeding years. Throughout the years, the music department was fortunate to have excellent instrumental tutors, the earliest being Ralph Davies, Doris Knusson (violin) and Stuart Knusson (cello). Of the many other tutors, mention should be made of T R Noble (brass) who taught for a considerable number of years.

By 1958, the School Orchestra had developed into a balanced ensemble and subsequently each year, performed in School concerts, Y Noson Gymraeg and Speech Days. The annual School Eisteddfod featured a new competition for a House instrumental group, the winners receiving the Clapham Shield. The repertoire was varied and interesting-one year the Ceredigion instrumental group performed the 'Toy Symphony.'

Several pupils distinguished themselves in the musical world and became professional players in such orchestras as the Liverpool Philharmonic, the B B C orchestras, the London Symphony Orchestra, the City of Birmingham Symphony Orchestra and others. One of the first members of the School orchestra was Gwenda Lewis who played the clarinet. She became the first Ardwynian to gain a place in the National Youth Orchestra of Wales, which when it was formed in 1945, was the first national youth orchestra in the world. This success was to be maintained annually by other musicians. Ardwyn was represented each year from 1955 by one or more pupils playing in the N Y O W.

In 1954, an outstanding pupil joined Ardwyn from Roundhay school in Leeds. He was Duncan Druce, a member of the National Youth Orchestra of Great Britain. He ultimately gained a first-class honours degree in music at King's College, Cambridge and a scholarship to study violin and composition at the The Royal College of Music. During those formative years of the School orchestra, Duncan, in his unassuming way would always be ready to help. No doubt, many will remember his performance of the second movement of the Mendelssohn Violin Concerto at the 1955 School Eisteddfod.

As a result of the enthusiasm and dedication of Betty Jones Davies, the choral work of the school burgeoned in parallel with the orchestra. At any one time, three choirs were functioning: the junior boys' choir, the girls' choir and the Sixth form mixed choir. The choirs performed annually in school concerts, every *Noson Gymraeg* and made particular contributions in the Christmas services of nine lessons and carols held in various places of worship in the town. By 1957 the orchestra was thirty-three players strong and with the choirs and individual performances, the School was able to stage a Christmas concert with twenty-four items on two successive evenings. The School magazine report thought that 'the whole programme was proof of an abundance of talent, of a well established orchestra and of disciplined and prolonged training and practice, all reflecting great credit on the pupils themselves and on their conductor, E Jones Davies.'

The School's contribution to the National Youth Orchestra of Wales had risen to six by 1959, each playing a different instrument - Gwenda Lewis clarinet, Faleiry Phillips harp, Susan Cox oboe, Julian Clapham bassoon, Ceredig Gwyn violin and Gruffydd Miles 'cello. The same year the Apollo Trio namely Ceredig Gwyn violin, Michael

Parrott 'cello and Paul Richard piano, won first prize in the youth section of the National Eisteddfod of Wales in Caernarfon.

As if not to be outdone by the abundance of musical talent in the School, an English Dramatic Society was launched. Gethin Abraham-Williams remembered that the idea originated among members of the Form VI Latin class 'though we were adamant that we had no intention of producing the work of either Plautus or Terence !.' Directed and produced by Gethin Abraham-Williams, the first production was J B Priestly's 'Laburnum Grove' in the King's Hall in June 1957 which produced a profit of £45. The 1958 production was in the hands of Rhona Ryle. The choice was the stage production of Louisa M Allcott's 'Little Women' which was played to a packed King's Hall under the auspices of the Festival of Wales.

Following preparatory work during the summer vacation, the junior and senior play-reading groups presented three one-act plays produced by G Abraham-Williams and Kenneth Sharpe, in the Parish Hall in September 1958.

The dramatic society delighted a good audience at the Parish Hall in June 1959 with another Night of Plays. The three one-act plays were again the unaided efforts of the pupils themselves and reflected well on the producers John Reeves, Sion Rees and Alan Christian, ably served by Philip Edwards as stage manager. The proceeds of the evening went to the Ockenden Venture.

The third 6B play was a very ambitious choice, a verse play-'The Lady's not for Burning' by Christopher Fry. Its reviewer in the *Ardwynian* thought:

> It was a difficult play for amateur production on two counts. First, the period dress and settings and second, and by far the greater task, the speaking and declaiming of the verse dialogue. The former difficulty was well tackled but several of the actors found the words quite a burden. Nevertheless the effort was a most commendable one and the very process of learning the verse and building the sets was a valuable experience. It is certainly good to aim high, as the effort will bring its own lessons and rewards. Gwenllian Jones, the producer must have worked hard and is to be congratulated for facing the task.

The hectic pace was maintained with a full length play 'Mystery at Blackwater' by Dan Sutherland based on the Wilkie Collins novel 'The Woman in White'. The play produced by Gethin Abraham-Williams with the cast of sixth-formers and recently-left pupils was highly praised. Its production in the King's Hall and at Machynlleth in September 1959 raised £120 for World Refugee Year.

For their second Night of Plays in the session 1959-60, the junior and senior members of the dramatics society staged four one-act plays to a sparse audience on a bitterly cold January 1960 evening. Production was in the hands of Janet Carter, Susan Brenells and Alan Christian and again Philip Edwards managed the stage and lights. All this thespian activity prompted a note in the 59-60 edition of the *Ardwynian*:

> Last year we recorded the fact that no fewer than fourteen one-act plays and a three-act play had been produced in public by School pupils the previous session. The figure this year has gone up to two full length plays and eighteen one-act plays. Over one

*Above:
Mayor W. G. Rowlands
addressing the pupils
at the 1955
Sports Day.*

Left: A.T.C. School Squadron (led by their O.C. D. A. Young) in the Mayor's Service Procession June 1955.

The A. D. Lewis Years — 1954-1971

Top:—Chaired Bard 1958 Gethin Abraham Williams.

Rev. Emlyn Lewis, officiating.

Middle:—Prize Day 1956 E. Jones Davies head of music conducting the orchestra.

Bottom:—Cast of 'Mystery at Blackwater' 1959 Kenneth Sharpe, Mary M. Davies, David E. Jones, Cissian Jones, Anne Thomas, Gethin Abraham Williams, Janet Carter, Myfanwy Gray-Jones, Catrin Gapper, Ruth Morgan, Brynhild Clapham

hundred and thirty parts were played, and allowing for some duplication of roles, probably over a hundred different pupils have 'had a go' on a public stage in the space of two terms. This is a remarkable achievement.

The figures quoted include the four English and four Welsh plays written and produced by the pupils for the Mortimer Green and Goronwy Owen House trophies and the productions of the Welsh Night plays under the direction of the staff of the Welsh department.

Rhona Ryle, who was involved with dramatics remembers her arrival in the School in 1954 as a third former.

> I had previously attended a very prim and prissy girls' grammar school in Surrey. At my initial interview, AD Lewis stressed strongly that I would encounter a culture shock -Welsh language, male teachers, male peers and all sorts of differences. Despite his forebodings I settled in quickly and found staff and pupils extremely friendly and caring. I had no Welsh at all and was two years behind in Latin. I became an immediate challenge to a fearsome figure, one Beynon Davies, who was determined that this alien, daughter of the director of the land-grabbing Forestry Commission, should be instantly converted to all things Welsh. He thereupon gave up his dinner hours and intensively coached me in both Welsh and Latin. I remember being petrified of him, but it was all worth it as I achieved 'O' level passes in both subjects when I reached year 5. What an amazing man!
>
> I have nothing but praise for the teaching staff. Standards of discipline were high, we all worked hard and I have no memory of any scenes of disruption or of any truancy among my peers. The social life was well provided for. I loved the drama, the House plays, the eisteddfod in the King's Hall and a memorable School trip to Edinburgh overnight by train. It was rumoured that Roy James drove the train all the way back to Aberystwyth.
>
> Academic standards were high and it seemed fairly usual for pupils to achieve nine or ten passes at 'O' level.

There appears to have been no School Magazine produced in the session 1955-56, the first lapse since 1923. However the 1956-57 edition and the thirteen subsequent annual issues were produced under the editorship of W Beynon Davies. To emphasise the change, the newly appointed art master Hywel Harries had designed a new cover which was used on all subsequent issues. The School crest had been redesigned and the title *Ardwynian* had been dropped. The editor, in a note, explained that the Magazine recorded the successes of pupils and also reflected the manifold activities of the School. 'In collecting material for it we have been impressed by the unexpected variety of the activities and surprised by the versatility of a great number of pupils.' Far greater use was made of the Welsh language than previously. The winning eisteddfod literary items were included at the expense of prize day speeches.

In September 1956 the long awaited kitchen-dining room came into use. At long last the ritual of arranging the trestle tables and benches in the main hall each lunch time which had gone on under the direction of Dan the caretaker for so long was no more.

The new building was clad internally with facing brick and with its large windows, was a very attractive acquisition. Hywel Harries, having been consulted about pictures to adorn the walls, typically produced his own mural measuring eight feet by four feet of views of the town- 'A Composite of Aberystwyth'. Within two years he had completed a companion mural depicting various aspects of life in Cardiganshire. The pictures are splendid examples of Hywel Harries' wonderful artistic talents and also testify to his readiness at all times to give freely of his time and talent.

The only other new building to be built on the Ardwyn site was the science wing which when it became operational in 1961 provided much needed modern chemistry and physics laboratories. Further development was impossible because of lack of space and the PTA spearheaded a move to provide a new school on another site. As far back as 1951, the Governors were in favour of acquiring the whole of Erw Goch farm, near the site of the secondary modern about to be built at Cefnllan. By 1962 the issue had developed into a new school or a new college of further education. In 1965 fields of the Erw Goch farm were purchased for a new school with the college of further education to occupy the vacated Ardwyn premises. However, that year the Labour education minister Anthony Crosland issued his infamous circular 10/65; the Department of Education and Science now required education authorities to submit plans for comprehensive education. As a result everything was halted and the School, now bursting at the seams with more than 720 pupils, had to make do with several mobile classrooms which somehow were squeezed in. By renting the Llanbadarn road dairy buildings from the College, the accommodation problem was further eased.

The 1956-57 Magazine reported that E E Forster, after thirty-seven years of devoted service to the School had retired in July 1956. Pleasure was taken in that she had decided to spend her retirement years in the town she had served so well. However a local paper carried a different story with a headline 'Ardwyn teacher resigns on a question of principle.'

> I have resigned on a matter of principle. I handed my resignation to the Headmaster last Wednesday. He asked me to reconsider my decision and the Governors did the same. I refused absolutely. I also insisted that there should be no speeches or farewells. I dislike hypocrisy.
>
> It is understood that the reason for Miss Forster's resignation arises out of certain arrangements made at the school during the absence of the senior mistress earlier in the year.
>
> A friend said: Miss Forster has always been the most outspoken and courageous member of staff at Ardwyn. She has always hated injustice and was frequently the spokesman for the rest of the staff. Now that a situation has arisen which she felt was an affront to her self-respect, she has shown the same uncompromising attitude. Her resignation is within her tradition. Those who know the circumstances admire her courage.
>
> Miss Forster will take up a position at a leading girls' school in Warwickshire in September.[88]

Because of recurring ill-health, Sam Mitchell, the senior master, had to retire in January 1958 and died later that year. He had joined the staff in 1921 after serving in the

Great War with the Denbighshire Yeomanry and later the Royal Welch Fusiliers. W G Rowlands and R D James wrote the following tribute for the Magazine:

> The passing of 'Sam Mitch' as he was affectionately known by two generations of his pupils at Ardwyn, has taken away a loveable and engaging personality who had left his mark on the district. Having completed his education at UCW Aberystwyth, he settled down as a master at Ardwyn. He made a big impact as a games teacher, while in the classroom he was, perhaps, an unconventional figure who owed his teaching success to his personality and originality. Nothing gave him greater pleasure than to see his former pupils excel in sport in later life.
>
> He served again in the 1939-45 War and on his return to Ardwyn, he perhaps did some of his best work as careers advisor and helped many pupils seek successful careers. He completed his work as deputy headmaster of the School he had served so well.
>
> What is not so well known is that Mr Mitchell was an artist of no mean ability, and his watercolours and oil paintings will long be treasured by his friends. He was a most modest and unassuming man who delighted to be in the company of the ordinary man, where his generosity, geniality and true humility won him a host of friends.

George Rowlands, head of the English department, succeeded Sam Mitchell as deputy head. In 1955 WG Rowlands had served as Mayor of Aberystwyth, the first Ardwyn member of staff to become 'chief citizen'. He recalled in a Magazine article that Aberystwyth had borough status since 1277 with the privilege of appointing a mayor and corporation. Documents relating to the Middle Ages had been lost but the names of all mayors of the last three hundred years were recorded and he took pride in seeing his name added to the list. During his year of office he had the pleasure of welcoming the Queen and the Duke of Edinburgh to the Borough when they officially opened an extension to the National Library on the 8 August 1955.

David Herbert Jenkins joined the staff in 1920 as a young man of twenty-four. Perhaps at that time he had little thought that he would set up a record of long service of nearly forty years which was unlikely to be exceeded. George Rowlands, on DH Jenkins' retirement in December 1959, recalled that he had served under four Ardwyn Headmasters and had witnessed major alterations to the buildings and a doubling in the number of pupils. He had helped shape the lives of thousands of young men and women and had the good sense, in 1936 to marry one of his former pupils Evelyn Lumley Jones. David Jenkins had for many years organised the annual sports and tennis teams but probably was much more at home in his other spheres of activity-the inter-house eisteddfod, and *Y Noson Gymraeg* which had proved such an attractive and abiding feature of School life.

> David Jenkins was an excellent colleague and a great favourite in the men's staff room. He was modest and unambitious, twice refusing promotion to the position of deputy headmaster. He had a keen, quiet sense of humour always enjoying the many quips and witticisms of his fellow teachers, and frequently surprising everybody by his unexpected contribution to the discussion. For the thirty years I served with him at

Ardwyn, I found him kindly, cooperative and good humoured, with an encouraging word for the newly appointed teachers, many of whom had formerly been his pupils.
So with real gratitude, Ardwyn says, 'Goodbye, Mr Chips!.'

Dan Evans also retired in 1959 after thirty two years of diligent work as caretaker, serving three Ardwyn Headmasters. His replacement John Williams was the last in a line of men who had, very successfully, performed a vital job in the life of the School. Without having the authority of a teacher, he had to gain the respect and confidence of the pupils. There was also the need for diplomacy and tact in dealings with the staff.

Doris Mitchell had been appointed in 1942 for the wartime period while her husband Sam was on active service. 'Ma Mitch' became a much loved teacher and many came to appreciate her wise counsel in time of need. As well as teaching general science she developed a pre-nursing course in the lower sixth which set many girls on the road to that honoured profession. Her temporary appointment lasted eighteen years, a period which she considered to be the happiest time of her life. There was genuine regret when retirement came in 1960.

The award of further State scholarships in the latter half of the Fifties brought the total for the decade to twelve making that period the most successful in terms of that premier distinction. The year 1955-56 was particularly bountiful; head girl Heather Lewis gained a State scholarship and an open scholarship to the University of London, Duncan Druce an open scholarship to Cambridge and the Royal College of Music, as well as entrance scholarships to the U C W.
Heather Lewis also had the distincton of representing Welsh Girl-Guides at the World Guides' centenary camp at Manila in the Philippines in January 1957. The colourful account, in the *Ardwynian*, of her journey by sea and by air, two weeks camp and the hospitality of Filipino, Chinese and Indian families makes fascinating reading.
Travelling for most pupils was restricted to the annual school trips, each organised down to the minutest detail by W G Rowlands. The third visit to Dublin in twenty years took place in 1957, in the following years Edinburgh, Windsor, London airport, and in 1960 Portsmouth and Southampton were visited.
But some Ardwynians travelled further afield; A T C cadet Sgt Peter D Davies secured a RAF flying scholarship which took him to the U S A for three weeks in the summer of 1958. Susan Brenells spent 1958 in a school in North Carolina having been awarded an American international scholarship. Margaret M Jones was chosen to represent Urdd Gobaith Cymru on a three week visit to Russia, visiting Moscow, and Leningrad while Linda Williams, became the second Ardwyn girl in two years to represent her country in an international Girl Guide camp, this time in Sweden. The first school exchange holiday was arranged with the Stenwijk school, northern Holland. In August 1957, Ardwyn pupils and their parents were hosts to the Dutch children with a return visit to Holland the following summer of a party led by the Headmaster A D Lewis. Although the Dutch connection was not maintained, following a number of visits by teachers from Freiburg, each of whom spent a term at the School teaching German and other subjects, a strong association developed and was maintained for many years by exchange visits of pupils.

In the autumn of 1957 an all-girls team took part in the BBC radio series Top of the Form. After defeating the boys of Canton High School, Cardiff in the first round, they were beaten by the girls of Dr Williams' School, Dolgellau in the next round.

By 1957 television had arrived in Aberystwyth and former pupil Henley Thomas was seen in the role of 'Morgan Evans' in 'The Corn is Green', and he also appeared in Galworthy's 'Strife'. In 1960 he played the central character 'Huw' in 'How Green Was My Valley' serialised by BBC Wales, followed by leading roles in three Alun Owen plays, as well as a Royal Shakespeare Company production of 'As You Like It' in the Aldwych Theatre and their premiere production of 'Afore Night Come'. An earlier *Ardwynian* had recorded his success in gaining a Leverhulme scholarship at the Royal Academy of Dramatic Art and his first engagement-a small part in 'Tea and Sympathy' at the Comedy Theatre. He well remembers his stage debut whilst at Ardwyn during the war years, in the chorus of 'Mikado', and 'Gondoliers', followed by major roles in 'Princess Ida' and 'Merrie England.'

From this time onwards pupils were frequently seen on the small screen particularly in Welsh language programmes. T W W had a series of programmes entitled *Troeon Gyrfa* in which school pupils interviewed a distinguished former pupil of their school. Ardwyn were involved on two occasions in the autumn of 1959, the subjects being the Rt Revd. John Richards, Bishop of St Davids and Dr T Ifor Rees, the former British Ambassador to Bolivia. The pupils involved were Marian Morgan, Catrin Gapper, Gwenllian Jones, Elwyn Lewis, John Hefin Evans, and Elwyn Elias.

The 1961-62 issue of the School magazine congratulated two boys on their effort in bringing out the Ardwyn School Newspaper. 'We have seen two issues of it and hope they will get all the support they deserve.'

> After five years of inconspicuousness at Ardwyn, I started a school newspaper with Clifford Thomas as joint editor and Chris Loosely as business executive. This ran for four issues and consisted of eight pages of duplicated typescript. There had been attempts at school newspapers before but this was the first controlled by pupils.
>
> AD Lewis asked to see the first issue in draft. He did not interfere, but actively encouraged our venture and later my own entry to journalism. We gave it up at the end of 6B to concentrate on advanced level. A year or two later, Ron Lewis, later of Harlech TV, revived it. After more than thirty years as a journalist, I can therefore say that I started as an editor and worked my way down (and Down Under) to being a reporter.[89]

After leaving Ardwyn in 1963 Howard C Jones was at the *Cambrian News* for seven years then moved to the Western Mail as sub-editor before emigrating to Australia in 1982. He has written more than ten books including 'Aberystwyth Yesterday' and 'Aberystwyth Borough 1277-1974'. He will be remembered as 'Will O'Whisper's of the *Cambrian News* for ten years from 1970.

Many features of school activity, ephemeral though they might be, are the result of initiatives by the pupils, often without any contribution by the staff. Ardwyn encouraged this and the chess club, after several false starts, became a permanent feature of

The A. D. Lewis Years — 1954-1971

School life after 1956, strongly supported by the town club. That year Michael Walker played in the British youth championships. Aneurin John, the first president of the club also distinguished himself by being selected for the Welsh secondary schools' chess team to play against the home countries in Dublin in July 1959. The club had progressed sufficiently to enter the *Sunday Times* national schools' chess tournament, reaching the Welsh semi-finals in 1959 at their first attempt. These matches were played over the telephone with contestants fortified by the teas provided by Violet Jones and the senior girls. Three pupils were invited to play in the Welsh national championships. By the end of the decade the club was providing players for the town and Mid-Wales teams; the 1960-61 magazine reported 'standards had risen rapidly, competition for places in the School team was becoming very fierce, with no player being able to rest on his laurels.' Despite encouragement no girls were ever tempted to the boards. Powys were the first winners of a House chess competition for which former pupil Emrys Williams of the town chess club generously donated a trophy to be presented annually to the winning House. In 1963 the team reached the Welsh zone final of the *Sunday Times* competition but were unable to play the deciding game against a Newport school because of 'an absurd time limit.' There followed two lean years when loss of senior pupils and the inexperience of the younger pupils proved to be a great handicap. By now other Cardiganshire schools were promoting the game to such an extent that a county tournament became viable. Emrys and Dewi Williams of Aberystwyth provided another trophy-the 'Cardiganshire Shield' for the competition and Ardwyn were the first winners in 1966-67 defeating Aberaeron, Tregaron, Dinas and great rivals Cardigan. However the following year Cardigan got their revenge, but the School team were consoled by getting first and second in the Mid-Wales Championships through Robert Cooper and Melville Jones. The latter also became the Cardiganshire under-18 champion. In the remaining four years before reorganisation, Ardwyn won the shield on three occasions.

Under AD Lewis the 'Welshness' of the School was greatly enhanced; the teaching of Welsh throughout the School was re-established and the annual eisteddfod went from strength to strength. It had always been a joyful occasion with the opportunity to dress outrageously in the House colours, wear rosettes, colourful hats and decorated mascots. It was also the chance to make a great noise-the only School function where this was possible, although one raised finger from the Head or Beynon Davies brought instant silence for the competitors to perform. A great deal of effort was put in by staff and pupils in the weeks preceding St David's Day. Extended breaks allowed for the chief choral practices to be held; in theory every pupil was a member of a choir but the 'growlers' had been identified by staff like Idwal Davies in the case of Gwynedd, and instructed 'to keep mum' during the competition.

Practices for such items as the octet would take place in the houses of pupils during the evening and as a result of the effort put in by so many, standards were very high. The *Cambrian News* of 4 March 1955 reported the adjudicator as saying that she had never experienced such a high standard of choral singing in any school eisteddfod. The violin playing of 15 year old Duncan Druce was rated as 'outstanding.'

The eisteddfod of 1957 was won by Ceredigion for the first time for 16 years. Gethin Abraham-Williams won the first of his two bardic chairs that year.

> In 1957 I got first prize for a short story about a whistling kettle. It was a typical teenager's effort drawing on Agatha Christie, Conan Doyle, and the Ingoldsby legends. But the highlight was winning the chair with a poem on the Setting Sun. I was fortunate to the win the chair again the following year, but it is the first one that stands out in my memory. I hadn't the slightest idea that I was in the running for it and it was only by chance that my mother and aunt were in the audience to see the ceremony.[90]

Two additional trophies were donated the following year. The prefects of 1956-57 had presented a shield for the short speech competition and the Katherine Clapham instrumental music cup awarded initially to the winner of the instrumental solo competition but later for an instrumental group.

> The climax of the year's cultural activities was the eisteddfod when the School took over the King's Hall for the whole of St David's Day. I recall my friend John Wyn Evans (now Dean of the Cathedral at St David's) turning up at the eisteddfod with a huge raw leek attached to his lapel and declaring that if our House, Gwynedd, won the eisteddfod cup he would eat the leek before our eyes. Gwynedd were triumphant that year, and Wyn was true to his word. When I was in the lower sixth I won the chair; the poem I wrote now strikes me as a rather pretentious effort, but the chair itself (made by woodwork teacher Idwal Davies) has a place of honour in my home, not least because the inscription on it, 'ARDWYN 1963', brings back memories of a time of great happiness and uncomplicated friendships.[91]

Ardwyn pupils also competed in the Urdd National Eisteddfod. Elwyn Elias recalled being one of the party of eight competing in the *Dawns Werin* trained by his form mistress Marian Hughes that gained first place, much to their surprise. In 1959, a girls'-group won the Cerdd Dant event in the Mold Eisteddfod. The School Magazine took great pride in recording the achievements of seven pupils of art teacher Hywel Harries. Examples of their work had been displayed in the art and craft pavilion at the 1959 National Eisteddfod held in Caernarfon.

As he had won the eisteddfod chair twice, and was runner-up once, during his last three years at Ardwyn, it came as no great surprise to learn that Peter Davies was the chaired bard at the Urdd National Eisteddfod in Holyhead in 1966. As well as his achievements in many of the eisteddfod competitions he was remembered for his great character acting in the House plays and the *Noson Gymraeg* dramas.

Barbel Edwards, won the senior girls' solo in the 1965 eisteddfod. That year she entered the Royal College of Music and in the summer of 1967 was the soprano soloist at the concert given by the National Youth Orchestra of Wales in Pontypool.

Beryl Potts (Richards) who had also graced the School eisteddfod and opera stage in the late Forties won the rose bowl as a soloist at the Woodstock festival of music in the summer of 1967.

The Welsh ethos in the School was also heightened by the annual Welsh Night. On his retirement in 1959, DH Jenkins who started the series of cultural evenings in 1939, wrote an article in Welsh in the 1959-60 Magazine to mark the coming of age of *Y Noson*

The A. D. Lewis Years — 1954-1971

Noson Gymraeg 1958—"I'r Clochdy fel Arfer"
Janet Miles, Peter Davies, Ann M. C. Davies, Lilian Pritchard
D. W. Meredith, Llinos I. Jones, John Hefin Evans.

"Ty ar Werth" – Noson Gymraeg — December 1963
John Wyn Evans
Mary Jones, Marlene Davies, Mary Evans, Jennifer Farrow.

The History of Aberystwyth County School (Ardwyn) 1896-1973

Noson Gymraeg — 1953 — "Michael"
John Evans, Elizabeth Morris, Dafydd Hughes, Bethan Bebb, Hughie Hughes,
Llinos I. Jones, Deulwyn Morgan, Edna Ellis.

Noson Gymraeg — 1956 — "Wing Lŵ a'i Helbulon"
Back: Rhun Owens, Margaret Radford; Middle: Graham Jones, Wyre Thomas, Byron Howells.
Front: Mari Griffiths, Hazel Jeremy, Alwyna Jones
This party won the Drama Cup (under 19) at the Urdd National Eisteddfod,
Llandybie, May 1957.

Gymraeg. He recalled that following the spectacular success of the Gilbert and Sullivan operas, it was felt by some that there was need to express the Welsh spirit in the School, particularly through the medium of drama. It was decided that children throughout the School, from the youngest to the oldest, would have the opportunity to take part. The pattern of the event did not change throughout its thirty-one year history. At the outset, there was a concert of miscellaneous items including choral pieces, specially arranged by the music specialist, vocal and instrumental solos, *canu penillion*, and frequently Welsh recitations by a group of children who had learned Welsh while at Ardwyn. The School orchestra also contributed items. Then followed three short plays produced by members of the Welsh department. By the time of his retirement DH Jenkins had himself produced twenty-one plays. Up to 1960, some 56 dramas were staged, including some translated from the English by Mari Carter and Beynon Davies. The fine tradition continued when Beynon Davies succeeded to the headship of the Welsh department ensuring a further eleven years of excellence, strongly supported it must be said by many Welsh-speaking members of staff. Hywel Harries gave years of service behind the scenes, turning youngsters into adults with skilful application of grease paint. Equally skilled were Idwal Davies and his boys in making scenery. A succession of music teachers also need to be recognised for their contribution to this cultural feast - William Roberts, Beryl Morgan, Gerwyn Thomas, and E Jones Davies. Unlike many schools, Ardwyn did not possess a hall sufficiently large to stage drama productions. The Welsh Night productions were particularly nomadic. First venue was the Parish Hall, then the Buarth Hall, from there to Siloh schoolroom. The woodwork department provided a portable stage in the School gymnasium and that became its home for many years before fire regulations caused another move this time to the Little Theatre, Bath Street. That venue soon became too small so for eight years from 1955 the King's Hall was used. Back to the Parish Hall for 1964 and 1965. The next two years back to the King's Hall and for the last *Noson Gymraeg* in 1968 the UCW Examination Hall.

> I entered Ardwyn in September 1957, from *Yr Ysgol Gymraeg* in Aberystwyth. It must have been a promising intake; all four of the Evan Morgan scholarships came to Ardwyn that year, and three of the winners were from *Yr Ysgol Gymraeg*. We were also the first cohort of pupils born after the end of the Second World War.
>
> My first-year form was known as 1AW; the W a recognition that we were mother-tongue Welsh speakers. We were fortunate to have as our form teacher Mari Carter, a caring and warm-hearted lady who helped everyone settle into the new environment.
>
> One of the great events in the School calendar was the annual *Noson Gymraeg* (Welsh Night) and in my first year I took part in an extraordinary play which featured a dragon. I was the creature's speaking part, and behind me I had a tail of four or five other boys who were enclosed in a colourful costume made by Hywel Harries, the art master, who was also the play's producer. As the dragon came on the stage I was to blow smoke, i. e. blackboard chalk which had been reduced to white dust. In my enthusiasm I managed to draw in a mouthful of the chalk and could hardly find breath to speak my lines, let alone blow out the 'smoke' which I was to produce.[92]

Elystan Morgan (1943-50) considered that in spite of its excellent qualities Ardwyn was not as Welsh as many would have wished.

> In this of course, the School was no different to the majority of grammar schools in the towns of Wales. Yet it could boast rich seams of Welshness in its educational and social life as well as 'high days and holidays' such as the St David's Day Eisteddfod, and the 'Welsh Night'. No pupil could have attended classes taken by D H Jenkins or W Beynon Davies without becoming aware that the language and literature of Wales had a special significance of their own and realising that Welsh nationhood was a priceless gift to be preserved and safeguarded at all costs.

During the Christmas Term 1955, the pupils became involved for the first time with the toy card collection in aid of the National Institute for the Blind Sunshine Homes. It became an annual event lasting for eighteen years; in Ardwyn's last year, 1972-73, a record total of £500 was raised which prompted a visit from an Institute officer who presented the School with a certificate of merit and revealed that the Ardwyn annual collection was consistently the highest of any school in Wales. Over the years more than £4,500 had been collected.

Other charities were supported; the 1964-65 Magazine noted that in two years £920 had been raised for the RNIB, Oxfam and the Freedom from Hunger Campaign. It also detailed the activities of the newly formed and self-governing sixth-form social service group chaired by Christine Edmonds.

> The objects are to do social work in the town-visiting the housebound, doing their shopping or any odd job. Its aim is not only to alleviate hardship but also to educate young people to be of service to others and to be a means by which they act on an individual basis. Those who took part agree that it proved a valuable and satisfying experience. There is something more concrete to report in another field in which the committee has been active, that is in raising funds for charity. The carol singing group collected £21 which was donated to Multiple Sclerosis research, a disease which affects mainly those in their early twenties. A donation to medical research might be a regular consideration by future committees. Help was given to the Friends of Ockenden during their flag day and assistance at their summer fair has been promised.

The first 'Own Clothes Day' realised £30; pupils were allowed to wear clothes other than their School uniform on payment of a fee. Over many years, and continued in the daughter schools, this custom became a popular fund raiser. Following the 1965 School Eisteddfod, a concert was arranged, with the cooperation of the music department, of the winners of the stage competitions. Once again the talents of pupils in music and recitation were affirmed with the evening brought to a close by items from the sixth form choir and the singing of what had become the School Hymn, *Gyfrannwr Pob Bendithion*, to a tune composed by E Jones Davies. The proceeds of £20 went via the social service committee, to the Freedom from Hunger Campaign. Each subsequent Magazine chronicled the activities of the social service group which went from strength to strength in fund raising and other community activities.

The Ockenden Venture was strongly supported through the years mainly by the pupils organising a stall at their summer fair. Presumably with the Head's permission, apples collected from the school orchard were sold to the canteen and to pupils. This might surprise those less altruistic pupils who looked forward to the autumn School dance as an opportunity to 'scrump' apples from the Head's garden! A large quantity of old School Christmas cards found in a cupboard were sold and added to the sum collected from carol singing, allowed a donation to the Richard Dimbleby fund for cancer. The old peoples' homes in the area were regularly visited and many concerts given there provided enjoyment to both sides. What was probably the first sponsored walk in the area took place in 1967. Tradespeople, friends and parents supported the 16 mile walk from Borth via Taliesin to Aberystwyth which raised £60 for mentally handicapped children. That same year the sixth form girls agreed to assist the W V S with the hospital canteen on Sunday afternoon and soon took complete charge, school holidays included. Not to be outdone, the boys took on the task of cleaning the League of Friends bus each Saturday.

Former senior mistress Dr Ethel Jones welcomed the group's visits to her in her old age, as did Mrs Diddier a former School cleaning lady who was reported to have enjoyed her 80th birthday cake provided by the pupils.

Fund raising continued through the Sixties by running school dances, own clothes days, Miss Ardwyn and Mr Ardwyn competitions. Photographs of staff as infants provided a 'Guess the Baby' competition; 'Guess the Headmaster's Weight' contest also proved popular and profitable.

The more energetic in the social services group regularly tidied the churchyard at St Michael's. The grass cutting was voted the 'most strenuous of all our activities particularly on a hot Saturday afternoon in July.'

On two evenings in September 1961 a concert in aid of the King George V Jubilee Trust was given in the King's Hall. The senior pupils responded to a request from the Mayor Ald W G Kitchin and played a major role in cooperation with experienced artistes. Richard M Jenkins, the deputy head boy arranged and produced the programme and acted as compere. As well as individual musical items, there were performances by the girls' choir conducted by Menna Bennett Owen, and the Apollo Trio. Appearing on stage for the first time were 'The Night Riders' comprising John Humphries, Ernest Watson, Peter Lydiard, Barrie Tudor Evans and Christopher Edwards. They became a very popular group of musicians playing at school dances and elsewhere. A group of senior boys presented a one-act play 'Birds of a Feather.'

For the following two years the revues were repeated with the proceeds going to charity. On each occasion Philip Edwards looked after the stage management and lighting-'by experience and devotion he has attained great proficiency with stage lighting and effects'. Indeed after graduating from Imperial College, Philip worked for BBC Television and for twenty-two years has been lighting manager at the Royal Northern College of Music opera theatre as well as running his own theatre lighting business. Another example of how an interest encouraged by the School developed into a career.

As a result of the enthusiasm and commitment of botany teacher Cecil Goodwin, a School camera club established in 1960, was soon making a name for itself. A well-equipped darkroom providing facilities for film processing and enlarging, increased membership to such an extent that a junior class and beginners' class were formed in addition to the usual club evenings. The standard of members' work was quickly reflected in successes gained in photographic competitions. In 1962, Glyndwr Hubbard and Monica Thomas each gained first prize in the Welsh area 'Junior Photographer of the Year' competition, with Monica going on to win the national premier award in the colour section. Both winners were presented with their awards by Christopher Chataway MP at a luncheon in the Dorchester Hotel, London. The following year in the same competition, Graham Birch and James Thorn were equally successful and received their awards from Dame Margot Fonteyn at a luncheon at the London Savoy. The ceremony was covered in the national papers and screened on B B C Wales TV. Cecil Goodwin, in his Magazine report descibed 1964-65 as 'the most successful year for the School Camera Club', with good reason. For the third year in succession, two out of three first places came to Ardwyn and another trip to the Savoy for Rowan Lindley and Martin Campbell. The efforts of other club members in the same competition were highlighted by having their entries exhibited at the international photo-cine fair at Olympia which meant that with the winners, there were ten exhibits from the School on display. There were more honours to come; club members had been submitting prints monthly for a year to a competition organised by the *Amateur Photographer* magazine for school camera clubs. The School Club had headed the points table throughout the year and ended as winners with fifty-three points out of a possible sixty.

By now the School eisteddfod had recognised the talent to the extent of having four classes in the photography section. National prizes continued to come to the School; Terry Jenkins, Julian How and Timothy Pritchard, winners of a competition sponsored by the television company T W W, had the exciting experience of being interviewed on television.

Although subsequent years did not bring similar success in competitions, the Club continued to thrive. The acquisition of the U C W dairy buildings in 1967 allowed the botany department to move from its cramped quarters in D2, at the same time providing a new home for the camera devotees. Assistance was given to a sixth-form botany study of Ynyslas sand dunes and a start made on a long-term project to produce a complete photographic record of Aberystwyth and district for future generations to have an idea of what the town looked like. Another project was the reproduction of 'Old Aberystwyth 'photographs borrowed from friends and relations. By 1970 former members of the camera club were distinguishing themselves in the photographic world. Edward Pritchard, a freelance professional photographer was responsible for a full-page advertisement in the *Observer* colour supplement for 'Dubonnet' while Graham Birch, a Liverpool University student was overall winner in the All-Britain inter-varsity photographic competition with firsts in the open and portraiture sections.

J C Goodwin also found time to run an angling club which met during the lunch hour. The activities included fly tying, rod making, advice on choice of equipment and instruction in handling and casting with a fly rod.

The Magazine of 1970-71 reported on another dairy building activity. Supported by the teacher in charge, an animal house situated behind the main building became a naturalists' paradise. Rabbits and guinea-pigs were bred successfully and a large number of budgerigars were used for the practical teaching of genetics in the upper School. Tropical birds, goldfish and turtles ensured that the pupils' interests never waned and there was no lack of carers even during school holidays.

With the demise of the rowing club in 1953 maritime pursuits were not resumed until the Sixties. The Headmaster, A D Lewis an enthusiastic sailor, purchased a sloop for the use of the School. With a large keel and the tidal vagaries of the harbour waters, sailing in the good ship 'Mersey' was not without its thrills and scrapes but many pupils and staff were grateful for the experience and their first sailing lessons from the Head and Alwyn Williams. Thus encouraged, many pupils bought or built their own sailing dinghies; Martin Jones, the first club captain was ably supported by the other founder members David Wareing, David and Maurice Kyle and Philip Astley. In the magazine item, 'Sailing in 1964', the club captain wrote of the remarkable standard of enthusiasm and proficiency attained in a short time. Fine weather and great enthusiasm had contributed to the success of the season which had lasted from March to November. The school yacht and sailing dinghy had been in great demand and junior sailors coached by the more experienced helmsmen achieved a remarkable standard of proficiency. Claiming that the sport was second to none for exhilaration and amusement, the captain hoped that more pupils could be tempted to join the Ardwyn sailing club.

Perhaps the exhilaration came from the deliberate capsizes for which the record was fifteen in one day; it was all part of the training for the crews to handle such a mishap in the safety of the harbour. For many years Ardwyn sailors dominated the local regattas and successfully competed as far away as Bala and Chester where the opposing helmsmen were often of national standard. In the last few years of the School, with fewer private boat owners, membership had dwindled but the project of building four Mirror dinghies in the woodwork department would ensure that the traditions built up in the previous ten years would be perpetuated in the daughter schools.

Cross-country running had figured as a House competition from the Thirties, but few if any boys did any serious training for the event. Indeed it is true to say that for many, the actual race was the only occasion that the course had been run. In the early years of the Fifties, reports of the events were very despondent, particularly regarding the very few entries for the senior event; in 1954 both Powys and Gwynedd were eliminated from the competition because of their failure to provide entries for the senior race. Wynne Hughes the PE master, reporting the results of the 1956 races, observed that 'the cross-country event was the most gruelling and stenuous of all school activities and should be preceded by an adequate period of training.' But the situation was to change dramatically; the autumn of 1958 saw the first Ardwyn harriers team formed mainly through the persistence of Elwyn Lewis. The opening fixture against the U C W 'Freshers' was narrowly lost but both matches against Towyn were won. Fixtures were difficult to arrange but the captain Elwyn Lewis, winner of the House senior event in 1958 and 1959, expressed the hope that a full fixture list would be possible in the future and that 'in the years to come Ardwyn would become as noted for its harriers as it is for its rugby players.' Prophetic words indeed.

By now Wynne Hughes had joined the College physical education department and his replacement, Hywel Mathews gave strong encouragement to the sport. The difficulty with lack of fixtures was mitigated by the introduction, in 1960, of county and national cross-country championships. Ardwyn took pride in being the only school to enter two full teams for the county trials at Aberaeron and the selection of seven boys for the senior county team of eight runners, captained by Elwyn Elias. Ardwyn also supplied the junior captain in Gwyn Price Evans. In the national championships at Newtown, Christopher Loosely did exceptionally well to come third out of a field of

The History of Aberystwyth County School (Ardwyn) 1896-1973

Senior Hockey XI 1967–68

Lindy Martin, Sian B. Davies, Verona Davies, Sandra Morgan, Meryl Thomas, Miss M. Edwards.

Glesni Roberts, Nona Davies, Sian Roberts, Effie Richards, Susan Ellis.

1st Team 1961–62.

Caren Fleming, Catrin B. Davies, Mrs. C. Griffiths, Beryl Jones, Ann Williams, .

Margaret Edwards, Anna Pugh, Dinah Thomas.

1957 Tennis Team.

Miss Shirley Dann Ruth Evans, Hazel Dix, Alice Henley.

Pat Edmonds, Pat Meigh, Valerie Thomas.

The A. D. Lewis Years — 1954-1971

Prefects 1958–59

*Head Girl:
Rhona Ryle*

*Head Boy:
Peter Davies*

1st XV 1958–59

*Capt.
Jimmy Thomas.*

Harriers 1962

Gwynfor Roberts, Peter Price, Robert Williams, Ifan Jones, Geoff Evans, John Evans, Colin Hancock, Roy Jones, H. Mathews.

Richard Evans, Derek Davies, T. G. Evans, Christopher Loosely (Capt), T. Gwyn Evans, Terry James.

ninety runners in the junior event and two weeks later won the Aberystwyth Promenade race in record time. For Chris Loosely this was the start of a brilliant athletics career; his success whilst a fourth-former, in the House senior race in 1960 was the first of four such victories. The record number of 134 boys who took part in the cross-country races that year was an indication of the new enthusiasm for the sport. Pupils ranging in age from twelve to eighteen, inspired by the dedication of Chris Loosely, Terry James and Richard Evans, were keen to join them on training runs. A total of 196 runners took part in the School races in 1962 including 40 seniors;. Arfon ended a five-year sequence of wins by Ceredigion. That year, after a comfortable win in the county championships, Loosely won the senior race in the Welsh schools championship at Newtown from a field of 90 runners, with his inseparable training companion, Terry James a commendable ninth. Hywel Mathews proudly noted that this was the first occasion that the School had obtained a winner's certificate from any national athletics event.

> I was located in a hut near the finish with all the other county managers, each seated at a desk to record the results as they came in after crossing the line. Being in the hut I missed the finish but I do remember the pleasure in Loosely's face at being the first runner through the door to record his win. Cardiganshire and Ardwyn had made its presence felt on the national cross-country scene.[93]

In 1963, after his third success in the House competition, Chris Loosely became the first winner of the 'K Ian Evans Cup' presented by the parents of Ian Evans in gratitude to the School for all the benefits their son had derived. Ian held the School mile record for some years; a State scholarship in 1959 led to a brilliant career at Cambridge plus an athletics Blue-the first ever for an Ardwynian.

Loosely repeated his triumph in the national championships in 1963 and 1964; in addition he became Welsh A A A youth cross-country champion. He was selected for the Welsh under-twenties team to run at San Sebastian, Spain, where he was the first Welshman home, coming fourteenth out of an international field of thirty-two runners. He also represented the Welsh secondary schools as a miler in international events, becoming the first Ardwynian to earn a Welsh athletic vest at track events. (In 1959 Paul Edwards had become the first Ardwynian to win an international vest – as a shot-putter.) He remained a very modest young man, whose great concern was the encouragement of others, particularly juniors, to follow in his footsteps.

In his review of the harriers' activities in 1963-64, his last year at School, Chris Loosely considered that the season was the busiest and most successful to date. Such was the enthusiasm and dedication, a junior section of the club was founded and meetings increased to two a week. He took pleasure from watching the progress of Ardwyn's future champions and commended the loyalty and support of his club members, one of whom was prepared to forfeit his place in the rugby team in order to run with the harriers. Such team spirit bound a number of good individuals into a brilliant team. 'The season had a fitting climax. The Cardiganshire team containing seven out of eight Ardwyn harriers, came second to Glamorgan in the national championships. This achievement gave me infinitely greater pleasure than my third winner's certificate and when I look back on my days at Ardwyn I shall always be proud to have been captain of such a wonderful team.' He paid tribute to the support received from Hywel Mathews who had moved to teach at Machynlleth.

> I have thought hard, 37 years later, about the success of the Ardwyn harriers in the late 50s and early 60s when I was PE teacher. As in most things I think that it was a combination of factors. The School had a tradition of annual House competitions for boys at three age groups so the formation of a harriers club was logical. Many of the harriers were not involved in any other winter sport, so they were able to devote all their time and enthusiasm to running. There was no clash of sports for boys like Elwyn Lewis, Ian Evans, Chris Loosely, Thomas Gwyn Price Evans, Terry James and Richard Evans-I could name many more. They simply enjoyed the fun and sport of cross-country running and were very good at it. Others played rugby in winter and those like brothers Gwynn and Gary Davis, who peaked athletically after I left, managed to combine both sports. The winter running provided the perfect base for middle and long distance track athletics. Undoubtedly the PE teacher at the time influences what happens and my recollections of my short time at Ardwyn, which seems to have coincided with success nationally in cross-country and distance running, is that there were some outstanding athletes in the School at the time. However, without the existence of the Aberystwyth Athletic Club and specifically the inspiration and coaching of Ron Cullum, I doubt whether their success would have been as great.[94]

It is true to say that the harriers club operated without a great deal of help by the staff who were heavily involved in the so-called major school games. Forty years on, the work of Ron Cullum is remembered with gratitude by so many. A former Ardwyn pupil, he founded the Aberystwyth Athletic Club in 1955 to provide opportunities for young people to take part in track events and cross-country running. In 1963, at the tender age of 38, he ran the mile in the Welsh Games at Cardiff in the time of 4 minutes 20 seconds. He was also largely responsible for the formation in 1968, of the Mini-Minor Soccer league providing competitive soccer for hundreds of boys and some girls.

Ron Cullum provided leadership for the group of young distance runners in the town, advising on standards to aim at, and supervising their training.

> Thinking back for the reasons why we did so well at distance running in the Sixties, Chris Loosely was a big inspiration and has to take a lot of the credit for being the first to break the south Wales dominance. We were all greatly helped by Ron Cullum who blended us into a team and the experience of running against the Aber. University lads was a great incentive to improve our standards.[95]

The loss of Chris Loosely was not as traumatic as might have been feared, in fact new heights were reached the following season, under the captaincy of Richard Evans. The seniors were unbeaten, the result of several nights a week training at the Vicarage field. UCW Freshers were beaten in the opening fixture, followed by the first win against the junior leaders regiment, Tonfannau. Schools from north Wales, Cheshire and Lancashire were beaten when Ardwyn was the first school team home in the Beaumaris to Bangor road race at their first attempt. With the School dominating the County teams once again, there was great disappointment in the cancellation, due to bad weather, of the national championships; Cardiganshire had high hopes of winning for the first time. Half the Aber A C was composed of Ardwynians who helped the club clinch the North Wales League title in its second attempt eclipsing such well established teams such as Wrexham and Shrewsbury Athletic Clubs.

The newly appointed P E master Peter Duggan sensibly adopted a new pattern for the House competition. After a month's training before the event, those achieving a set standard, gained points which counted towards the competition. The new arrangement meant that only those capable of doing so ran, even so, more than 120 runners took part. The senior race was run on a new 4 mile course, designed to be more suitable for the selection of a team for the county championships. Terry James was the winner in a time it was said was unlikely to be beaten for many years. Gary Davis in winning the junior race, and the 'Ian Evans trophy' for an outstanding performance, gave a glimpse of his future capabilities. Arfon won the Adler cup for the third successive year.

Despite predictions, Gary Davis in winning the School senior race in 1965, beat the previous year's time by 29 seconds. The harriers improved on the previous record season when both juniors and seniors were undefeated; notable victories were recorded against Llanelli Grammar School and Llandovery College. The same two schools plus Trinity College, Carmarthen were later defeated in a quadrangular match, proving if proof was needed, that Ardwyn was the dominant force in Welsh schools cross-country. The School's impact was even felt in the north of England when against Welsh and English opposition the Ardwyn harriers retained their hold on the Bangor road race title. For the Welsh schools championships at Newtown, Ardwyn supplied seven out of the eight members of the county team; Gary Davis took first place, four seconds ahead of team mate and club captain Richard Evans. Gary retained the title the following year and despite the departure of Richard Evans and other long serving members, but strengthened by the arrival of Frank Thomas from Dinas School, Ardwyn retained an unbeaten record for the senior team for the third consecutive year. A new and prestigious title was added to the accumulating honours-the Gilwern road race. Gary Davis took first place with the team prize also coming to Ardwyn despite the presence of the redoubtable Birchfield Harriers and Bristol A C.

> I had some natural ability but after Chris Loosely won the Welsh schools title again in 1964, I was determined to emulate him. From finishing in 45th place in the junior race in 1965 I won the senior race the following year. I was training twice a day, going out in the lunch hour most days. We all trained incredibly hard, possibly too hard, it got a bit fanatical. My best race for Ardwyn was the national in 1967 when I won by 300 yards; it was a great feeling to smash the big boys from Glamorgan.
> To be summoned to the Head's office was like an invitation to death row. At my first visit I received four strokes of the cane for leaving my satchel out in the rain; the second was to receive his congratulations. He had heard on the radio of our win in the Gilwern road race. I didn't have the courage to tell him that the team had to hitch-hike there and back to do it.[96]

When Gary Davis left for university, Frank Thomas took over the leadership of the harriers. Frank had, as a fourteen year old, held the unofficial world record for the 10,000 metres (6 miles) under 16 years age group. His team mates remember him as an incredibly brave runner; he maintained the School tradition by winning the Welsh

The A. D. Lewis Years — 1954-1971

Schools title in 1968. For the first time Ardwyn filled all eight places in the county senior team at that event. Llandovery College were comprehensively defeated early in the season at junior, middle and senior levels, and Frank Thomas had successes in the West Wales and Welsh youth championships and inevitably the senior race in the House competition which Ceredigion won for the second successive year.

In the Magazine report on the harriers 1968-69 season there were indications that the superlative performances of the the past were coming to an end. With the departure of Frank Thomas there appeared to be no natural leader and it was reported that meetings were now irregular and enthusiasm seemed to be on the wane. However, in the county championships, the junior and senior races were won by Dennis Hughes and Richard Pugh to maintain the series of Ardwyn victories since the inception of the competion in 1960. Although there were brave efforts from Richard Pugh and Stephen Nantlais Williams in the Welsh Schools championships, for the first time in seven years, an Ardwyn boy had failed to win the title.

The activities and accomplishments of the Ardwyn cross country runners have been chronicled in some detail because they deserve a special place in the history of Ardwyn sport. In fact they must be the most successful School team in the long history of the School. No sports team got anywhere near their consistency over such a long period as eight years and certainly no team produced athletes who could say that they were the best in Wales and even further afield. Their record was particularly meritorious since for the most part, they were self-motivated and virtually independent of the School. There was of course a spin-off for track and field athletics.

Quite soon after he was appointed to the PE staff, Wynne Hughes, in an effort to improve standards in track and field athletics, introduced athletics as a major games activity towards the end of February each year. The performances in the inter-House athletic meeeting of May 1956 showed a marked improvement; javelin, shot and discus events for the girls were included in the programme in line with the policy of the Welsh Schools AAA. Hurdles events for boys and girls appeared in the programme for the first time. Iwan Jones who had captained the School at rugby, soccer and cricket and was victor ludorum in 1955, won the sprint events and triple jump. Colin Creasey, who had earlier won the cross country race, added the half-mile and mile to his accomplishments; his time of 4 mins 55 secs for the mile at last broke the twenty-one year record of Ifan Davis.

The seven-year old 440 yards record of M Magor was claimed by Glyn Dudlyke. A new record too for Peter Wright in throwing the senior discus 109ft 9ins. In winning the hurdles and 220 yards events, Elizabeth Lee was the most successful girl athlete, in the previous year she was victrix ludorum, the last occasion for the medals to be presented.

Eight Ardwynians made the county team with Creasey and Glyn Williams achieving a commendable 6th and 4th place in the mile and 880 yards respectively in the national meeting at St Helen's, Swansea. The following year, Glyn Williams, after breaking the 440 and 880 yards records in the School sports, went on to gain second place in the 880 yards at the Colwyn Bay national meeting. Obviously the work of the coaches was bearing fruit; at the county meeting, Ardwyn won three of the seven trophies, were runners-up in three and also claimed six of the seven relay titles.

In the 1958 inter-House sports, Ceredigion secured the Nanteos cup after being second to Arfon for six successive years. Thirteen records were improved upon including the girls' senior 100 yards, which Mair Evans had held since 1941; Marilyn Richards clocked 11. 6 secs, a time never bettered in the remaining years. Showing his versatility, Glyn Williams, renowned for his middle distance running, equalled the 220 yards time of 24. 8 secs first recorded by David White eleven years earlier. Paul Edwards gave a glimpse of his talents in breaking the middle high jump and weight records. Competing as a senior the following year, Paul won seven events, a feat which must be regarded as the outstanding track and field achievement in Ardwyn's history. He gained a standard certificate at the national sports and later had the distinction of becoming Ardwyn's first international in any sport when he was selected to put the weight for the Welsh Schools AAA against Scotland.

Iwan Thomas, new to the event, created a new record in the hurdles at the county meeting. At the national held in Haverfordwest, the Cardiganshire bus arrived just in time for Iwan to get into his blocks-he came a very close second. As a senior, his 110 yards hurdle record stood for five years.

During the Sixties records continued to tumble and more Welsh international vests came to the School. As in the case of the harriers, Ardwyn track and field athletes could now compete successfully against the best in Wales. The dedication, fitness and success of the harriers had permeated the School at all levels and performances in track and field soon showed a similar level of excellence. The Headmaster A D Lewis strongly encouraged his pupils to achieve the highest standards academically and on the sports ground; he was a regular and vociferous supporter at most of his School's sporting encounters and was chairman of the Aberystwyth Athletic Club for many years.

Given that Ardwyn was the largest school in Cardiganshire and from 1962 was fortunate to have use of the U C W cinder track for training and for its inter-House competition, the record of Ardwyn in the county sports was still a proud one. In the sixteen years from 1956 to 1971, the senior girls and senior boys claimed the county trophies thirteen and twelve times respectively. In that period the girls averaged two trophies per county meeting and the boys just over one. The university cinder track became available in 1962 with a resulting improvement in standards particularly in the jumps, where the cinder approaches helped in the breaking of the ten-year old senior long jump record by T Glyn Evans and the junior triple jump by Gwynn Davis. Davis also improved the 80 yards hurdle time and won the long jump-the start of an illustrious athletic career.

In the previous year, Christopher Loosely, running in the middle mile, had run a faster time than the senior mile winner so it came as no surprise to see him break, by .7 sec, the 1960 record of Ian Evans. He improved the mile time again in each of the following two years. The county team was dominated by Ardwynians, 22 boys and 11 girls. As a result of their performances in the national competition, Anna Pugh became the first Ardwyn girl to represent her country, her event being the shot and Christopher Loosely gained selection for Wales as a miler.

Christine Griffiths was appointed PE mistress in 1960; her no nonsense approach to her duties and generosity in the time she devoted to coaching, soon saw an upsurge in the standard of the girls' sports generally.

In terms of success in the county competition, 1963 must rank as the outstanding year. The girls swept the board, gaining fifteen first places and all three age group trophies. The boys secured three out of four cups, missing the junior title by one point.

The biggest athletic meeting ever to be staged at Aberystwyth took place on Saturday 13 July 1963 when the national championships were held at the U C W Vicarage fields. The following Monday the headlines in the sports section of the *Western Mail* read: 'Loosely sets up new schools record in the mile event'. He had run a 4 min 24 sec mile clipping .6 sec off the six year old record. He was described as 'one of Wales' most promising young hopefuls'. In the same meeting, the victory of Terry James in the steeplechase was seen by very few people as it was held at the Penglais cinder track. However later in the afternoon he received a well-deserved ovation when he was a close second in the 880 yards event.

Ardwyn PE master Hywel Mathews, as organising secretary of the national meeting, was congratulated on his meticulous organisation and Bill Groom, the U C W grounds-man, always cooperative and amiable, was commended for the long hours put in preparing what was regarded as the best grass track in Wales.

Anna Pugh and Christopher Loosely, two of twenty-seven Ardwynians representing their county in the national that year, both gained their second Welsh vest and were joined in the schools' international by Terry James.

In the 1963 School sports, Ceredigion won the cup for the fourth successive year; the Magazine noted the outstanding achievements of Terry Davies in winning the three junior throws and Gwynn Davis in winning four middle events, including a new record in the hurdles. In the national competition, 1964 saw 'the greatest triumph yet' when, in Brecon, four first places were gained, Christopher Loosely-mile, Terry James-steeplechase, both at senior level, Richard Lloyd-100 yards and Gwynn Davis-triple jump, both at middle level.

Not a year passed without records being broken. In the 1967 sports, 24 records were improved and 6 equalled. In some cases changes in the age group structure, new events and metrication were responsible and it must be said, several claims which when researched could not be substantiated. It is only possible here to recognise the outstanding performances and those whose records were never surpassed during the lifetime of the School.

The records set up by Paul Edwards in 1959 and 1960 in the javelin-141 ft 9 ins, discus-115 ft 7 ins and weight 39 ft 7 ins were never improved, despite claims to the contrary.

The legendary Chris Loosely, in addition to his two appearances for Wales as a miler, improved the School mile record three times. His best time, run in 1964, 4 mins 28.4 secs was beaten by Gary Davies in 1967 by 2.4 secs, a time time never surpassed. It is of interest to note that Gary's father, Ifan held the mile record for twenty-one years. Loosely's 880 yards time of 1 min 58.2 secs was never surpassed.

Gwynn Davis as a junior, had achieved national standards in two events early in his athletic career; after gaining first place in the triple jump in the middle age group in the national competition, he was selected for Wales in that event. He left School holding three records, two of which, a triple jump of 44 ft 3 ins and a long jump of 20 ft 6.5 ins were never improved.

Injury problems caused Gwynn to give up triple jumping and instead of competing in that event in the schools' international in 1965, he elected to run the 440 yards at the Welsh Games and won. As a first year university student he represented Wales in the world junior cross-country championships despite an earlier apathy to that sport. He

Ardwyn Sailing Club 1962

A. D. Lewis (Head) at the helm of the school boat "Mersey" with I. L. Davies engineer & crew.

The A. D. Lewis Years — 1954-1971

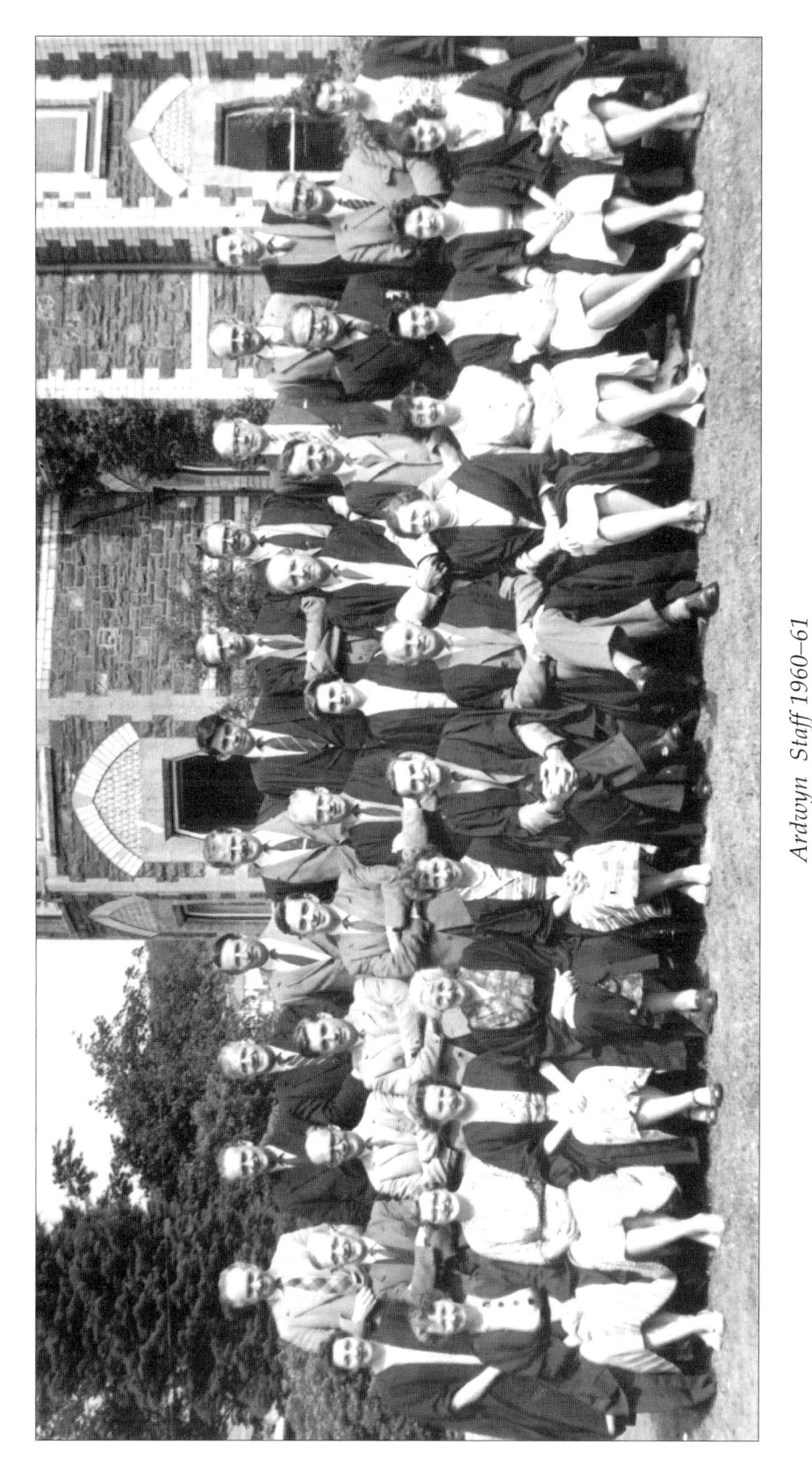

Ardwyn Staff 1960–61

Back—Hywel Harries, Idwal Davies, Ken Jones, Noel Butler, Huw S. Lloyd, H. Mathews, Carl Chadwick, David Sansbury, Morgan Price, A. Jones, John Taylor.

Middle—Rhiannon Roberts, Maurice Chapple, R. Everson, J. C. Goodwin, Aneurin Jenkins-Jones, L. O. Lewis, C. Griffiths, W. Beynon Davies, Leslie Davies, Roy James, R. J. Lloyd, Mari Carter.

Seated—E. W. Williams, L. C. Thomas, E. Jones-Davies, G. Winkler, G. M. Mainwaring, George Rowlands, A. D. Lewis, Gwen Herbert, Violet Jones, E. Beacham, June Treharne, Mary Owen.

subsequently ran many times for Wales including the Commonwealth Games at Edinburgh in 1970.

> My first School sports, when I created a new record for the long jump, 14 ft 2 ins, if I recall correctly, was a day of great joy. I suppose that distance was beaten eventually, but I was certainly proud of it. I also remember 'Moc' Price mis-reading a triple jump of mine as 30 ft 6 ins and not 36 ft. He wouldn't budge and I thought it was the end of the world. I also remember Mr Price for his amazing ability to draw a perfect circle on the blackboard unaided.[97]

Gary Davies emulated his older brother Gwynn in 1966 gaining a Welsh vest after a second place in the mile at the national meeting.

In 1964, Terry James created a new School time for the 220 and 440 yards, won first place in the national 880 yards and represented Wales for the second time as a steeple-chaser.

Anna Pugh, as well as representing her country in two internationals, created School records in the shot and javelin; her shot put of 29 ft 3/4in was never improved.

Margaret Edwards was a talented and versatile sportswoman; she dominated the sprint events in her age group between 1959 and 1963. Appointed to the School as PE teacher in 1967, she was unable to coach a pupil to beat her own record 28.8 secs for the 220 yards!

J Richard Lloyd was described by the athletics captain Terry James as 'the finest sprinter Ardwyn had ever produced.' Such statements are often made but usually without conspectus and knowledge of past 'greats'. However, he did win most of the sprints he ran during his School career; in the 1964 inter-House sports he created new records in the middle 100, 220 and 440 yards events and won all three races in the county meeting. This earned selection for the national where he was placed first in the 100 yards; no Ardwyn athlete had won a national sprint title, which perhaps vindicates the claim of 'best ever.' Injury and other factors prevented Richard competing at senior level when he seemed set for further honours.

As a junior, Menna Beasley gained first place in a hurdles event and second place in the 100 yards at the Connah's Quay national championships in 1965. At the same meeting Sian Davies and Lynda Jenkins were placed fourth in the senior 440 yards hurdles and 880 yards respectively; both held School records in those events which were never bettered.

In 1965 Peter Hughes created a new 440 yards record of 52.5 secs as did Tom H Williams in the 220 yards with a time of 23. 1 secs. The following year the twenty-four year old 100 yards record of Colin Lewis of 10.4 secs was improved by Tom Williams by .1 sec, running of course on a cinder track.

Representation at international level was maintained by Richard J Evans when he was selected to run the 1500m steeplechase for Wales in 1965 and again the following year having won the event in the national; he gained a creditable second place in the international match between the home countries.

As experienced athletes left School, there seemed to be a never ending succession of replacements imbued with the desire to emulate the feats of their predecessors. Competing as a junior in 1965, Ian Jones won four events; he later established new middle group records for School and county in the two sprint events and javelin as well as reaching the finals in his events in the national. Before leaving, he added the county record in the pole vault to his list of accomplishments. Brian Williams was another who showed his versatility early-his feat of creating new junior records in both sprints and shot were described as 'outstanding on the day'. Frank Thomas, another dedicated runner gained his first international vest as a steeplechaser in 1967 and repeated his successs the following year as a miler, having won the senior mile at the national. No further international honours in track and field came Ardwyn's way although it is difficult to understand why Danny Clues did not get recognition after winning the 440 hurdles at national meetings in 1969 and 1970. Nevertheless in the ten years from 1959, Ardwyn athletes earned Welsh representation on thirteen occasions.

Verona Davies must have created a record in winning the javelin event in her age group on six occasions in the inter-House sports as well being a winning hurdler and sprinter. In the 1969 sports she broke the nine-year old discus record of Margaret E Jones with a throw of 83 ft 5 ins and the javelin record of Anna Pugh with a throw of 97 ft. Nona Davies and Pamela Bowen were both able athletes who established new records at School and county meetings in the late Sixties.

For some, competitive athletics did not cease on leaving School. Gary Davies turned to road racing and as a Sale harrier won the Derwentwater 10 mile race, outsprinting a future British Olympic marathon runner to beat Ron Hill's record. In 1983 he ran in the London marathon and won the inaugural mid-Wales marathon.

Chris Loosley had an outstanding record as a runner at U C W representing British universities and Wales, though it was generally agreed that he had a raw deal from the Welsh selectors. Loosely was close behind the Australian Ron Clarke in a six mile race in the White City when the latter broke the British record.

At the age of 45 years, Frank Thomas is still running for the Welsh veterans. He ranks fifth in the UK and in 1994 ran a half-marathon in 68 minutes.

Perhaps the proudest record of all belongs to Richard (Dic) Evans. He represented Wales on six occasions in the world cross-country event, being captain for four years. Dic can claim to have represented Wales in one athletic event or another for thirty years consecutively; with over a hundred appearances for his country, he is Wales' most capped distance runner. He has also represented Great Britain in the marathon on four occasions. He was the first Welshman home in the inaugural London marathon in 1981 in 27th place. In his running career he has competed with the best in the world-Gordon Pirie, Brendan Foster, Kip Keino, David Bedford, Steve Jones and he beat the Finn Laise Viren in a cross-country race at the Crystal Palace.

On St David's Day 1992 he broke the world record for the veterans 50 mile track event. Dic had the distinction of being a selector for the 1992 Olympics and has been British and Welsh team manager for cross-country and road running.

Following the twelve State scholarships awarded in the ten year period 1950-59, a further four were gained before the award was abolished in 1963. A list of the twenty-three State scholarships awarded to Ardwyn pupils is given as an appendix. In the last ten years of the School's life, many pupils gained the three distinctions at Advanced level which would have merited a State scholarship. During this period, a record thirteen Oxbridge places were obtained, including open scholarships gained by Huw Ceredig,

Alun Ellis Jones, David J Gowan, Paul Nevin, and Stephen Nantlais Williams. Philip Henry Jones later gained an open scholarship from UC Swansea to Jesus College, Cambridge as did Ceri Davies from UC Cardiff to Jesus College, Oxford. Simon Read, Alan Thomas, Leslie Williams, Ann Evans, Alun Edwards and Ann Morrison secured their Oxbridge places by virtue of the brilliance of their A-level results. A further nine pupils obtained open scholarships to the colleges of the University of Wales and one each to the Universities of London and Manchester.

Gareth Rhys Thomas after gaining first class honours in civil engineering at Imperial College, London was awarded a research fellowship at Cornell University, USA. Alwyn H Jones who had entered UC Cardiff as a State scholar in 1957 gained first class honours in Classics and was elected to a research studentship at Cambridge. By the late Fifties, university aspirants were becoming more adventurous; no longer were they content to opt for their home town university college.

Distinctions came too for activities out of School. Paul Brenells and Philip L Edwards had gained the highest award in Scouting and had the honour of taking part in a march past by Queen's Scouts from all over Great Britain at Windor Castle in April 1962. Susan Astley and Naomi Clapham had also qualified for the Queen's Guide award; only once before had a Cardiganshire guide been so recognised. In 1964, when she was head girl, Susan was chosen as sole representative from Wales at the international guide camp in Sweden, the third Ardwyn girl to receive that honour in seven years. That same year, Wendy Lyn Christian Jones was the first Ardwynian to receive an award under the Duke of Edinburgh award scheme. She was invited to Buckingham Palace to receive the certificate; she had previously been presented with her gold medal by Sir Ifan ab Owen Edwards. The tasks connected with the awards were in forms of social service carried out under the auspices of Urdd Gobaith Cymru.

As has been previously noted John Morris had been instrumental in establishing a debating club in the School and had secured a landslide victory for the Liberals in a 1948 mock election. Within ten years of leaving Ardwyn he was in Westminster having won Aberavon as a Labour candidate in the 1959 General Election. Following the 1962 Election, John Morris was joined on the Labour benches by Dr Jeremy Bray, MP for Middlesbrough, who had spent a short time in the School in the early years of the Second World War when his father had been minister at the English Methodist Church. After unsuccessfully contesting a by-election in the Wrexham division for Plaid Cymru at the age of 22 years, five years after leaving School, Elystan Morgan was elected as Labour MP for Cardiganshire in March 1966, ending almost eighty years of Liberal domination.

Elystan Morgan MP made his maiden speech on 6 May 1966 during the second reading of the Agriculture Bill. He opened by paying tribute to his predecessor for his industrious constituency work of close on 21 years.

> I hope I shall be able to emulate not only the quality of constituency service but, if one may be so bold, also the length of his tenure.
> Cardiganshire, for nearly 50 years has been represented by members of the legal profession. The people of Cardiganshire have obviously not said with St Luke

'Woe unto you, lawyers! for ye have taken away
the key of knowledge.

Michael Joplin (Westmorland) followed the fairly lengthy maiden speech and commented:

> I have always hoped that at some time when I was in the House I should have the good fortune of following an Hon Member who had made his maiden speech. I now have that opportunity and I am glad to have it. I never believed that I should sit through a maiden speech which I should enjoy so much that I was able to congratulate the Hon Member, as I congratulate the Hon Member for Cardigan, with such feeling. I welcome him to the House; he has made a most enjoyable speech with great knowledge and lucidity. I am sure that the House agrees with me when I say that I hope we shall hear from him often.[98]

> Despite the sharp edges of many recollections, some things, in particular, value judgements of people do change with the passage of time. From the perspective of forty to fifty years many reappraisals of fellow pupils have occurred with the benefit of experience and hindsight. The vast majority of these were for the better. Not all, however, were confined to fellow pupils. In particular, there was the case of Miss Forster, whom I regarded in my boyish ignorance as representing a somewhat unprogressive and less than sympathetic spirit. One fine day in 1966, however, on my unexpected election to Parliament, Miss Forster lept off her Hercules bicycle in Terrace Road, ran across the street and hugged me, explaining that I was the only successful Labour candidate that she had voted for since her Suffragette days. It must have been a very mutual re-appraisal![99]

The *Ardwynian* noted that there were now three former pupils of Ardwyn holding Labour seats, two of them with posts in Wilson's government. John Morris had moved to the Ministry of Transport and Jeremy Bray had taken Morris' former post at the Ministry of Power. The confident predictions of the editor that Elystan Morgan would soon make his presence felt in the House were realised when he served as Under Secretary of State in the Home Office between 1968 and 1970. At the same time John Morris was promoted from Transport to Defence while Bray moved to the Ministry of Technology. Re-elected in 1970, Elystan, in the following four years, added to his growing reputation as opposition spokesman on Home and Welsh affairs. It was generally thought that had he not lost his seat to the Liberal, Geraint Howells in the second election in 1974, he would have become the Secretary of State for Wales. Elystan Morgan resumed his legal career; he was made a life peer in 1981 and a circuit judge in 1987. In 1991 Lord Elystan Morgan was appointed a Vice-President of the University of Wales, Aberystwyth.

Geraint Howells, an Ardwynian of the Thirties, served the constituency diligently and well for eighteen years. When defeat came in the 1992 Election his services to his native county were rewarded with a life peerage. Dr Jeremy Bray and John Morris QC continue in Westminster, the latter still on the opposition front bench currently shadow attorney general. Michael Hilary Roberts who spent a short time in Ardwyn when his

'The Perfect Changeover'
Caren Fleming and Anna Pugh at the County Sports, 1962.

Dic Evans

who became Wales' most capped distance runner. He has represented his country in one athletic event or another for thirty years consecutively with over a hundred appearances.

The A. D. Lewis Years — 1954-1971

Athletics Team 1959–60.
Winners of the Lower Junior & Senior group at the 1960 County Sports.

Aberystwyth Athletic Club 1964
made up of mainly Ardwyn athletes, six of whom represented Wales at schoolboy & senior level. Coach and mentor Ron Cullum is centre front row.

father was vicar at Holy Trinity church, served as the MP for Cardiff North-West division from the Seventies until his early death. Thus Ardwyn provided Westminster with seven Members of Parliament when Ernest Evans and Goronwy Owen, MPs from the Twenties are added to the list.

On May 18 1899 a conference of governments met in The Hague to discuss the general question of peace. May 18 was adopted as the anniversary of the beginning of the official discussion of peace in time of peace; that day became known as World Peace Day or Goodwill Day. In 1922, the suggestion, made by the Revd Gwilym Davies, that the boys and girls of Wales might join once a year in a greeting to the children of the world was enthusiastically adopted by the schools of Wales and by the newly formed Urdd. The BBC was not in existence but the greeting was 'wirelessed' in the Morse Code on May 18 1922 through a government station in Great Britain and by the Eiffel Tower in Paris. In later years the BBC broadcast the Message of Goodwill or *Neges Ewyllus Da* on May 18 each year in the Children's Hour programme and from its Empire station. There was no response from anywhere until 1924 when messages were received from Poland and Sweden by the Revd Gwilym Davies at the Temple of Peace, Cardiff. A year later, replies came in scores and increased to hundreds from all parts of the world until 1938. With the outbreak of war, silence fell upon country after country in Europe and with the spread of war in the Pacific, no reply came from lands in the Far East. The founder of the Goodwill Message lived in retirement in Aberystwyth from 1940 until his death in 1955 and presumably donated his papers relating to the Message to the School since the Ardwyn archives contain the telegrams and letters sent in reply to Revd Davies. Those received after cessation of hostilities are particularly poignant. Children from a school in Lyon, writing on 22 May 1946, named members of their class who lost parents during the war in prison camps and in the field, and expressed the hope that the world would always remain at peace. Polish children from a displaced persons centre in Brunswick, W Germany wrote that they were glad to be remembered by the childen of Wales and regarded liberty and loyalty as the most precious things; 'our slogan is to love our neighbours and we will always be ready to contribute to peace on earth'. The first occasion that Ardwyn pupils were actively involved was remembered by the deputy head boy, a noted poet.

> An important feature of School life involved participation in the annual Goodwill Day message started in 1922 and still running. In May 1958 a number of us were involved in sending a tape-recorded message to schools in America and Israel.
> A feathered bird conveyed the note,
> That Bronwen of our folklore wrote;
> Another bird of man's design
> Brings you today this Celtic line.[100]

A photograph exists of the recording session in the Central Hall of the School. Head girl Gwenda Lewis is seen reading the message together with fellow sixth formers and the Headmaster. It was ten years before further reference was made to the Goodwill Message when the Headmaster reported to the Governors that the text of the message had been drawn up by the sixth form and broadcast by two pupils. For the first time a

Chinese version of the greeting had been prepared by the parents of Chinese pupils in attendance, an indication of the growing cosmopolitan nature of the School.

A former missionary in Persia, John R Richards, who was appointed Bishop of the See of St David's in 1956 was the guest speaker at prize day the following year. He spoke of his days at Ardwyn recalling that from Miss Dalley they had learnt discipline and confessing that in every class except hers, the pupils did everything they should not have done ! Dr DJ Davies had taught him moral courage and David Samuel, the value of religion. The latter was not averse to wielding the stick when necessary.

Another old Ardwynian, Dr Richard Phillips, former lecturer and research director at the UCW agriculture department, in his prize day address in 1958, pleaded for a more considerate outlook towards the rural areas and recognition of the importance of rural areas in the well-being of the nation. The following year a senior government civil servant Blaise Gillie of the Ministry of Housing, Cardiff reminded the audience that education was increasingly affected by the need to earn a living, but he hoped that they would not cease to pursue knowledge just for the pleasure of it.

Headmaster AD Lewis took the opportunity to speak on the defects of the 11 plus examination, regretting that there was no second chance as there was in the GSE examination. Those present were reminded that an education advisory body, in a 1954 report, had recommended that the process of selection for secondary education should allow a small number of grammar school places to be filled at each individual school by alternative methods to the 11 plus examination. He criticised those pupils who left prematurely after giving a signed declaration to stay until 16 years of age; they lacked the will to work, lacked interest in study, had insufficient perseverance and ambition and had no parental encouragement. These early leavers had taken the place of other suitable children who would have stayed the course. These observations probably served as a means of giving a public explanation of his action earlier in the year when he had admitted a 13 year old boarding school boy who had not qualified through the 11 plus test for a grammar school education. An item in the minutes of the county higher education committee read:

> Ardwyn Grammar School-Exclusion of pupil:Resolved that as a pupil admitted to the School in May 1959 could produce no academic criteria acceptable to the Committee to prove his suitability for admission to the School, the Headmaster be asked to exclude him immediately.[101]

In November 1959, the *Cambrian News* reported that the county education committee had agreed, at a meeting on 5 November, to allow the boy, whom they named, to remain at Ardwyn. In an acrimonious meeting, where it was reported that the chairman, Ald Gwarnant Williams had to raise his voice frequently, Ald John John, the mayor of Aberystwyth gave notice of a motion 'that the education committee give consideration to allowing a further test for the children who were not able to gain admission to Ardwyn on the 11 plus test.' The Ardwyn Governors, in their July 1959 meeting had recommended that the education committee appoint a sub-committeee to investigate the case. The examination board met on August 27 and after hearing the Headmaster's reasons for admitting the boy, declared the Headmaster's action as irregular and in future no child must be admitted without passing the 11 plus test. The boy would have to submit himself to a test arranged by the Director of Education Dr J Henry Jones. It was after the director had reported to the 5 November meeting that the boy was allowed to remain at the School.

The Headmaster AD Lewis, interviewed by the *Cambrian News* said:

> I am very pleased about it for the boy's sake because the admission to the School has been justified. Some national newspapers have mis-represented the issue. They had given the impression that he was the only pupil at the School who has not passed the entrance examination. That was not so. There were over a dozen pupils there who had not been passed by the LEA. Some were transfers from other grammar schools outside the county or even the country. Others were admitted for health reasons and there were special cases such as twins. When one twin failed the examination and the other passed, it was always wise to admit both. Having scrutinised the boy's work at the other school attended I was satisfied the boy was up the Ardwyn standard. My assessment was confirmed at the end of the year when, although he had been here a short time, he came through better than 39 others who had been here all the time.
>
> There were special health reasons why the boy should attend a day school rather than a boarding school where he had been following a grammar school course. There is no machinery for the transfer of a pupil between the ages of 11 and 15 years from a boarding or private school to a local authority grammar school. It's an anomaly. That is why I took this decision. There were also other reasons which I cannot divulge why I could not follow the usual course of admittance.[102]

A *Cambrian News* editorial in the same edition was headed 'Why the 11 plus secrecy?'

> It would appear that the machinery is quite flexible for the transfer of such pupils to a grammar school. There is little doubt that many parents in the town who are quite rightly up in arms over the matter, would long ago have been storming the gates of Ardwyn had they known of such flexibility of entry.
>
> What has irritated them further is that the authority retreated into the conclaves of secrecy by referring the matter for the private consideration of the examination board which has plenary powers.

From 1956, reports in the Magazine of prize day speeches were very brief if mentioned at all. The accounts in the local press concentrated on what the Headmaster had to say with scant attention paid to the words of the guest speaker. In his annual report on each prize day in the Sixties, AD Lewis never failed to comment on the serious accommodation problems in the School with more than 700 pupils on the roll. Despite the completion of the new science wing in 1961, new buildings were still required; only five of the nineteen teaching rooms were up to Ministry of Education standards; seven of the twenty four forms had no form room and there was need for a library, assembly hall with stage, adequate playground and playing fields.

> A good staff as I have in Ardwyn, will create a good school in the most unpromising surroundings. But it is wrong to compel them to work for years in unsatisfactory conditions which can be improved by simple administrative procedure.

This theme was consolidated by Ald D Rees Morgan, chairman of Governors, who said that the School should be blown up and a new School built. 'We should have looked for a suitable site a very long time ago; we cannot keep adding on.' His comments, of course, became headlines in the local paper.

That AD Lewis was a reformer by nature came through in his speeches. He spoke of the serious problems facing the country in the scarcity of university places available:

> We are told the country needs more and more trained people and that means a vast development of higher education. We are much too ready in schools and other academic circles to dismiss young people and label them non-university types unless they are gifted academically. We are inclined to take the honours course as our criterion, clinging to the concept of education as a ladder for the talented rather than an enriching experience for all. Providing higher education only for the intellectual or social elite is inadequate for modern needs. We cannot afford the present wastage rate. I have been told that a London medical school rejects 20 out of 21 candidates.

The Headmaster wished to see more pupils spending three years in the sixth form; they would be more mature entering the university and better equipped to work independently. Universities often felt that first year students had been spoon fed. He regretted the abolition of State scholarships but welcomed the non-academic sixth form trend. There was no stigma attached to sixth formers who did not attend university or college.

John Morris MP, guest speaker in 1961, told the pupils that they were privileged to be educated in Wales. Far too many parents were too keen to send their children to schools in England.

E D Jones, Librarian of the National Library, welcomed the growth of the Welsh language as an educational force and believed that the language, literature, history and traditions of Wales were the priceless heritage of all Welsh children. 'I tell you this because I think it is more important than ever today to ensure the survival of Welsh as a living language.'

Maj Gen Lewis Owain Pugh, of Glandyfi, the guest speaker in 1963, was the only military man to address an Ardwyn prize day audience. As secretary of the Council for the Preservation of Rural Wales, he was naturally concerned with the conservation of the Welsh countryside, and appealed to his listeners to be on their guard against damage to its natural beauty. He thought that the greatest threat to the Welsh language was the influence of television, which was almost totally in the English language and had an accumulative effect in conditioning one's mind to the use of English.

The Headmaster, revealed that nearly half of the School were now in the fifth and sixth form. The sixth form had increased in numbers from 63 ten years ago to 140 at the present time. Five classes in the upper sixth had 20 or more pupils. No doubt as a riposte to taunts in committee, he reported that 49 out of the 70 in the previous year's sixth form, had entered university or college. 'How can committeemen say we allow people into the sixth form who should not be there?'

In another of his annual reports, A D Lewis drew attention to the difficulty of running the School on a very tight budget with the staff having to operate their departments on a shoe string.

The History of Aberystwyth County School (Ardwyn) 1896-1973

1957/58
Murals painted by Hywel Harries
Above: Composite of Aberystwyth
Below: Composite of Cardiganshire

Since the local authority do not have the resources to meet the heavy financial burden of an efficient, up to date, modern system of education, surely the time has come to reconsider the whole financial basis of administering schools, even if it means making a dent in the image of the sacred cow of local control.

The Headmaster was unable to be present at the 1965 Prize Day owing to the serious illness of his wife. The guest speaker was the chairman of the Mid Wales Development Association, J Llefelys Davies. As the former general manager of the Milk Marketing Board he spoke on business as a career. He was one of the few people from a Welsh school who, after an academic training, had gone into business. The tendency in Wales was for the best pupils to go into the professions which led to the belief that Welsh people were not prepared to take some of the risks of life but opted for the 'safe' careers. The speaker believed that there were going to be great opportunities for the best pupils in the world of commerce. Salaries in business could be very high and there was nothing wrong in being ambitious. Some of his listeners thought he over-emphasised the material rewards at the expense of pursuit of vocation or mission. In his present position he was trying to see where mid-Wales was going in the future. It had suffered from depopulation more than any part of the country. He would like to see more people in mid-Wales which would result in larger towns thus creating more scope for the young people to stay and enliven their lives in the area.

By 1966 the talk was no longer of the erection of a new building for Ardwyn but following the Department of Education circular 10/65, energies had to channelled into the establishment of a comprehensive school in the town. Elystan Morgan MP, the guest speaker that year, was unable to give an indication when the government would approve the re-organisation plans but said 'I cannot promise you results but I can promise to be your advocate at all times. The heritage of 70 years of education linked with Ardwyn will not be lost-it will enriched by the change.'
The Headmaster's report was mainly concerned with reorganisation of secondary education in the town stating that it was aimed at the abolition of the 11 plus examination and widening and improving the School so as to give all children equal opportunities.

> I commend the Ardwyn teachers- the ones with most at risk in terms of status, financial reward, and teaching satisfaction, for their forebearance and open mindedness. It would not have been surprising if, like their grammar school colleagues elsewhere, they had led an opposition to all plans for re-organising their School out of existence. The staff of Ardwyn had the courage to enter the arena in the conviction that it is within and not against the comprehensive school that the battle is to be fought.

He returned to the question of sixth form size. Public and direct grant school headmasters had drawn attention to the high proportion of their pupils who stayed for sixth form work quoting an average of 58 percent. For the State grammar school the figure was 38 percent.

> At Ardwyn the figure in the last few years had varied between 54 percent and 67 percent, a fact which is certainly not uncomplimentary to us. Yet at meetings of our local

education committee baseless statements have been made about our sixth form, making me wonder whether we at Ardwyn have committed some heinous offence by building up one of the biggest sixth forms in Wales. Furthermore these other schools are proud of the high proportion of pupils admitted to university and claim these figures too as a measure of their efficiency and value; here again our record is far above the national average. Indeed we have been blamed for accelerating the depopulation of the countryside by our very success in pursuing these courses.

In what was the last Ardwyn prize day, December 8 1967, the guest speaker was the Archdruid of Wales, the Revd D Gwyndaf Evans whose long journey from north Wales had been made tortuous by a heavy and unexpected overnight fall of snow. There is no record of his address but Donald Evans of the Welsh department and a former crowned bard at the National Eisteddfod had composed a poem of welcome which was sung to harp accompaniment by Mary Lynne Davies.

The Headmaster spoke of the reluctance of pupils, boys and girls to take up engineering and technology careers; the shortage of these specialists was the major reason why Britain failed to exploit ideas it was good at conceiving. A career in these disciplines offered attractive salaries, foreign travel, and work which was visibly a service to humanity. Perhaps the reason partly lay in the education system and partly social snobbery which made people turn their noses up at work-soiled hands and clothes. He also urged parents not to allow their children to drift into teaching because they couldn't think of anything else to do. A drifter would be a useless member of the profession and a menace to a school and the community. If a person had the ability to get into a college they could succeed in any number of occupations. 'Most doors will open if you push hard enough.'

He welcomed the Plowden Report with its emphasis on the importance of home-school relations. Ardwyn had long recognised the value of regular contact with parents which was embodied in the School's thriving PTA. Looking to the future, it was only natural to speculate on the pattern of education when the new comprehensive school came into being. The comprehensive school was in danger of becoming something everyone knew about, but very few understood. Its true aim was to provide something educationally richer and more varied than the present schools were able to do. Unless it did that the campaign for reorganisation throughout the country would have been criminally misconceived.

AD Lewis announced to the Governors in September 1968 that following consultation with the staff, it had been agreed that in future there would be no prize day. For some time school leavers had shown a reluctance to appear at the function to collect their prizes and examination certificates. Many years earlier the date of the event had been changed from February to December to coincide with the Christmas vacation of university and college students. The decision to abolish prize day was explained in the Magazine -'there is a feeling that perhaps much of what is done on such occasions is no longer relevant'. It was also reported that no head prefects or deputies had been nominated for that year.

AD Lewis was always generous in his praise for his staff and many of those he appointed remained at the School until its closure and then taught in the daughter schools. E W Williams served for 18 years as head of French ably supported by WJ Taylor who joined her department in 1960 direct from university and spent the whole of his teaching career in Aberystwyth. In 1957, Huw Spencer Lloyd, a former pupil, joined the science department and Ken Jones, a former UCW rugby captain was appointed to teach geography and history; both were involved in the coaching of the School rugby XVs for many years.

DC Chadwick, English and Rhiannon Roberts, Welsh, Gareth Emanuel, Classics, Wyn Richards, geography, and Moira Convery, physics, joined the staff in the late Fifties-early Sixties and all spent the rest of their teaching careers in the town. After over ten years as senior mistress Gwen Herbert, whose sight was failing, decided to retire and a popular choice as her replacement was Violet Jones, domestic science teacher.

W G Rowlands retired in 1964 after 34 years as English master, the last five as deputy head. His friend, colleague and neighbour Roy James wrote an appreciation in the *Ardwynian* that year

> William George Rowlands was born in Gilfach Goch just before the end of the 19th century. He was deeply influenced by his family life in the little mining valley about which 'How Green was my Valley' was to be written. From the sixth form in Bridgend County School he passed straight to service in France with the Royal Welch Fusiliers in 1917. He was wounded, badly gassed and temporarily blinded, yet he was only 20 when his birthday came on Armistice Day 1918. After graduating from UCW he spent six years at Alexandra Road school before joining Ardwyn. He married into a well-known Aberystwyth family and though he had no children of his own he was to become a 'South Wales uncle' to dozens of children partly through his great interest in Aberystwyth's children's choir. He has an encyclopaedic knowledge of local families, which has, among other things, been of the greatest help to his younger colleagues in getting to know Ardwyn pupils. George Rowlands was deeply saddened by the outbreak of war in 1939 and the inevitable casualty list of former Ardwynians. He organised the sending of letters, gifts and copies of the School Magazine to servicemen and women all over the world and threw himself into his job as local company commander of the Home Guard. For a man of none- too- robust health, he amazed his friends by what he could get done in 24 hours each day. As a councillor, alderman and mayor, he was highly successful, speaking with direct commonsense and simplicity on all matters. He was particularly fitted to the position of deputy headmaster, bringing efficiency and humanity to a job with special problems. Much of the smooth-running of the School resulted from the quiet work he had carried out in his book-store office known naturally to him as his 'cwtch'.

The School and the whole town were shocked and saddened in September 1969 by the news that WG Rowlands together with his brother-in-law Tom Griffiths had been killed in a car accident near Nancy when they were returning from a stay with friends in Freiburg, in Germany.

Richard J Lloyd succeeded to the post of deputy head combining those duties with the headship of the chemistry department for many years. He was an exceptional teacher of his subject and had the knack of getting the best out of his pupils. One remembers, on entering the fifth form-the School Certificate year, how he cast his eyes around the class and audibly counted the number of pupils he expected to gain distinctions. He was rarely disappointed, somehow you knew what was expected of you. Later, as the Higher/Advanced level practical examinations dawned, he and his fellow science teachers, would spend many out- of- school hours including week-ends preparing glassware and other apparatus in order to provide the best possible conditions for success.

After seventeen years in the School Gwyneth Winkler retired from teaching German. She had successfully re-established the subject after the war

> Mrs Winkler taught me Latin for two years and then was successfully persuaded to start German classes. I was the only one of the first small group to survive and take my O-level German, though the subject thereafter became part of the main curriculum. Known for her short temper and the missiles, notably textbooks, which were hurled at slackers in the back rows, Gwyneth Winkler was in fact warm and generous, freely giving of her time and resources to those who demanded them. I kept in touch with her long after her retirement; in fact she was, according to her son Eddie, chuckling over a letter just received from me on the day she died after a long and stressful illness.[103]

K F Loates succeeded as the head of German in 1965 and quickly set about establishing a link with a German school.

> I had been a German teacher for 10 years and always had the wish to make possible, closer contacts between German and British pupils. Having grown up in the war years I knew all too well how frustrating and almost pointless it was to learn a foreign language without getting to know the foreign country and its people.[104]

Following an application to the Central Bureau for Educational Visits and Exchanges for a twinning with a German school, in December 1966 came a letter from a Herr Fritz Pratschke accepting a 'partnership'. The writer was an English and geography teacher at the Altkonigschule in Kronberg which he described as a beautiful small town near FrankfurtMain, situated at the foot of the Taunus mountains in the centre of West Germany. A party of thirty Ardwyn pupils led by Ken Loates visited Kronburg during the Easter vacation 1966 on the first exchange visit. To welcome the visitors, the Union Jack and the flag of West Germany flew side by side on the Kronburg Rathaus (town hall)for the first time. Reporting on the success of the visit, Ken Loates hoped that the exchanges would continue at regular intervals and looked forward to the visit of the Kronberg pupils in the summer. Whatever his hopes and aspirations were, it is unlikely that he envisaged the partnership achieving its silver anniversary which it did in 1994. The twinning survived reorganisation, Penglais, one of Ardwyn's daughter schools happily maintained the link. It has gone from strength to strength, and is likely to be the longest lasting exchange in the country. Some families have participated up to four times. To celebrate the 25 years of exchange Fritz Pratschke, who had led all twenty-five visits to Aberystwyth, produced an anniversary booklet in which he explained why the exchange was so desirable to him.

> Experiencing the end of World War II and the life of a refugee, made me seek contacts with a British school as soon as I started teaching English at my first post-A K S. I was, and still am, deeply convinced that communication through the learning of foreign languages, experiencing cultural differences and friendships are the best guarantee for peace and understanding among the peoples of Europe.
>
> When I consider that with nearly 800 participants so far, there is no valley or village around Aberystwyth where there has not been a pupil from A K S; Aberystwyth is nowhere outside the U K better known than in Kronberg. This is reason enough to be a little proud and to hope that efforts on either side of the Channel to continue the exchange programme will succeed in the years to come.[105]

In addition to the language exchange, reciprocal visits have been made by orchestras and choirs of the schools as well as adult choirs from the two areas. On several occasions the mayors of the two towns have made exchange visits and former exchangees, in order to advance their proficiency in the German or English, have had temporary employment arranged in the respective towns. Many enduring friendships have been forged over the years; Jane Rumsey Williams later Thomas took part in the first exchange and has maintained her strong connection with Helga Kraft her exchange partner. In 1994, Jane's son Garrod, and godson to Fritz Pratschke was the first of the second generation to visit Kronburg.

A report by the accompanying teachers of the November 1989 visit to Kronburg vividly encapsulates the epoch making events of that time.

> When the dates for the visit were arranged last year, no-one could have foreseen the momentous events which were to unfold during the fortnight's stay.
>
> In another year the shining memories would be of generous German hospitality, family life and food in a foreign culture, taking part in school lessons in a foreign language and the comradeship of shared experiences inherent in any extended stay away from home. Added to that would have been the unforgettable sight of the fortified barrier which divides the two Germanies; that combination of wire mesh, vehicle traps, audible and visual alarms, patrolling dogs and observation towers which since 1953 have kept the population of the German Democratic Republic from visiting family and friends in the West.
>
> When the group visited the border near Hunfield on 6 November, the pupils were already excitedly exchanging pieces of news about amazing happenings in the G D R -the million-strong demonstration in Berlin and 10, 000 refugees crossing into West Germany each day. Then at a camp playing host to 250 East German migrants, mostly families with young children, who had arrived the day before, the pupils were brought face to face with the human realities behind the television pictures. After that visit the news followed thick and fast. Tuesday the government resigned, followed by the Politburo, on the Thursday night the border opened- all seen by the pupils through the eyes of the families with whom they were staying. The television pictures must have been impressive in any country, but for the pupils to witness and take part in the tide of emotion which engulfed a nation last week was for them a rich and deeply moving experience.[106]

The silver anniversary of the exchange was celebrated by a joint orchestral and choral concert in September 1994 in the Great Hall, Penglais, followed by reciprocal festivities in Kronburg.

Pamela Munday formerly head of German at Penglais School in explaining the endurance of the exchange, pointed to the devotion and single-mindedness of Fritz Pratschke. Headmasters, and staff had always given strong support; parents not only provided hospitality but encouraged their offspring to take advantage of a rewarding project.

> The most important factor however has always been the upholding of a vision-that participation in an exchange should be an all-round learning experience-much more than an opportunity to practice a foreign language, much more than a holiday or school outing, much more than a concert. Pupils who participate return home changed-they mature, they grow up, they widen their understanding of another culture and of each other.

Following on the success of the early Fifties, the Ardwyn netball players reached even greater heights in the remainder of the decade and beyond. Indeed it is true to say that the Sixties were the golden era for Ardwyn netball; it is one thing to defeat school teams in Cardiganshire but the real test was beyond the county boundary.

Elizabeth Lee captained an increasingly confident and capable first VII for three years from 1954; in 1957 in fifteen games played by the first and second teams, the only defeat came from Merioneth champions, Barmouth. During this period there were a succession of P E teachers but in 1960 Christine Griffiths was appointed and the following six-year period proved to be the most successful period in the history of girls' team games as well as in athletics.

> For netballers in particular, lunchtimes were never to be the same again. After-school practice and games became more and more frequent with each and every lunch time devoted to practice, much to the dismay of some players. Christine's stance was 'No practice, no game' and since we all wanted to play (and win) we endured the seemingly neverending lunchtime practices stoically. Our digestive systems probably suffered untold damage! However the hard work was rewarded with much success.[107]

Christine Griffiths initiated county tournaments in both winter games; from the first netball competition in 1961, the senior team won the title for twelve successive years and the juniors for eight years. By the end of the 1967-68 season, all teams, there were frequently five teams fielded, had remained unbeaten for six years.

By virtue of winning the county tournament, the Ardwyn VIIs automatically represented mid-Wales. This gave the players the opportunity to gauge their standard against stronger counties. One of the first sorties into this territory came with the tournaments at Conwy and Colwyn Bay in the north and Cwmbran in the south. The standard in the former was much the same as that in Ardwyn but netball in south Wales was on a different level and a great deal of experience was gained from those early games. There was great satisfaction when eventually, mid-Wales (an all-Ardwyn VII) soundly defeated south Wales at Llanelli in 1965 and north Wales in 1966 to achieve an enviable double. The Magazine correspondents were generous in their thanks to their mentor

The A. D. Lewis Years — 1954-1971

> Our successes must be attributed to the care and encouragement given us by Mrs C Griffiths. It is her lead and training that has made the game of netball reach such a high standard in Ardwyn. She has given up much of her spare time to train us and improve our play in every way.

After six years, Christine Griffiths left the School in July 1966, to start a family. She would have been well satisfied with the high standards her coaching had achieved. Her policy was to develop the game throughout the School. She took a great interest in all the achievements of her players and especially those who brought honours to the School such as the late Caren Fleming who was the first Ardwyn girl to attend a CCPR course during the summer of 1962. After captaining the senior team for two years, Verona Davies, along with another fine athlete, Lindy Martin reached the last ten places in trials for the Welsh schoolgirls netball team. Lindy narrowly missed selection but Verona went on to play for Wales in 1969 confirming that Ardwyn netball had reached the zenith. Another factor in the success was the team spirit which the girls had developed. By the time senior level was reached most of the team had been involved in competitive netball for six years with an understanding of each others play developed to a high degree. It is probably significant that Anna Pugh, Catrin Beynon Davies, Wendy Bray, Verona Davies and Sian Beynon Davies each served as team captain for two successive seasons.

Christine Griffiths would also have been pleased when some seventeen years ago a group of Ardwyn old girls formed the Aberystwyth Netball Club which has played league and friendly matches throughout Wales. Leading the formation of the Club were such notable players as Zena Evans(Shattock), Marilyn James(Richards), Gwen Thomas(Hawkins), Margaret Haynes(Daniel) to be joined later by Beryl Varley(Jones), Sian Jones (Beynon Davies), Susan Jones(Clark), Gaynor Hamer, Sandra Jones(Morgan) and Ann Morgan (Richards)

The 1956-57 captain of hockey Beti Rowlands who was also head girl that year, writing in the Magazine, said that for many years the standard of play in hockey had been undistinguished but there were signs of improvement. In the following three years just three matches were won; however in September 1959, a P E mistress who was a Welsh ladies' hockey international, was appointed. Although her stay was just one year, the coaching of Rose Watkins brought a great improvement, the only game lost to a school was against Llandysul. She was succeeded by Christine Griffiths and for the next six years the seniors were unbeaten by a school team, although there were defeats by the mixed adult teams of Trawscoed and Ardwyn staff whose 'greater bustling tactics' proved too great on occasions. Needless to say the county tournaments went to Ardwyn until three no-score drawn games in 1966-67 allowed Aberaeron to spoil the sequence. It was not until the following season that the first goal, in eight annual county tournaments, was conceded by the seniors. In 1962-63 the School and county captain was Margaret Edwards and although the 'big freeze' caused many games to be cancelled, her teams had a successful season; great pleasure was derived from the defeat of Aber Ladies. Following success in the south Wales hockey tournament, in a county team with six Ardwynians, Margaret Edwards and Anna Pugh were selected as reserves for the south Wales team. Greater honours were to come in later years for Margaret Edwards

1st Rugby XV, 1961–62. Captain: Richard Jenkins

Cricket XI, 1962. Captain: Anthony Evans

Boys' Athletics Team, 1962.

with selection for the Welsh ladies' hockey team. By 1962, there was great strength in depth with five teams being fielded when the opposition could be found. As with netball, the time and energy devoted to improvement of technique and fitness by the PE mistress was acknowledged; 'to her must go much of the credit for the success of the teams '. The greatest distinction came to the School captain, Zena Shattock when she was selected for the Welsh schoolgirls hockey XI in February 1963, the first Cardiganshire girl to be so honoured. When Margaret Edwards was appointed as PE mistress in 1967 she had already been 'capped' for Wales. In the following years she travelled widely as an international player making twenty-three appearances for her country. However it would seem that for the School hockey players the golden days were over; in the remaining years more games were lost than were won.

Following the successful years of the mid-Fifties with the advantage of playing rugby for two terms, there followed a lean period. No player with the experience of Iwan Jones, who had dominated the play of the first XV for many seasons, emerged. Having retired from the active coaching of the team, Roy James took on the role of critic and Magazine correspondent, to show that his writing flair and lucidity was not confined to cricket.

He was hard on those boys who found tackling a difficult art. To some players it comes easily and there are those who derive as much pleasure from saving a try by a great tackle as scoring a try. Aled Bebb was one such boy, no giant but one who was born to be a scrum-half. One ageing rugby master prone to coach by example, after being hit by a perfect knee high tackle from this eleven year-old wisely decided that runnning with the ball when Bebb was around could damage one's health and it was time to stop showing off. Roy James thought that in rugby there was room for all types of boys, whose varying physical gifts could be adapted by an experienced coach. One of his great joys was to see lads who had previously made little progress in the game, obviously thoroughly enjoying themselves in the timetabled games lessons, particularly in vigorously tackling their best friends.

The 58-59 side of Jimmy Thomas was strengthened by the arrival from Haileybury School of Paul Edwards, a first class centre three- quarter who added great scoring power to an already thrustful back division which included JR Thomas, Alan Christian, Alun John, and Elwyn Elias. The size limitations of the School field were overcome by the use of the college and the town rugby pitches which gave ample opportunity for skilful back play, which in the opinion of the critic was the best he had seen in the previous eleven years. He also commented that it was not the function of a school, as is all too often assumed in some quarters, to provide players for adult clubs, but merely to teach boys to play well and sportingly at all times and to observe honourable practices such as meeting the obligation of fixtures and to behave well on and off the field. It was all the more pleasant to record new friendships made with such schools as Whitgift (Croydon) and Ogmore Vale, which were new to the Ardwyn fixture list.

Tony Ford, now professor of chemistry at the University of Natal, Durban remembered an after-the-match escapade.

> In my last year at Ardwyn, we had played at Dolgellau and after the game and lunch,

just before boarding the bus to return home, someone spotted a large stuffed alligator on a corridor shelf with a smaller one behind it. It seemed like a good idea at the time to take the smaller one as a souvenir, since it was not likely to be missed. It was smuggled aboard the bus and put in the safe keeping of Sandy Davies. It was quite near the end of term and we were entertaining Whitgift School who were on tour. The alligator was taken to the match as a mascot and later brought to the evening dance in the School hall. I happened to be carrying the beast when it caught the eye of Dewi Lewis the Head who wanted to know where it had come from. My friends suddenly remembered that they had things to do so I was left to provide an explanation. I think I said something like my cousin was a merchant seaman and had brought it back from Port Said and had donated it to the rugby team as a mascot. Dewi seemed to like that story. We thought we'd got away with it until, some time after I had left School, Dolgellau discovered the loss and for some reason connected its departure with Ardwyn. After Dewi Lewis had received a request for its return from the Dolgellau headmaster, he was reported to have said 'So it didn't come from Port Said after all then.' The rugby team had the task of finding a replacement since the original could not be found and eventually one was procured from the Half Moon shop and presented to the north Wales school.[108]

The successes of that season with just two games lost by the first XV in eighteen matches encouraged the coaches to take on strong south Wales sides like Llandeilo, Amman Valley and Gwendraeth the following year. The side captained by John Hefin Evans played above themselves and several first class games were played on the town ground. That the team lost to the south Wales sides was due to lack of confidence rather than anything else. The best game of the season was that against Gwendraeth led by the Welsh secondary schools' captain Ken Jones later a British Lion. The score of 9-nil to Gwendraeth was, if anything, flattering to the south Wales side. However a notable victory was registered against Pembroke Dock for the first time in many years.

The fielding of a first and second XV, together with an under 15 and a bantams XVs (years one and two) ensured continuity and match experience. The Sixties saw a great improvement in the standard of rugby football played; there were several claims in annual reviews recorded in the Magazine, that the season had been the best ever. Such a claim was made in 1961-62 when three games only were lost, one of which was against adult opposition in the shape of the Town second XV. Leon Gibson, now the chief executive of Ynys Mon district council, was the writer.

> The past season has been one of the most successful in the history of the School. The team, when playing together exceeded the wildest expectations of the masters in charge of rugby. A light but very mobile and intelligent pack of forwards provided a very fast set of backs with countless opportunities to run the ball, thus producing the very entertaining and highly successful play typical of Welsh schoolboys.
>
> The steady improvement of the standard of play is well illustrated by the deserved victory over the famous Gwendraeth Valley grammar school. One would have expected the School to lose to this renowned south Wales side, whose rugby is of a higher quality than that to be found in Cardiganshire. The School players rose magnificently to the occasion to record its first ever win against such reputable opposition. This

notable victory was achieved by consistent team-work, in which backs and forwards combined effectively to outplay the opposition at their own game. It is to be noted, as throughout the season, that Ardwyn's success was due to excellent team spirit rather than the brilliance of individual members.

Then came the big freeze of 1962-63 when no rugby was played from 15 December to 2 March. As well as a victory over Pembroke, the season will be remembered for a cruel stroke of luck to Glyndwr Hubbard. While playing so well in the final trial to choose the fifteen to represent the Welsh secondary schools, he sustained a broken leg. Gone was the best chance the School ever had of a Welsh cap at the under 18 age group. Another 'best ever' claim in 63-64 with just four defeats but victory in a county senior seven-a-side tournament.

Peter Duggan took over boys' physical education in September 1964. An inexperienced first fifteen improved as the season progressed; a handsome win against a strong Tenby side and a draw with Gwendraeth added up to a satisfactory season. But it was reported that the highlight of the year was a short tour undertaken during the Easter vacation to play two London schools both of whom were defeated. Peter Duggan was thanked for arranging the first ever tour by an Ardwyn team as he was for his efficient coaching, enthusiasm and inspiration during the season.

> I can recall the absolute joy of a sports mad kid, blessed with a little talent, being given an opportunity to express that ability in new fields. I rememeber my first rugby lesson taken by Hywel Mathews, when I had some exhilarating runs with the ball, no doubt in hopelessly undisciplined fashion, and basking in the attention I received. In the early games for the bantams against Abermad, I couldn't have weighed more than five stone and no doubt pretty ineffective because I was such a lightweight. I remember when we won the west Wales sevens tournament and a tour to London when Peter Duggan saved my life by removing a mountain of blankets my solicitous team mates had piled on top of me after I had developed a high temperature-a consequence of tackling some six foot monster all afternoon.
>
> Although some of us got to the early trial matches, south Wales schoolboy rugby seemed impossibly powerful by comparison. I got to a west Wales stage and I can recall two scrum halves playing, one was Gareth Edwards and the other Selwyn Williams who later also played first class rugby. I was prevailed upon by my co-centre to play outside centre and as a results I never saw the ball all afternoon, he just ran straight every time with no intention of ever giving me a pass.
>
> There were many rugby enthusiasts among the Ardwyn staff who created an atmosphere in which one strove to do well and I always felt appreciated. My father told me after one game that he'd heard Roy James joke to some fellow- spectators 'we'll be alright this year if Davis doesn't go north'.[109]

Richard S Lloyd led a fine 1965-66 side who amassed a record 72 tries, averaging four per game. Games master Peter Duggan was able to persuade the legendary Carwyn James to speak at the inaugural rugby dinner that year. Another rugby celebrity, Cliff Morgan, came the following season, which in terms of performance had not been up to standard; the four teams had won just 15 out of 38 matches played. 1967-68 was also a lean year with the ignominy of defeat by all the other Cardiganshire schools. However on route to Dublin to watch the international against Ireland the first XV managed to defeat Holyhead. At under 15 level, Brian Williams narrowly missed selection for the Welsh schools' team.

Normality was resumed the following season under the captaincy of David Keyse when a record 300 points were accumulated. There was great disappointment for Ian Jones, prevented by bad weather from attending the final WSSRU trial; Ian was the reigning School sprint champion who used his great pace to good effect on the rugby field.

Perhaps it was the newly acquired scrummaging machine, but 1969-70 could rightly be claimed to be the best in Ardwyn's rugby history. Garrod Roberts' side scored 98 tries and in amassing 388 points, beat the redoubtable Tenby, Gwendraeth and Cowbridge. The only defeat came playing at Tregaron where victory was always rare. The under 15s team won all their matches and were delighted with the progress of Geraint P Jones who reached the final Welsh trial but failed to gain that elusive first Welsh rugby cap for Ardwyn.

Each Magazine review of an Ardwyn team sport invariably referred to the contribution made by the School groundsman. John Lewis had, since 1939, been responsible for the maintenance of the playing field and tennis courts. a task he had carried out single-handedly and with great skill. Many pupils will remember the after-the-match teas which he and his wife prepared in the tiny kitchen of the School pavilion during the Forties.

He retired after 39 years of dedicated service in December 1968, replaced by John Richards, an amiable countryman who proved to be dedicated and popular not just for the seemingly endless supplies of fruit he would bring from his own garden for distribution to the children.

There were great hopes in 1971 when the rugby captain Brian Williams advanced through the various WSSRU trial matches that at last the School would gain a representative in the national team. Although he was a member of the Welsh squad, he failed to gain selection. The same fate befell Clive Evans in the under 15 age group. The highlight of a season which was not the best, was a visit to Christ College, Brecon where, in closely contested games, first and second XVs were narrowly beaten.

Ardwyn cricket continued to prosper during the Fifties under the management of Roy James, whose devotion to the summer game bordered on the fanatical. The Magazine continued to be a means of promulagating his views on the game and reliving the delights of the previous summer. After more than twenty years of use, the School field was suffering from subsidence, a consequence of its previous life as the town's refuse dump. Such was the variable quality of the cricket square that use was made of the splendid College facilities in the summer of 1956. 'The boys were always welcome visitors on this ground particularly when supported by the excellent teas made by the senior girls.' During the autumn, the School cricket square was ploughed and re-seeded and was ready for limited use the following summer. The net facilities had previously been upgraded which had 'brought a remarkable improvement in the standards of a new generation of players.' Ieuan Williams was the most successful bowler and 'was in no way flattered by his figures, for his effortless run-up and high easy action together with accurate length, were more impressive on good wickets against excellent batsmen than on poor, wearing ones.'

> One looks forward to the new season with great hope, in what is perhaps the most civilising of all games. Cricket has a wonderful charm and social discipline of its own, and many a summer evening on the School field, the writer has felt like the Sussex farmer of 1739, whose wife wrote to his son: 'Last Monday, your father played at cricket, and came home pleased enough, for he struck the best ball in the game, and wished he had not anything else to do but play cricket all his life'.[110]

The new square had played well and credit was given to the diligent work of groundsman John Lewis who had prepared a true and easy paced wicket. The best innings the coach had seen in ten years was credited to David Edwards who hit 47 runs in a long awaited defeat of the College Staff XI. Batsmen were reminded of the essentials a) play good balls defensively and b) score off every bad ball mercilessly-the average bowler would soon be demoralised. Roy James also wrote that the whole basis of cricket rested on the willing cooperation of hard-working coaches and the patient practice of youngsters prepared to put in time and work to achieve skills over a long period. 'No other game asks so much but also gives so much.'

Despite a wetter than usual summer in 1958, the team which had been carefully built up over the years was as good as the coach had seen in ten seasons. There was always the feeling that Ieuan Williams, a great schoolboy left-arm medium-fast bowler and his supporting bowlers would be much too good for schoolboy and average adult opposition. This comfortable background saw the batsmen get on with the job in the best of spirits. Derek Dawson and Jimmy Thomas were a splendid opening pair and their excellent calling and running between wickets usually demoralised other school bowlers. Strength in depth allowed a team, with its stars taking part in a postponed athletics meeeting, to tie with a powerful Senior Commoners XI. In the newly instituted league seven-a-side tournament, the School seven humbled Ceredigion the town side, in the quarter- final but bad nerves saw four runs-out in the semi-final which the School should have won, but even so the league leaders, Llwyn-y-gog, were taken to the last over by skilful bowling. In a bout of justifiable self-congratulation Roy James was prompted to write 'there are not many grammar schools in Wales where cricket has been taught and learned as conscientiously as at Ardwyn.'

He had praise for the dedication of the players, many of whom made the long walk to the School field at lunch time to practice. As a result, several boys of only average ability turned themselves into fieldsmen of exceptional merit and at the same time improved their batting out of all recognition.

A glance at the fixture list showed that the only schools sides played were Tregaron and Aberaeron; the reason given was that most schools had neglected their cricket squares. As a do-it-yourself effort, masterminded by the the craft teacher Idwal Davies, an artificial wicket was laid in the square and was ready for use in the 1960 season. The coach, in defending its acquisition, declared that for far too long, in local cricket, bowlers of average ability had received far too much assistance from worn grass wickets, while young batsmen had been unable to apply the technique they had learned on a true surface in the nets. Despite one of the wettest summers in living memory, 1960 was one of the most successful seasons, the Banks XI being the only team to inflict a defeat and that in the sevens tournament. Arnold Thawley, a boy who was never seen without a cricket ball in his hands, on or off the field, topped both the bowling and batting averages. Alun John, Tony Ford and Elwyn Elias were batsmen singled out for praise. The latter had also caught the eye of Phil Clift the Glamorgan C C coach, who 'had said nice things generally about the the School cricket standards.'

Despite the success of Ardwyn cricket the reports gave a veiled concern about its future. In 1961 Roy James produced his last annual report before handing on the responsibility. He wrote of the good standard of cricket played by a relatively small group of players and was concerned at the very low standard of the majority of boys; the 'long tail' in House matches supplied evidence of this.

> Some of the juniors showed promise so there was hope for the future so long as Trevor Bailey's views were respected-'There is no such thing as a born cricketer, but boys of average talent and a fair measure of ball-sense and timing can make themselves into very good cricketers by hard work, intelligence and regular practice; natural ability on its own, will never get anyone anywhere in the hard exacting discipline of cricket.'

Bryan D Jones had first appeared in the School nets in 1956 as a second former, obtained his colours the following year and in all stood as wicket keeper for five seasons; the last in 1961 when he led the side. His contribution was acknowledged in the review of that season.

> Bryan Jones was a good captain but was also the best schoolboy wicket-keeper that the writer has seen, but he would be the first to admit that he enjoyed splendid support from his fielders with their fine catching, good ground work and splendid full-pitch throwing -in. It is attention to these valuable' bits and pieces' that transforms an average cricket side into a very good one - and a good looking one as well.

The Magazine report of the 1961 cricket season stated

> 'no other summer activity can give so many years of enjoyment after leaving school, if the game is learned properly during years 11 to 18.' How very true. Since hanging up my bat after 40 years of playing, I have a lot for which to thank the reporter. His name? Roy James.
>
> We will all have memories of Roy, that ill-tempered blackboard-duster thrower, whose willingness to give up his spare time to help small boys share the game he loved went far beyond what could be expected.
>
> Net practice, down by the gas works, surrounded by stinging nettles and enveloped by the smell of gas. Roy gave up his time from after school until... well who knows? Mondays, Wednesdays and Fridays. Matches Tuesday evening, Thursday evening and Saturday. Homework... what was that? Memories of Roy shouting (did he ever speak quietly?) 'open your legs' to some flat-footed batsman in the nets. Memories of being bamboozled by his spin bowling as he hobbled on his built up shoe. Memories of how he taught me to keep wicket. 'First lesson, crouch down so your nose touches the bails; that's where you stand for medium and slow bowling. 'I was terrified but never forgot that and always did it for the next 40 years.'
>
> I only got the better of him twice, both when I was captain. First was when he

expected to play against a college team of advanced physical training students. 'Very strong team, you'll need my experience'. 'Sorry Mr James, I need athletic fielders for this one, but you can umpire.' He used to go very red when angry. We won by lots so he grudgingly spoke to me afterwards. The second occasion was in a Teachers/Parents v First XI where he stood batting between us and victory. I got the bowlers to bowl at his gammy leg. Inevitably we got him out. I'll always remember the exchange as we left the field.

> Roy: You..... you wouldn't give anything away, would you?
> Me : Mr James, I've had a good teacher haven't I
> A pleasurable grin spread across his round, red face as he limped away.[111]

As can be gleaned from the above recollection, the coach Roy James frequently turned out for the School XI when the opposition was an adult team. However as well as relinquishing the pen he also gave up his playing involvement in 1962 but still coached the side. He must also have used his powers of persuasion to extract more funds from the Governors to provide a much needed practice net near to the School. Again Idwal Davies, who never believed his duties were confined to the workshop, and the caretaker John Williams, were responsible for its construction. The new correspondent and club secretary Geraint H Jenkins already showed a perspicuity which later helped him scale the academic heights. He was concerned at the dearth of cricketers at Ardwyn and was amazed at the team's continued success. In addition to the captain Anthony Evans, the batting responsibilites were shouldered by Gwylon Phillips, Vivian Reeves, Geraint Jenkins with John James a future star. A new School record was claimed for an opening stand of 76 by G Phillips and A Evans against Padarn hostel. Obviously the record books were not consulted since, as previously cited, in 1939, 120 runs were put on for the first wicket by Jim Pinsent and Bob Williams. The summers of 1962, 63 and 64 continued to be bounteous with more or less the same team fielded, captained in turn by Evans, Phillips and Jenkins. The latter wrote that he had previously subscribed to the view that' fast bowlers and wicket-keepers were, if not exactly mad then pretty odd', donned the pads and gauntlets for the first time in his career and apart from a few minor mishaps, enjoyed himself immensely. Geraint Jenkins appealed to boys of the middle school to attend net practices and show some interest especially now that facilities were provided within the School premises. 'It is disheartening to see only first team members practising regularly while many boys with the ability to become good cricketers either show an appalling diffidence or prefer to indulge in tennis-a game far better suited to the opposite sex'. The team was well served in these years by the medium pace bowling of Geraint Evans who topped the averages for two years. Anthony Evans headed the batting averages in 63 and 64 and more than thirty years later was still making lots of runs.

In the remaining years of the decade, the play was inconsistent and in some years only a handful of matches were played. There were however several high spots. In a rare school match, Tregaron were beaten in an close, exciting match. This was in 1967 when, unusually three players, including two brothers, scored half-centuries even though only six matches were played. Garrod Roberts scored 66 not out against the NLW. Rupert Madgewick and captain Geraint Roberts achieved half-centuries against WPBS and shared in a third wicket partnership of 110, claimed to be a record stand for

Ardwyn. These runs were scored from a total of 163 for 3 wickets in only 24 overs! The last occasion brothers played together in the cricket XI was in 1939 when the Pinsent brothers graced the field. With Geraint Roberts leading the side for the second year, all four matches were won including one of the best results for some years in the defeat of the Senior Commoners with Garrod hitting an undefeated half-century, 'a victory brought about by the three main essentials of overs matches-a sound opening partnership and tight bowling supported by good catching.'

The use of the College swimming baths continued to be popular and the House swimming galas were always keenly contested affairs. In the eleven years up to 1960, Arfon boys claimed the swimming cup for each of those years and in the twenty years from 1952 the Arfon girls' team won the trophy on sixteen occasions. The baths supervisor and swimming instructor Jim Blaze retired in 1961 after serving since the baths were opened in 1939. His instruction in life saving, which had brought so many awards to the Ardwyn pupils over the years, was carried on by Ron Arthur who had been appointed to the staff of the College physical education department with special responsibility for swimming. He soon established an Ardwyn life-saving club and for ten years gave unselfishly of his time to train pupils in the art of life saving at the evening meetings. Hardly a year passed without the Magazine recording a long list of life saving awards gained. 1966 was a fairly typical year, thirty-seven boys gained the preliminary life saving award, seven the advanced award and three the RLSS bronze medallion. The girls obtained five intermediate certificates, sixteen the bronze medallion and one a bronze cross.

A glance at the records show that the better competitors were those who, being children of College staff, were able to use the College baths regularly. In 1964, the PE mistress said that lack of this facility should not be a handicap, with the sea at their doorstep and cited Jane Fleming Jones the strongest swimmer in the gala that year, as an example of the standard that could be attained without regular use of the baths. The swimming arrangements changed in 1966 when it was decided to give instruction to first and second years only, the aim being to teach every pupil to swim before entering the third year and with a thorough knowledge of all strokes and to make a start on life saving techniques. The gaining of the advanced life saving test was the qualification to join the life saving club. In 1968 the Corporation, for the first time, provided lifeguards for its beaches and senior boys in the club were employed in this role doubling as deck chair attendants.

> Some of the fondest memories of my schooldays stem from my involvement in the founding and running of the lifeguards. Several other Ardwynians were founder members including Richard Arthur, Peter and Paul Norrington Davies, Elwyn Isaac, Alan Rees and Roger James and we were led by a former Ardwynian Paul Kidson. The life guards provided a forum for social interaction coupled with competitive lifesaving whilst serving a community need. I believe that they are still going strong twenty-five years later.
>
> The Ardwyn life saving club also gave me a chance to learn to play water-polo with the College students and later I captained the Welsh universities at the sport and at swimmming.[112]

The A. D. Lewis Years — 1954-1971

Cast of School Play "She Passed Through Lorraine", King's Hall, July 1961. Produced by Richard Jenkins.

Winners of the 'Cerdd Dant' and 'Canu Deusain' at the Urdd National Eisteddfod, Rhuthin, 1962.

One of the lifeguards, Alan Rees also played water polo and remembered two well built young men joining the College team. They turned out to be Special Branch officers who were at the College in advance of Prince Charles who spent the summer term 1969 at the UCW prior to his investiture as Prince of Wales.

Stuart Sherman was another accomplished swimmer who never failed to win his events in the swimming gala for six years from 1967. Inevitably he became a life saver and took an active part in surf lifesaving on a competitive level. Stuart represented Wales on ten occasions, five as captain and made two visits to Australia. As a board paddler he competed in world championships in Bali and Hawaii and was ranked fifteenth in the world at that contest and dominated board racing and the iron man events in Britain between 1970 and 1986.

In the middle Sixties, two long established House competitions came to an end. There is no record of the boys' gymnastic event being held after 1960, the girls competition survived a few years more. Despite the keenness of AD Lewis, who invariably officiated, the boxing tournament was not held after 1963. Two years earlier the first recorded knock-out had occurred but criticism of poor preparation was regularly voiced.

> One minute can be a very long time indeed for those who have done little or no training. Many of the contestants found this fact only too true as they gasped for breath with their hands hanging limply by their sides. The fatigue resulted in far too much wild and aimless swinging and slapping with the open glove.[113]

It was probably the Headmaster who gave the final knock-out blow so to speak. On the last occasion the event was held, in his summing up, he commented that boxing skills were being abandoned for the sake of a fight. Probably to the relief of many, that was the end of the sport at Ardwyn.

If some activities were coming to an end, others, some of them transient, took their place

Basketball was introduced in the late Sixties through the enthusiasm of several boys including three Chinese pupils Edmund and Arthur So and Charles Yu and with the encouragement of Peter Duggan. A team was entered in the College league and not surprisingly, suffered a series of defeats at the hands of teams which contained several of the College first team. An inter-House competition saw Arfon running out winners in what was regarded as an exceptionally good game. With interest growing, the School was able to field four teams in a College tournament. With the loss of Richard Arthur and Alan Rees it was a case of rebuilding in 1969-70 but lack of height and experience was a handicap. However in the House matches, Ceredigion proved unbeatable at senior and under 15 level. The awarding of colours at the end of the 1970-71 season was recognition of the high standard that had been achieved in a short time. Following reorganisation school basketball continued to flourish.

On July 12 1960, twenty boys took part in the first cycle race. The twenty-five mile circuit included Ponterwyd, Devil's Bridge, Penparcau, Pen-y-bont bridge The course started and finished at the School entrance in Llanbadarn road and was known to the cycling fraternity as 'around the twenty-five.' The age range and variety of cycles involved necessitated a handicapping system devised by one of the enthusiasts, John Swaffield. The winner was Roger Garraway of Gwynedd with a time of 1hr 28mins 10secs which became the standard time. The Headmaster was so impressed with the enthusiasm and organisation that he donated a cup for House competition. The competition ran for six years; Robert Williams won the event on two occasions, breaking the record each time. Michael Collison subsequently claimed the record but in 1965, on the last occasion it was held, a cloudburst in Devil's Bridge drastically reduced the number of finishers. Although its life was relatively short, the venture was another example of the encouragement which was always given to the initiative of pupils.

A somewhat bizarre activity was taken up following an appeal from the UCW tiddlywinks club, frustrated by the lack of opposition. After ascertaining that it was a serious invitation, the idea of winking had an enthusiastic reception. More than ten sixth-formers were in involved in several matches with the students whose captain it was reported, held a world record- he had potted 5,000 winks in under three hours. It was later reported that 'despite ridicule from the rest of the School', Ardwyn had made quite a name for itself in tiddlywink circles. After four years however, despite appeals to fellow pupils to swallow their pride and join in the game, interest had waned. The last report in the 1969-70 Magazine referred to their first victory over the freshers and a high position in the College leagues.

Despite the variety of sporting activities available not all pupils were motivated to participate.

> I've never made it a secret that I don't like organised sport. Considerable periods of my young life were devoted to avoiding games in school. Despite headmaster A D Lewis' exhortations that sport(meaning rugby) was good for body and mind, my puny body definitely felt that running around icy slush and horizontal rain was not good for it. However I suppose it stimulated my mind to seriously study avoidance tactics.
>
> The main boys' sport at Ardwyn was rugby with cross-country running an alternative and cricket in summer. At this latter sport my short sight resulted in hopeless performance. For years I was convinced that cricket balls were totally invisible at distances greater than ten feet. They miraculously became visible just in time for me to dodge out of their way to my stumps. At least in rugby the ball was larger but so were almost all the other players.
>
> Early avoidance strategies were not a success. I can still recite all ten items in the country code, learned by rote as a punishment from the Head for being caught crossing fields near Pen-y-bont on a totally inept short cut from the cross-country course. However the Head was right, my mind did improve, at least in the study of avoidance tactics and my pallid pipe-cleaner legs were saved from much of the five-mile senior cross-country course by cutting across to Cefnllan and brewing tea at home until the tail-enders were observed passing our gate.
>
> In the sixth form the pinnacle of games avoidance was devised with my friend Pip Nelson. As both of us were involved in the stage crew of the School dramatic society

> we were given the keys to the drama store. This was a long dank catacomb under the C-block balcony, half filled by scenery flats and other props. At break time we locked ourselves in the store, plugged in a battered electric fire, tuned in our transistor radio and reclined in battered armchairs doing our homework until all possibility of games was over. Later on an electric kettle provided brews of tea and coffee. This ruse had several advantages; it enabled us to swear truthfully we had never left school premises, homework actually got done on time and the games staff were relieved of the responsibility for two of the most useless sportsmen ever to avoid gracing a games pitch.[114]

Terry Whitaker might have had an aversion to organised games but he was able to survive the physically demanding experience of a total of five years as a marine biologist with the British Antarctic Survey. However in April 1982, he was one of a group of BAS scientists who had the misfortune to be captured, along with a platoon of Royal Marines, when Argentine forces invaded the island of South Georgia, the action which precipitated the Falklands war. Dr Whitaker had the rare distinction of being awarded the prestigious Polar Medal for distinguished service in Antarctica.

During the Sixties there was a burgeoning of outdoor activities some of them initiated by the Headmaster. His view on these pursuits was emphasised in his report at the 1966 Prize Day.

> It has often been said in the past, and as a committed games man I agree, that we have attached too much importance to games at the expense of other social, cultural and out-door activities like camping, sailing, climbing and trekking. We play games because we enjoy them, not because of any supposed character building virtues in them. In any case, organised out-door activities have now become varied with something for everybody not just the person who happens to have good muscular co-ordination and good ball sense.

At the suggestion of the Headmaster, in 1964 an expedition club was formed under the leadership of Bryan J Davies. In the first year Plynlimon and Cader Idris were climbed in severe winter conditions. Indoor activities included a slide talk on the Snowdon Horseshoe by David Sansbury and aspects of mountaineering by a member of the College mountaineering club. In the summer of 1966, three members of the club, using youth hostel accommodation attempted to climb all fourteen peaks over 3,000 feet in Snowdonia. Their efforts were thwarted by driving rain and sleet.
From these beginnings, the club evolved into a climbing and mountaineering venture. Rhys P Davies reported a successful winter climb, in conditions of severe snow and ice, of the Idwal Slabs. Another development was orienteering; more than fifty senior pupils took part in the first competition at Cwmere, with the eager cooperation of staff members Moira Convery, Dinah Thomas and Ken Loates.

An undertaking involving several disciplines not to mention adventure and risk was initiated by a group of Talybont boys led by Simon Hughes, augmented later by others from Aberystwyth.

The A. D. Lewis Years — 1954-1971

The North Cardiganshire Mining Club was formed in 1966 to explore and survey disused lead mines in the area. In collaboration with the UCW caving club, several inaccessible levels at the Cwmystwyth lead mine were re-opened and more than 14,000 ft of underground workings accurately surveyed. Valuable contributions to the industrial archeology of the area were made. A 16 ft diameter underground water wheel was found in the Cwmeinion mine in the Artist's Valley, two underground lift cages were discovered in the Bwlch Glas mine at Talybont and the Cwmystwyth mine produced, amongst other artefacts, a full set of rock drilling equipment (circa 1900) the retrieval of which involved wading through chest-deep ice-cold water in mid-winter. Examples of old mining equipment were donated to the Llywernog mine museum and the Ceredigion Museum. For many of the mining club members what started as a hobby became a career. Several became mining geologists- Robin Hill is employed by the South Africa Chamber of Mines in Johannesburg, Stephen Godden travels the world as a consultant mining engineer, Simon Hughes, after a period in Nicaragua as mining development engineer, is a consultant in mineral exploitation and David Roberts works in the aggregates industry.

After graduating from Imperial College, John Ashton gained a PhD at Aberystwyth working on the lead, zinc and gold mines of mid and north Wales. He is currently assistant chief mine geologist at the Navan zinc and lead mines in Ireland, one of the largest and technologically advanced mines in the world.

His interest in mineralogy was kindled at an early age by enlightened parents who accompanied him to the old mine tips of north Cardiganshire to collect mineral specimens. He later became an enthusiastic member of the mining club.

> Initially, knowledge of such matters as lighting equipment and safety was virtually non-existent but helped by some members of the UCW caving club and old Ardwynian Terry Whitaker equipment and safety awareness gradually developed. However a letter to the *Cambrian News* criticising our lack of experience in mine exploration caused much concern at the School and to parents. As a result our activities became clandestine for a while and acquired a thrilling mystique sufficient to ensure that most of us who were involved followed careers in the mining and extractive industries. In fact no one involved with the club ever suffered more than a minor scratch despite the potentialy dangerous surroundings, a fact which I am convinced is due to those involved gaining experience and safety-awareness in a tightly knit group which was well able to cope with the risks involved. To the great credit of the School, the club was supported financially which enabled us to buy essential equipment such as ropes and expensive flexible wire ladders.
>
> John Phillips of the UCW geology department was also a good friend to the club.
>
> The achievements of the club were considerable and involved visits at least once a week to one of the local mines. The surveying and mapping of many ancient mine levels including some of the old pre-gunpowder 'coffin levels' at Talybont and Cwmystwyth proved invaluable experience for those of us who now work full time in working underground mines.
>
> Other memories include spending more than one New Year's Eve in camps underground as well as a sponsored stay by eight of us in Level Fawr, Cwmystwyth for a full week.[115]

No 561 (Ardwyn G S) Squadron, Air Training Corps became one of the permanent features of School life. From the early Fifties, the annual review of the squadron's activities, usually written by the senior cadet, never failed to appear in the *Ardwynian*. From those reports it is possible to assemble an accurate lineage of the aircraft used by the RAF in the following twenty years.

After four years as its commanding officer David G Sansbury resigned his commission as did Noel Butler his assistant. Welsh master DA Young took over the command in 1955 and built up the membership to a record thirty-seven. The high percentage of proficient cadets brought congratulations from the highest quarters in the RAF. The cadets enjoyed their Easter camps at various RAF stations, flying in Sunderlands at Pembroke Dock, Chipmunks at St Athan, and in Canberra bombers at Cambridge; two cadets, John Stephenson and Peter Davies, were the first in the unit to gain glider pilots certificates.

D A Young was the last Ardwyn master to command the unit; when he moved from Ardwyn in 1958, Dr RF Walker of the UCW took over with continued success. Head boy Peter Davies won a flying scholarship and a trip to the USA which included a meeting with President Eisenhower in the White House. Not all the activities were in the air; mountaineering courses and initiative exercises were developed culminating in a demanding two-day trek of 35 miles in the hills of mid-Wales carrying a full pack of equipment. For their efforts the three-man team won the Dimond expedition trophy in 1962 and retained it for a further three years. With success in aircraft recognition and dinghy drill competitions together with awards during Easter and summer camps for marksmanship, drill and smartness, 561 Squadron was establishing a reputation for excellence. No doubt the loyalty of the cadets was a vital factor in the success of the unit. Many retained their allegiance for the whole of their stay in the School typified by Michael J Lewis, who reached the rank of flight sergeant after six years of service and who was held as an example for others to follow. He also reached the heights in the world of film music as a composer, conductor and producer during his twenty-five years in Hollywood.

One cadet had the unforgettable experience of flying through the sound barrier in a Hunter jet trainer and viewing his home town from a height of 14,000 feet.

After a period as a civilian instructor, William Jones served as commanding officer for six years from 1962. Ardwyn cadets were selected, in competition with the other units in the Wing, for visits to Singapore and Canada and trips to RAF stations in Germany became almost an annual event.

Iwan Thomas and T Glyn Evans had the honour of representing the Welsh ATC rugby XV while BJ Davies, WOB Davies and Michael Nichol were selected for the national expedition over the 'Roof of Wales', a ten-day, 170 mile trek from Bala to Porthcawl.

Such was the reputation built up by the squadron that a member of the public who had followed the activities of the unit and had admired the work and bearing of the boys, gave a dinner as a token of esteem.

While at camp in Easter 1967, the cadets had a flight in the newly introduced Hercules transport plane over the stricken oil tanker 'Torrey Canyon' aground near the Scillies, just a day or so before it was sunk by RAF bombing.

On his retirement in 1968, Flt Lieut William Jones received the Lord Lieutenant's certificate for meritorious service. The new CO, Flt Lieut JR Lloyd assisted by PO Don

The A. D. Lewis Years — 1954-1971

Shaw introduced other activities such the Duke of Edinburgh award, and community involvement. When a parents/cadets organisation was formed funds were raised to purchase a go-kart.

As a result of the keenness and enthusiasm of its officers the ever-increasing membership reached forty; Cdt Cpl Michael Williams was chosen as a Welsh representative for an exchange visit to Canada in the summer of 1967 and Sgt Hywel Thomas won a trip to a RAF station in Germany, to maintain the record.

Hywel later was accepted by the RAF as a trainee pilot.

1970 was judged to be the best year in the history of the squadron. At the Easter camp at RAF Brize Norton, in competition with other squadrons in a variety of activities, 561 brought back the trophy for the best ATC unit in camp. They also enjoyed around-Britain flights in V C 10 and Belfast aircraft.

Following stringent interviews, medical and aptitude tests at the Biggin Hill selection centre, three cadets, Hywel Thomas, John Wall and Tim Williams gained flying scholarships. This number was a record for the Corps nationally. All three subsequently completed the necessary flying hours to qualify for a private pilot's licence.

Although the squadron moved to their new headquarters in Plascrug in 1976 it proudly retained the Ardwyn name in its title- No 561 Aberystwyth and District A T C (Ardwyn) Squadron. When the commanding officer Don Shaw retired in 1986 after fourteen years service, former Ardwyn cadet John Wall succeeded him and still serves. In 1991 the squadron and the Air Training Corps nationally, celebrated its fiftieth birthday. Since 1986 it has admitted girls and continues to be a most successful and attractive youth organisation never failing to be well represented at the Remembrance Day service and Mayor's Sunday parade.

The Parents-Teachers Association continued to prosper with the strong encouragement of AD Lewis. As a pressure group they were able to persuade the LEA to provide musical instrument tuition which led the the establishment of the School orchestra. Their move to have the ditch adjacent to the playing fields piped was unsuccessful but plans to build an ambulance station on the Waun near to the proposed development of the new school was reversed by the planning authorities after protests by the PTA. Strong support, including canvassing county council members, was given to the campaign to have a new science wing and a new kitchen-dining hall built. In 1962, as previously recorded, the Association led a move to build a new Ardwyn on the Erw Goch site. The Association was fortunate in having a succession of wise and able chairmen who usually served for two years- Richard I Aaron, E D Jones, Ll B Bebb, J E Meredith, W J Lewis, Jac L Williams, John Medway, T Arfon Owen, C H Houlder, and in the final year, Charlotte Johnston broke the male dominance.

During the Fifties the terminal meetings usually included a guest speaker frequently with a careers bias. Other occasions were devoted to discussions of the School curriculum. Resolutions adopted included one which deplored early specialisation and in particular the enforced choice between Latin and mathematics at the end of the second year. A question on the possibility of a choice between Welsh and French in the science stream provoked a very lengthy discussion on the position of Welsh in the curriculum. One opinion was that the policy of the LEA in enforcing the teaching of Welsh to school-leaving age was to be deplored. The Headmaster explained:

a) that the view that the object of Ardwyn was to preserve Welsh 'to the last ditch' was exaggerated.
b) that, given the cooperation of parents, the choice of Welsh at one of four levels did not impose heavy burdens on the children.
c) that no pupil at the Schol was being deprived of the second language required for the purpose of matriculation.
d) that a time-table could not be drawn up to be criticised item by item by the Association. Recommendations would be considered but no promise could be given that the curriculum could be revised accordingly.[116]

The Magazine invariably carried a report, compiled by the secretary, of the activities of the P T A with a frequent appeal for a more representative support. 'There is much that we have done, within the limits of our functions, to promote the welfare of the School, but although interest has been well maintained among the faithful few, there are still regrettably far too many parents who are entirely indifferent to our aims.' In the Sixties the form of the meetings changed. It was recognised that guest speakers were not essential and that parents preferred meetings where they could meet the staff on a one-to-one basis to discuss their problems. The refusal by the staff to wear name-tags at these encounters was no doubt an inconvenience but both parties recognised the benefit of such meetings.

With the abolition of prize day, the public were denied the annual reports of the Headmaster. However he did give an account of activities and provided some statistics which were recorded in the minute book of the P T A. Those notes also provide an invaluable record of the machinations of reorganisation of secondary education in Aberystwyth. Giving reasons for the 'unlamented' demise of prize day, when questioned, AD Lewis explained that the cost of hire of the Kings Hall had become prohibitive, the work involved had become excessive and there was an indifference or hostility towards the institution by all concerned.

At the Association A G M in 1969 the Head spoke of his concern about the increase in smoking and drinking by his pupils. 'Ardwyn could not hope to be isolated from the national trend of lax standards of behaviour' and thought that, in the first instance, it was a matter of home discipline. The following year he spoke of the menace of drug-taking in the country as a whole which should not be ignored. The authorities had pinpointed the danger points in a community as universities, grammar schools, and boarding schools and there seemed no good grounds for thinking that Cardiganshire was an exception. Such was the concern of parents that Dr Moir, the UCW medical officer and a police sergeant were invited to address the parents amd staff at the next meeting. Dr Moir outlined the position in the country as a whole and in the town of Aberystwyth. He listed the motives for drug-taking and Sergeant Thomas revealed that in Dyfed, between 1969 and 1970 convictions for possessing cannabis had trebled and there had been nineteen drug related offences where previously there had been none. He concluded his talk by showing the various forms of drugs and demonstrated a burning of cannabis.

A D Lewis commented on the press publicity given to the School. With three former pupils sitting as Members of Parliament, the School had been dubbed 'The Welsh Eton'. This sobriquet was even more relevant when consideration was given to four other for-

The A. D. Lewis Years — 1954-1971

1st Hockey XI, 1963. Captain: Zena Shattock.

First Rugby XV, 1969–70. Captain Garrod Roberts.

mer pupils, Elwyn Lloyd Jones, Daniel Gruffydd Jones, Alwyn Jones and Basil Thomas who had reached high positions in the Civil Service.

The Headmaster revealed that 54% of the 11 plus age group had been admitted to Ardwyn in the 1969-70 session, usually the figure was around 43%. When one considers that the intake into grammar schools in most large towns was often less than 10%, it would appear that Ardwyn was already a comprehensive school!

He referred to criticism that he crammed as many pupils as possible into the School to boost his own salary and departmental allowances. He had also been criticised for not transferring pupils to Dinas when it was apparent that they were not suited to an academic course of study. He spoke of the great reluctance of parents to allow such a move regarding it as a demotion. In 1970 the School roll stood at 768 pupils with a sixth form of 180 where there were 58 combinations of courses. There was no creaming for advanced level, all the upper sixth members followed a full A- level course. Of the sixth-form leavers in the previous year, 36 had gone to universities in Oxford, Wales, Birmingham, Bradford, Manchester, Warwick, and York, 3 to polytechnics, 8 to colleges of education, 13 to technical colleges and 6 to do nursing. Despite the large intake each year, Ardwyn could boast of a figure of 59% of pupils gaining five or more O-level subject passes when the national average was 24%.

When it was reported that due to financial contraints, there was a shortage of text books for the children, the PTA set up an appeal fund and invited parents to contribute. More than £280 was raised in the first year but on the advice of the Headmaster it was agreed that text books should not be purchased from the fund. It was the responsibility of the L E A to provide such basic items. He was concerned that the LEA members were ignorant of the function of a P T A and wondered how to promote a better understanding. When it was revealed that the Governors had the power to coopt members from the now defunct Old Pupils Association, moves were made to obtain representation of the P T A on the governing body; it came in the last year of the School. The appeal fund was an important income for the School with more than £300 raised annually; the ultimate decision on its use was left to the Headmaster who saw it as a means of providing equipment and facilities which could not be covered by the normal resources of the School.

After many years of campaigning for a new school building for Ardwyn, the P T A, after the decision in 1965 to re-organise secondary education on comprehensive lines, took up the battle to establish such a school. The Ardwyn staff after due consideration, recommended that a unitary comprehensive school be established, a decision supported later by a parent referendum. However the L E A were in favour of a two-tier system with a junior and senior school using the Ardwyn and Dinas sites. A D Lewis led the revolt against this idea stating that the scheme chosen should be the most sound educationally, 'expediency should not be the main issue'. He later expressed disgust at 'the insinuations against the Ardwyn staff in the education committee' and urged the P T A not to accept any interim scheme. There was a change of heart, the first of many, when the L E A included a new school in the 1968-69 building programme and gave assurances that there would be consultation in the planning stages. Disappointment came when a letter from Shirley Williams, Secretary of State for Education stating that the new school was not in the 68-69 programme and unlikely to be considered for the following year. A private firm of architects was commisioned by the LEA to draw up plans in consultation with the teaching staff. R J Lloyd reported to the P T A that there was deadlock between the staff and the Department of Education and Science over the laboratory requirements in the new school with the latter determined to reduce the figure of thirteen labs to eight. Early in 1970 the D E S decreed that on financial grounds, a unitary comprehensive school was out of the question. Speaking at a P T A meeting in February 1971, Dr J Henry Jones, Director of Education, described a unitary comprehensive, which would cost £500, 000, as 'an idealistic dream' and outlined the three possible alternatives. The first was no change, as favoured by the Ardwyn and Dinas staff. This brought an immediate rebuttal from A D Lewis who declared that the staff were opposed to the interim solution of a two-tier system. The second possibility was a two-tier system of junior and senior comprehensive schools. and thirdly, a scheme not previously publicly discussed, an English medium school and a bilingual comprehensive school. He concluded by stressing the increasing disquiet felt by parents and primary school teachers at the separation of children into modern and grammar schools at the age of 11 years. The Ardwyn deputy head R J Lloyd reminded the director that Ardwyn staff had five years previously, fought for comprehensive education against the wishes of others. They felt that a two-tier system would not adequately preserve grammar school education for those pupils able to benefit. Although A D Lewis was due retire in July 1971 he remained adamantly opposed to the two tier plan. In his last P T A meeting in May 1971 he said he deplored the decision of the full education committee to adopt the two-tier scheme. It could be defended only on the grounds of expediency. He felt that many parents and primary school teachers were concerned only to abolish selection at 11 plus, without giving due consideration to what happened at the secondary school stage.

From the first edition of the School Magazine in 1904, the Old Pupils' Notes proved to be a valuable source of information on the achievements and distinctions gained by former pupils.

Ardwyn counted a large number of clergymen among its *alumni* of whom four reached the rank of bishop. The first was Timothy Rees who became Bishop of Llandaff in 1931, he had been a boarder at the Ardwyn School pre-1896. Mention has previously been made of John Richard Richards, who after distinguished service as a missionary in Persia, was appointed Bishop of St David's in 1956. The 1970-71 Magazine recorded the retirement of the Rt Revd John Richards and his return to Llanbadarn Fawr where he had spent his childhood. The same issue congratulated another former Ardwynian H J Charles on being consecrated as Bishop of St Asaph. There was of course no *Ardwynian* to announce the appointment of Cledan Mears as Bishop of Bangor in 1982, a position he held for ten years.

> I was a pupil in Ardwyn from 1934-40. If bodily weight is anything to go by, they must have been some of the happiest days of my life. My weight in the sixth form was 11 st 4 lbs; ever since I have been a stone less. There must be a simpler explanation than that as prefects who helped to serve the dinners, we were always privileged to receive a second helping.
>
> The staff at the time were a mixed bag. Unfortunately the most talented of them were not always the best teachers or disciplinarians. I owe a debt to Richards in geom-

etry, James in history, Mainwaring and Rowlands in English, Dr Rae in Latin and Dr Jones in French. I shall always hold in high esteem Major Stimson, who was responsible for the gymnastics. I continued to learn from him during my three years at Aberystwyth college where he enabled me to gain full colours in the university team.

I remember with affection the annual operas. I can still sing to myself some of the pieces from the Mikado, the Gondoliers, Pirates of Penzance, and Ruddigore. In the last of those, as one of the ghosts who emerge from the portraits on the wall, the strains of 'When the song of the breeze rings through the trees and the bat in the moonlight flies'.. etc, still return without effort to the memory.

As to events that effected school life, there was the build up to the second world war. Storm clouds in this respect were always looming on the horizon and when 1939-40 came, we soon became aware that the war scenes of the continent were not that far away, when pupils ahead of us in School were called up to HM Forces. We were obliged to think what this would mean to us personally and as time wore on we came to our various conclusions as to what our obligations would be in that respect.[117]

In 1960 the School rejoiced in the news that David Elwyn Lloyd Jones had been appointed principal private secretary to the Chancellor of the Duchy of Lancaster, a minister with a seat in the Cabinet. His distinguished war service in the Burma campaign for which he was awarded the M C, has already been instanced.

The central commitment to his life was education. Between 1961 and 1969 he was an assistant secretary in the Ministry of Education, taking responsibility under ministers for the full range of non-university further and higher education. The central focus of his activity and his major achievement in those years was helping create the British polytechnic system. He saw the expansion of the polytechnic system as a way of reducing the disturbing gap in qualification levels between Britain and many other Western societies. He served as under-secretary Department of Education and Science 1969-80; he had a high regard for the talent of some of the ministers but as he saw it, the high turnover of ministers hindered effectiveness. The average tenure of office of a secretary of state for education was then less than two years, scarcely giving anyone time to master the brief before moving to another job. After his retirement he viewed with great sadness the changes in the educational scene. Central control appeared to him to be becoming stronger and the era of expansion replaced by severe cuts in funding.

Some of the notes he left revealed a good deal of his thinking on education. 'Maybe', he wrote 'there is a reversion to basic English cynicism about education.

As David Lloyd George put it- 'the Welsh have a passion for education, the Scots have a respect for it and the English no objection to it'. 'Perhaps', he continued, 'we need an injection of Welsh passion to restore the traditional belief in education to see through these grim years of recession.'[118]

Arthur Hughes Jenkins left Ardwyn in 1926 after gaining a school certificate. Five years later he was sworn in as a constable in the Cardiganshire constabulary and after five years as desk sergeant in Aberystwyth he resigned in 1945 to join the Hong Kong force. The start of a meteoric rise was his appointment as chief constable of the Falkland

Islands in 1948. He became deputy chief of police of Grenada, West Indies in 1951, chief of police of St Vincent, West Indies a year later, and spent ten years in British Guiana retiring in 1964 from the post of deputy commissioner of police. He was awarded the Colonial Police Medal and the Queen's Police Medal for distinguished service.

> The long walk from Penrhyncoch to Bow Street railway station, the ten minute train ride into Aberystwyth and then the walk of not less than a mile to Ardwyn School for several years from 1922, in my case, was a necessary evil for some of us before the advent of school buses. I can remember they were hard times economically and a stop at Pain's shop on the way to Ardwyn to buy a pennyworth of broken biscuits was almost an event. During my last year at school, if the weather was cold I seem to remember that my father's overcoat was always a little on the large and heavy side.
>
> A school strike in the early Twenties meant that Ardwyn pupils of under school leaving age had to attend their elementary schools, in my case Penybontrhydybeddau. This meant a walk of over two miles from my home in Penrhyncoch. The railway strike in 1926 meant a long walk from Penrhyncoch to Aberystwyth and back to attend school at Ardwyn.
>
> I have other happy memories of meetings, long after school days, with former school friends. I met Willie Ellis in St Vincent in the West Indies. He always drew pictures of beautiful sailing ships at our back table in the geography class. As captain of a Canadian bauxite carrying ship on its way from Demerara to Canada, he stopped off to see me in St Vincent a quarter of a century later.[119]

Described by a contemporary as 'the most prolific scholar of my generation in Ardwyn', Geraint H Jenkins left School in 1964 after successfully captaining the cricket XI and gaining the A-level prize in history. He went on take a first class honours degree in history at University College Swansea and was appointed lecturer and later senior lecturer at the UCW Aberystwyth. He gained his PhD from the University of Wales in 1974. A prolific author, his books and articles in Welsh and English are regarded as 'fundamental contributions to the field of Welsh history in the seventeenth and eighteenth century' and he has been described 'as one of today's outstanding historians in Wales.' In 1989 he was appointed to the grade and title of Reader by the University of Wales who also commissioned him to write the illustrated history of the University of Wales to mark its centenary in 1993. Dr Jenkins was further honoured with the award of a personal chair in recognition of his outstanding contribution to the understanding of seventeenth and eighteenth century Welsh history. Professor Geraint Jenkins is currently director of the University of Wales Centre for Advanced Celtic Studies based in Aberystwyth.[120]

Early in 1991 the Environment Secretary, Michael Heseltine annnounced the appointment of former Ardwynian, Dr David Slater as Her Majesty's chief inspector of pollution. David Slater entered the UCW in 1959 with a College scholarship in chemistry. Following lecturing posts in Ohio State university and Imperial College, London, he became a consultant in industrial risk assessment and led the investigation into the Flixborough disaster in 1974. He also worked in India during the aftermath of the Bhopal chemical disaster and was involved in work on the major oil spillage by the

Exxon Valdez. Dr Slater was made an honorary professor by the UCW in 1992 and in the 1996 New Year Honours list he was appointed a Commander of the Order of the Bath.

Headmaster A D Lewis was appointed chairman of the Mid-Wales Hospital Management Committee in succession to Dr David Jenkins a former Ardwynian who in 1969 secured the important post of Librarian of the National Library of Wales. When Dr Jenkins retired in 1980 he was succeeded by Prof Geraint Gruffydd who had also been an Ardwyn pupil for a time in the Forties.

> His instructions were precise. Unless I was by his gate by 8 am he would have started on his two-mile trek from Penrhyn-coch to Bow Street without me and I would have to run for it. As Arthur Hughes Jenkins was a near six foot fifth former, and I a good deal shorter, I soon realised how severe was my handicap. Even at that time he revealed his caring, disciplined nature which was to take him to high office in law enforcement. However, I saw to it that I was on time, for he had promised to be my guide and mentor into the new world of Ardwyniana.
>
> As a raw recruit I was soon initiated into the new life-the strengths and foibles of the staff and prefects, and much more. By the time we arrived at Bow Street I had mastered an Ardwynian survival course including how to avoid detention.
>
> On the train there were endless introductions to lads and lasses-from as far afield as Glandyfi, Eglwys-fach, Borth and Llandre. One soon heard tales of the sea, of the Ynyslas tree stumps and of the Borth Bog witches. Equally fascinating was the lilt of a different dialect spoken by the pupils who had joined the train at Glandyfi. It was, at first, intriguing to hear Eglwys-fach pronounced Eglwys-fech and 'nawr'inverted to 'rwan'.
>
> I was greatly enlightened when informed by David Davies, Glandyfi, that he could take me to the actual spot where you could draw a line across the road between Tre'r-ddol and Furnace where north and south Wales actually met!
>
> Life was no less interesting in the school yard. During break-times the first year boys were confined to a small triangular playground. Its one redeeming feature for me was that during the first few weeks of the session it became an open-air book market. In those days we were obliged to buy our own text-books, and for the last of my purchases I well recall being cornered by an older pupil who wished to sell me 'The World', for geography. New at five shillings, I was firmly offered it as a good bargain for three shillings. It must have been a fourth or fifth generation copy- without front cover and half the title page and the final page index, it had been 'conveniently' broken into three sections 'for ease of transport'. Bidding continued after lunch and we eventually agreed on one shilling.
>
> Later in life, as Keeper of Printed Books in the National Library and fairly knowledgeable about the antiquarian book trade, as I glanced down upon Ardwyn's playground I always recalled my apprenticeship with refreshing amusement.
>
> My first headmaster, C Lloyd Morgan, toured the School with the air of a genial commander notwithstanding his loss of a leg during the Great War and the need to rely heavily on his sturdy walking stick. One of my highlights then was to listen to his reading and appreciation of English poetry in a rich and sonorous voice which would

have done credit to a professional actor. It was an experience never to be forgotten.

Occasionally he would visit the playground chatting freely with us about our personal interests. He would stand on the fringe of a crowd of lads listening to what he called 'the melody of spoken Welsh' and encourage us to speak it while playing.

Sport was never my 'forte' partly because of chest trouble and steaming spectacles. I had a fairly strong shot and at one time was proudly picked for Gwynedd football team. My generation will well recall our football pitch on the Plascrug tip – mud patches surrounding each lagoon. Every footballer has his ne'er to be forgotten moment of fame!

We were pressing hard around Arfon's goal when the ball landed on an island of grass, only to be cleared effectively beyond mid-field. I stood some ten yards from our goal-alone and palely wondering. Both packs turned heel baying like the Gogerddan hounds. Suddenly, I saw the wizard, Bill Price move ahead with unnerving speed which had attracted the interest of first division managers. If he arrived before me he would certainly score for he was unstoppable. Almost breathless, I arrived a yard or two before him and kicked as hard as I could. The ball flew out of his reach followed by a clod of mud which caught him full face.

During the 1926 railway strike we had no option but to take the five mile walk to school- and back again. It may have been half term, we had a free afternoon and after enjoying my sandwich lunch made my way towards the National Library drive hoping thereby to cross the fields to the Waun as a short cut to Capel Dewi. I was aiming to jump the fence near the lodge when I froze as a burly voice of authority questioned whither I went. I nervously explained my manoeuvers and to my relief he even pointed me a foot-path which would ease my journey. I later learned-much to my amusement-that my helpmate was none other than Sir John Ballinger, the first Librarian of the National Library. Thus the world goes round; it was my only meeting with my eminent predecessor.[121]

Many Ardwynians had long careers as regulars in the armed forces; probably no one attained higher rank nor achieved greater distinction than Captain Edgar Brown RN. His obituary in the *Daily Telegraph* 8:2:95 detailed his career. He left Ardwyn in 1937 to join the merchant navy; some months before war was declared he joined the Royal Navy as a midshipman engaged on flying duties. At the time of Dunkirk, and two days short of his twenty-first birthday, while searching for shipping off Calais, his Albacore was 'jumped' by a dozen Me 109s. His aircraft was badly damaged and he had to have a piece of cannon shell removed from his head. 'I can't remember much about that birthday,' he recalled. Brown was mentioned in despatches for his part in obtaining detailed information on Japanese positions in the Malay peninsula. He survived the post-war axe and accepted a permanent commission as a lieutenant. In 1955 he was given his first command and was later promoted captain after a spell on the carrier *Victorious*. He commanded the frigate *Nubian* in the Persian Gulf where he was also senior naval officer and naval advisor to the Shah of Persia prior to the latter being deposed. In November 1967 he was informed by the Admiralty that he was to be the next captain of *Victorious* then undergoing modernisation. However his chance of attaining flag rank disappeared when a serious fire broke out on board and she was subsequently scrapped. Captain Ed Brown was appointed CBE in 1970 and on retirement in 1975 he enjoyed another career as secretary of the King George's Fund for Sailors. His researches into the welfare of elderly seafarers uncovered real need to which the Fund responded. He was appointed CVO for his charity work in 1984.

Peter Norrington Davies who left School in 1969 seems to have had the distinction, as far as the School records show, of being the only Ardwynian to have gained entry to the Britannia Royal Naval College. During the three years spent at Dartmouth, he qualified as a civilian pilot but opted for the submarine service. He served on *HMS Andrew*, an 'A' class submarine, which was the last British submarine to fire a shell. After two years as a navigator on *HMS Orpheus*, he had a shore posting as a submarine controller which allowed him to play first class rugby for the Royal Navy XV, appearing twice at Twickenham against the Army and the Royal Air Force in the inter-services tournament. A period as navigator on the nuclear-powered submarine *Conqueror* followed, although he was successfully pursuing a commanders' course when that vessel had the argument with the *General Belgrano* in the south Atlantic in 1982.

His first command, of *HMS Walrus*, lasted for more than three years, followed by an operations post at Northwood in charge of all British submarine movements. Peter left the navy in 1988 and later became harbour master in his home town, coinciding with the opening of the Aberystwyth marina. His brothers Paul and Patrick, also Ardwynians, are both battalion commanders holding the rank of Lt Colonel, in the Royal Regiment of Wales.

Ardwyn has another connection with RNC Dartmouth. Stephen Cannon (1952-57), gained a Masters degree in quantum physics at UCW Aberystwyth in 1965. After a short period with GEC he was commissioned into the Royal Navy in the instructor branch. Following some time afloat, he spent many years lecturing at the Britannia Naval College retiring in 1983 with the rank of Lt Commander to join Ferranti, the electronics giant. However the navy ties were too strong and he returned to Dartmouth as a civilian lecturer where he still serves.

Another 'first' was the acceptance of David Martin, in 1968, for a civil airline pilot training course at Hamble. In the face of ferocious competition he was congratulated on being the first ever Cardiganshire pupil to be selected for this training. David subsequently had a successful career as a commercial pilot with South Africa Airways.

The summer vacation of 1967 saw the most ambitious school trip to date. 170 pupils and 9 members of staff along with other schools in the county took part in an educational cruise to the Mediterranean. The *SS Devonia*, formerly the troopship *Devonshire* which had transported some fathers to and from theatres of war, carried their children to Vigo, Lisbon and Gibraltar.

The venture was repeated in 1970 when the party embarked on *SS Uganda* from Swansea docks to visit the islands of Madeira, Teneriffe and Lanzarote, spectacular examples of the activities of Vulcan. A visit also to Tangier which included a fascinating stroll through the Kasbah. During days at sea, pupils were kept busy with ample recreational opportunities, lectures on the sites visited and evening entertainment. Later in the autumn, parents and friends were invited to a cruise evening at the School to view films and slides taken by staff and pupils.

Another 'first' was a skiing holiday in February 1969, for 31 pupils accompanied by teachers Peter Duggan and Dinah Thomas. After a week of coaching and skiing in the Austrian Tyrol, excellent progress was made by most and happily there were no broken limbs. Thereafter, skiing trips abroad became annual events.

But two pupils were off to warmer climes; the first pupils to be accepted for Voluntary Service Overseas were head girl Nonna Dummer, who went to Bihar, near Calcutta and Christopher Adams to the Solomon Islands.

Although prize day had been abandoned for what many saw as paltry reasons, the inter-house eisteddfod was indestructible and continued to excite pupils, Welsh speakers and non Welsh speakers alike. The wooodwork master Idwal Davies had always made a miniature bardic chair for presentation to the winner of the chair poem competition as well as a baton for the leader of the winning House choir. However in the 1967 festival, the King's Hall stage was graced by a new bardic chair crafted in oak and upholstered in red leather. The chair had been made by two A-level woodwork students, Peter Humphreys and Anthony Morris under the direction of Idwal Davies. E Jones Davies, head of music, who was always heavily involved in the preparation and direction of the eisteddfod had, that year, composed the anthem which was the test piece for the chief choral competition. At the 1970 eisteddfod, the contest for the chair poem was a family affair. Stephen Nantlais Williams gained first place for a poem written in English and second place for a poem written in Welsh; his brother Paul gained third place. The following year Paul was awarded first place in the competition as well as third but due to illness he was unable to be present to be chaired.

At the end of the 1969-70 session, after thirty-nine years of loyal and devoted service to the School, Violet Jones, teacher of domestic science and senior mistress, retired.

Generations of Ardwyn girls were grateful to their beloved 'Miss Jones' for the thorough training she gave them in the art of house craft. Those who studied her subject at advanced level realised the extent of her devotion and desire to see them following in her footsteps to train as 'domsci' teachers. Boys too came under her tuition in hygiene lessons. Basil Thomas recalled such a lesson. ' Miss Jones taught us hygiene from which I remember that one should be sure to dry between one's toes thoroughly and that walking exercises every muscle in the body, which is my excuse since then for doing nothing more strenuous.'

As is true of many devoted teachers, Violet Jones felt strongly that her contribution to the life of the School should not be confined to the classroom. Whenever a School function required the provision of refreshments she would spend many hours with her equally devoted 'girls', in preparation. She probably reached her zenith in the eagerly anticipated opera soirees held to reward the diligent work of all those involved in the annual opera productions. Her sumptuous suppers on those occasions were greatly appreciated and marvelled at, particularly during the period of wartime rationing. She also catered for the parent-teacher meetings and the many after-school activities, concerned that the pupils should not miss their tea. Violet Jones was always receptive to the problems brought to her, even though some might be considered trivial to a less enlightened teacher. Tearful girls distraught perhaps by a broken boy-girl friendship, knew that from Miss Jones they would not get ridicule just sympathy, comfort and sensible advice.

Her well merited and popular appointment as senior mistress in 1961, meant that her

The A. D. Lewis Years — 1954-1971

responsibilities, particularly those involving counselling were increased, but her zeal, experience and sensitivity ensured a successful outcome. With her retirement, the School and staffroom lost one of its most colourful characters. Her colleagues expressed the hope that she would have a long and happy retirement. Her friends would testify that this she patently enjoyed. She died in 1995 in her ninetieth year after 'enjoying each day as it came' as she vowed she would.

Gwyneth Mainwaring who had been head of English since the retirement of WG Rowlands in 1964 took on the additional duties of senior mistress.

Also retiring was Morgan Price. He had spent fourteen years teaching mathematics throughout the School with much success as many of his pupils would testify. In the remaining years of the School, Doreen Harris (mathematics), Margaret Baron (domestic subjects), Emrys Harries (economics), Rheon Hughes and Stuart Coleman (chemistry) Keith Lewis (mathematics), Loveday Edwards (science) and Bethan Evans (RE) were appointed and faithfully served or are serving one or other of the daughter schools.

W Beynon Davies relinquished the editorship of the School Magazine in 1970 after being responsible for the previous fourteen issues. His replacement was W John Taylor who maintained the high standard for the remaining three years of the School.

The intense activity in the field of drama of the late Fifties was maintained for much of the next decade with the initiative coming mainly from the senior pupils. The series of one-act plays was continued for several years with the indefatigable Phillip Edwards stage manager of all four one-act plays in 1961. In the annual full length play, Susan Brenells was given great credit for her polished production of 'Fools Rush In' (Kenneth Horne). The fifth play in the series, staged by the lower sixth was Lionel Hayle's 'She Passed Through Lorraine' which gave ample opportunity for a wealth of costume change and scenery. The reviewer considered the performance to be convincing both in staging and speaking and delighted an appreciative and expectant audience. It was well patronised considering the time of the year and reflected great credit on the producer Richard M Jenkins and the stage manager Philip L Edwards.

A change was made in 1962 when the whole school was involved in the staging of Bertolt-Brecht's 'Caucasian Chalk Circle'. It was considered to be a play admirably suited for a school cast inasmuch as it had a great number of parts to offer, was fluid in its action and did not depend on a near professional timing for its effect. It also gave the opportunity for costume and lighting effects; the result in both cases was pleasing to look at. Production was by staff members B J Daniels, G M Mainwaring and E W Williams with Philip Henry Jones as assistant producer. More than fifty pupils took part.

The following year it was back to an unaided pupil production, when a group of enthusiasts from the middle and upper School delighted an appreciative King's Hall audience with their performance of Agatha Christie's 'Ten Little Niggers'. The production team of Glyn Jones, James Thorn and Alun Ellis Jones were complimented on a smooth and successful presentation.

The following four years saw no drama productions other than those of the House drama competitions and the Welsh Night plays.

However with the exception of 1969, members of the English department staged a drama production in each of the remaining years. 'A Man For All Seasons'(Robert Bolt), the choice in 1967, was a bold venture and a colourful and enjoyable spectacle. A critic considered it to no easy play for such a young cast to put over and their success spoke highly of their ability and hard work. Special mention was made of Dafydd Jones as Sir Thomas More and Richard London as Thomas Cromwell who built up and sustained the tension between them remarkably well. Shaw's 'Androcles And The Lion' was an excellent choice the following year; it gave the opportunity for many pupils to appear on stage without having to do or say too much. This production by AW Cox delighted a good audience on two evenings in the university examination hall. 'The Queen And The Welshman' (R A Sissons) was the play selected for the 1969 production but circumstances cause a delay until January 1970. Meanwhle A W Cox had emigrated to New Zealand so C H Riden also of the English department took over responsibility for its production which was done most efficiently and convincingly. The main characters- Queen Katherine, Sir Owen Tudor and the cynical Villiers, played by Sara Pennington, Richard Williams and Lawrence Horner - were, to the reviewer, very convincing because of the very subdued shyness of the Queen and Sir Qwen, and the sly and sinister under-playing of Villiers. It was a good presentation by all concerned and a convincing testimony to some steady team-work. In A D Lewis' last year as Head, two plays, translations from the work of Eugene Labiche, a nineteenth- century French comedy-writer were performed. Staff members Philip David and Wendy Smith were responsible for the production of 'Spelling Mistakes' and 'An Italian Straw Hat' though they acknowledged that it had been a team effort with pupils from all years involved. Margaret Baron, domestic science teacher and KB Edwards, who had taken over responsibility for the geography teaching, organised the making of the costumes.

Much of the religious influences Ardwyn sought to diffuse to its charges were through the statutory morning assemblies and religious education lessons. It is probably true to say that, in what was becoming an increasingly secular world, for many of its pupils these activities were irrelevant but not for all.

> Beynon Davies was thought of as a very strict disciplinarian but I still remember some of his lessons as the place where I learnt truths for the first time. I can picture his face as he tried to impress us with the impact of the name 'Yahweh' for God. I subsequently became a believing Christian in the summer vacation between the lower and upper sixth and have an idea of what Beynon was trying to convey to his naive RE pupils. During my last year in School I led a Bible study group during lunchtime once a week and remember a class full of colleagues. During my years in London as a medical student and later, a small group of ex-Ardwynian Christians used to meet at Westminster chapel to hear Dr Martyn Lloyd- Jones, formerly of Tregaron, preach and would, often as not, spend the remainder of Sunday together. Regulars included, Anne Lewis, Catrin Gapper, Gwen Aaron and myself.[122]

A branch of the Students' Christian Movement was formed in 1967 meeting weekly under the chairmanship of Nesta James. The society was able to attract the local clergy to speak on various topics as well as hearing from missionaries on leave from Singapore and Kenya. Discussions, Bible study groups and religious films also figured in the meetings; many members took time to visit the elderly and lonely.

A D Lewis gave strong encouragement to the development of a Christian ethos in the School, as his comments in the 1966 prize day address indicated.

> In these exciting and in many ways perplexing times I think it is wonderful that so many of our young people do participate in really worthwhile activities, many of them involving direct service to the community; I honestly believe that most of the young people concerned derive their inspiration to help their fellow men from their Christian upbringing. Speaking in Welsh, he thought that the last two lines of the School hymn provided a goal for many Ardwyn children:
> *A gwisg ni oll ag awydd*
> *Gwasnaethu dynol ryw*
> (Dress us all with the desire to serve mankind.)

Alan Rees, at Ardwyn 1963-70, now a hospital consultant, regarded his time in the sixth form to be too heavily focused on academic achievement with no real attempt at a broad education.

> If you had chosen the sciences you could forget about art, literature or politics although D C Chadwick's Use of English course was very stimulating and a breath of fresh air. Ken Jones who supervised the prefect system was an effective buffer between a very regimented, authoritarian Head and the 'little rebels without a cause'. Many of us remember Ken's wise words of counsel with affection.
>
> Nevertheless the School gave me a good start in life. The emphasis on an academic education was probably a product of the natural Welsh emphasis on education, the fact that Aberystwyth is a Town/Gown society and unless higher education was pursued there was little alternative locally other than local government or agriculture.

Rhona Ryle, head girl in 1959, held a contrary view.

> The sixth-form was a very stimulating period. We were encouraged to take a great deal of responsibility. Prefects organised all sorts of functions and ran the whole detention system. We were allowed to replace the ghastly box-pleated tunics and round felt hat for the luxury of grey pleated skirts, thick grey lisle stockings and green berets. Miss Mainwaring went round with her ruler to ensure that skirts were regulation length.
>
> I particularly remember the ritual of assembly. The whole School sat cross-legged in neat rows in the Hall, boys on the right and girls on the left in complete silence. The staff would file in and then the head prefects would march to the Head's study, knock at the door and say 'The School awaits you, sir.' We would then escort him to the Hall where he would conduct assembly-an imposing figure in gown and mortar board.
>
> My parents moved from the town when I was in the lower sixth so I was left in digs on my own. I shall always be grateful for the care and attention I had from the staff at the time. Roy James and Noel Butler made me most welcome in their homes. A D Lewis used to invite me for Sunday lunch and even gave me a glass of sherry on occasions. My feelings for Aberystwyth were so strong that I decided to remain there for university. The town always felt like home to me and that was, I am sure, due to my

happy experiences of Ardwyn. I am also sure that the reason why I and so many former Ardwynians choose to spend their retirement days there is a desire to return to our roots. I realise now what a stable staff the School had; so many of them spent their entire careers at Ardwyn. That surely must have played a large part in laying strong foundations for generations of pupils.

The end of the summer term 1971 marked the closing of an era with the retirement of A D Lewis after seventeen years of service as Headmaster. Magazine editor W John Taylor wrote:

The past seventeen years have seen the School grow in size and stature; there has been an increase of more than two hundred pupils since the 1954 figure of 540. During this period, the Headmaster has been instrumental in acquiring extra land both for the School grounds and the playing fields and it was largely through his untiring efforts that improvements and extensions were made to the inadequate buildings with additions to the C block and the provision of a laboratory block, a dining hall, a library and several mobile classrooms. He, too, is responsible for the attractive appearance of the grounds by his thoughtful planning and judicious purchasing of flowers and plants. Mr Lewis has maintained Ardwyn's strong traditions and high level of attainment in academic, musical and sporting activities: success in public examinations consistently exceed the national averages; the School regularly supplies youth orchestras with fine instrumentalists while Mr Lewis himself fostered choral singing of a high standard. He deserves great credit for his deep concern with the moral education of the pupils and he has instilled in his charges a keen sense of responsibility for the welfare of others, especially the aged, afflicted and infirm. He can be justly proud of his part in initiating and guiding the social services group.

On a more personal level, Mr Lewis was most approachable and sympathetic while refusing to sacrifice the principle of firm discipline. The relationship between him and his staff has been one of mutual respect and esteem. His devotion and attention to his wife, the late Rhiannon Lewis, during her long periods of illness, were a continual source of admiration.

The Headmaster's energies were not confined to Ardwyn; he has played an active part in the life of the community at large. His interest in sailing and good works are combined in his contributions to the Royal National Lifeboat Institution, as a crew member, committee member and sometime assistant secretary, while he is a former Commodore of the Aberystwyth Yacht Club. Services to the UCW include membership of the Court of Governors and the College Council. His devotion to the Welsh language and culture is testified by his work for Urdd Gobaith Cymru; he is now the movement's vice-president. Recently he was chosen as chairman of the Mid-Wales Hospital Management Committee and is a co-opted member of the Cardiganshire Education Committee.

The staff and School take this opportunity of expressing their gratitude to AD Lewis and of wishing him a long and happy retirement with good health and plenty of fine weather for his great interests-farming and sailing.

AD Lewis owed a great debt of gratitude to RJ Lloyd, appointed his deputy in 1964.

In addition to being an inspirational teacher, Dick Lloyd had extraordinary powers of organisation to which AD Lewis and his successor CG Suff gave free rein.

> There was Maldwyn (assistant groundsman) who would great me cheerfully every morning at the School gates. One morning however the cheer was replaced with a scowl. I asked him what was wrong. He nodded towards the Headmaster's house. 'Its him, he has just said', "Maldwyn, brush that drive, trim that hedge, cut that lawn and clean up that garden. Then come and see me after prayers and I'll give you the day's work". No sooner had he said that we both burst into roars of laughter.[123]

W Beynon Davies also retired in July 1971 after spending 27 years at Ardwyn. Appointed in 1944 to teach Latin, he took charge of Scripture teaching in 1948 and from 1959 had been head of the Welsh department. For a time towards the end of the war he had coached rugby. Throughout his time in the School he had been an inspiring and gifted teacher if a little formidable. The School Magazine carried a tribute written by two of his colleagues Gareth Emanuel and Donald Evans.

> His concern for the well-being and education of the pupils has never been confined to classroom teaching; the continued success of the eisteddfod, the Welsh Night, Magazine and other activities have been principally due to his energy and enthusiasm. His dedication to work and duty, his wide knowledge and scholarship and his love of all things Welsh will be missed. We thank him for his unremitting service and wish him many years of good health and happiness.
> *'O quid solutis est beatius curis !'*

Ceri Davies, head boy in 1963-64, now a senior lecturer in Classics at the University of Wales, Swansea, owes 'an immense debt of gratitude' to Beynon Davies.

> He ranks among the greatest interpreters of literature whom I have known at any level. No-one was under any misapprehension that, with Beynon Davies in the School, Welsh was a subject which mattered. Indeed, he put the WJEC to shame by rejecting their inadequate 'O' level syllabus in Welsh literature and offering his own much more demanding and worth-while course. So we read a selection of medieval Welsh prose and some of Dafydd ap Gwilym's *'cywyddau'* for 'O' level, along with some of the best of more modern literature. 'You read Shakespeare and Hardy in English literature', he said. 'You must read their equivalents in Welsh.' I had no doubt that, along with Greek and Latin, Welsh would be my third 'A' level subject. During those two sixth-form years to listen to Beynon Davies expounding literature was a cultural experience in itself. His asides opened up all sorts of vistas, and the care with which he marked our essays revealed the man's stature as a teacher. He was not one who would abide laziness in any pupil; but he had the right to speak, because he worked so hard himself. His many writings and learned publications bear eloquent witness to his commitment to his subject and to the stature of his scholarship.

C. G. Suff, B.A., Headmaster 1971-73.

CHAPTER FIVE

THE CHARLES G SUFF YEARS

1971 - 73

Charles G Suff became the fifth Headmaster of Ardwyn in what was the School's seventy-fifth year. Hailing from Alltwen in the Swansea Valley, he had a distinguished career in both academic and sporting activities at University College, Swansea. An honours graduate in history, Charles Suff went on to research under Professor Glanmor Williams, the history of Swansea between 1660 and 1835. He represented his college at rugby, cricket and badminton and was an opening bat for the University of Wales XI. After teaching posts at Holywell and Bishop Gore, Swansea he joined the staff of Trinity College, Carmarthen where he held the position of senior lecturer until his appointment to the Ardwyn Headship.

Acknowledging the 75th anniversary of the foundation of the School, Charles Suff wrote in the *Ardwynian*:

> We honour the founders of the School and those who followed in their steps. We also trust that in the 1970s we can maintain their ideals of education in its fullest sense and even add a few ideals of our own.
>
> In an article in the Jubilee Magazine (1946), the Headmaster (DC Lewis) expressed a wish that a comprehensive school be built in Aberystwyth and stated that 'this would require a new school built on a more suitable site'. It seems likely that this wish will be fulfilled in the not too distant future. Whatever happens to Ardwyn in the reorganisation, we hope that its tradition will form a solid and realistic foundation for the future of secondary education. The editor of the Jubilee Magazine concluded his article on 'Ardwyn 1896-1946' with the words-'Long may Ardwyn flourish'. In this 75th anniversary year, may we amend this phrase and express the hope that 'the spirit of Ardwyn' will flourish in the years to come.

The new Headmaster was taking over at a time when the future of secondary education in the area was in the balance. Much of his time in the remaining two years of Ardwyn would be taken up with resolving the many problems posed by reorganisation. Plans for that were still in a state of flux and reflux.

At his first PTA meeting in November 1971 C G Suff emphasised the value of cooperation between parents and staff and invited parents to call on him if there were any problems. 'The aim of the School is not to be simply a "nine to four workshop" but rather a way of life in which each child can reach full potential.' The Director of Education, Dr J Henry Jones who was due to retire at the end of the academic year, reported on the current state of the plans for re-organisation. In May 1971 the education committee had agreed that a senior comprehensive school be established on the

Ardwyn site and a junior comprehensive on the Dinas site with a new bi-lingual school for 450 pupils to be built with the sum of £285,000 which had become available from the D E S. A further sum of £300,000 had been requested to modify the existing schools. Dr Jones added that the Secretary of State for Wales had praised the introduction of Welsh-medium secondary schools in Flint and Glamorgan and this was the approved policy of the Cardiganshire education committee; the scheme would have to be completed by 1973. PTA chairman CH Houlder wondered whether the wishes of the parents had been followed as the situation had been altered since the questionnaire had been completed. There were many other expressions of concern but a proposal to stage a further meeting for a full discussion was not favoured.

By May 1972 re-organisation plans had again been modified. More money had become available from the DES to build additional facilities on the Dinas site for a unitary English-medium comprehensive school while the Ardwyn site would accommodate the Welsh bilingual school. Phasing would start in September 1973 to be completed in two years.

W J Phillips, who had been deputy director of education since 1965 succeeded Dr Henry Jones as director in 1972. To him fell the onerous task of implementing the reorganisation. That the transition was smooth and generally trouble free is a tribute to his organisational powers. He had the foresight to involve the staff of the schools in his plans. They in turn were eager to use their professional expertise in the design and equipping of laboratories and other specialist rooms. With his technical and design skills, craft specialist Idwal Davies, appointed an additional deputy head in 1972, also played a vital part in the planning stages.

With the reorganisation plans finally determined, the work of the School continued as in previous years. An innovation in January 1972 was the visit of a group of American girls from the Sandford School, Ohio. These pupils, forming the Sanford Bell Choir gave a concert which comprised classical music, traditional songs and novelty numbers. An enthralled audience were generous in their acclamation of this entertaining and convivial group. To reciprocate, Ardwyn pupils staged a *Noson Lawen* with harp and piano playing, singing and dancing.

There was genuine regret when R D James was forced to resign on health grounds at Christmas 1971. He had been on sick leave for more than a year.

> The departure of Robert David James, known to all as Roy, after spending the whole of his teaching career at Ardwyn, is a great loss to the School. A dedicated, erudite and inspiring teacher, deeply interested in human geography, he is largely responsible for the initial encouragement and subsequent success of numerous lecturers and teachers of geography in departments at university and school level. But he also contributed widely to the corporate life of the School, notably in sport where his profound knowledge of both rugby and cricket enabled him to recognise and develop talent with skilful coaching. He overcame the disability of a war-time injury on the cricket field, where he bowled at a vicious speed off a short run, broke many bowlers' hearts at the crease and proved a dextrous catcher in the slips. His expenditure of time and effort, organising and inspiring Ardwyn cricket is much appreciated. In addition to his aca-

The Charles G. Suff Years — 1971-1973

Senior Netball Team 1971
Eryl Davies, Carolyn Weston, Angela Nelson
Kay Morris, Lindy Martin, Sian B. Davies (Capt.), Nona Davies, Sian Roberts.

Senior Hockey Team 1970–71
Eryl Davies, Jane Rosser, Simone Ryley, Angela Nelson, Pam Bowen, Eleri Morgan
Valerie Cowan, Sian B. Davies, Sian Roberts (Capt.), Nona Davies, Lindy Martin.

Sian Roberts, Nona Davies, Valerie Cowan with Senior Girls' County Athletic Cup, College Track, May 1971. Ardwyn girls won three sections out of four.

Nona Davies winning the 100m Senior Girls' event at the County Sports, UCW Track, May 1971.

demic and sporting prowess, his breadth of knowledge, his sense of humour, and his sparkling wit made him a superb raconteur and after-dinner speaker, while the mens' staffroom regularly rocked with laughter when Roy was in full spate.[124]

R D James died on 24 March 1973 whilst visiting his beloved family home at Aberdare. He passed away still asking about that afternoon's rugby international. The sad news brought sorrow to the School and town alike for he was widely known, extremely popular and well loved for his enthusiasm, spirit and humour. Roy lived a full life and excelled in everything he set out to do.

The impending closure of Ardwyn was not allowed to disrupt the well established routine of the School.

The 1972 Eisteddfod, the first to be arranged by the new head of Welsh, Mari Carter, was a triumph for Odette Jones; as well as leading Powys to their second successive victory, she conducted the winning choir, won the girls' solo and piano duet with Linda Thomas. Later that year, Odette gained a choral scholarship to the Royal Holloway College, London. Powys won the Edwards Eisteddfod Cup for a third successive year in 1973, compensating for their lack of success between 1952 and 1971

After successes in School eisteddfodau over many years, Geraint Hughes of Bow Street, gave Ardwyn another 'first' at the Bangor National Eisteddfod in 1971 when he won the scripture recitation competition in the 12-16 age group. The following year at the Haverfordwest festival he went even better winning two first places in recitation events. To add to the joy, Elysteg Edwards also gained a first prize in the folk-song solo 12-16 age group.

Marian D Jones also achieved a national distinction by winning a first prize in the 1972 *Western Mail* St David's Day essay competition. Her essay, written in Welsh, was re-printed in the *Ardwynian* of that year.

The Christmastide School concert, so long a feature of the School was as successful and popular as ever. As well as a varied programme of vocal items, there were performances by the octet wind ensemble, junior and senior girls' choirs and a sixth form choir. The School orchestra had never been stronger, totalling almost fifty members. Indeed due to the increase in numbers a new junior orchestra had been formed. As many as forty-five pupils belonged to the county orchestra, which under the expert direction of the county music organiser Alan Wynne Jones practiced fortnightly at Aberaeron. An annual course was arranged each Easter culminating in a highly successful concert at the Great Hall, Penglais. In its last year, Ardwyn provided the leader of the county orchestra, in Andrew Pearson who had contributed greatly to the School's musical activities. A record number of seven pupils and a former pupil were selected for the National Youth Orchestra of Wales to maintain an eighteen year representation. Success would not have come without the dedication of the music staff and it must be said, the resolution and perseverance of the musicians and the support and sustenance of parents.

Many other individuals attained success in various activities.

For the first time in its history, an Ardwyn boy gained selection for a Welsh soccer team while still a pupil. David Pugh became a youth international, playing against Ireland in January 1972; a proud Headmaster presented him with his 'cap' in morning

The History of Aberystwyth County School (Ardwyn) 1896-1973

Wyn Owen Evans

receiving his Welsh Youth Cap from C. G. Suff, Headmaster, 1973.

David Pugh

represented Wales Youth v Ireland at Wrexham, 29th January, 1972. Wales won 3-1.

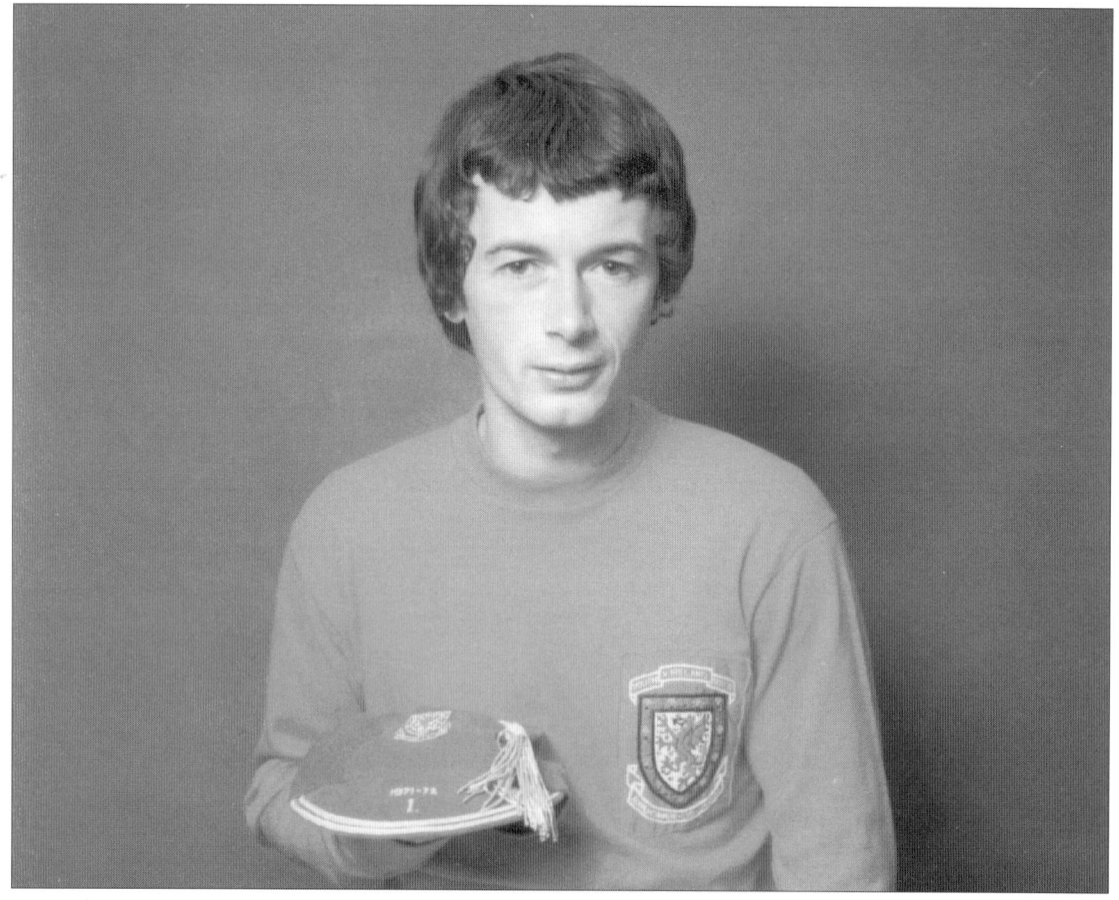

The Charles G. Suff Years — 1971-1973

Noel Davies

Welsh School's Cap (under 15 years) Rugby Union Wales v. England, January 1972.

assembly. At the young age of sixteen years, David was a regular member of the Town XI and had made a strong contribution to sport in School.

The following year Wyn Evans continued the trend, gaining selection as a goal keeper for the Welsh youth against Scotland. He went on to gain two more caps that season and attracted the attention of Liverpool and West Bromwich Albion.

For the record, the following former pupils had previously gained youth soccer caps shortly after leaving School: John D Jones (1950), Ronnie Smith (1951), Ronald Thomas (1953), Dyfed Elias (1956).

For the first time since 1954, an issue of the *Ardwynian* (the last edition) carried an account of the activities of a School soccer team. The Headmaster was thanked for permitting the formation of a senior soccer XI; captained by Stuart Sherman, the side had drawn with Machynlleth, who in days gone by had always provided the sternest of tests, and had beaten Llanidloes 3-1. The hope was expressed that soccer would be continued in future years, with a return to former glories and perhaps more international honours.

C G Suff who had been appointed headmaster-elect of Penglais School had informed the Governors that soccer would be played alongside rugby and paid tribute to the work of the Mini-Minor league in catering for more than 500 boys who played in the league.

Despite having played rugby since the Thirties and exclusively since 1954, Ardwyn had never produced a schoolboy international rugby player until Noel Davies won selection for the Welsh Schools' under 15 year group against England in 1973. A coach-load of enthusiasts travelled to Cardiff to give him support. Ardwyn teacher Ken Jones, who had been the first Cardiganshire teacher to be elected to the Welsh Secondary Schools Rugby Union committee, became its chairman in the 1971-72 season, an honour richly deserved for his tireless work in that sphere. Although there were several near misses, Ardwyn was never able to produce a W S S R U under 18 year group international.

Not for the first time, the School magazine took pride in recognising the achievements of pupils who had gained distinctions in their youth movements out-of school. Eirwen Davies, Lyn Spencer Lloyd and Anna Sabacchi joined the elite group who had been awarded the Queen's Guide certificate, the highest honour in the Girl Guide movement.

In each of the last two years of Ardwyn, a pupil gained the coveted Evan Morgan scholarship of the U C W Aberystwyth. Paul Nantlais Williams, took up his in 1972 and subsequently gained a first class honours degree in philosophy despite very poor health. Ann Eleanor Evans however had to refuse her scholarship on gaining an entrance award to Girton College, Cambridge to read Classics. Huw Rhisiart Davies secured an entrance scholarship to Manchester University in 1973.

Huw Madoc Davies was in the penultimate cohort of Ardwynians to sit ordinary level examinations in 1972; it was as a Penglais pupil based at the old Ardwyn site that he gained advanced level qualifications which took him to UC Cardiff and a first class honours degree in chemistry. After a PhD at Norwich, he joined the brain-drain to the United States. In 1995, still in his forties, he was appointed to the chair of organic chemistry in the University of Buffalo, New York State. As a synthetic organic chemist he builds molecules into complex structures which may have useful biological properties. His work in developing a synthetic medication for cocaine addiction has attracted millions of dollars in federal and private aid.

Ald D Rees Morgan, elected to the governing body in 1927, was for twenty years its chairman until his retirement in 1961. He was succeeded by former Ardwynian, Ald Mrs G C Evans who held office until reorganisation in 1973. Both gave great service and leadership, and strongly supported successive Headmasters in all their aspirations, particularly in the fight for additional buildings and new School premises. They were aided by Governors who sought to do their utmost for the School and the records indicate that harmony and cooperation prevailed, in contrast to the early years when it seemed that some were intent on promoting themselves rather than the welfare and progress of the School.

At the penultimate meeting of the Governors in March 1973, the chairman thanked the Ardwyn PTA for their gift of £250 saying 'We are very conscious of the good support they give.' The Headmaster remarked 'PTAs are often accused of interfering, but we work very cordially at Ardwyn and get on very well. I think we can develop further the PTA relationship.'

The Headmaster reported that 56 pupils had applied for university and 53 had been conditionally accepted. Others had been accepted at polytechnics and colleges of higher education.

At the close of the 1971-72 session, J Cecil Goodwin who, for eighteen years, had been head of the botany department, left to take up the post of schools service officer in biology at the National Museum of Wales. Reference has already been made to the contribution he had made to fostering many extra-curricular activities notably photography, angling, and fly-tying. He had created a naturalists' paradise in the dairy buildings, where the emerging concept of environmental conservation had been developed. In a national competition organised by the Institute of Biology entitled 'The Countryside in Winter', the sixth form botany class had gained first prize and their entry exhibited at the National Library and the National Museum of Wales where it formed part of a larger 'Man and the Countryside' exhibition. The same group of pupils gained a second prize in a competition again organised by the Institute of Biology with the theme 'Nature Conservation in the School area.' In conjuction with the School camera club and as part of their advanced level studies, pupils were preparing an ecological survey of the sand dunes at Ynyslas with a view to producing a tape-slide lecture pack for the use of future A-level classes.

Mari Carter, appointed in 1957 to the Welsh department, left at Easter 1973 to join the UCW administrative staff as a translator. Her replacement, Mary Davies, was the last of over 200 entries on the register of teaching staff.

W Leslie Davies, who had been head of Classics since 1949, was taken seriously ill during the last year of Ardwyn and after a courageous fight died the following year.

> When I started my third year, Leslie Davies became my Latin teacher, and my interest in the language and in the Ancient World in general grew apace. I suppose he for his part, must have seen some promise in me, because after about half a term, he approached me and said that he understood that I was the pupil who had expressed an interest in beginning Greek. If I was still so inclined, he was willing to teach me during some spare minutes he might have. And so began my learning of the second of the classical languages. In Forms 4 and 5 Leslie Davies secured some hours on the timetable for Greek, and I enjoyed my individual 'tutorials' with him. I continued with both Latin and Greek into the sixth form by which time Leslie Davies was joined by an immensely able colleague in the person of Gareth Emanuel. Classics became my subject at university, and has provided me with my bread and butter ever since. I have often asked myself what was the secret of Leslie Davies' success as a teacher. He was by no means a popularizer. I think some pupils found his method of teaching too demanding. There was also about him a shyness, not to say a remoteness, of character. I could not say that, even at the end of my time at Ardwyn, I knew him well. But I have never met his equal as a teacher of language. He had a remarkable gift for imparting understanding of philological principles to those who were interested enough to try to follow him, and his sensitivity to the complexities of the two classical languages gave me-and several others before and after me-a priceless foundation for our further studies. He seemed to assume that I would go on with Greek and Latin in the sixth form, and somehow it never occurred to me to do otherwise. In my sub-

sequent work I have studied and written about writers from Wales who wrote in Latin (especially during the Renaissance) or who were interested in the classical tradition. I was also a member of the New Testament and Apocrypha panel of translaters for *Y Beibl Cymraeg Newydd* (The New Welsh Bible), published in 1988. These pieces of work are all, at least in part, expressions of what I owe to Leslie Davies and Beynon Davies for what they gave me.[125]

The 1972 School play was a comedy by Robert Bolt, 'The Thwarting of Baron Bolligrew' performed on two evenings in May in the U C W examination hall. Produced by Phillip David of the English department, the play starred Richard Morris, Glyn Edwards, Paul Convery Dyfed Bowen, Liz Pearce and Jonathan Thomas. with a further cast of twenty-four.

For its last play, the School presented Nikki Marvin's 'The Legend of Scarface and Blue Water' to packed audiences for four performances in April 1973 in the newly opened Theatr y Werin. The *Cambrian News* critic considered the play 'an excellent choice, for it involved a very large number of the pupils and by its use of several media -music, dancing, mime as well as speech- made a fitting climax to the School's theatrical tradition of presenting over the years, Gilbert and Sullivan as well as 'straight' plays.'

The *Ardwynian* report claimed that the production had thoroughly disorganised the spring term.

> Even the safety of home was challenged as frantic souls were chased away from their mothers' linen cupboards where they were rummaging for the enormous quantities of sheets needed to clothe a cast of ninety-six. Aberystwyth's chemist shops soon ran out of brown, green and autumn gold dyes and weary assistants in the dressmaking shops are still reaching for rolls of inch-wide tape for headbands and trimmings every time they see an Ardwyn uniform.
>
> The sets for the play were particularly beautiful and are a credit to the skill and inventiveness of Hywel Harries and his team of helpers. The stage was a whirl of colour and movement as the technical facilities of the theatre were used to the full. The 'flying' of the totem pole was an unparalleled success with the younger members of the audience. The School was fortunate in having the specialised talents of E Jones Davies and a parent, M V Johnston, whose music and dance sequences made this play so delightfully different from most other schoolplays. The music was in part, written by fourth-form music pupils, Meryl Goodwin, Catrin Roberts, Wyn Thomas, and Dawn Mills and was scored by Betty Jones Davies, the School's head of music, who also wrote much of the music herself. The School orchestra performed with notable success on all four occasions.
>
> Ken Loates' skill in teaching judo has now received the town-wide acclamation it deserves since the stunning fight sequence between Dancing Bear and Grey Hawk was seen on the stage -the first action seen by the audience as the curtain rose.

Tribute was paid to the producer Jennifer L John of the English department whose indefatigable energy and unfailing enthusiasm provided the inspiration for a show worthy of Ardwyn's final year. The entire production personified the 'Ardwyn spirit' which had prevailed throughout its seventy-six year history. The many members of staff, pupils, and parents who had worked so hard at a variety of tasks and whose cooperative efforts had achieved a concordance which could only result in a triumphant success.

The opening of Theatr-y Werin on the Penglais campus in September 1972 provided a great cultural benefit to the town and from the first week, Ardwyn pupils eagerly became involved in its Saturday morning drama classes. Having suffered from the lack of a suitable hall and stage facilities in School, Ardwynians were at last able to gain new skills in many aspects of drama production. As well as acting, there was the opportunity to manipulate sound and lighting effects, building and painting scenery and the fun of using make-up. Others found satisfaction in ticket selling and ushering the public to their seats. The 'Scarface' production was just the first in a long line of similar enterprises staged by local schools; the theatre had finally filled a void in the cultural life of the district.

While he had become a familiar face on the television screen as a newscaster, former Ardwynian John Edmunds was also a distinguished scholar who had translated from the French a number of classical works by Racine, Corneille and Moliere. Two had been broadcast and stage productions were planned for the Bristol 'Old Vic' and Birmingham in which John Edmunds would appear.
In March 1973, the School received a visit from Dr Edmunds, accompanied by the actress Rosalind Shanks. The visit had been arranged by his former English teacher at Ardwyn, Gwyneth Mainwaring. The audience of sixth formers and staff were thrilled by the performance of prose, poetry and drama readings.

In recognition of Ardwyn's last year as a grammar school, a team was entered for the B B C's 'Television Top of the Form'. Carys James, Annette Jones, Alun Edwards and Gareth Price were seen on television on April 8 1973. Despite the encouragement of a coachload of supporters taken to Cardiff, the team lost to Whitchurch High School in the first round by 63 points to 56 in a closely contested free- scoring quiz.

As a result of the enthusiasm and vision of the members of the Ceredigion Antiquarian Society, a museum was established in Aberystywth and housed for ten years in Vulcan Street. Its curator was Dr John Owen a former Ardwynian. In 1982 the museum moved into the restored Edwardian Coliseum theatre to house the growing collection. As a result of the dedicated work of Dr John Owen, the Ceredigion Museum has become a popular tourist attraction with its displays of archeology, local folk-life, a cottage of 1850, agriculture, geology, dairying and various crafts as well as changing exhibitions allowing artists and others to display their work.

The Aberystwyth Yesterday exhibition has delighted thousands of visitors and locals for over two decades. The collection, amassed by former Ardwynian Margaret Evans (Bowyer) and located in the first floor hall above the railway station, consists of thousands of items representing the town's development over a century and a half and is still growing. In recognition of her diligent community work, Margaret was awarded the M B E.

Charles Suff, like his predecessor, strongly encouraged the charity and community service activities of his pupils. The social service group, mainly sixth-formers, continued to support a wide range of charities; in the last two years nearly £1,200 was raised in various ways. Long standing activities such as helping at the WRVS hospital canteen and cleaning the League of Friends bus continued as well as staging concerts at the Deva, Avondale and Bodlondeb homes for the aged. Regret was expressed at the death of an old friend, Mrs Didier. This lady had been constantly visited by members of the group led by Andrew Lewis and had played an important role in her life in her final years.

Perhaps it is not generally known that the now flourishing 'Radio Bronglais' was set up in 1972 as the Bronglais Hospital Radio Service run by a group of fifteen Ardwynians helped by a few students of the UCW. In the early days it broadcast four nights a week, two nights being devoted to patients' requests, one to a selection of music chosen by the DJ himself and the fourth night, in conjunction with the 'Talking Newspaper', a taped version of the *Cambrian News* was played.

In the late Sixties, when the LEA developed a careers advisory and youth employment service, M Wyn Richards took on the responsibility of careers teacher at Ardwyn and organised, in conjunction with the county careers officers, the first careers convention in March 1968. Following the success of the first convention, it was repeated in May 1973, with more than fifty advisors representing almost the whole range of possible careers. Being able to obtain first hand information from experts in a particular field was of great benefit and a number of young people were set on the road to their chosen career. Wyn Richards was able to develop a comprehensive careers library at the School and was available to offer vocational guidance and provide an effective link with the County advisory service.

School excursions were continued with visits in the summer of 1972 to Norway led by RJ Lloyd and IL Davies, while E Jones Davies was responsible for a School contingent on a county organised visit to the Saltzburg music festival. The following summer, Interlaken was the location for a party of 84 pupils and staff who flew from Cardiff to Zurich. This was officially the last Ardwyn trip although pupils had been saving for many months before embarking on a cruise in December 1973 to Greece which involved an outward flight to Naples and a return flight from Tangier. In between there were opportunities to see Stromboli, Vulcano, Katakolon, Athens and Palma, Majorca. One cannot help but contrast these visits made by pupils in the last years of Ardwyn with those taken more than seventy years earlier, when a School excursion meant a picnic in Rhydyfelin or Llyfnant Valley.

By 1972 plans were underway to establish a town twinning between Aberystwyth and St Brieuc. Over the Easter weekend a number of Ardwyn juniors who played soccer in the mini-minor league, visited the picturesque Breton city reputedly named after a Cardiganshire Saint 'Briog'. Ardwynians encouraged the link by corresponding with pupils in the *Lycee Rabelais*. At Easter of the following year Ardwyn was well represented at the inaugural twinning ceremony when an official party from St Brieuc visited the town. Many pupils acted as hosts to the visitors and played in the sporting fixtures which had been arranged. At the twinning ceremony W John Taylor, teacher of French, translated the official speeches and read the French version of the address delivered by the mayor of Aberystwyth. E W Williams, head of French, introduced, in French, Welsh and English, the musical items at a celebration concert at the King's Hall. Art teacher Hywel Harries was commissioned to provide the official gift presented to the official St Brieuc delegation - a fine painting of the Aberystwyth harbour at low tide. It is satisfying that the link between the two towns has lasted for more than twenty years.

The first rugby XV were also making contacts with overseas countries. In the 71-72 season touring sides from Paris and British Columbia were welcomed and defeated. On a visit to London to see the England -Wales game, a match with Beverly High School was fitted in and ended in a convincing win of 34-0. In the following season, two events stood out. The first tour abroad, to Czechoslovakia where both games, in Morovia and Prague ended in wins for Ardwyn. The only regret was that the stay in Prague could not have been longer. The other event was the award of a junior schoolboy cap to Noel Davies previously instanced.

In the last two years, the fortunes of the hockey team did not change. Although Sian Roberts, Sheila Cowan and Jane Rosser deservedly gained selection for the county XI, only two wins were gained by the senior eleven.

In keeping with their outstanding record from the early Sixties, the senior netball team suffered just one defeat in the same period, which meant that in the eleven-year spell since 1962, four games had been lost and their record of victories in the county tournament had been extended to twelve years.

In the penultimate year the cricketers played ten matches, in the previous seven years the average number of games played per season was just over five. Andrew Lewis, the captain reported a renewal of interest; two games were won and Simon Hill and Alun Edwards topped the batting and bowling averages respectively.

In 1972, for the first time ever, the School sports had to be abandoned due to bad weather. However the girls won twelve events in the County championships and the senior girls' shield. Five girls represented the county at the national meeting. There was no record available of the boys' results. Sian Roberts was the outstanding sports woman of her era; she captained the hockey and netball teams and won the 80 m hurdles, high jump and javelin at county level. Ardwyn can also claim to have nurtured Jane Lloyd Francis who was emerging as a talented hurdler and high jumper having overcome a serious leg injury a few years earlier. In 1974, as a Penglais pupil she represented Wales in a senior international in the hurdles, the following year won the high jump at the Welsh Games with a record of 1.58 m. In 1978, at 21 years of age, Jane won the high jump at the Welsh AAA championships for the third successive year, broke her own high jump record with a leap of 1.70m and equalled the Welsh record. Her feat almost earned qualification for the Commonwealth Games. As a student at Loughborough university she won the British university and Welsh pentathlon (high jump, long jump, shot, 100m hurdles and 800m) and between 1974 and 1979 represented Wales in the hurdles, high jump and pentathlon. If this was not enough, Jane added the javelin and

200m to her repertoire and in 1979 competed for Wales in the heptathlon ! Having spent five years at the School before reorganisation, Ardwyn can rightly claim her and add her name to the roll of the athletic elite.

Another future international athlete Ieuan Ellis, was at Ardwyn for one year before becoming a Penglais pupil. Like Ardwynians of an earlier era he benefited from training with the Aber AC, but his mentor was Dic Evans. A rigorous training programme brought success on the track, cross-country and road, as a schoolboy and later as a senior. After winning his first Welsh cross-country vest in 1977 as a sixth former, Ieuan represented Wales eight times in the world cross-country championships as well as on the track at 5,000 m and 10,000 m. He was placed eighth in the 1986 London marathon and qualified for the Welsh team in the Commonwealth Games when he was placed seventh; he also ran for Great Britain in marathon events. After running his fastest ever marathon in Beijing in 2 hours 13 minutes 21 seconds, Ieuan won the inaugural Kathmandu marathon in 1993. He claims that his success at running was due to an aversion to playing rugby, being the smallest in his year. He enjoyed the 'punishment' of lapping the playing field while his fellows wallowed in the mud.

In his editorial in the last issue of the *Ardwynian* 1972-73. W John Taylor wrote:

> Ardwyn Grammar School ceases to exist at the end of the present school year. It is a time of sadness and nostalgia, of apprehension, hope and expectation. It is a time for looking back-to the proud traditions and achievements of more than three-quarters of a century. It is a time for looking forward-to fresh opportunities and success in the two new schools which come into being in September 1973. Let us hope that both Penglais (English-medium comprehensive school) on the present Dinas site and Penweddig (Welsh-medium comprehensive school) which will inherit the present Ardwyn buildings, will be able to establish and maintain reputations and traditions to rival Ardwyn's proud record.
>
> The present magazine is the last *Ardwynian* ever to appear, and is a final, permanent record of the achievements and activities of the School as it nears its demise. Past numbers bear witness to the success of Ardwyn pupils in all walks of life, with reference to many distinguished names in academic, cultural, religious, political and sporting activities, all bringing honour and credit to the School. May these people, along with the traditions and reputation of Ardwyn, long be remembered with pride and affection.

In the same issue, the Headmaster, CG Suff wrote:

> As the last Headmaster of Ardwyn, I am indebted to my predecessors. The variety of their contributions created a secure foundation for the new educational developments and one can look forward with confidence to the schemes of 1973 with the knowledge that a firm educational foundation has been built up over the years. In this the School has justified its motto *'Nerth Dysg ei Ymdrech'*.
>
> However Heads may come and Heads may go, but the stability of a school, as AD Lewis maintained, depends on the quality and degree of continuity of its staff. Ardwyn has been very fortunate in its staff and I have been fortunate in my present

staff. Words cannot really express the extent of my gratitude to the staff and in particular to my deputies, RJ Lloyd, GM Mainwaring and Idwal Davies. I have also been extremely fortunate in my Governors; over the years they have worked ceaselessly for Ardwyn and have given me every support in implementing improvement schemes and educational innovations. No Head could wish for a better chairman of Governors than Mrs GC Evans, she has steered each meeting with skill and good humour during the last critical years in the history of the School.

Now that plans for the reorganisation of secondary education have been officially approved, seventy-six glorious years of Ardwyn have come to an end. May I re-iterate the hope expressed in last year's School Magazine that the 'spirit of Ardwyn' will continue to flourish in years to come. Let us have faith in our new schools and wish them every success. 'Tomorrow to fresh woods and pastures new.'

Perhaps the last words can be left to one of the most distinguished of Ardwyn's sons.

Looking back at our days at Ardwyn-even in the most objective and critical light- one cannot avoid coming to the firm conclusion that the educational experience we enjoyed, compared favourably with the best that Wales and Britain had to offer. Of course there were more distinguished and expensive institutions, but my own view will always be that the sum total of what Ardwyn had to give us was quite magnificent. The staff were in the main people of outstanding ability and of absolute dedication. Several generations of such people had contributed to an ethos of good learning and God-fearing standards of duty and integrity which equalled academic achievement in importance. I suspect that the size of the School was not altogether irrelevant. It was just big enough for a realistic range of disciplines to be taught, but also small enough for each child and teacher to know one another.

The pride and affection we feel towards Ardwyn is not the product of indulgent sentimentality but is a true assessment of the irredeemable debt of gratitude we all owe to our splendid old School.[126]

Epilogue

A PERSONAL REMINISCENCE BY ARDWYN'S LAST HEADMASTER

C Lloyd Morgan one of my predecessors as Headmaster of Ardwyn, in an article to the Jubilee magazine (1946) claimed that the School had a dynamic quality 'and that it was a quality of such power that a Head was not required to lead; instead he very gladly followed, and at times was willy-nilly swept along by the torrent.'

When I was appointed as Headmaster in 1971, I was more than glad that the special 'dynamic quality' which Major Morgan thought was 'inherent and indestructible' still lived on. Glad -because my appointment came as a surprise not only to me but also, I suspect, to many others in Aberystwyth. Although qualified as a teacher and lecturer with some twelve years experience, I had very little administrative experience. Thus I was thrust onto a sharp administrative learning curve but admirably supported and helped by a dedicated staff and governors who were imbued with a vitality which epitomized Lloyd Morgan's assessment of Ardwyn.

I doubt whether such an appointment could take place nowadays. Here was an 'amateur'- probably one of the last 'amateur' Heads to be appointed in Wales- who had not served an apprenticeship as a deputy head and had not undergone the now seemingly compulsory management training necessary for Heads.

Furthermore, there were no informal interviews prior to the formal interview at Swyddfa'r Sir in Aberystwyth. The interview was professional in every sense but thankfully did not include the psychometric testing devices of the present era.

Having been appointed, I was rushed to be medically examined by Dr A Butler and was taken by the Deputy Director, W John Phillips, to see the School for the first time. As we entered the gates of the School, I remember him saying *'Dyma dy diriogaeth'* (Here is your territory). On that fine May day, I was introduced to R J (Dick) Lloyd (deputy head) and G M Mainwaring (senior mistress) outside the Head's study, followed by a short tour of the school and grounds and also the School House which was to be the family home until 1976. It was a very warm welcome indeed!

My memories of the staff are vivid. In my twenty-five years experience as a Head, I cannot recall a more dedicated, enthusiastic and loyal staff. Ardwyn had cast its magic spell over all of them; they lived for and would have died for the School. It is invidious to single out individuals when the School and I were indebted to all. However, when memories come flooding back, faces appear -associated with the following events which are focused strongly in my mind's eye.

Meeting the Director of Education for Cardiganshire, Dr J Henry Jones, one was confronted by a scholar, a man of letters with a razor-sharp mind. He was a leader but also a friend whose help and guidance I greatly appreciated. It is of interest to note that my letter of appointment from Dr Jones assessed my gross salary in 1971 as £3,475. His successor, W John Phillips was also an able leader who successfully implemented the comprehensive plans for Aberystwyth -which was no mean task.

It was with trepidation that I approached my first School Assembly. Having overcome that hurdle I recall with pleasure those gatherings; they were formal, meaningful occasions with enthusiastic hymn singing of the highest standard. The annual carol service was more than a School event, it was a town occasion which ensured that the large town chapels were 'full to the brim' on those celebration days.

The annual School Eisteddfod was also a great school and town event. However, it was awesome for the Head to chair and lead when the exuberance of the pupils was given full rein.

Remembrance Day services at the King's Hall, attended by members of staff and senior pupils are recalled not only for the solemnity of the occasion but also for the cold blasts of wind that one encountered on the promenade on leaving the service.

The School had a full and active sporting life. Good tennis courts and playing fields enabled a number of pupils to gain county and international honours. However it was my controversial decision which allowed soccer to be played on an inter-school basis during these last years. Even though I am a stalwart rugby supporter, I still believe my decision was justified.

One must not forget the beautiful Ardwyn grounds, meticulously kept by the ground staff. On fine sunny days, it was indeed idyllic to be able to live in the School House and enjoy the grounds after official school hours.

It was a great shock to learn that my appointment also included being chairman of the Ardwyn No 561 Squadron A T C. To a number of pupils, this was an important aspect of their school life. The standard of training and discipline was extremely high which made the squadron rank as one of the best in Wales.

Above all however, the School was about academic work and the standards achieved at Ardwyn were second to none. No praise is great enough for the quality of teaching and guidance given to pupils, supported by the immaculate organizational framework which emanated from the experienced and methodical deputy head-Dick Lloyd. A master time-tabler, I can honestly state that he was the first and the very best deputy in my long career as Headmaster. Ardwyn was synonymous with academic and general educational success. It was an institution treasured by the town of Aberystwyth. Its passing and the establishment of two new comprehensive schools-Penglais and Penweddig was in keeping with the educational ethos of the 1970s. However on reflection, after over twenty years of headship, mainly in comprehensive schools-Penglais and Bishop Gore,

Swansea- I can look back with gratitude on my own educational upbringing in Pontardawe Grammar School and also to my initiation to the headship at Ardwyn. Grammar schools should take pride in their achievements and the opportunities offered to children from a wide variety of backgrounds.

Ardwynians can reflect and bask in the glory of their School. Seventy six years of Ardwyn formally came to an end in 1973 but I have no doubt whatsoever that its spirit, so well captured in its motto *'Nerth Dysg Ei Ymdrech'*, will not only be remembered in Aberystwyth but will live in many a heart world wide.

Charles G Suff

Appendix A

ARDWYN OPERATICS

(including the 1946 Jubilee Magazine article written by
'Alpha' reviewing the productions from 1929 to 1945)

'A significant movement in the training of the young and a happy augury in the future development of operatic and dramatic art in the country'. Such was the Press comment on what was a great innovation for the School in 1929. On the initiative of the Headmaster, DC Lewis, it was decided, that Christmas term, to depart from the usual run of School concerts and to undertake the production of a Gilbert and Sullivan comic opera, the one chosen being 'HMS Pinafore'. It was a great venture and one undertaken with full confidence and by splendid team-work, that confidence was fully justified.

Throughout the term strenuous efforts were made; Charles Clements as musical director, Major HF Stimson as producer and BG Arnold in charge of the dances-what a fine team! They brought out the best of the excellent talents available among the pupils, while SE Thomas and E Forster saw to it that the costumes were worthy of the occasion. Need one say that the performance on 18 Decembers 1929, at the Coliseum, was a great success and it seemed that the new venture was likely to become a permanent feature of our School life. So indeed it has proved, for ever since we have given performances at Christmastide to delighted audiences.

'Pinafore' then became the first of a series-a single performance, which brought a balance to the School treasury of £42 7s 8d. It gave the opportunity to many pupils to make a mark as actors and singers, and to many more to swell the chorus and become acquainted with delightful music and stagecraft.

It is not the intention of this article to enlarge on the performances of individuals in every play in the long series that has been undertaken since that first performance, but merely to let fancy roam, choosing some features which specially appealed. It shall be be a random roaming over the years with certain memories standing out and being duly noted.

The performance of 'Iolanthe' in December 1930 filled the Coliseum for two nights with very appreciative audiences. There was every justification for the appreciation shown of principals and chorus. Memories crowd of David Sansbury as Strephon; Douglas Galloway as Lord Chancellor; Elsie Williams as Iolanthe and Evelyn Lumley Jones as Phyllis. Delightful! That sums up the whole production. Oh yes, it is interesting to note that the orchestra was composed of past and present pupils-really and truly a completely School show.

'The Gondoliers', 1931-the School's most ambitious effort so far, but one which proved well within the powers of the selected party. It added to reputations already made and made new ones. It is here that the School is fortunate in that it can rely on a 'carry-on-section' of experienced pupils while newcomers are being made familiar with the footlights. Of this performance we recall the Press comment: 'The singing, acting, and dancing reached a very high level of excellence and as no expense had been spared in procuring suitable costumes, this most ambitious production rejoiced the hearts of the packed houses and brought well-deserved fame on the fair name of Ardwyn'. It also produced £52 for the School treasury and a delightful soiree-incidentally this became a permanent after-opera feature-for those who took part.

Two nights and a matinee for school children. That was the rule for 'Princess Ida' in 1932 at the Parish Hall. Though there were limitations inspired by the smaller stage, there is no doubt that this was a very pleasing production and one which deserved praise.

'No entertainment associated with the Christmas season at Aberystwyth is anticipated with greater eagerness and enjoyed with greater pleasure than that provided by Ardwyn School before breaking up for the holiday'. That was a comment made many years ago and it is certainly even more true now than ever before. One has only to be present when seats are being booked to realise the wide appeal our operatics have made.

The performance of the 'Pirates of Penzance' in 1933-again in the Parish Hall, was notable in two respects: Major Wheldon of the Welsh department of the Board of Education was a distinguished and appreciative visitor on the second night. Secondly, the singing of Gwyneth Williams as Mabel, was so delightful as to gain for her an audition at the invitation of R D'Oyly Carte. We shall not easily forget her rendering of 'Poor wand'ring one.'

The next play in the series-'The Mikado' 1934 was presented in the Municipal Hall, as the King's Hall was then known. This was an outstanding show, with a first-rate collection of principals and a splendid chorus. We recall the fine performances of Willie J Griffiths as the Mikado, Derek Butler as Ko-Ko, Arvian Jones as Pooh-Bah, Jemuel Edwards (later to be a victim of World War II) as Nanki-Poo, Eirys Thomas as Katisha, and Gwyneth Williams as Yum-Yum. What a fine team and how they captured the audiences! Nearly 3, 000 people paid for admission allowing a gift of £100 to be made to the infirmary.

'Patience', 1935, is associated with the memories of the sweetness of Evelyn Christian as Patience, the dramatic ability of Eirys Thomas as Lady Jane, the fine acting of Arvian Jones as Bunthorne and the delightful singing of the chorus, so ably costumed by Miss Forster.

It had been rumoured that 'Patience' would be the last of our productions, but the demand was so great that rumour became a lying jade, and 'Merrie England' was decided on for 1936 - a break in the G&S series, but a delightful break and what a colourful presentation at the King's Hall and what a financial success. First- rate interpretations were given by Meg Lewis as Queen Elizabeth, Ethel Williams as Bessie, Sheila Budge as Jill-all-alone, and Jeremy Edwards as Raleigh. Incidentally, this was the first appearance of William Roberts as musical director, he having succeeded Charles Clements. A very successful debut for Mr Roberts and continued success for HF Stimson and Miss Arnold.

The years 1937 and 1938 saw the production of some lesser known plays: 'The Rose of Persia' by Hood and Sullivan in 1937, and ' The Sorcerer', preceeded by 'The House with the Twisty Windows' as a curtain- raiser in 1938. The musical plays were produced by the Stimson, Roberts, Arnold team while GM Mainwaring produced the the curtain-raiser. Once again the infirmary benefited to the extent of £75, this being a contribution towards the obtaining of new X-ray apparatus.

The cast of "Patience", 1935.

Left:
Merrie England, 1936.

Right:
Iolanthe, 1930
Phyllis:
Evelyn Lumley Jones

Stephan:
David Sansbury

Below:
HMS Pinafore 1941

John A. Benbow,
Ann Ansley,
David A. Leech,
Mary Benbow,
Humphrey D. Williams,
Elsie Rowlands.

Utopia Limited, 1948
Nia Rowlands, Marian Hughes, Mary Owen, Pam Bilton, Sheila Bumford, Monica Webb.

Left:

The Rebel Maid, 1947

*Meurig Major,
Barbara Rees,
Joseph Torri*

Right:

Merrie England, 1946

*Sir Walter Raleigh: - John Cheshire
Queen Elizabeth: - Beryl Richards*

Another break in the team of producers came in 1939, for Miss Arnold had left and the dances necessary for 'Ruddigore' in that year were arranged by her successor Betty Jones.

The Gilbert and Sullivan cycle had now taken its full turn, and there was speculation as to the next move. Should the opera cease ? Should productions other than G & S be considered ? There is a charm about the work of those composers which never dies and it really was grand to find that the decision was for- repeats. So the new series started in 1940 with 'Iolanthe', after a ten year interval. Newcomers to the stage in no way let the School down, rather did they show that for several years to come, the material for splendid performances was there. Incidentally a brother and sister made reputations, for Mary Benbow as Phyllis and John Benbow as Lord Chancellor, gave fine performances.

HMS Pinafore again was the chosen piece for 1941. Repeat performances, after a lapse of years, usually invite comparisons. We shall refrain from making these and content ourselves with saying that the operatic company reached new heights and reached new records. Nearly £300 was taken and the profits were earmarked to provide a portable stage for use in the gym.

So great has been the reputation gained by these Christmas productions that in 1942, it was decided to book the King's Hall for three nights. Even so, the demand for tickets was so heavy that a special matinee was arranged for school children. Four performances and each one a great success. The opera ? That was the 'Pirates of Penzance'. In this Mair Evans created a precedent for us by being the first girl to take a male role, playing the part of Frederick in fine style. We enjoyed the quiet restrained acting and singing of Gwyneth Davies as Ruth. She was a newcomer who ably performed her part. The 'two veterans of our stage', Mary and John Benbow, were excellent as usual, while the audiences greatly appreciated the performance of Colin Lewis as Sergeant of Police- and what a fine squad he had.

It is really remarkable how the right performers turn up year after year-both for singing and acting. The 'Mikado' in 1943 gave proof of this for John Platt brought the house down with his portrayal of Ko-Ko, while Mair Jones as Yum-Yum thrilled the audience with her delightful singing. Donald Macpherson's Mikado was a polished performance, and Joan Evans as Katisha also impressed. And what a grand chorus.

One's happiest memory of "The Gondoliers' in 1944 centres around the singing of Seymour Evans and Peter Potts as the Duke and Marco respectively, and of Valmai Benjamin as Tessa. Who can forget the stately Gavotte in which the Duke gives a lesson in deportment to Marc and Guiseppe and the Duchess and Casilda ? Or the abandon- and perfect execution- of the Cachucha ?

William Roberts, our music director, left us in 1945 and was succeeded by Beryl Morgan. To her fell the task of preparing for the next opera-'Princess Ida'. It was no small task to undertake, but Miss Morgan soon showed that musically, Ardwyn performances would be maintained at the high level already reached. The work of the principals and chorus was first-rate and she has every reason for satisfaction in this, her first appearance before an Aberystwyth audience. We cannot pass over this play without referring to the singing and acting of John Cheshire as Cyril-the hit of the evening; of John Humphries as King Gama; of Margaret Isaac as Ida and the two sisters, Beverly and Beryl Richards as Lady Blanche and Melissa.

So we come to 1946. Ere this magazine appears the School would have performed 'Merrie England' and present indications show that another great success may be looked for.

And great success it was; the local press reported that the usual high standard of excellence of these annual productions had been maintained on a scale which would have done credit to any professional company.

Some of the highlights of the performance were the rendering of 'Who were the Yeomen' by Islwyn Oliver as Earl of Essex, 'Dan cupid hath a garden' by John Cheshire as Sir Walter Raleigh and 'O who shall say that love is cruel' by Beryl Richards as Bessie Throckmorton. Meurig Magor, who had been called to fill a gap at short notice was commended for his playing of Walter Wilkins.

1947 saw the first performance by Ardwyn pupils of 'The Rebel Maid' (Words: AM Thompson and G Dodson; Music:Montague Phillips) It was reported to be 'enthusiastically received as ever by packed houses at the three evening performances'.

Though all played their part admirably, mention must be made of the central figure-The Rebel Maid- played to perfection by Beryl Richards, for whom the part seemed to have been made, so natural was the charm and loveliness she gave to it. However, it was the three funmakers, Abigail(Barbara Rees), Solomon Hooker (Meurig Magor) and Septimus Bunckle, the inn-keeper (Joseph Torri) who at times, stole the show. Magor in particular was outstanding in all his guises, his singing voice added to the lustre of his performance.

The staging of a lesser known G & S work, 'Utopia Limited' in 1948 was again a new venture. For two nights, the King's Hall was packed and the 'tumultuous applause at the final curtain was well merited'. As King Paramount, Joseph Torri was again well cast, being able to give to the part just the right tinge of assumed dignity, flashes of natural humour or a farcical interpretation of royalty affronted, as the occasion demanded.

The singing of Ronald Miller as Captain Fitzbattleaxe and Beverly Richards as Princess Zara added a weighty contribution to the success of the performance. The reviewer doubted whether Meurig Magor's superb playing of Scaphio could have been bettered even by one more accustomed to the stage.

For the 'coming of age' of the Ardwyn light opera series, 'The Pirates of Penzance' was the choice in 1949-the third occasion for it to be staged by Ardwyn. Gwyneth Mainwaring in her review in the *Ardwynian*, commented that Sullivan wielded the strange power of stilling our critical faculty and filling our memories with melodies that we are unable to forget. Brian Thomas as the Major-General was picked out for 'his brilliantly executed patter-song', as was Brian Martin's 'Policeman's lot is not a happy one'. Eurogwen Davies and Ronald Miller as Mabel and Frederick also gave a memorable rendering of the Roundelay. Sixth-former Gareth Davies was given a special word of praise for his part in the production.

In 1950 the choice was 'HMS Pinafore', the third occasion it had been performed in the series and the first production for the newly appointed music teacher, Gerwyn Thomas. The indefatigable Major Stimson, had been persuaded out of retirement to produce his twenty-second Ardwyn opera.

The hopelessness of the sailor's love for the captain's daughter was well portrayed

*Utopia Limited,
1948*

*Emyr Jones,
Tom Williams,
Francis Edwards,
Peter Hughes,
Ronald Miller,
Brian Thomas*

*Pirates of Penzance,
1949*

*Pirates of Penzance,
1949*

314

with a fine dejected air by Delwyn Tibbott; the scheming of the villain-Brian Martin was executed with conviction. John Carpanini carried the weight of gold braid well. Of the singing, the most powerful was that of John Wintle, but the choruses were well balanced and tuneful. Eurogwen Davies also had power well blended with sweetness while Eirwen Evans gave an unfaltering performance which lent confidence to the rest of the cast.

There was genuine regret when it became known that the 1951 opera 'The Gondoliers'-the twenty-third in the series, was to be the last. The production costs had increased enormously while receipts had diminished. The 1951 production would not have been possible without the support from more than 150 patrons.

Seasoned campaigners Delwyn Tibbot, John Wintle, Brian Martin and Eirwen Evans all gave mature performances while the newcomers to the role of principal, Barbara White, Howys Spencer Lloyd, Anne Devina Evans, Iwan Jones and Ivor Williams all fitted in well. The colourful, energetic dance-the Cachucha, performed by the chorus was one of the highlights.

In 1952 the customary opera was replaced by a very successful Christmas concert. However the following year, in an effort to clear the deficit of the organ fund, it was decided on a final opera production. In the Coronation year of 1953 the choice of 'Merrie England' was appropriate; success was assured when Major Stimson, agreed to be the producer. In an effort to reduce production costs, Violet Jones and her girls made the costumes while Idwal Davies and art teacher Don Harvey organised the making of the sets.

For E Jones-Davies, in her second year as head of music, this was her first experience as musical director of an Ardwyn opera.

The report in the *Ardwynian* written by sixth-former Norma Christie, praised the performance as a whole but considered that Janet Ward-a stately Queen Elizabeth with her rendering of 'O, Peaceful England', was one of the highlights. Sheila Phillips was an appealing Jill-all-alone while William Watkins as Walter Wilkins was the 'comic turn' of the evening; his 'Fish Song' with the girls of the chorus brought repeated applause. Benny Wigley as Raleigh and Brynley Griffiths as Earl of Essex gave skilful portrayals.

So, the Ardwyn operas came to an end. When he initiated them in 1929, did DC Lewis envisage their survival for twenty-four years? The School was fortunate in having a succession of enthusiastic music teachers who were able to obtain the best from their pupils. Then of course there was Major Stimson, responsible for all twenty-four productions. 'The effects of his patient care towards the children, his unerring sense for effective grouping, his enthusiasm and admiration for the work of Gilbert and Sullivan are unmistakable.'

DC Lewis frequently trained the chorus, and members of staff did a great deal of unobtrusive work behind the scenes. Gwyneth Mainwaring and David Sansbury himself a star performer when a pupil, shared the task of libretto director in the later performances. Art teachers with their pupils were responsible for the make-up, PE staff arranged the dance sequences while needlework and woodwork departments had their important parts to play in costume and scenery production. A glance at the opera programmes shows that many former pupils were proud to be part of the orchestra

'Alpha' also gave credit to the pupils who took part.

> They entered fully into the spirit of the productions and spared neither time nor effort to benefit by the instruction given them. Their reward-the appreciation of the audiences, a feeling of having done their best and brought honour to the School.

It could also be added that the stage experience developed their sociability, team spirit and confidence. Another attraction for the principals was of course, missing the Christmas terminal examinations, while all participants had the 'soiree' to savour early the following term.

Merrie England 1953
Earl of Essex, Brinley Griffith
Queen Elizabeth, Janet Ward

Merrie England 1953
Sir Walter Raleigh, Benny Wigley
Bessie Throckmorton, Mererid Phillips

THE SCHOOL AT WORK

Chemistry Laboratory. Form VIA

Domestic Science Room

Art Room

Dining Hall

The Girls Yard c.1939.

The Tennis Courts

Appendix B

STATE SCHOLARSHIP WINNERS

1931 Miriam Davies

1936 Lilian Williams

1939 Gareth Wyn Evans

1942 Evan John (Jack) Jones

1946 Paul Roberts, John E Watkin

1949 William G Edwards

1950 Ronald Miller

1951 Ann Butler, Terry Thorpe Edwards, Daniel Gruffydd Jones

1952 Eleanor Jones, Margaret Meredith

1953 Roger T Griffiths

1955 Michael Blayney

1956 Heather M J Lewis

1957 Alwyn H H Jones

1959 M C Anne Davies, K Ian Evans

1960 Marian E Morgan, David R Clayton Jones

1962 Sian Evans, Roger J Owen

State Scholarships ceased to be awarded after 1962

Appendix C

DANIEL THOMAS SERVICE and LEADERSHIP PRIZE *

DALLEY SERVICE LEADERSHIP PRIZE **

Year	Daniel Thomas	Dalley
1923	Percy Evans -	
1924	W M Whitehouse,	Dorothy Evans
1925	W M Whitehouse,	Gwyneth Davies
1926	T Seaton,	Mary E Lewis
1927	Evan R H Davies,	Eira Lloyd
1928	Ernest George -	
1929	Hywel N Ellis,	Elwyna Thomas
1930	Herman Benson -	
1931	John Edwards,	Gweno Ellis
1932	J Arthur Jones,	Annie Davies
1933	Glanville Griffiths,	Annie Davies
1934	Glanville Griffiths,	Margaret Morgan
1935	W E Griffiths,	Nancy Rees
1936	D Llewelyn James,	Eirys Thomas
1937	Dewi Ellis,	Meg Lewis
1938	Gwilym Williams,	Sheila Budge
1939	Alec Clarke,	Sheila Budge
1940	D Rowland Edwards,	Olwen Jones
1941	Edward Ellis,	Janet Mountford
1942	Evan J Jones,	Menna Davies
1943	Harry Hallam,	Mair Evans
1944	John H Edwards,	Margaret Griffiths
1945	Islwyn Fisher Davies,	Dorothy Vandanelli
1946	Wm J B Richards,	Gwenda James
1947	Gwilym Phillips,	Sheila Green

1948	Tom Williams,	Gwyneth Benjamin
1949	Tom Williams,	Beryl Richards
1950	Ceiriog Evans,	Lilias Edwards
1951	Colin Wooldridge,	Hilary Evans
1952	S Merfyn George,	Eirwen Evans
1953	Ifor Davies,	Enfys Owen
1954	Thomas J Davies,	Janet Ward
1955	William Watkins,	Llinos Phillips
1956	Richard H Edwards,	Heather Lewis
1957	Stuart Jones,	Beti Rowlands
1958	Anthony Russell-Jones,	Gwenda Lewis
1959	Peter D Davies,	Rhona Ryle
1960	D Elwyn Lewis,	Marion E Morgan
1961	Elwyn Elias,	Catrin Gapper
1962	Gerwyn Watkins,	Gwyneth Morse
1963	Thomas Glyn Evans,	Esyllt Beynon Davies
1964	Ceri Davies,	Susan Astley
1965	Dewi Davies,	Delor Jones
1966	Martin Jones,	Nesta James
1967	Richard Cameron Morgan,	Christine Williams
1968	David Hunt,	Nonna Dummer
1969	David Keyse,	Beverly Evans
1970	Elgar Hopkins,	Glesni Roberts
1971	Leslie Williams,	Eleri Morgan
1972	Keith Williams,	Olwen Evans

* C Lloyd Morgan awarded the Headmaster's leadership prize to boys, from 1923 to 1928, after which it became the Daniel Thomas service and leadership prize.

** Irene Dalley, the Headmistress awarded her leadership prize to the girls from 1924 to 1931, thereafter it became known as the Dalley service and leadership prize.

Appendix D

SAMUEL EXHIBITIONERS

1929	Arthur Jones, Gwynne Morgan
1930	Howell Watkins, Douglas Galloway
1931	Howell Watkins
1932	Wm J Griffiths, Bradley Jones
1933	Wm J Griffiths, J Bradley Jones
1934	Wm J Griffiths, Dewi Ellis, David Mason
1935	Dewi Ellis, Iorwerth Isaac
1936	Iorwerth Isaac, D Maldwyn Mason
1937	Elwyn Lloyd Jones, Ninian Lewis, Robert P Williams
1938	Robert Parry Williams
1939	Eddie Ellis, John Mason
1940	E William Jones, Malcolm Wilkinson
1941	George A Holmes, Evan W Jones, Malcolm Wilkinson, Richard W Williams
1942	George A Holmes, Richard Williams, John Ellis Williams
1943	Islwyn Fisher Davies, W T Edwards, Russell Ward, John Watkin
1944	D Teifi Edwards, D Cyril Thomas, Richard J Williams
1945	Ieuan Davies, David Jenkin, Wyn Parry Williams, Ceredig Thomas
1946	John Cheshire, D Maurice Davies
1947	James W Ll Jenkin
1948	Brian Thomas, Daniel Gruffydd Jones
1949	Terry Edwards, Brian Martin

1950	Brian James, Robert Ward
1951	David H Jones, P Eurfyl Owen
1952	William Watkins, Alan Jones
1953	Richard Edwards, Phillip Manning, Alan Parry
1954	Peter Caul, Emyr Winstanley
1955	No record available
1956	Alwyn Jones, Basil Thomas
1957	Anthony Russell-Jones, David Slater
1958	Anthony Ford, Aneurin John
1959	David Thomas, James Robin Thomas
1960	Howard Jones, John Swaffield
1961	Francis M B Carpanini, Richard M Jenkins
1962	Howard C Jones, Philip Henry Jones
1963	Huw Ceredig, Martin Edward Evans
1964	Rhys Jenkins, Gerran Thomas
1965	Lynn Jones, Richard C Morgan
1966	Rhodri Ceredig, David Hunt
1967	John Aaron, R Stephen Evans
1968	Elwyn Isaac, J Alan Rees
1969	No record available
1970	David Richards, Paul Nantlais Williams
1971	Alun Lloyd Edwards, Gareth Roy Edwards
1972	Huw Madoc Lynne Davies, Barry Paul Lionel

APPENDIX E

CHAIRED BARDS OF ARDWYN

1924 Dilys Pugh
1925 Hughie Hughes
1926 Hugh Jones
1927 Idris Thomas
1928 Idris Thomas
1929 Hywel Ellis
1930 Gwen Hughes
1931 Gwen Hughes
1932 Harold Charles
1933 Ivor Snell
1934 Marian Lloyd
1935 Marian Lloyd
1936 John I Hollings
1937 Dd Alun Jones
1938 John I Hollings
1939 Gwladys Hughes
1940 Margaret Bowyer
1941 John Mason
1942 Irfon Williams
1943 Eifion Jones
1944 Mary Humphries
1945 Mary Humphries
1946 Sian Davies
1947 Sian Davies
1948 Sian Davies
1949 Francis W Edwards
1950 Elystan Morgan
1951 Thelma Nelson
1952 Llywela Morgan
1953 Thelma Nelson
1954 Tom Davies
1955 Heather Lewis
1956 Heather Lewis
1957 Gethin Abraham Williams
1958 Gethin Abraham Williams
1959 Brynhild Clapham
1960 Peter Davies
1961 Helen Davies
1962 Peter Davies
1963 Ceri Davies
1964 Clifford Thomas
1965 Dewi Emrys Davies
1966 Katherine Davies
1967 Mair Williams
1968 Mair Williams
1969 Heledd Jones
1970 Stephen Nantlais Williams
1971 Paul Nantlais Williams
1972 Catherine Johnston
1973 Lowri Williams

The eisteddfod cup donated by Prof Edward Edwards was first competed for in 1923. Over 51 years, the cup was won by Arfon on 15 occasions, by Ceredigion 11, by Gwynedd 15 and by Powys 10.

Appendix F

MEMBERS OF THE NATIONAL YOUTH ORCHESTRA OF WALES

1956 Gwenda Lewis

1957 Gwenda Lewis

1958 Gwenda Lewis

1959 Gwenda Lewis, Faleiry Phillips

1960 Gwenda Lewis, Faleiry Phillips, Susan Cox, Julian Clapham, Ceredig Gwyn, D Gruffydd Miles

1961 Ceredig Gwyn, D Gruffydd Miles, Michael Parrott

1962 Ceredig Gwyn, D Gruffydd Miles, Bethan Miles.

1963 Ceredig Gwyn, D Gruffydd Miles, Bethan Miles

1964 Ceredig Gwyn, D Gruffydd Miles, Bethan Miles, Michael Williams, Rhodri Ceredig.

1965 Huw Ceredig, Rhodri Ceredig, D Gruffydd Miles, Bethan Miles, Michael Williams, William Evans, Elsbeth Jones, David Thomas.

1966 Huw Ceredig, Rhodri Ceredig, D Gruffydd Miles, Bethan Miles.

1967 Rhodri Ceredig, Bethan Miles, William Evans.

1968 Rhodri Ceredig, Ann M Davies, Brian Sansbury

1969 Rhodri Ceredig, Ann M Davies, Brian Sansbury.

1970 Arthur G M Davies, Ann M Davies, Brian Sansbury

1971 Arthur G M Davies, Gareth John, Andrew Pearson

1972 Arthur G M Davies, Gareth John, Andrew Pearson.

1973 Fay Evans, Dale Evans, Ruth Walters, Arthur Gwyn Davies, Gareth John, Gareth Price with former pupils Andrew Pearson, Ann Morgan Davies.

APPENDIX G

WELSH SECONDARY SCHOOLS' INTERNATIONALS

1959   Aneurin John CHESS
Paul Edwards ATHLETICS (Shot)

1962   Christopher Loosely ATHLETICS (Mile)
Anna Pugh ATHLETICS (Shot)

1963   Christpher Loosely ATHLETICS (Mile)
Terry James ATHLETICS (Steeplechase)
Anna Pugh ATHLETICS (Shot)

1964   Zena Shattock HOCKEY (v South of England)
Gwynn Davis ATHLETICS (triple-jump)
Terry James ATHLETICS (Steeplechase)

1965   Richard Evans ATHLETICS (Steeplechase)

1966   Richard Evans ATHLETICS (Steeplechase)
Gary Davis ATHLETICS (Mile)

1967   Frank Thomas ATHLETICS (Steeplechase)

1968   Frank Thomas ATHLETICS (Mile)

1969   Verona Davies NETBALL

1971   Brian Williams WSSRU squad

1972   David Pugh SOCCER (Youth v Ireland)
Noel Davies RUGBY under 15 gp v England

1973   Wyn Evans SOCCER (Youth v Scotland)

Appendix H

HEAD PREFECTS

1922-23	W D Percival Evans M Angharad Hughes	1934-35	William J Griffiths Nancy Rees
1923-24	Wallace M Whitehouse Nancy Charman Dorothy G Evans	1935-36	Melvyn Lewis Nancy Rees
1924-25	Wallace M Whitehouse Gwyneth J Davies	1936-37	Dewi M Ellis Ada L Owen
1925-26	Thomas Seaton Mary E Lewis	1937-38	Jack Thomas Meg Lewis
1926-27	Ieuan R H Davies J Eira Lloyd	1938-39	Jim Pinsent Meg Lewis
1927-28	D Ernest George E Brenda Williams	1939-40	D Rowland Edwards Olwen Jones
1928-29	Richard E Thomas David T Davies H Marise Loveday	1940-41	Eddie Ellis Mona Lewis
1929-30	Herman Benson H Marise Loveday	1941-42	Roy Pinsent Menna Davies
1930-31	John Edwards Gweno Ellis	1942-43	Colin Lewis John A Benbow Mair Evans
1931-32	Howell Watkins Annie Davies	1943-44	Harry Hallam Margaret Griffiths
1932-33	Ivor Snell Annie Davies	1944-45	John H Edwards I Fisher Davies Mary J Evans Myrtle Williams
1933-34	Ivor Snell Glanville Griffiths Margaret Morgan	1945-46	I Fisher Davies John Watkin Gwenda James

1946-47	John Edmunds Wyn Parry-Williams Margaret Evans	1961-62	Gerwyn R Watkins Gwyneth Morse
1947-48	Gwilym Phillips Gwyneth Benjamin	1962-63	T Glyn Evans Esyllt Davies
1948-49	Tom Williams Beryl Richards	1963-64	Ceri Davies Susan Astley
1949-50	Norman Nichols Lilias Edwards	1964-65	Dewi Emrys Davies Delor Tudor Jones
1950-51	Colin Wooldridge Gwen Owen	1965-66	T Martin Jones Nesta James
1951-52	Dafydd R Thomas Eirwen Evans	1966-67	Richard C Morgan Christine Williams
1952-53	Brian Martin Enfys Owen	1967-68	David Hunt Nonna Dummer
1953-54	Janet Ward I David Morgan		
1954-55	William Watkins Llinos Phillips		
1955-56	Richard H Edwards Heather Lewis		
1956-57	Colin Creasey Beti Rowlands		
1957-58	Anthony Russell-Jones Gwenda Lewis		
1958-59	Peter Davies Rhona Ryle		
1959-60	Elwyn Lewis Marian Morgan		
1960-61	Elwyn Elias Catrin Gapper		

Appendix I

ARDWYN ANNUAL ATHLETIC SPORTS

	VICTOR LUDORUM	VICTRIX LUDORUM
1927	Goronwy Lewis,	Eira Lloyd
1928	J D Davies,	Gwyneth Owen
1929	George Williams,	Lilian Silver
1930	George Williams,	Nellie Price
1931	Leslie Thomas,	V Davies & K Roberts
1932	Noel Butler,	Gwen Davies
1933	Noel Butler & L Thomas,	Gwen Davies
1934	Derek Butler,	Pegi Davies
1935	Ifan Davis,	E Vera Jones
1936	Danny Lewis,	Pegi Davies
1937	Denis James,	E Vera Jones
1938	R Killin Roberts,	E Vera Jones
1939	R Killin Roberts,	Rona Davies
1940	D Rowland Edwards,	Marjorie Williams
1941	Ken Allen,	Marjorie Williams
1942	Colin Lewis,	Menna Davies
1943	H Hallam,	Barbara Bray
1944	H Hallam & Idris I Jones,	Ellen Watson
1945	Idris I Jones,	Nancy Jeremy
1946	David White,	Joyce Jones & Menna Davies
1947	David White,	Dawn Ramsey
1948	Trefor Evans,	Joyce Jones & Beryl Richards
1949	Meurig Magor,	Beryl Richards
1950	Dafydd Thomas,	Marina Edwards
1951	David Hughes,	Mary Owen
1952	Dafydd Thomas,	Mary Owen
1953	Hefin Elias & John Wintle,	Mary Evans
1954	Geraint Jones,	Mari Jones
1955	Iwan Jones,	Elizabeth Lee
1956	No further awards.	

Appendix J

STIMSON GYMNASTIC CUP HOLDERS

1929 Hywel Ellis & Dick de Lloyd

1930 John Lewis

1931 John C Wilkinson

1932 David Sansbury

1933 Derek Butler

1934 R Nancarrow & R Wilkinson

1935 Melvin Lewis

1936 Dewi Ellis

1937 Ninian Lewis

1938 Gareth Howell & Killin Roberts

1939 Gareth Howell

1940 Kenneth Allen

1941 Colin Lewis

1942 Jim Mitchell & Meirion Morgan

1943 Ifor Williams & John H Edwards

1944 John Cheshire

1945 Wm T Edwards & Eric Morgan

1946 Wynn W Hughes

1947 S. Gassner & B Lewis

1948 Frank Collinson & Tom M Williams

1949 James W Ll Jenkin

1950 Dafydd Rhys Thomas

Appendix K

CHAIRMEN OF GOVERNORS

Alderman Peter Jones 1894-96

Dr H Lloyd Snape 1896-98

Richard Richards 1898-99

George Davies 1899-1900

Mrs Jesse Williams 1900-01

Revd Thomas Levi 1901-02

Mrs W Griffiths 1902-03

Prof R W Genese 1903

Ald Caleb M Williams 1903-13

Prof D Morgan Lewis 1913-15

Ald C M Williams 1915-16

Revd R J Rees 1916-18

Prof D Morgan Lewis 1918-22

Prof Edward Edwards 1922-25

Richard Richards 1925-27

Revd T Noah Jones 1927-30

Vice Principal Ed Edwards 1930-33

Ald J Barclay Jenkins 1933-38

Ald D Rees Morgan 1938-43

Revd Herbert Morgan 1943-45

Ald D Rees Morgan 1945-61

Ald Mrs G C Evans 1961-73

REFERENCES

1. Ardwyn Jubilee Magazine 1946 p 3 D C Lewis
2. Ibid p 6 T J James
3. Ibid p 21 D Jonathan Jones
4. Ibid p 23 D O Morris
5. The Old Black and Greens Aberystwyth Town FC 1884-1984 p 252
6. Ardwyn Jubilee Magazine p 20 S E Thomas
7. Ibid p31 T Ivor Rees
8. Ibid p21 D Jonathan Jones
9. Ibid p19 S E Thomas
10. Ibid p22 W Tom Williams
11. Ibid p18 S E Thomas
12. Ibid p18 S E Thomas
13. Ibid p18 S E Thomas
14. Ibid p21 D Jonathan Jones
15. Ibid p25 T O Pierce
16. Ibid p29 John Rees Thomas
17. Ibid p21 D Jonathan Jones
18. Aberystwyth Observer editorial 17 July 1902
19. Educational Developments in a Victorian Community Dr W Gareth Evans U C W 1990
20. Ardwyn Jubilee Magazine 1946 p26 T O Pierce
21. Ibid p36 Richard Phillips
22. U C W Aberystwyth 1872-1972 E L Ellis p68
23. Ardwyn Jubilee Magazine p30 John Rees James
24. Ibid p24 D O Morris
25. Ibid p33 John Morris Jones
26. Wales and Medicine ed John Cule Gomer Press Llandysul
27. Ardwyn Jubilee Magazine p40 Dorothy Sulston
28. Ibid p38 Gildas Tibbott
29. Ibid p40 Dorothy Sulston
30. Ibid p33 Emrys Williams
31. Ibid p38 Gildas Tibbott
32. Ibid p41 John R Richards
33. The Old Black and Greens p47
34. Ardwyn Jubilee Magazine p44 David Idris Jones
35. Ibid p42 John R Richards
36. W D Percy Evans - conversation 7:4:92
37. Ardwyn Jubilee Magazine p37 Gildas Tibbott
38. Cadfan Evans - conversation 12:3:91
39. Ardwyn Jubilee Magazine p48 Rhiannon Aaron
40. Rhiannon Aaron - conversation 8:12:92
41. Ardwyn Jubilee Magazine p52 Gweno Lewis
42. John Julian Jones -correspondence 15:8:94
43. Ardwyn Jubilee Magazine p52 Gweno Lewis
44. Ibid p4 D C Lewis
45. Ibid p52 Gweno Lewis
46. Jim Pinsent -correspondence 28:11:93
47. Jim Mitchell -correspondence 6:11:93

48. R Killin Roberts -correspondence 3:12:93
49. John Lewis -correspondence 7:3:93
50. Ardwynian July 1936 D C Lewis
51. Ardwyn Jubilee Magazine p57 E L Ellis
52. Ibid p56 Lilian Williams
53. Dafydd Morris Jones-correspondence 24:1:94
54. Ardwyn Jubilee Magazine p57 E L Ellis
55. Pegi Morris Jones -correspondence 10:1:94
55a Ibid
56. Ibid
57. Lilian M Williams -correspondence 8:11:93
58. Roy Pinsent -correspondence 16:12:90
59. Emlyn Edwards -correspondence 14:4:94
60. John Edmunds -correspondence 25:10:93
61. Teleri Bevan -correspondence 6:8:93
62. Emlyn Edwards -correspondence 14:4:94
63. Roy Pinsent -correspondence 16:12:90
64. The Old Black and Greens p99
65. Lilian M Williams -correspondence 8:11:93
66. Herbert Williams -correspondence 8:12:93
67. Delwyn Tibbott -correspondence 6:11:93
68. Emlyn Edwards -correspondence 14:4:94
69. Ardwyn Jubilee Magazine p62 W G Rowlands
70. Delwyn Tibbott -correspondence 6:11:93
71. Lord Elystan Morgan-correspondence 26:8:94
72. Delwyn Tibbott -correspondence 6:11:93
73. Ibid
74. G Rhys Edwards letter Welsh Gazette Dec 1947
75. D Elwyn Lloyd Jones letter Welsh Gazette 1:1:48
76. John Edmunds -correspondence 25:10:93
77. Ibid
78. Ardwynian July 1950 editorial
79. Ibid October 1951 M T Chapple
80. John Cheshire -correspondence 10:3:94
81. Dafydd Morris Jones-correspondence 24:1:94
82. E L Ellis -correspondence 12:4:93
83. Les Chamberlain -correspondence 2:11:94
84. Roger T Griffiths -correspondence 30:4:95
85. Les Chamberlain -correspondence 2:11:94
86. U C W Aberystwyth 1872-1972 E L Ellis p298
86a Hefin Elias -correspondence 25:10:94
87. Elwyn Elias -correspondence 25:4:94
88. Cambrian News 19:7:56
89. Howard C Jones -correspondence 15:12:93
90. Gethin Abraham -Williams -correspondence 14:7:94
91. Ceri Davies -correspondence 2:11:94
92. Ibid
93. Hywel B Mathews -correspondence 10:1:95
94. Ibid
95. Gary Davis -correspondence 20:2:94

96. Ibid
97. Gwynn Davis -correspondence 6:3:94
98. Hansard 6:5:66
99. Lord Elystan Morgan-correspondence 26:8:94
100. Gethin Abraham-Williams- correspondence 14:7:94
101. Cards CC Higher Educ Comm Minute 784 1:7:59
102. Cambrian News 6:11:59
103. Basil Thomas -correspondence 18:1:94
104. 25th Anniv Booklet Kronberg/Ardwyn/Penglais exchange 1994 p17 K F Loates
105. Ibid p40 Fritz Pratschke
106. Ibid p96 P Munday, G Kelly, A Pearson.
107. Beryl Varley -correspondence 12:3:95
108. Anthony Ford -correspondence 23:2:94
109. Gwynn Davis -correspondence 6:3:94
110. Ardwynian 1956/57 p36 Roy James
111. Bryan D Jones -correspondence 20:1:95
112. Melville Jones -correspondence 2:10:95
113. Ardwynian 1957/58 Wynn W Hughes
114. Terry Whitaker -correspondence 2:3:94
115. John Ashton -correspondence 6:3:95
116. Ardwyn P T A Minute Book 25:3:57
117. Rt Rev Cledan Mears -correspondence 16:12:93
118. The Times - obituary D Elwyn Lloyd Jones July 91
119. A Long Beat - autobiography A H Jenkins- Gee 1994
120. Aber Alumni UWA Autumn 1989 and PROM Winter 1993
121. Dr David Jenkins CBE -correspondence 14:12:95
122. Elwyn Elias -correspondence 25:4:94
123. R J LLoyd -correspondence 9:9:95
124. Ardwynian 1971/72 ed W John Taylor
125. Ceri Davies -correspondence 2:11:94
126. Lord Elystan Morgan -correspondence 26:8:94

LIST OF SUBSCRIBERS

Rhiannon Aaron, Aberystwyth
Kenneth Abraham, Cardiff
Gethin Abraham-Williams, Dinas Powys
Alan Adams, South Africa
Robert Lynne Adams, Ynys Mon
Mildred Atkinson, Aberystwyth
Betty Bailey, Aberystwyth
Aled Bebb, Goginan, Aberystwyth
Roy J Beddington, Aberystwyth
Anne G Benbow, Birmingham
John A Benbow, Birmingham
Teleri Bevan, Llandaff
Jean Bodrero, Carmarthen
Margaret de Bolla, Eglwysfach, Powys
Jane R Bonner, Aberystwyth
Peter Bourne, Borth
Meg Bowen, Aberystwyth
Carys Briddon, Tre'rddol, Powys
Gordon W Burns, Aberystwyth
Derek W Butler, Stourbridge
Noel R Butler, Aberystwyth
Charles & Margaret Bumford, Aberystwyth
Mari Carter, Bow Street, Dyfed
Stephen Cannon, Yelverton, Devon.
Les & Carol Chamberlain, Wrexham
Phyllis Chavasse, Aberystwyth
Alan Christian, East Morton, West Yorks
S A Cheetham, Chester
Gilbert W Clarke, Porthcawl
Jim Clements, Aberystwyth
Elaine Comber, Malvern, Worcs
Eileen Craine, London
Ron Cullum, Aberystwyth
Menna Cwyfan-Hughes, Bodorgan, Ynys Mon
J Richard Daniel, Gravenhurst, Ontario
Ambrose Davies, Aberystwyth
Alun Davies, Woolton, Liverpool
Beti Davies, Cheadle, Cheshire
Ceri Davies, Sketty, Swansea
Dewi Emrys Davies, Cardigan, Dyfed
E Jones Davies, Aberystwyth
Eleri Davies, Aberystwyth
Gwyneth Davies, Aberystwyth
Islwyn Fisher Davies, Aberystwyth
Jeff Davies, Llanon, Dyfed
J E Wynne & Mary Davies, Aberystwyth
John Ceredig Davies, Aberystwyth

Mary Beynon Davies, Aberystwyth
Nansi A Davies, Aberystwyth
Nonn Davies (Gwynn), Llandaf, Cardiff
Peter D Davies, Norwich
Pegi Morris-Jones, Brithdir, Dolgellau
Tom Davies, Cheadle, Cheshire
Tomos L Davies, Epsom, Surrey
W Islwyn Davies, Aberystwyth
Gwynn Davis, Bath
Gary Davis, Sandwich, Kent
W H Dinning, Royston, Herts
Lawrence Drizen, London
Christopher Edwards, Haywards Heath
D Rowland & Nonna Edwards, Aberystwyth
David Teifi Edwards, Barnet, Herts
Derek Edwards, Aberystwyth
R Emlyn Edwards, Solihull
John Hugh Edwards, Aberystwyth
Margaret Edwards, Aberystwyth
Maureen Yvonne Edwards, Llanilar, Dyfed
Peter Edwards, Aberystwyth
Philip L Edwards, Glossop, Derbys
Richard H Edwards, Hawarden, Clwyd
R Graham Eklund, Aberystwyth
Elwyn Elias, Edgbaston, Birmingham
J Hefin Elias, Cardiff
E L Ellis, Aberystwyth
Rolant J Ellis, Aberystwyth
Gareth Emanuel, Aberystwyth
Margaret Escott, Reading
Adrian Morgan Evans, Cardiff
Audrie Evans, Haverfordwest
Bethan Evans, Aberystwyth
D Cadvan Evans, Aberystwyth
The Ven David Eifion Evans, Bow Street, Dyfed
D Rhiannon Evans, Bangor, Gwynedd
Derwyn & Rosemary Evans, Capel Seion, Aberystwyth
Dic Evans, Abermagwr, Aberystwyth
Eifion B Evans, Bristol
Herbert Evans, London
H M Evans, Sheffield
John Hugh Evans, Croydon, Surrey
J E Evans, Llanrhystud, Dyfed
John Martin Evans, Llandeiniol, Dyfed
Margaret Evans MBE (Bowyer) Aberystwyth
Martin Evans, Abbots Langley, Herts

Mary Evans, Aberystwyth
Peggy Russell Evans, Aberystwyth
R Oliver Evans, Chester
Seymour Prosser Evans, New Quay, Dyfed
T Evans, Portsmouth
T Gwyn Price Evans, Crymych, Dyfed
Trevor W Evans, Llandybie, Dyfed
Olwen Everson, Aberystwyth.
Lyneth Farr, Newmarket, Suffolk
R Ieuan Felix, Heswall, Wirral
Tony Ford, Durban, South Africa
J Barrie Foulkes, Worthing, West Sussex
Rosemary Francis, Roundhay, Leeds
B M Frost-Smith, Penrith, Cumbria
Christine (Caffrey) Garside Clitheroe, Lancs
Myfanwy Gate (Hughes), Ripponden, West Yorks
Leon Gibson, Penmynydd, Ynys Mon
A W Gilbey, Aberystwyth
David R Gorman, Preston, Lancs
David Greaney, Aberystwyth
Michael John Griffiths, Y Felin Heli, Gwynedd
William I Griffiths, Aberystwyth
John Grogan, Stockport, Cheshire
R Geraint Gruffydd, Aberystwyth
Jane Anne Hall, Hartlebury, Worcs
Margaret & Alan Harget, Sutton Coldfield
C M Harries, Aberystwyth
Doreen Harris, Bow Street, Dyfed
Lyn S Hawkes, St George, Abergele
Heledd Hayes, Cardiff
Gwyneth Hayward, Penn Bottom, Bucks
Alan H Heaton, Harrogate, N Yorks
M Heiron (Greenwood), Shrewsbury, Salop
Simon F Hill, Bournemouth
Robin W Hill, Johannesburg
J H Richard Hurst, Aberystwyth
Gwen Hitchcock, Eastbourne, E Sussex
Howys Spencer Hooper, Bournemouth
Andrew Hoskins, Walsall, W Midlands
Nick Hoskins, Swanmore, Hants
Richard Hoskins, London
Glyn & Wendy Hubbard, New Zealand
Kai & Anna Hubbard, Borth, Dyfed
Mr & Mrs Alwyn Hughes, Blaenannerch, Dyfed
Beryl Evelyn Hughes, Aberystwyth
Elwyn & Lilias Hughes, Aberystwyth
Glenys M Hughes, Aberystwyth
Helen Hughes (Savage), Blackwood, Gwent
Jennifer A Hughes (Farrow), Aberystwyth
John H Hughes, Aberystwyth

Mabel Hughes, Aberystwyth
Mary Hughes (Savage), Blackwood, Gwent
Walford Hughes, Borth, Dyfed
William Gwynfor Hughes, Rhiwbina, Cardiff
Wynn & Mair Hughes, Aberystwyth
Dafydd Ifans, Penrhyncoch, Dyfed
Dafydd Alun & Hilda Isaac, Tre'ddol, Powys
Richard Iorwerth Isaac, Aberystwyth
June W Jack (Guy), Bromsgrove, Worcs
Carys Lloyd James, Solihull, W. Midlands
Eleanor James, Llandre, Dyfed
Elsie James, Aberystwyth
Tom & Sheila James (Robins) Finchley, London
Brenda Jeeves (Owen), Taliesin, Powys
James W L Jenkin Trinity, Jersey, CI
Alison Jenkins (Farrow), Aberystwyth
Dr & Mrs David Jenkins CBE, Penrhyncoch
Eddie Jenkins, Norwich
Evelyn Lumley Jenkins, Aberystwyth
Jane Jenkins, Devil's Bridge, Dyfed
Nansi Jenkins, Harrow, Middsx
Robert David Jenkins, Llanfarian, Aberystwyth
Huw John, Victoria, Australia
Mary John (Owen), Porthcawl
Pamela & Alun John, Penrhyncoch
David A Johnston, Aberystwyth
Alun Ellis Jones, Bow Street, Dyfed
Brian Nepaulin Jones, Aberystwyth
Bryan & Valeri Jones, Wotton-under-Edge, Glos
Carys A Jones, Ffurnais, Machynlleth
Christopher & Christine Jones, Macclesfield
Daniel Gruffydd Jones, Aberystwyth
Dafydd Morris Jones, Aberarth, Dyfed
Dewi Jones ,Halifax, W Yorks
Dilwyn Morgan Jones, Blaenplwyf, Dyfed
Dilys Wynn Jones (Thomas), Llanfihangel-y
 Creuddyn, Dyfed
Eleri Jones Barry, S Glam
Mr & Mrs Emrys Jones, Blaenanerch, Dyfed
Esyllt Jones (Beynon Davies), Casllwchwr,
 Abertawe
Ethel A Jones, Derry Ormond, Lampeter
Gareth Jones, Islington. London
Geraint Jones, Aberystwyth
Gwyn & Helen Lloyd Jones, Mumbles, Swansea
Howard C Jones, N S W Australia
Hywel T Jones, Aberystwyth
Ian Jones, Cwmrheidol, Aberystwyth
Idwena Jones, Ashford, Middsx
Jano Jones, Llandre, Dyfed

Joan & Prys Jones, Churchdown, Gloucester
Jacob Ieuan Jones, Droitwich Spa, Worcs
John Julian Jones, Dudley, W Midlands
J D Rowland Jones, Llanilar, Dyfed
M Gwenda Jones, Aberystwyth
Marcia Jones, Aberystwyth
Margery Jones, Rotorua, New Zealand
Mary Wyn Jones, Aberystwyth
M Julian Jones, Pembroke Dock, Dyfed
Mel Jones, Holmfirth, W Yorks
Menna Wyn Jones, Aberystwyth
Meryl Jones (Thomas), Carmarthen, Dyfed
Philip A Jones, Cambridge
Richard Jones, London
Revd Robbie Jones, Newport, Pembs
Sarah Mary Jones, Llanbadarn Fawr, Dyfed
Tom O Nepaulin Jones, Edmonton, Alberta
Valma Jones, Talybont, Dyfed
Wyn Jones, Crowland, Lincs
Mair Joynson, West Cross, Swansea
Allan Keall, Much Hadam, Herts
Gwilym Keeble-Williams, Barry, S Glam
David Keyse ,Worcester
Annette W Keyworth, Bow Street, Dyfed
Walter J King, Aberystwyth
Janet Kyffin, Aberystwyth
Valerie D W Laing, Tackley, Oxford
A Aeronwy Lewis (Crees), Capel Bangor, Dyfed
Antony Lewis, Capel Dewi, Aberystwyth
Colin Lewis, Dinas Cross, Fishguard
David Michael Lewis, Aberystwyth
Eifion Lewis, Aberystwyth
Elsbeth M Lewis, Aberystwyth
Gareth Lewis, Bow Street, Dyfed
Ian R Lewis, Aberystwyth
Janice M Lewis, Aberystwyth.
John Lewis, Aberystwyth
M Gwyneth Lewis, Aberystwyth
Ron Lewis, Carmarthen
E Lewis-Evans, Trawscoed, Aberystwyth
Sian Lewis, Llanilar, Aberystwyth
Mr & Mrs T Lewis, Manceinion.
Mr & Mrs Watts Lewis, Blaenannerch, Dyfed
Barry Lionel, Aberystwyth
Marise Lloyd Evans, Aberystwyth
Huw & Enfys Spencer Lloyd, Aberystwyth
Hywel Spencer Lloyd, Llanidloes, Powys
Ian Spencer Lloyd, Abergele, Clwyd
Richard Lloyd, Sutton Coldfield
R J Lloyd, Aberystwyth

Llyfrgell Gyhoeddus Aberystwyth
Llyfrgell Genedlaethol Cymru Aberystwyth
G I Lumley Aberystwyth
Rt Revd John Cledan Mears Cardiff
Ann Meire, Flint, Clwyd
Eirwen Marks (Evans), Ammanford, Dyfed
David Martin Bech, Luxenbourg
Lindy Martin, Otterton, Devon
Hywel Mathews, Merthyr Tydfil
Rosalind McNeill (Stephens), Hull
Geoffrey S Miles, Birmingham
R I Millichamp, Aberystwyth
J E Mitchell, Andover, Hants
Jane Moffitt (Adams), S Africa
Aneurin Wyn Morgan, Cwmrheidol, Aberystwyth
Arthur Morgan, Aberystwyth
David Morgan, Aldershot
Lord Elystan Morgan, Dolau, Bow Street, Dyfed
Tonwen M Morgan (Evans), Ferryside, Dyfed
Anthony John Morris, Borth, Dyfed
James H Morgan, Talybont
John Morris QC, MP, House of Commons
John Peter Morris, Aberystwyth
Llinos J Morris, Barnet
Richard Anthony Morris, Bow Street, Dyfed
N J Nichols, Farnham
J M Nicholson, Aberystwyth
Peter Norrington Davies, Aberystwyth
Buddug Owen OBE, Rhuallt, Clwyd
John D Owen, Aberystwyth
Mary Olwen Owen, Aberystwyth
Robert Wheatley Owen, Colchester, Essex
Myrtle Parker (Williams), Talybont, Dyfed
David Alan Parry, Llangefni, Ynys Mon
Phyllis Vaughan Parry, Aberystwyth
H Wyn Parry-Williams ,Dachet, Berks
Derek R C Pavey, Epsom, Surrey
Penglais School Aberystwyth
Marina Penny (Edwards), Bristol
Gwilym M Phillips ,Reading
Irfonwy Lloyd Phillips ,Rhosllanerchrugog, Clwyd
Ivor & Janet Phillips (Ward), Cardiff
Ray & Cath Phillips, Port Talbot, W Glam
W John Phillips ,Carmarthen
I D Gwynne Pickering, London
Jennifer Pickett (Chapple), Preston
David & Brenda Piers, Hereford
Lila Piette, Bow Street, Dyfed

B R W Pinsent, Bedford
P J N Pinsent, Bristol
Peter & Beryl Potts (Richards), Ontario, Canada
Afona M Pritchard, Borth-y-Gest, Gwynedd
Prof Gwyn Pritchard, Sketty, Swansea
Huw John Pritchard, Bangor, Gwynedd
Tegwen A Pryse (Ellis), Bow Street, Dyfed
David Pugh, Rhydyfelin, Aberystwyth
Enid Pugh, Aberystwyth
Mike Pusey, Victoria, Australia
Alan & Eleri Rees (Morgan), Whitchurch, Cardiff
John T Rees, Poole, Dorset
Eirlys Reeve, Rickmansworth, Herts
Lynn Rhys, Dinbych, Clwyd
E L Richards, Aberystwyth
Gerwyn Richards, Aberystwyth
James Arwyn Richards, Penrhyncoch, Dyfed
John Richards, Aberystwyth
Malcolm H Richards, Aberystwyth
Beryl M Roberts, Aberystwyth
R R Killin Roberts, Telford, Shropshire
Janet Roberts (Owen), Bow Street, Dyfed
Rhiannon Roberts, Bow Street, Dyfed
Margaret Robins-Craven, London
Rhiannon E Roderick (Phillips), Llangwyryfon, Dyfed
Delor Tudor Rogers (Jones), Barry, S Glam
Jane Rosser, Aberystwyth
Elisabeth Royle-Evans, Capel Dewi, Aberystwyth
Bethan Rowlands (Lloyd Jones), Bristol
Ellen M Rowlands, New Cross, Aberystwyth
E Lynda Rowlands (Davies), Llangathen, Dyfed
Gwenda Rowlands-Rudge, Aberystwyth
Idris Rowlands, Llandeilo, Dyfed
Leonard Rufus, Bow Street, Dyfed
Gwenda Rumsey-Williams, Aberystwyth
Anthony Russell-Jones Shawley, Worcs
Beti Sallis Bargoed, M Glam
Maynard B Samuel, Capel Seion, Aberystwyth
Richard Colin Samuel, Wallasey, Cheshire
Brian Sansbury, Bow Street, Dyfed
Michael Sansbury, Sketty, Swansea
Marilyn Sillett (Richards), Newark, Notts
Bruce D Sinclair, St Andrews
Eric Slater, Aberystwyth
Deborah Slay, Rippingale, Lincs
Gregory Slay, Chichester
Sheila A Smith (Burnford), Evesham, Worcs
Jane Smyth (Ellis), Abermad, Aberystwyth
Ann Sneath (Havard), Birmingham

Lenora Stanford (Thomas), St John's, Newfoundland
Catrin Beynon Stephens (Davies), Abertawe
David & Anna Subacchi, Aberystwyth
Charles G Suff, Ammanford, Dyfed
J Sutton (Williams), Aberystwyth
Avarina Mary Taylor, Aberystwyth
Helen C M Taylor, Rathmines, Dublin
Jennifer Taylor, Cardiff
W John Taylor, Aberystwyth
Mair Turner (Evans), Aberystwyth
Mike & Nona Taylor (Davies), Aberystwyth
Alan Vaughan Thomas, Clarach, Aberystwyth
Beryl Thomas, Aberystwyth
Dafydd Rhys Thomas, Retford, Notts
Delia Thomas, Aberystwyth
Dewi Thomas, Llangunnor, Carmarthen
Eluned Thomas (Hughes), Weybridge, Surrey
Elwyn Thomas, Llandre, Bow Street
Gerran Thomas, Aberystwyth
Gwyneth Margaret Thomas, Clarach, Aberystwyth
Harold Thomas, Cardiff
Henley Thomas, West Malvern, Worcs
H Alun Thomas, Aberystwyth
Ian Ashley Thomas, Clarach, Aberystwyth
Iwan & Jane Thomas (R-Williams), Llanilar
Alun and Kay Thomas (Bowen), Llanbadarn Fawr
Mary E Thomas, Bow Street, Dyfed
Mary E Thomas (Owen), Caerdydd
Ronald Thomas, Sheffield
T A Thomas, Penrhyncoch, Aberystwyth
Wendy Lynne Christian Thomas, Caerfyrddin
Delwyn Tibbott, Cardiff
Ann Tomkinson, Cardigan
Joseph Torri, Nuneaton, Warwicks
David H Trevena, Aberystwyth
William Troughton, Aberystwyth
Beryl Varley (Jones), Aberystwyth
F Vellani (Slater), Aberystwyth
Alan G Walker, Westbury-on-Trym, Avon
Helen Wallis, Solihull
Rannveig Wallis, Carmarthen
M Kathleen Waplington (Owen), Gerona, Spain
Gwyneth Mary Ward (Thomas), Twickenham, Middx
Sian Ward (Pritchard), Llanbedr, Barmouth
A M Watkin, Tre Taliesin, Powys
John & Gwyneth Watkin (Benjamin), Ottawa, Canada

Revd John G E Watkin, Llandudno, Gwynedd
Gerwyn & Eleanor Watkins, Cowbridge, S Glam
John Anthony Watts, Aberystwyth
G H Lorraine White, Cowes, I O W
Terry Whitaker, Aberystwyth
Alexander Cecil Whitehill, Penrhyncoch
D Tecwyn Wilkinson, Sutton Coldfield
Parch a Mrs Aled W Williams, Llanddewi Brefi, Dyfed
Delyth Williams, Caernarfon, Gwynedd
Delyth A Williams (Morgan), Whitchurch, Cardiff
Elgan Moelwyn Williams, Newtown, Powys
Enid M Williams (Jones), Aberystwyth
Henry E Williams, Devil's Bridge, Dyfed
Herbert Williams, Cardiff
Ivor E N Willaims, Aberystwyth
Ifor W Williams, Aberystwyth
Jane Williams, West Hendon, London
John Ellis Williams, Aberystwyth
John Emrys Williams, Bishopton, Renfriwshire
John Williams, Aberystwyth
Julian Williams, Cardiff
Lilian Williams, Llanfairfechan, Gwynedd
Margaret G Williams (Isaac), Cardiff
Margaret Myrtle Williams, Talybont, Dyfed
Richard J Williams, Rugby, Warwicks
Roger & Glenys Williams, Llandysul, Dyfed
R W Williams, Guildford, Surrey
Tom & Barbara Williams (White), Colwyn Bay
Victor H Williams, Bow Street, Dyfed
Mary Wilmshurst, Yeovil, Somerset
John T Wintle, Worcester
M H J Woodman, East Grinstead, W Sussex
Olwen E Wannacott (Williams), Bristol
M Wynne-Griffith, Aberystwyth
Menna Yarwood (Lewis), Sheffield
Ysgol Penweddig, Aberystwyth